Thinking about children

Thinking about children

Sociology and fertility in Post-War England

JOAN BUSFIELD
Lecturer in Sociology
University of Essex

MICHAEL PADDON
Senior Lecturer in Social Sciences,
Manchester Polytechnic

Cambridge University Press

Cambridge
London   New York   Melbourne

Published by the Syndics of the Cambridge University Press
The Pitt Building, Trumpingtron Street, Cambridge CB2 1RP
Bentley House, 200 Euston Road, London NW1 2DB
32 East 57th Street, New York, NY 10022, U.S.A.
296 Beaconsfield Parade, Middle Park, Melbourne 3206, Australia

Library of Congress catalogue card number: 76-22986

ISBN 0 521 21402 5

First published 1977

Printed in Great Britain at the University Press, Cambridge

(30/7/90)

223064

*For our parents
and Lindsay*

Contents

Preface

When we began this book we intended it to be the report of a survey of the 'social determinants of fertility', based on questionnaire interviews with some 300 women and most of their husbands, who were living in Ipswich in 1969-70. Our aim was to elucidate the factors influencing the couples' pattern of childbearing with a view to explaining both the changes in the birth rate in England in the post-war period and the differences in levels of fertility between various social groups. What we have written is now both less than and more than this. On the one hand, though the purpose of the study has not changed very markedly over time, our ideas about the value of survey research for answering the sorts of questions that interested us have. Our growing awareness of the limitations of research using structured and closed-ended questionnaire techniques and of the particular weaknesses of our own survey has diminished the importance we attach to the data that we obtained by this method, and its role in this book is now relatively minor. Instead we have made use of data from a variety of other sources, especially our own preliminary pilot study of 50 women, carried out in the same town in 1966-7. The interviews were much more open in their structure than those for the survey and the quality of data obtained at this stage of the research is very different. It is these interviews that have provided the bulk of the data for the substantive portions of the book.

On the other hand this book, like any other report of sociological research, provides an account of the research activity itself, and in this instance the account may be just as interesting as much of the substantive content of the research. Most reports of research tend to gloss over the activities involved in producing the final account. Although the 'methodology' sections outline the basic procedures used, much of the detail gets lost; all we have is the finished product and relatively little information as to how it was achieved. To some extent this is inevitable; as ethno-methodologists have shown us, providing an 'adequate' account can be an infinite task, and is usually sensibly routinised. However, whether desirable or not, with this research the conventional gloss was impossible to achieve. For the research was carried out by several people, and we found, as the work progressed, that we did not agree amongst ourselves: we did not agree about the value of certain theoretical approaches, about the way to understand and interpret the data we had obtained, or about what conclusions could be drawn from our material. Moreover no amount of discussion could reconcile our differences, for they are differences not only about specific methods and specific theories, but also about the nature of sociological activity itself. Such disagreements reflect the state of sociology and, where they exist, do not yield a ready compromise.

For us there were two alternatives. The one was to incorporate the disagreement within the covers of the same book and to attempt some dialogue between ourselves in the account of the research that we offered. The other was to present two separate accounts of the research, for the strongest disagreement was between the two of us who had worked the longest on the research, Joan Busfield and Geoffrey Hawthorn. Initially we chose the first alternative since this would allow some direct debate between us. In time, however, the necessity of adopting the second became more obvious. The problem was that even where we did agree about some of the details of an argument we did not agree about the way the point should be made, or about the sort of language that should be used to make it, so that the common ground between us came to seem smaller and smaller. We finally decided, therefore, to write two separate accounts of the research that we had carried out together. In theory at least the advantage of writing two accounts of the same empirical research is that it makes rather forcefully the familiar point that data is not neutral, waiting to be collected and displayed according to its inherent truth and reality; any data can be understood and interpreted in a variety of different ways. In practice we will in the end, almost certainly have used so little of the same material from the large amount we collected that the way in which the data has been interpreted and each account constructed will be less visible than we had anticipated. Nevertheless, we hope that comparison of two studies that focus on the same questions and draw upon the same body of research data will provide a better insight into contemporary sociological activity than other simpler research presentations. To our knowledge we will be unique in presenting as co-researchers alternative accounts of one body of research material. We do not advocate that this should be the standard method of reporting, not least because other research teams agree more closely than we did. But this does not make a single account less selective or biased: it is just less obviously so. With two accounts, however divergent, the 'cover up' is less successful.

II

This book has, therefore, a double nature. On the one hand we discuss certain general theoretical and methodological issues in sociology by examining the history of one project, and the assumptions on which it was based. On the other we offer the beginnings of an explanation of marriage and childbearing in post-war England which draws on the substantive data obtained from that project. This twofold nature has created problems of structure and organisation, which we have handled in the following way.

In our introductory chapter, after some preliminary comments about the nature of the study, we outline the demographic changes in post-war England in their historical context and consider some of their implications for family life. The first section of the book then deals with theoretical questions. In Chapters 2 and 3 we discuss two dominant theoretical traditions that have influenced attempts to explain patterns of marriage and childbearing: the Malthusian and the utilitarian. We conclude the first section by outlining in Chapter 4 our own theoretical presuppositions. This chapter is an essential preliminary to the methodological chapters that follow. Together with Chapter 5 it provides some account of how we reached the particular ideas, interpretations and conclusions that we put forward in the substantive chapters of the book.

The second section, focussing on questions of research design, describes both the development of the research and our retrospective judgements on the decisions that were made. Chapter 5 provides a chronological history of the research covering both the pilot and survey stages, which briefly describes its institutional and intellectual context and origins. In Chapter 6 we point to some of the main errors of the research when judged by conventional methodological standards, whilst in Chapter 7 we question an underlying premise of its design: that a survey was the best method of data collection available to us. Those more interested in our attempt to explain patterns of marriage and childbearing may wish to skip this section of the book, at least initially.

The third and final section presents our ideas about marriage and childbearing in post-war England. Chapter 8 deals with the ideological context of marriage and considers some of the factors that have encouraged increasing proportions to marry, and to marry at younger ages over this century up until recently. In Chapter 9 we turn to childbearing itself and describe some of the common ideas and beliefs that provide a context for decisions about having children in this society. Having examined this common set of ideas, in Chapter 10 we look at ideological variation, and set out a number of ideological perspectives which are associated with different images of family life and different ideas about family size and spacing, and also have implications for contraceptive use. Following this Chapter 11 turns to questions of uncertainty, conflict and change in ideas about family size and spacing, examining how these are effected by negotiation between husband and wife as well as their effect on contraceptive practice. Chapter 12 concentrates exclusively on the problem of realising intentions about having children and considers both the role of contraception and the more general influences on its use, apart from those intentions. The subsequent and concluding chapter draws together the threads of the previous arguments of the book by pointing to some of the factors that have contributed to trends in family size and spacing in post-war England.

III

The number of those who have contributed to this research at some time or other is enormous and we could not hope to mention them all. Financial support for the pilot study was provided by the Nuffield Foundation, and for the survey by the Social Science Research Council. In addition the Department of Sociology at the University of Essex gave funds on a number of occasions for research assistance and data analysis.

Janet Cabot and Brenda Corti gave especial help with data collection and analysis; Diana Barker and Liz McGovern both acted as research assistants on the project at different times and were a valuable source of information and testing ground for our ideas; Phil Holden's regular help with computing was essential to us; Marion Haberhauer and Penny McHale helped to transform chaotic drafts into ordered typescripts; Diana Gittins, Stephen Hatch and Alan Ryan all spared some of their time to comment on drafts of various chapters; and Ruth Cohen helped with the proof reading.

Though Geoffrey Hawthorn does not agree with much of our argument, we are especially grateful to him for refusing to accept our view of sociology in general and of this research in particular, thereby forcing us to clarify our own ideas. Without the part that he has played this would be a different, and we believe, worse book.

Finally, Michael Lane has contributed to the research in a variety of ways, not least by pointing to numerous infelicities of style and argument in the drafts for this book; by advocating the view that a sociological text should not deter the reader with arid and confusing professional jargon; and by rejecting the belief that consensus and conformity are necessarily a moral good.

To them, to the men and women who talked to us so freely and willingly about having children, and to all our friends and colleagues, past and present, who have given help and support, we would like to express our thanks.

1. Introduction

The birth of a child is invariably regarded as a momentous, if not always desirable event both by its parents and the wider society wherever it occurs. The creation of a new life is an occurrence imbued with much meaning and is often surrounded by ritual, ceremony and myth. Of course, its precise significance varies. To an Indian farmer the birth of a son is an occasion for great rejoicing for sons provide essential labour to work the land. As one asserted, 'without sons, there is no living off the land. The more sons you have the less labour you need to hire, and the more savings you can have'.[1] In contrast, to an Icien woman the birth of a child, though an occasion ideally requiring thanksgiving and celebration, in practice adds one more burden and difficulty, for a child makes demands on the supply of food which is almost always insufficient. Because of this a mother may leave her baby on the ground when she is gathering food 'almost hoping that some predator will come along and carry it off'.[2] To parents in our own society the birth of a child, especially the first, is normally a joyous and significant occasion, for children are widely regarded as an essential part of marriage and family life. As one woman said to us about having children, 'that is married life, really', whilst another commented, 'it's not a family unless you've got children'.

While the birth of a particular child may be significant only for the parents and family into which it is born, the birth of children in general is of great significance to the wider society to which the family belongs. *Rites de passage,* of which our society retains only a vestige in the christening ceremony, are the public recognition of the importance of new members to the social order. Society also recognises the importance of children in a rather different sense; leaders and rulers may, for instance, be interested in the size of the households of which their community is composed for purposes such as taxation; they may be interested in the number of births in the community, regarding the new members as potential manpower for military or economic purposes. At times such interests may take an extreme and striking form as when Hitler in 1935, desiring to perpetuate the Third Reich, proclaimed of women: 'Every child which she brings into the world is a battle which she wins for the existence or non-existence of her nation',[3] or when Mussolini in 1927 argued that:

To count for something in the world, Italy must have a population of at least 60 millions when she reaches the threshold of the second half of this century . . . It is a fact that the fate of nations is bound up with their demographic power . . . Let us be frank with ourselves: what are 40 million Italians compared with 90 million Germans and 200 million Slavs?[4]

Nor have such chauvinist sentiments been restricted to avowed Fascists. Faced with the prospect of the declining birth rate in Britain in the 1930s Neville Chamberlain in 1935, when Chancellor of the Exchequer, had this to say:

I must say that I look upon the continued diminution of the birth rate in this country with considerable apprehension . . . the time may not be far distant . . . when . . . the countries of the British Empire will be crying out for more citizens of the right breed, and when we in this country shall not be able to supply the demand.[5]

It was from concerns like this about the size of population and the level of births, amongst others – though by no means always associated with such forceful nationalism – that a science of demography developed: a discipline concerned to record and measure numbers of persons, as well as the vital events of births and death, and the incidence of disease, marriage, migration and so forth, which constitute the dynamic forces that produce change and fluctuation in the size of populations (a concept itself first used in the seventeenth century).[6]

Our concern in this study is with one aspect of childbearing – with the quantity and tempo of childbearing in post-war England. In that sense our study is demographic. In other respects it is not. For demography is defined not only by its immediate subject matter but also by specific disciplinary traditions: traditions to which our own study does not conform. Demography has concentrated on, and been most successful in developing techniques of measurement and prediction (as its original name, political arithmetic, implied); in contrast the concern of our own study has been first and foremost with the *explanation* of demographic phenomena. The empirical data that we have collected does not (and was not intended to) match up to the standards of demographic measurement and compares unfavourably in this respect with data available from other sources.[7]

Moreover, in focussing on the explanation of demographic phenomena rather than on measurement and prediction, we have drawn on ideas and ways of thinking that stem far more from sociology than from the traditions of economics and political economy to which demography has always been more closely bound.[8] More especially, in attempting to explain patterns of childbearing in post-war England we have found it necessary to turn back to, and examine the meaning and significance of children to the parents themselves, and to consider their ideas and beliefs about having children, as well as their ideas and beliefs about the family's social and economic circumstances and life more generally – concerns which demography, with its emphasis on aggregate phenomena and on techniques of measurement, has tended to eschew. Indeed the emphasis on measurement has not only meant that demography has given relatively low priority to explanatory questions, it has also influenced its approach to explanatory issues in other unfortunate ways.[9]

In the first place, demographers have tended to concentrate on producing *demographic* explanations of demographic phenomena. That is to say they have examined the influence of the conventional demographic variables (which can be measured relatively easily) on one another – such variables as age, population size, fertility, marriage and so on – rather than moving outside this set to other social and economic factors, even though most demographers recognise that in many cases there is a need to do so to produce satisfactory explanations of demographic phenomena. In that sense demographers have concentrated on the immediate correlates or causes of demographic phenomena and have often left others to concern themselves with extending the explanation beyond that point. Second, the concern with measurement has exacerbated, as well as reflected the empiricist orientation of the discipline; not only has measurement tended to become an end in itself, but 'looking at the facts', and preferably easily quantifiable facts, has often dominated any explanatory activity. Hence the atheoretical, survey-based approach of much of the research.[10]

Finally, and related to this, the emphasis on measurement has involved an atomistic and asocial approach to demographic phenomena which is antithetical to the more holistic and social approach that we argue in the following chapters is necessary for the task of explanation. From the point of view of measuring population growth it is reasonable to treat populations as sets of isolated individuals, to treat births and deaths, marriage and migration as events that happen to people, to abstract them from their social context, and to regard them as identical. Yet if one wants to explain changes in patterns of marriage and childbearing or even variations in the level of deaths, we have to accept that these events have both personal and social meaning which is not uniform in time and place, and we must accept that they often result from, and are affected by, the definite and intentional actions of those immediately concerned, and others. Of course, demographers do not always ignore action when dealing with explanation (it would be difficult to do so), yet neither of the two dominant theoretical traditions in the study of fertility, which we discuss in the following two chapters, pay much attention to the social and cultural context in which births occur.

Nonetheless, though we draw on sociological rather than demographic or economic traditions in this book, sociology does not provide us with much direct support, since, with the occasional significant exception, sociologists, especially in this country, have shown rather little interest in demographic phenomena. We have discussed elsewhere some of the few sociological theories in which population growth has been held to have an impact on the nature of social relationships.[11] But the task of explaining changes in population growth has attracted, if anything, even less sociological interest. What is especially surprising is the lack of interest shown in childbearing, as opposed to childrearing, by sociologists of the family. Presumably the sociologists' lack of interest must have resulted in part from the development of demography as a separate discipline, and must have been further exacerbated by, as well as reflected in, the fact that demography has been closely tied to economics: an example of the detrimental effects of disciplinary boundaries. Patterns of marriage and childbearing are just as much family and social phenomena as demographic and economic ones.

Demography must, however, provide the starting point of our explanatory activity for we need both to outline the changes that have occurred in the quantity and tempo of childbearing in post-war England, and to relate them to other demographic changes during the period and before. Let us, therefore, consider first the changes and variations in the birth rate in post-war England, and examine their immediate demographic origins.

I: The demographic changes

The initial aim of our study was to account for changes in the crude birth rate in England since 1950; our dominant and more specific aim has been to account for differences in patterns of childbearing – in family size and the timing of births – within the population over the same period. The post-war period has been characterised by some marked fluctuations in the birth rate as Table 1:1 shows. After an immediate and expected post-war bulge in births the crude birth rate for England and Wales moved towards the level of the late 1930s (around 15.0 live births per thousand population) where it was expected to remain. But this did not happen. The first sign of a new increase became apparent in 1956 and the rate continued to rise steadily from then, reaching a peak of 18.7 in 1964, the highest level since 1947. Since then the birth rate for England and Wales has declined just as steadily and was 13.0 in 1974 the most recent year for which complete figures are available. (The provisional figures for the first two quarters of 1975 suggest that the overall rate for 1975 will be even lower.)[12] The figure for 1974 was the lowest ever recorded for England and Wales and the low level, which indicates, albeit imperfectly, a reduction in fertility, is already beginning to attract wider attention. Before that the lowest rates had been in the early years of the war (14.1 in 1940 and 13.9 in 1941) and around the height of the depression (14.4 in 1933).[13]

By comparison with the longer term changes in births over the previous century (the crude birth rate for the period 1871-80 was 35.3) neither the increase between 1956 and 1964 nor the subsequent decline appears to be of much demographic significance.[14] Were it not for the broader demographic

TABLE 1:1   *Crude birth rate for England and Wales, 1945-1973*

Year	Total live births per 1,000 population of all ages	Year	Total live births per 1,000 population of all ages
1945	15.9	1960	17.1
1946	19.2	1961	17.6
1947	20.5	1962	18.0
1948	17.8	1963	18.2
1949	16.7	1964	18.5
1950	15.8	1965	18.1
1951	15.5	1966	17.7
1952	15.3	1967	17.2
1953	15.5	1958	16.9
1954	15.2	1969	16.3
1955	15.0	1970	16.0
1956	15.7	1971	16.0
1957	16.1	1972	14.8
1958	16.4	1973	13.7
1959	16.5	1974	13.0

Sources: *Statistical Review of England and Wales, 1972,* Part II, Table DI; H.M.S.O. 1974; *Population Trends,* I, Table 12; H.M.S.O. 1975.

characteristics of England this might well be true. As it is the low death rates and the relatively low level of migration make changes even of this magnitude vital to overall population growth. From a demographic point of view the period in which we are interested falls within the third and final stage of the so-called 'demographic transition': the stage in which population growth, after a period of rapid expansion, slows down because both birth rates and death rates are relatively low. But though relatively low neither birth nor death rates are constant, and the precise level of births, in particular, can make a difference to the level of population growth that is far from insignificant.

A simple example shows the extent of the contribution that different *fertility* rates can now make. The report of the Population Panel made three different projections of population size in 2011 taking 1971 as the base year and making varying assumptions about future fertility rates.[15] On the assumption that fertility would fall below the 1971 level to reach replacement level by 1977 (the low model) the population in 2011 would be 60.7 million. If the rate were to remain at the 1971 level over the whole period to 2011 (the medium model) the population would be 66.1 million by that date. Were the rates to rise above the 1971 level to reach, by 1981, a gross reproduction rate of 1.37 (the high model) the figures would be 74.3 million. Differences of the order of 13.6 million (22%) are not insignificant. Of course these projections assume that the particular fertility rates are then sustained at a constant level over a longish period of time which would be most unusual. It is the continuing fluctuations in the level of the different factors that makes the task of projection so notoriously difficult and erroneous.

When we examine the period since the eighteenth century we can see the full magnitude of the demographic changes that have occurred in the last three centuries. In the first decades of the eighteenth century both death rates and birth rates were relatively high, though it would be wrong to suppose that childbearing was at a maximum. Not only was the age at which women married relatively late, but by no means all women married, and there was also sporadic control of childbearing within marriage. A number of local studies indicate that some sort of birth control, almost certainly withdrawal, must have been used by married couples to restrict childbearing in the pre-industrial period.[16] Population growth during this, the first stage of the demographic transition was generally low. The size of the population of England and Wales in 1700 has been estimated at 5.8 million persons.[17]

The initial growth in population that marked the beginning of the second phase of demographic transition, the stage of rapid population growth, began in the 1740s, but only took on significance with hindsight. Initially the growth seemed to be part of a 'normal' fluctuation as Habbabkuk describes:

At first sight the growth was no more rapid than in many earlier periods. But the growth of earlier periods had sooner or later been reversed. The growth which started in the 1740s was not reversed. It was not only reversed; it accelerated.[18]

We can be almost certain that this new growth was not only the result of lowered death rates but also of somewhat higher birth rates than in the pre-industrial period. However, whilst the initial declines in the death rate were not exceptional, as the declines progressed it became clear that a radical change in the pattern of mortality was taking place. Between the period 1701-50 and the period 1801-30 the crude death rate in England and Wales declined from 32.8 to 22.5, according to one estimate.[19]

Declines in the birth rate followed a century later; though they did not become visible in the figures for the crude birth rate until the late 1870s there is evidence of some reduction in family size from the 1860s onwards.[20] The decline in the birth rate continued steadily until the 1930s to be followed by the fluctuations that we have already documented. The changes in the rate of population growth that resulted are shown in Table 1:2. From a growth rate of 1.4% per annum in the decade 1871-81 the rate declined 0.4% per annum in the period 1931-39.

Analysis of the patterns of marriage and childbearing in the period since 1850 shows that much of the initial decline in the birth rate was due to changes in the age at marriage. Though marriage already occurred at a late

TABLE 1:2   *Intercensal population changes for England and Wales 1801-1971*

Year	Population size	Mean annual rate of intercensal increase
1801	8,892,536	—
1811	10,164,256	1.32
1821	12,000,236	1.67
1831	13,896,797	1.48
1841	15,914,148	1.36
1851	17,927,609	1.22
1861	20,066,224	1.13
1871	22,712,266	1.25
1881	25,974,439	1.35
1891	29,002,525	1.11
1901	32,527,843	1.16
1911	36,070,492	1.04
1921	37,886,699	0.48
1931	39,952,377	0.54
1939	41,460,000	0.37
1951	43,757,888	0.54
1961	46,104,548	0.52
1971	48,749,575	0.56

Note: The figure for the population in 1939 is a mid-year estimate.

Source: Office of Population Censuses and Surveys, *Census 1971, Age, Marital Condition and General Tables,* Table 1 London H.M.S.O.; 1974

age by the standards of many other countries, in the last decades of the nineteenth century it was generally postponed even longer.[21] Control of childbearing within marriage remained episodic, though its use increased during the second half of the nineteenth century, and it has only been in the twentieth century that it has played a major role in producing low birth rates.[22] During this century, however, changes in the age at marriage have made little contribution to the declines in the birth rate; indeed, as Table 1:3 shows, the age at which men and women marry has declined over most of this century, especially since the 1930s, reductions and fluctuation in the birth rate notwithstanding. The long steady decline in age at first marriage marks a definite change from the pattern of preceding centuries.[23] Before this century the age at marriage had been relatively high, with both men and women commonly postponing marriage to the second half of their twenties. Furthermore, the decline has affected all social groups. The common pattern, at least for the last century, has been, with some interesting exceptions, that those with higher occupational status have married at later ages than those of lower occupational status, and this pattern has been maintained (with perhaps a small decline in the differentials) despite the overall reduction in age at marriage; thus those in lower status occupations have experienced declines in age at marriage no less than those in the higher status occupations. The changes are documented in Table 1:4.

TABLE 1:3   *Mean age at first marriage, of men and women in England and Wales, 1901-1973*

Period	Bachelors	Spinsters
1901-5	26.90	25.37
1906-10	27.19	25.63
1911-15	27.49	25.75
1916-20	27.92	25.81
1921-25	27.47	25.57
1926-30	27.36	25.54
1931-35	27.43	25.53
1936-40	27.51	25.38
1941-45	26.76	24.58
1946-50	27.15	24.54
1951-55	26.55	24.18
1956-60	25.90	23.49
1961-65	25.36	22.90
1966-70	24.64	22.47
1971	24.60	22.59
1972	24.85	22.88
1973	24.86	22.72

Note: Before 1941 divorced men were included with bachelors and divorced women with spinsters.

Source: *Statistical Review of England and Wales, 1973,* Part II, Table L; H.M.S.O. 1975.

TABLE 1:4   *Average age at first marriage of grooms and brides in Britain by groom's occupational group, birth cohorts 1900-29*

Year of Birth	Professional and managerial		Black-coated		Skilled manual		Other manual		Unknown occupations		All	
	M	F	M	F	M	F	M	F	M	F	M	F
1900-09	30.1	27.2	27.6	26.2	27.3	24.9	26.6	24.0	26.3	23.9	27.4	25.1
1910-19	25.9	25.7	28.7	24.6	26.1	24.1	25.9	23.8	23.0	23.0	26.8	24.3
1920-24	26.7	25.6	25.8	24.2	24.8	22.7	24.1	22.3	21.7	20.0	24.9	23.1
1925-29	26.3	24.2	24.8	22.6	24.0	21.8	24.2	22.0	25.5	22.5	24.9	11.3

Source: E. Grebenik and G. Rowntree, 'Factors associated with the age at marriage in Britain', *Proceedings of the Royal Society, Series B,* December 1963, p. 186.

Moreover the decline in age at marriage during this century has been paralleled by a less striking, but nonetheless significant, increase in the proportions of men and women marrying at some time in their lives as Table 1:5 shows.

TABLE 1:5 *Proportion of persons ever married (out of 1,000) in England and Wales, 1881-1960*

Age 40-44	1881	1891	1901	1911	1921	1931	1941	1946	1951	1956	1960
Males	878	871	861	852	863	887	888	881	891	897	890
Females	861	850	831	820	821	819	827	836	858	895	913

Source: *Statistical Review of England and Wales,* 1960, Part III, p. 23.

To a large extent, however, it has been changes in the quantity and tempo of childbearing within marriage that have made the greatest contribution to the reductions in the birth rate since the 1850s, especially to the reductions of the twentieth century. As Table 1:6 shows, over the last century family size has declined markedly, and the average number of children born to married women is now approximately half that of a hundred years ago. Of particular interest is the change that this has meant in the distribution of completed family sizes. Table 1:7 indicates that the proportions of women having families of five or more children has declined especially steeply. Since women still tend to start their childbearing early in marriage, one consequence of the reduction in family size has been a concentration of childbearing in the early years of marriage, and in many cases childbearing is completed within the first ten years.[24] As women are also marrying younger this typically means that childbearing is completed by the time a woman is thirty.

TABLE 1:6 *The decline in completed family size in England and Wales, marriage cohorts 1861-1939*

Marriage cohort	Family size	Marriage cohort	Family size
1861-9	6.16	1910-14	2.82
1871	5.94	1915-19	2.46
1876	5.62	1920-4	2.31
1881	5.27	1925-9	2.11
1896	4.81	1930-4	2.07
1900-9	3.30	1935-9	2.03

Note: Mean ultimate family size of marriages contracted when woman was under 45.

Sources: Table 5:17, Wrigley (1969) Table 5:7; *Statistical Review of England and Wales,* 1973, Part II, Table QQb. London H.M.S.O. 1975.

TABLE 1:7   *The relative frequency of families of different sizes in Great Britain, for marriage cohorts 1870-1925*

Number of births	Marriage cohorts				
	1870-9	1890-9	1900-9	1915	1925
0	83	99	113	150	161
1	53	95	148	212	252
2	72	136	187	235	254
3	86	136	157	159	144
4	95	122	120	95	77
5	95	100	84	59	45
6	94	83	63	35	27
7	89	65	45	21	18
8	83	52	32	15	10
9	73	40	33	19	6
10	62	30	15	6	4
11 plus	115	42	14	6	2
	1,000	1,000	1,000	1,000	1,000

Note: Live births to completed marriages contracted when woman was under 45.
Source: Wrigley (1969), p. 198.

The demographic picture in the post-war period has been more complex, as the fluctuation in the birth rate would lead us to expect. Although both the mean age at marriage for men and women continued to decline and the proportion marrying continued to increase after the war, recently there has been some change in these trends. On the one hand, when we examine the proportions marrying at different ages, rather than the overall mean age at marriage, we find that the increase in the proportions of men and women marrying before 20 was halted in 1966 and since then the proportions have fluctuated, though their most recent level has been higher than that of 1965.[25] On the other hand since 1971, the decline in the mean age of first marriage of both men and women has itself been halted and there have been some signs of a reverse.[26] In consequence over the period till 1965 the trends in marriage were favourable to, and must have contributed to the rise in the birth rate; since then, though the change in patterns of marriage did not coincide exactly with the change from an increasing birth rate to a decreasing one, there has been some reversal of previous trends, so that changing patterns of marriage may once more be making some contribution to the changes in the birth rate.

The changes in marital fertility that have played an important, though not exclusive part in producing the changes in the crude birth rate in the post-war period, are most unlikely to have been solely the result of changes in the tempo of childbearing within marriage. Although figures for completed family size for the period are mainly estimates, and involve a degree of unreliability that is greater for the most recent cohorts, we can be fairly certain that women marrying in the second half of the 1950s and the first half of the 1960s will end up with larger families than those who married in the first half of the 1950s or in the decade from 1965.[27]

Analysis of the distribution of family sizes over the post-war period also indicates that changes in mean family size primarily involve shifts in the relative proportions having one or two children, or none at all, and that the bulge in births between 1956 and 1964 involved in particular a shift away from having only one child or none at all, rather than any shift to 'large' families. The trends are shown in Table 1:8. The decline in fertility since then has probably involved further reductions in those having larger (three or four) families and may also result in higher proportions remaining childless.[28] The evidence also indicates that the increase in family size over the period of the rise in the birth rate was most apparent among those who married relatively late.[29]

TABLE 1:8 *Family size distributions after 10 years of marriage in England and Wales, selected marriage cohorts 1951 to 1964 (for women married at ages 20-24 and married once only)*

Number of live born children	Year of marriage				
	1951	1956	1961	1963	1964
0	14	11	8	9	9
1	27	22	18	17	17
2	35	38	44	46	48
3	16	19	22	21	19
4 or more	8	11	9	8	7
Total	100	100	100	100	100

Note: The figures for 1964 are provisional.

Source: Pearce (1975), Table 4, p. 8

Differences in family size within the country associated with specific social attributes, such as social class or occupational group have tended to attract especial attention. Not only do they provide clues to the factors that influence childbearing (as well as affecting the overall level of growth of the population in question), but they also affect the distribution of those groups within the society – a subject that from time to time attracts a rather unpleasant eugenic interest.[30] The popular impression tends to be that large families are primarily a phenomenon of the poor and those of lower social status. In the immediate post-war period this may well have been true, though the actual proportion of large families (say five or more children) was small. The 1951 Census showed that, as in previous decades, those from the higher status socio-economic groups had on average fewer children than those from the lower status socio-economic groups, a differential that had only declined a little during the century.[31] By 1961, the pattern had begun to look rather different and the lowest fertility was to be found amongst those in the middle ranking socio-economic groups, as Table 1:9 shows, and the fertility of those in the highest socio-economic groups (albeit small numerically) was as high as that from the lowest. However, the relation between social status, poverty and family size is a complex matter, and having a large family is one factor that may itself contribute to family poverty as resources have to be spread more widely.[32]

TABLE 1:9 *Mean family size by duration of marriage and socio-economic group of husband, England and Wales, 1961*

Socio-economic group	5 years duration	10-14 years duration
1 Employers and managers (large establishments)	1.27	1.81
2 Employers and managers (small establishments)	1.34	1.78
3 Professional workers—self-employed	1.66	2.17
4 Professional workers—employees	1.39	1.86
5 Intermediate non-manual workers	1.25	1.76
6 Junior non-manual workers	1.20	1.68
7 Personal service workers	1.37	1.90
8 Foremen and supervisors—manual	1.27	1.90
9 Skilled manual workers	1.39	2.00
10 Semi-skilled manual workers	1.49	2.02
11 Unskilled manual workers	1.71	2.30

Note: Socio-economic groups 12-19 (such as farmers, own-account workers) which fall outside this hierarchical ranking from employers and managers to unskilled manual workers have been ommitted from this table.

Source: General Register Office *Census 1961, Fertility Tables,* H.M.S.O., 1966.

Unfortunately the fertility data from the 1971 Census have not yet been published. Nevertheless, a recent analysis carried out by the Registrar General, unsophisticated though it was, suggests that the differential in absolute numbers of births between social groups (the analysis was based on the Registrar General's five social classes) may have declined during the early years of the 1970s.[33]

Although the mean family size of different marriage cohorts must have fluctuated over the post-war period, there is evidence that the timing of childbearing within marriage has varied as well. Both the available cohort data (see Table 1:8 above, for instance), as well as period data indicates that there have been changes in the timing of births as well as the overall number.[34] Indeed it has been argued that the fall in the birth rate since 1964 has been primarily due to changes in the timing of childbearing within marriage. Such an argument is, however, no longer easy to sustain, and it is most unlikely that the lower birth rates of the early 1970s will not be reflected in smaller family sizes for those in the salient family building years.[35] It is, however, as we have already argued, very difficult to establish the respective role of the two factors for the most recent cohorts.

Two final factors need to be considered: changes in the age and sex structure of the population and changes in the level of illegitimacy. The overall changes in the proportions of women in the population of childbearing age (15-44) were not, for the most part, favourable to the rise in the birth rate from 1956-64.[36] Since 1963. however, they have been declining and have consequently been favourable to the decline in the birth rate since 1965. On the other hand, if we consider only the proportion of women in the population aged 20-9—the commonest childbearing years—then the picture is rather different. The proportion of females aged 20-4 in the population has increased steadily since 1961, after declining between 1945 and 1957, and the proportion of women aged 25-9 has been increasing since 1962, after declining up to that time since 1948.[37] Since, therefore, the changes in the proportions of women in the most common childbearing years have not been favourable to the changes in the birth rate, it is not possible to explain those changes by reference to the changing age and sex structure of the population.

The proportion of births that are illegitimate declined in the first years after the war and then rose steadily until 1968; since then it has fluctuated.[38] Hence though much of the rise in illegitimacy coincided with the overall rise in the crude birth rate and made some contribution to it, at other times the changes have not corresponded. Overall, given the low proportion of illegitimate births out of total births (less than one in ten when the ratio has been at its highest), the contribution of changes in illegitimacy to the post-war fluctuations in the birth rate can only have been small.

To summarise the demographic trends over the period since 1950, the period of our study, we may say that from 1956 to 1964 demographic changes favourable to a higher birth rate coincided, with the exception of changes in the age and sex structure of the population: the age marriage was declining, the proportions marrying were increasing, as was the rate of illegitimate births and marital fertility itself (we can be almost certain that this was both because family size was increasing and the interval between births declining). Since then the situation has been less clear-cut. Initially the reduction in the birth rate appeared in the face of continued declines in the mean age at marriage, increases in illegitimacy and rises in the proportion of women in the most important childbearing years. But gradually the overall demographic situation has changed so that more factors (in particular the changes in age at marriage) are now favourable to a decline in the birth rate. Nonetheless, there can be little doubt that changes in marital fertility have played an important part in the reductions in the birth rate since 1965.

Similar, though by no means identical, long-term changes in population growth have occurred in other industrial societies with much of the slowing up of growth coming from reductions in family size.[39] In France, exceptionally, the decline in births virtually coincided with the decline in deaths and predated the decline in the English birth rate by a century.[40] Furthermore, reductions in the age of marriage and an increase in the proportions marrying have also occurred in many societies, where marriage had tended to be late and the proportions marrying relatively low.[41] The post-war changes in the birth rate in England and Wales have also been paralleled in other societies, though not surprisingly, since we are looking at the details of short-term fluctuations, more variation is apparent. Many western European societies have experienced a 'peaking' of the birth rate, several at exactly the same time as England.[42] The notable exceptions are France, the Netherlands, Finland and Norway, yet in the last three the birth rate is currently falling as it is in most parts of western Europe. The picture elsewhere has been rather different. Eastern European countries, for instance, have not generally experienced a significant increase in the birth rate in the post-war period, and in some the birth rate has been at the low levels recently reached in western Europe for almost a decade.[43] In the United States the birth rate was well above that of western Europe during the 1950s, fluctuating around the mid-20s. In 1958 it began to decline steadily reaching a low point of 17.5 in 1968. It then started to increase as the children 'of the first post-war baby boom, with some delay, began their reproductive activity', but this demographic pressure notwithstanding, began to decline again in 1971.[44]

II: Demographic change and family life

The significance of changes in patterns of marriage and childbearing is not restricted to their impact on population growth and through that to certain economic and social changes. Changes in patterns of marriage and childbearing also have a direct impact on other features of society, especially the family. It is women, in their roles as wives and mothers, who are most directly and obviously affected by changes in the quantity and tempo of childbearing, since having children, and what we regard as its inevitable concomitant, looking after them, are defined as women's work. If, for instance, women bear a large number of children then the period of childbearing is long and the cost to a woman's health and well-being is likely to be high, since the physical difficulties of pregnancy and childbirth increase the more pregnancies a woman has (after the first). Although there are few societies where women have borne children at maximum possible levels (figure of an average of thirteen live births are the exception rather than the rule),[45] nevertheless the shift from an average of seven pregnancies per woman (the figure for mid-nineteenth century England) to two and a quarter (the approximate contemporary figure) would have been significant even if there had been no changes in medical standards during that time.

A woman is also affected by the time she has to spend caring for her children as well as bearing them. As the time and energy involved in bearing children have decreased and their chances of survival improved, so have the time and energy devoted to caring for them increased. This is one description of the process of change:

Women's familiarity with pregnancy was accompanied by a sense of alienation from the whole reproductive process that reduced them to mere instruments of destiny. Therefore one cannot talk of mother's loving or not loving their infants; these words cannot have today's meaning. Writings of the past confirm that what we mean by maternal love is a modern invention inseparable from the mastery over survival. Today each woman may consider pregnancy as a project which ninety-eight times out of a hundred will achieve completion and result in a child who will almost certainly survive her. She can look forward beyond the pregnancy itself: she is no longer the instrument of an attempt, but the mistress of a plan. She can look beyond the delivery to the upbringing of a child. Consequently her role is becoming less restricted to childbearing and more concerned with the upbringing of children.[46]

Whether or not we agree with the precise account that Sullerot gives of women's changing attitude towards their children, there can be little doubt that significant changes have occurred in ideas about children over the last century and more, and that demographic changes have contributed to, and facilitated them.[47] Of course, as Sullerot makes clear, an important factor has been the greater chance that any child would survive. Nevertheless, even without that, reductions in childbearing would be likely to influence women's attitudes towards having children and bringing them up. Concern for childrearing becomes possible in a way that is not practicable when family size is large. Indeed this has often been suggested as one important reason for having a smaller family and the tendencies may well reinforce one another.

Nevertheless, at least in societies like ours, it is the first few years of a child's life that impose the greatest domestic burden so that the current combination of small family sizes and early marriage means that the greatest burdens of childcare, as well as of childbirth, are faced early in marriage and are often over before a woman has progressed far beyond thirty. As the expectation of life has also increased (even more for women than for men) having children and caring for them no longer requires such a great proportion of a woman's life. Yet at present a woman is almost always expected to give priority to, and prepare herself for familial roles. This contradiction must surely be one factor contributing to the demand for greater equality between men and women. Rather than feminism encouraging small family sizes, small family sizes no doubt facilitate feminism.[48]

But it is not only women who are affected by changing patterns of childbearing. We have already suggested that the care and attention given to individual children appears to be influenced by family size and there is much contemporary evidence to suggest that at any particular time the children born into larger families are at a considerable disadvantage compared with those born into smaller ones in terms of their chances of success within the education system, subsequent occupation, income and so forth.[49] Of course the correlations could be spurious and family size itself may have little direct influence on a child's success within the education and occupational markets, but this does not seem likely; not only do the relationships hold up even when we allow for factors like social class, but we can also suggest good reasons why family size should affect a child's social progress, for which there is more direct supporting evidence. Though it is true that parents concerned for their children's success are likely to have small families, it is also true that small families make fewer demands on many of the resources that facilitate educational and occupational mobility. Money, time and energy are all more likely to be freely available in smaller families so that a child brought up in one is more likely to be better supplied in these respects.

Although belonging to a small family may improve a child's position by making more resources available, it may also, where the residential unit is the so-called nuclear family – parents and children living together – enhance parental power and influence and weaken that of the child. This in turn presumably increases the role played by parents in the socialisation of their offspring for good or ill, and this is no doubt an additional factor for the 'success' of children from small families. On the other hand, it seems likely that parents with larger families are more authoritarian and restrictive in their treatment of their children, but this does not vitiate the earlier point.[50]

Again family size must also affect the relationship between husband and wife. We know that having children is a turning point in the marital relationship, normally increasing the wife's dependence on her husband, their role diversification, and possibly, too, marital dissatisfaction, and it seems likely that family size itself also has a marked impact on the marital relationship.[51] It has recently been argued, for instance, that the reduction in family size has encouraged greater participation in family life by husbands. As Young and Willmott put it, 'if the size of families had not been limited husbands would not have found their homes as congenial as they have eventually done'.[52] However, the trouble with this argument is that the point of comparison is historically restricted. Large families have not always been associated with low participation in family life on the part of husbands or with very marked segregation of marital roles between husband and wife. Moreover there is a problem of causal direction, for though a number of studies have provided evidence of a negative correlation between segregation of marital roles and family size, it is arguable that segregation itself encourages a couple to have larger family sizes rather than the reverse.[53] What we can be sure is that a number of studies have shown a constellation of large family sizes, segregation of roles and lack of communication between husband and wife, and another constellation of small family sizes, greater sharing of roles and more communication between husband and wife; but the variety of ways in which we might interpret that information highlights, as have many of the relations we have discussed in this section, the complexity of the situation in which childbearing occurs.

It is this complex of interrelated ideas, actions and events that we have attempted to explore in this study.

Part I

The theoretical debate

2. Malthusian theories of population

Two traditions have dominated attempts to explain variation and change in patterns of childbearing. They have gained such widespread acceptance that they cannot be ignored even by those who find them wanting. The first and older tradition, springing directly from the ideas of the celebrated Thomas Malthus, seeks to explain the dynamics of population change, of which fertility is seen as but one component, in terms of the material conditions of man's environment. The other, more recent tradition, based on the theoretical ideas of utilitarian economics, explicitly sees itself as a development of the economic framework provided by Malthus, but concentrates on explaining variation and change in the level of fertility, and the decision making it involves. In order both to illuminate the characteristic terms of the Malthusian account and to highlight some of the fundamental problems and weaknesses it presents, this chapter is devoted to an analysis of the work of Malthus himself and to the development and application of his ideas in recent theories of population. The following chapter will consider the second tradition, that of utilitarian theories of fertility.

I: Malthus

It is Malthus who conventionally and rightly provides the starting point for any discussion of how to explain levels of childbearing. His work marks a turning point in the history of man's ideas about demographic processes, and his importance lies not only in the intrinsic interest of his ideas but in the extensive use made of them by subsequent authors.[1] His influence has been enormous; he has been both maligned and praised, but rarely ignored.

Malthus offers a theory of population that is broad and comprehensive in its scope: it combines an explanation of population change with a treatise about the future of mankind, as well as offering ideas about the factors that influence economic development and suggestions for social policy.[2] It is this that has made his work of such longstanding interest and intense controversy. Two aspects of his work in particular have been the subject of much debate. First, his 'principle of population': his belief that the potential rate of growth outstrips that of the means of production. Second, his belief that 'moral restraint', in particular the postponement of marriage, is the ideal solution to the threat of too rapid population growth. We shall not, however, be concerned with Malthus' work as a whole. Our concern is with its core: his ideas about how population change is to be explained.

21

Stated simply Malthus' population theory asserts, in his own words, 'that population constantly bears a regular proportion to the food that the earth is made to produce'.[3] If a population grows, he argued, beyond the level that can be supported by the available means of subsistence its growth will inevitably be checked. There are two possibilities; either disease and starvation will rapidly increase and the numbers dying will be higher than usual, or when the means of subsistence are in short supply, couples may postpone marriage and have fewer children than they would otherwise, so that the overall level of fertility may decline. These two processes he termed, respectively, the positive and preventive checks on population growth. Malthus placed much emphasis on the importance of these checks: an importance that he believed arose from the natural potential of population growth to exceed that of the growth in means of subsistence. It was because 'population when unchecked increased in geometrical ratio and subsistence for man in an arithmetic ratio' that sooner or later either positive or, preferably, preventive checks on growth would come into operation.[4]

This brief outline of Malthus' theory of population incorporates three ideas which have had a profound impact on subsequent theories of population change – ideas which, in combination, we take to be the distinguishing characteristics of a Malthusian theory of population. First, the idea that the fundamental factor influencing population change is what Malthus calls either the 'means of subsistence' or the 'necessaries of life' or what is nowadays more generally called 'resources'. For Malthus some shortage of the necessaries of life is the only *variable* influencing population size, for it is only such a shortage that checks population growth, as the following passage makes clear.

Yet there is no reason whatever to suppose that anything besides the difficulty of procuring in adequate plenty the necessaries of life should either indispose the greater number of persons to marry early or disable them from rearing in health the largest families.[5]

Childbearing, he suggested, is natural and only some lack of necessities stops people from having children in large numbers and stops those children from surviving in 'normal' proportions. The correct question is not therefore 'why do people have children?' There is no need to ask that question since bearing children is natural to mankind. The correct questions are 'why do not people always have as many children as they can?' and 'why do not those born always survive as long as they normally do?' And the answer to both is to be found in the availability of the means of subsistence. Malthus makes it clear, therefore, that for him this is the *one* reason why people do not always have as large families as they might.

Food, he argued, is the most important means of subsistence to be considered, and it is the ultimate check on population growth.

It may be expected, indeed, that in civilized and improved countries, the accumulation of capital, the division of labour and the invention of machinery, will extend the bounds of production; but we know from experience that the effect of these causes, which are astonishing in reference to some of the *conveniences* and *luxuries* of life are very much less efficient in producing an increase in food; and although the saving of labour and an improved system of husbandry may be the means of pushing cultivation upon much poorer lands than could otherwise be worked, yet the increased quantity of the necessaries of life so obtained can never be such as to supersede, for any length of time, the operation of preventive and positive checks to population.[6]

But though food is the ultimate check on population growth, people may be concerned about other 'necessaries of life' and may postpone marriage and childbearing in order to guarantee them.

Although later authors have interpreted the means of subsistence more widely than Malthus, and tend, as we have said, to talk of 'resources' rather than of the 'necessaries of life', the emphasis on the overriding importance of material or economic factors in explaining demographic phenomena has remained. A typical contemporary use of resources as a key explanatory variable, in a theory of population which by our criteria is Malthusian, is that outlined by Kingsley Davis in his paper 'The theory of change and response in modern demographic history'.[7] Although Davis explicitly rejects the framework of 'ordinary population theory which assumes the sole "population factor" to be some ratio between the population-resources ratio and the collective level of living', his objection is to its concern with absolute need and not to its concern with resources.[8] In his view it is not the fear of hunger but the fear of 'invidious deprivation' – a fear of lower standards vis-à-vis other groups – that checks family size (in situations of low mortality). Davis argues, in other words, that it is not absolute but relative deprivation by which men are affected.

The dominance of the belief in the importance of material resources as the key factor influencing levels of childbearing as well as overall population size can be understood in terms of the connection that came to exist between economics and population studies.[9] Since economics has been the discipline concerned with the distribution of scarce resources, any phenomenon that has to be explained in terms of resource levels was properly within its province; and once population studies had come to be closely allied with economics it was only natural to explain population levels by reference to resources. The circle was self-reinforcing; and it has meant that much of the debate in population theory has focussed on *how* resources affect population growth rather than whether they do so. The contribution of most sociologists who have entered the arena, such as Davis and Banks, has been to address themselves to the former question rather than the latter.[10] There are exceptions to this emphasis, of course, the work of Judith Blake, for example.[11]

The second distinctive feature of Malthus' population theory which has has a major influence on subsequent population theory is the idea that there is some sort of regulation or adjustment of population size to the level of the available means of subsistence. Resources are important in Malthus' theory not just because they influence population change, but because they *regulate* population growth. More specifically the implicit model underlying the Malthusian theory of population is of a homeostatic system: if population growth exceeds the level that can be sustained by the means of subsistence it will be checked; if it does not growth will be possible until such a point is reached. Hence there is, at least in theory, a point where population is in balance with resources – a point of equilibrium. From this point of view the positive and preventive checks become 'equilibriating mechanisms', the means of adjusting population to resources. Malthus does not himself explicitly use the language of homeostasis in describing population change, though he does talk of checks, balances, regulation and so forth, and it has been left to subsequent authors to bring out the implicit homeostatic model more clearly. Habakkuk, for instance, whose work we shall consider in a moment, specifically uses terms like homeostasis and equilibration.[12] The model has also been developed by other authors who use the notion of 'optimum population': a notion that has attracted much interest despite the numerous problems it raises.[13] Homeostatic ideas are also very marked in recent theories of the regulation of animal population.[14] Their emergence in the latter work is especially interesting since in this instance they provide an indirect path from Malthus via Darwin.[15]

The final distinctive feature of Malthus' theory which needs to be emphasised is the idea that in the process of regulation it is the size of the *population* that counts, and changes in fertility and mortality are merely the means whereby the adjustment of population to resources is effected. Hence the explanation of changes in levels of childbearing can only be part of an explanation of population change as a whole. The theory stresses the interdependence and substitutability of demographic factors in the system; it is what Flew calls 'the relatedness of the various variables' that has to be recognised.[16] It is population size that is influenced by the necessaries of life; hence, fertility, mortality and migration should not be viewed as independent factors to be separately explained with population size as the mere aggregate of them all. Instead they should be viewed as interrelated and complementary factors: the alternative means whereby a balance between population and resources is achieved. In consequence, positive and preventive checks will often tend to complement one another:

The sum of all positive and preventive checks taken together forms undoubtedly the immediate cause which represses population; but we can never expect to obtain and estimate accurately this sum in any country and we can certainly draw no safe conclusion of two or three checks taken by themselves, because it so frequently happens that the excess of one check is balanced by the defeat of some other.[17]

Kingsley Davis gave contemporary expression to this Malthusian idea when he described the interrelatedness and complementarity of demographic factors by using the term 'multiphasic response', which denotes that a reduction in population growth may be achieved in a number of different ways; either by abortion, or by contraception, or by the post-ponement of marriage, or by migration or by a variety of other means.[18] In this sense different demographic changes are essentially substitutes for one another.

II: A contemporary adaptation

One recent explanation of population change that incorporates these three Malthusian ideas in its theoretical model is H. J. Habakkuk's *Population Growth and Economic Development since 1750.*[19] It therefore provides a useful framework for more detailed consideration of Malthusian ideas in contemporary form, and illustrates the problems to which they give rise when they are combined.

Habakkuk sets out to explain, in an avowedly Malthusian fashion, the population changes of the demographic transition in England. His summary interpretation of Malthus is as follows:

He was describing a mechanism by which population and resources were kept in line around a range of living standards and he was concerned with cases where population growth was warranted by resources as well as the more dramatised case of excessive population growth. The Malthusian model I propose to use is an equilibrating mechanism which operated on births and deaths from whichever side the initial disturbance came.[20]

In attempting to show how equilibrating mechanisms operated Habakkuk discusses all three stages of the demographic transition. But in judging how effective his analysis is we will consider only that period, the pre-industrial, in which a Malthusian account might be expected, *prima facie* to be most effective. Before industrialisation, increases in fertility were invariably matched by increases in mortality and the role of economic resources in checking growth is generally held to be crucial. Hence Wrigley, though unwilling to extend the analysis further, discusses the pre-industrial period in terms of homeostatic adjustment.[21] In contrast the rapid popula-tion growth during early industrialisation seems, at first-sight, to be evidence of the breakdown of Malthusian homeostasis; a view, however, that Habakkuk naturally rejects, arguing that since productivity was itself radically altered, the rapidity of population growth provides no evidence of the breakdown of equilibration.

Discussing population change in the pre-industrial era from his Malthusian perspective, Habakkuk attempts to specify the equilibrating mechanisms that then operated to link population to the level of resources. From the point of view of fertility he mentions three, of which the most important was age at marriage; 'Because marriage was associated with the setting up of a separate household births are linked with the availability of resources.'[22] In addition he draws attention to the proportions marrying (a factor which he does not consider in any detail) and the control of births within marriage. The latter, he points out, though it occurred, must then have been far less important than age at marriage in linking resources to fertility.

From the point of view of mortality Habakkuk suggests two possible mechanisms of adjustment. On the one hand 'the increase in population in relation to resources might reduce the normal standard of living to a level which increased the incidence of those diseases which were sensitive to the standards of nutrition, so that there was a rise in the level of mortality in a "normal" year'. On the other hand, 'the increase might raise mortality in the abnormal years of high death rates and increase the frequency of such years'. This would happen either because 'severe harvest failures were more likely to occur when population had become dense in relation to resources', or because 'a densely populated area was more vulnerable to those harvest failures which were due solely to the vagaries of the weather'.[23]

As an account of the way in which the level of resources could have influenced the level of births and deaths in a community all this is reasonable enough, although by no means uncontentious;[24] as confirmation that these processes should be regarded as a set of Malthusian equilibrating mechanisms for regulating population to resources it is far more problematic. Above all it is the *interpretation* that he gives to the demographic processes that is controversial. What grounds are there for regarding these processes as ones of equilibration? Habakkuk's mistake is to regard evidence of the influence of resources on the level of births and deaths as sufficient justification of his Malthusian equilibrating mechanisms. It is not.

Let us assume, for the moment, that Habakkuk is right in his account of the influence that resources exerted on the level of births and deaths and thereby on population size in pre-industrial England. There are nevertheless, in our view, two fundamental objections to the use of the homeostatic model to explain these changes. In the first place the homeostatic model cannot be tested in the form in which he presents it and cannot therefore be said to provide us with an *explanation* of the demographic changes to which it refers. This is because neither Habakkuk, nor Malthus himself, provide any clear way of identifying situations where the population is congruent with resources and those where it is not; hence it is impossible to determine whether or not any given demographic change does constitute an adjustment of population to resource levels. If we are to claim that the influence of resources on population constitutes a process of homeostatic adjustment it is an essential prerequisite that we know when population and resources are in balance and when they are not.

For Malthus it is the means of subsistence, especially food, that check growth but there is no clear indication either of the range of items that he regards as necessary or the amounts that are required, so that we cannot tell at any time whether or not population is adjusted to resources. In fact the operation of positive and preventive checks suggests rather different criteria of balance and imbalance. As far as the positive checks are concerned food is, as we have indicated, the prime necessity: the level that checks growth is the minimum necessary for survival (though even this will inevitably vary from environment to environment). If there is just enough food for survival then presumably a point of balance has been reached. In contrast with the operation of preventive checks the necessaries of life appear to be given a broader interpretation: a wider range of items is included and the standard set may be above an absolute minimum. Such a standard seems to be what is conventionally regarded as necessary, rather than the absolute biological necessities, but Malthus is far from clear about this.[25] At times he suggests that through prudence and foresight couples will postpone marriage and abstain from producing children in situations where the population would otherwise be checked by positive means; at other times he suggests they may act in this way well before such a point is reached in order to maintain or even to raise their standard of living. In this instance the adjustment occurs at a rather different level to that involved in the operation of positive checks. Do both count as points of balance between population and resources? In the latter case, even more than the former, we are given little guidance how to decide whether a particular change is one of adjustment or not. If all demographic changes are to be regarded as movements towards balance or as evidence of 'regulation' then the idea has very little explanatory value.

This problem is even more acute in the model formulated by Habakkuk. Not only does he use the more general term resources, which he nowhere defines, thereby giving us a far less clear idea of the factors that regulate population growth, but he explicitly (and rightly) recognises that the standards about which people will be concerned are set by conventions and are variable. To take account of this he has, therefore, to allow that some population changes may involve the establishment of a new point of equilibrium rather than the restoration of a former one.

when population increased more or less than resources, changes in births and deaths were set in motion which tended to bring them in line. But there might also be set in motion longer-term social changes which might permanently shift the relation between people and resources.[26]

But once Habakkuk introduces this possibility, the difficulty of deciding whether the system is in balance, and hence of deciding whether his interpretation is correct, is even greater, since there can now be more than one point of equilibrium. What by the previous standards – if they had been determined – would count as imbalance could turn out to be a new point of equilibrium: a matter that we could presumably only decide in retrospect. There could well be an asymmetry here: that people are more willing to take up an excess of resources in higher standards than to absorb a deficit of resources by a reduction in standards, but we are offered little guidance by Habakkuk either about the circumstances in which a new point of equilibrium might develop or about how to identify situations of balance or imbalance.

Against this it might be argued that determining the point of equilibrium is always, and rightly, an empirical matter; that if we observe population changes over time they appear as fluctuations around a particular point: the point of equilibrium. The trouble with this argument is that it is only plausible if we accept that there can be more than one point of equilibrium, since historically population change is not a question of fluctuations around a single point. But once having admitted that possibility we cannot readily establish the point of equilibrium by empirical means, for we have no good reason for saying that any given change constitutes a movement towards an old point of equilibrium, towards a new one, or whatever. In practice, no doubt, change would tend to be interpreted as movement towards a new equilibrium and lack of change as evidence that a new equilibrium has been reached. Yet if this is all we can say then the reason for and value of the homeostatic framework to explain demographic change is nil. The language of homeostasis adds nothing to our understanding of the processes involved. To talk of equilibrium and equilibration or of regulation and adjustment does not itself explain the dynamics of these population changes; it becomes merely a redescription of demographic change and stability: a new form of words that adds nothing to the explanation. It tells us very little about the conditions in which population growth will occur and when it will not. What we want to know is precisely what standards people do take into consideration when planning their family size, under what conditions standards are raised, when if at all, they are lowered, and so on: questions that neither Malthus nor Habakkuk answer.

The second major weakness of the homeostatic model when applied to population changes arises from the attempts that are made to incorporate into a single homeostatic framework both natural processes over which people have little control and those over which they have far more. Malthus himself treats as substitute checks on population growth two processes where the role of human agency is often likely to be very different. On the one hand we have increases in the numbers who die in a community from disease and starvation when resources are scarce, a process that presumably usually occurs with little intention or will on the part of those concerned. On the other hand we have reductions in the number of children born as a result of the intentional decisions of specific individuals.[27] Now, from the point of view of population statistics there is an equivalence: one person more or less; but to suggest that both can be subsumed within the same homeostatic framework and therefore *operate* in a similar manner is misguided. The regulation, if we want to use that term, involved in the mortality check through lack of resources that Malthus describes and the fertility check through lack of resources is clearly very different. One check is primarily 'natural': it is part of our biological make-up that if we do not have enough to eat we will die. The other is primarily a question of social rules, of conventional practices based on beliefs that it may be to one's personal advantage (or that of the community) if one has fewer children. Such rules are very different from the laws of nature: they can, for instance, be changed and they need not be followed.

Malthus, of course, recognised that the control of population growth by positive and preventive means differed considerably; he nevertheless felt it appropriate to incorporate both within the same model as if the mode of adjustment was the same, as well as the effects. If the homeostatic model is to be used at all it would seem to be more appropriate for the former than the latter since it derives from the natural sciences. It suggests an inbuilt, automatic process of adjustment, an idea of self-regulation, that fits the Malthusian positive checks better than the preventive ones.

To some extent Habakkuk does recognise the problem.

The equilibrating influences . . . resemble in some ways the mechanisms which it has been suggested tend to maintain the equilibrium in animal population. Precisely how these mechanisms work is not in fact a settled matter, but the resort to the restriction of births during seasons of famine does seem like the natural reaction of an animal population. But the longer-term changes in patterns of behaviour – in age at marriage, for instance, and in standards of living – were the result of decision after a process of reflection and reasoning, however rudimentary, and were therefore different in kind from the responses of animal populations.[28]

However, these comments are puzzling in two respects. First, it is not clear why Habakkuk suggests that the control of births after famine is not included in the category of reflective intentional action, whereas changes in age at marriage are, since he does not appear to regard changes in fecundity as the mechanism involved. More importantly, having pointed to the qualitative difference between events that involve intentional action and those that do not, he is happy to talk of both as parallel equilibrating mechanisms in a homeostatic system, forgetting the fact that the difference in operation is crucial and that where human agency is involved the idea of in-built automatic adjustment of demographic phenomena to the level of resources is much more problematic.

Suppose, however, we abandon the homeostatic language; we may still ask whether Habakkuk, or indeed Malthus, is right in the importance that is given to material resources in the explanation of population change. It must be remembered in so doing that the importance of resources in Malthusian population theory is enhanced by the homeostatic framework. They are important not because they are the sole influence on demographic processes but because they set the standards to which demographic processes adjust. Hence Habakkuk can admit, as he does, that in the pre-industrial period death rates were not responsive to resource-based factors alone (he points out that epidemics could raise the death rate above the normal level and that these are not to be explained solely in terms of resources – though even this admission does not go far enough for some) the important thing is that there should be some way of adjusting population to resources. This is all the Malthusian model requires. Resources are not the only influence, but they have the controlling hand.

Nevertheless, homeostatic language or no, the question remains of how important an influence on demographic processes material resources are. We would argue that their importance appears, from the evidence we have, to have varied culturally and historically and that only detailed empirical investigation can establish the precise role that they have played at different times and places. The evidence does suggest, however, simplifying the argument, that in the pre-industrial period material resources, rather narrowly defined – food, clothing, houses, tools – did often limit and influence the growth of population; that the ebb and flow of population like much else was often closely tied to and circumscribed by the material conditions of man's existence. How could it have been otherwise? Problems with the supply of food were perennial, as Braudel describes:

Famine recurred so insistently for centuries on end that it became incorporated into man's biological regime and built into his daily life. Dearth and penury were continual, and familiar even in Europe, despite its privileged position. A few overfed rich do not alter the rule.[29]

Indeed the overriding domination of man's life by his material circumstances and the routines developed to cope with those circumstances are what characterises pre-industrial society. Braudel comments:

Man was locked in an economic condition that reflected his human condition. He was an unconscious prisoner of the frontier marking the inflexible boundaries between the possible and the impossible. Before the eighteenth century his sphere of action was tightly circumscribed, largely limited to what could be achieved through physical effort. Whatever he did, he could not step over a certain line – and this line was drawn close to him. He did not even reach it most of the time.[30]

In such a society material resources set a boundary between the possible and the impossible for population growth, just as they did for so many other things. In contrast, in an industrial society while the boundary may still exist it is so much higher that it no longer sets the practical limits on population growth. Other factors start to become much more important. Not only do the increases in productivity change the material standards that can be achieved and to which people aspire, so that, as Kingsley Davis points out, the fear of invidious deprivation becomes more important than the fear of some absolute deprivation, but the need to be so greatly concerned about material resources diminishes. Our own study documents some of the concerns that influenced childbearing in England in the 1950s and 1960s and shows that material resources were by no means the only consideration.

Our objections to Malthusian population theory are, therefore, threefold. First that material resources are assumed to be the overriding influence on population growth which is not always the case. Second, that the homeostatic framework not only has little explanatory value but also leaves unanswered crucial questions about the way in which resources may influence population growth. And third, that the homeostatic model is extended to processes which are not similar in operation, and need to be analysed separately if they are to be understood.

It is true, nevertheless, that pre-industrial societies generally come closer to satisfying the conditions of Malthusian population theory than our own. They combine three characteristics more favourable to such a theory: an economic condition in which material resources were likely to have a considerable effect on population growth; an economic condition in which populations were more likely to fluctuate around the same level; and a situation where human agency may have played a lesser part in the demographic processes that occurred. Yet even in these 'favourable' conditions homeostatic notions are not only inappropriate to explain many of the demographic changes that did occur, but they do not help us do so.

3. Utilitarian theories of fertility

It is hardly surprising that resources have been given a central role in theories that focus on explaining variations in fertility alone, in view of their prominence in explanations of population change as a whole. In that sense most theories of fertility have been broadly economic, though not always exclusively so. It is, then, no less surprising that recently a number of authors have, in their efforts to explain differences in the timing and frequency of childbearing (whether temporal, cross-cultural or intra-societal), developed theories that are economic in a more specialised sense. Not only do they give prominence, even primacy to resource factors, but in their account of *how* these factors influence childbearing they use theoretical models borrowed directly from economics. In particular they have at their foundation the classic model of utilitarian man.

Theories of this type are variously labelled 'economic', 'new economic' and 'socio-economic' for the earlier, simpler versions have been modified in an attempt to cope with some of the complexities of the real world.[1] We shall term them utilitarian theories of fertility since they apply the utilitarian notions of classic economic thought to childbearing, though other more recent theoretical ideas from economics are often incorporated as well. Whilst they vary considerably in detail they have certain common features. They assume that a child is, at least in some respects, like any other good or commodity; hence having a child can be analysed as a decision to 'purchase', 'invest' or 'produce' a child and can be analysed in terms of the child's price or cost, the utility to be derived from it, its cost and utility relative to other goods or commodities and the resources available.[2] It is assumed that costs and utilities are assessed and compared and that, on the basis of the calculation, the household or family chooses the particular number of children that maximises its utility.[3]

The theories were originally developed in an attempt to explain the observed association between income or economic growth and fertility, and were initially sketched out in the work of Leibenstein and Okun, but Becker's paper 'An economic analysis of fertility', first published in 1960, is generally regarded as seminal.[4] His work relies almost entirely on the traditional theory of consumer choice (although brief mention is made of the 'production' of children) and concentrates its theoretical discussion on the various factors of tastes, income, costs and so forth. However, it gives little explicit attention to the underlying assumptions of the approach.

The modification and developments of Becker's framework have been rapid and numerous. Five developments have been of especial importance. First, there has been a shift of interest from the effects of differences in income on fertility to the effects of differences in the costs of children. Second, and related to this, the cost of the wife's time has been included in the price of children: it is given monetary value in terms of 'opportunity cost', that is the cost of income foregone by the wife.[5] This has also meant that time may be introduced as a further 'resource' constraining child-bearing. Third, more attention has been paid to the investment in 'human capital' that is involved in having children. Fourth, attempts have been made to develop models that allow the family unit to be treated at one and the same time as consumers and producers of children.[6] Fifth and finally, factors like 'coition' or 'sexual gratification' have been introduced as further economic goods or commodities in an attempt to handle the variable of contraceptive effectiveness in a more satisfactory manner.[7]

These are not, of course, the only developments; others have been made or suggested, such as Easterlin's claims that more attention should be given to the social influences on and variations in tastes.[8] Yet none of them have, in our view, significantly increased the value of the theories. They have changed certain important details and made the models far more complex. They have not, in most cases, changed the theories' central premises or the way in which they are constructed, and these are their fundamental defects. We intend to argue that utilitarian theories of fertility have not only failed to provide us so far with an adequate explanation of fertility, but are also unlikely to do so in the future. To that end we shall first outline in more detail the underlying premises on which utilitarian theories are based, then show why a direct evaluation of them cannot be avoided, and we will finally consider why they provide a poor foundation for any adequate explanation of patterns of childbearing.

Whilst there have been many critical discussions of utilitarian theorising in general there has been relatively little critical evaluation of utilitarian theories of fertility.[9] The most systematic critique so far has been that of Judith Blake.[10] However, not only is it no longer up to date (she deals primarily with Becker's original paper) but in our opinion she concentrates too much of her attack on the wrong point. Thus although she explicitly, and rightly, questions the analogy of children with consumer goods, she does not consider and evaluate the theories' other central premises. Furthermore much of the substance of her argument is an attempt to demonstrate that the correlations between income and childbearing do not provide empirical support for the theories. Yet, by adopting this strategy of attack, she fails to recognise that utilitarian theorising is an elusive and slippery creature (on this point as on others) and it is all too easy for the theorists either to introduce modifications to the theories in the face of contrary evidence, or to point to qualifying factors to account for any discrepancy between the theory and correlated data of this type, rather than to accept that the theoretical approach has no value. One response to attacks like hers has been the shift of interest to the effects of differences in the price of children rather than of differences in income. Whilst this is important, since it raises significant questions about the differential cost of children, it does not alter the central premises of the theories or the way in which they are constructed, which are the real weaknesses of utilitarian theorising about fertility, here as elsewhere. Let us begin, however, by outlining the basic premises of the theories in more detail in order to make our argument clearer.

I: The foundations
The basic premises of utilitarian theories of production and consumption can be outlined very simply. Here is Herbert Simon's description.

There are two principal species of economic man: the consumer and the entre-preneur. Classic economics assumes the goals of both to be given; the former wishes to maximise his utility, which is a known function of the goods and services he consumes; the latter to maximise his profit. The theory then assumes both of them to be rational. Confronted with a pair of alternatives, they will select that one which yields the larger utility or profit, respectively.

Beyond these postulates—that he is rational and that his goals are specified—the theory assumes nothing about the psychological characteristics of economic man. The factors that determine his behaviour (apart from those already mentioned) are entirely external to him. The consumer is constrained by a fixed budget, say, and by the prices of goods and services; the entrepreneur is faced with determinate supply schedules for his products, and a technologically determined production function. The economist predicts their behaviour, to the extent that he is interested in it without subjecting them to tests either or intelligence or of personality.[11]

What form do the premises take when this economic model is extended to the sphere of childbearing? We want to outline five central ones (many other assumptions are made in any particular theory as we shall see). In the first place the theories make two initial premises in order to assert the relevance of the utilitarian model to childbearing. First, that children are an economic good or commodity or to use Easterlin's phrase, that 'fertility behaviour reflects a balancing of preferences against certain resource constraints'.[12] This premise is the core of the controversial analogy of children with consumer durables, and in terms of utilitarian theory it means that children are assumed to have both costs and utilities, which, in combination with the level of available resources, determine family size. Both costs and resources are given some monetary value, and the assumption is that, other things being equal, a higher level of resources will therefore lead to higher fertility. Willis' formulation of this premise is more complex and more precise, but essentially the same. His aim, he says, is to consider 'those characteristics of children that provide satisfaction (or dissatisfaction) to their parents as commodities produced with time and goods according to household production functions'.[13] The second, related premise, is that children and other goods or commodities are, at least to some extent, substitutes; that not only are their respective costs and utilities potentially comparable, but that comparisons are indeed made between them, and children are viewed as alternatives to other goods or commodities. This premise is not usually distinguished from the first but is integral to the approach, particularly when the emphasis is on the effects of differences in the price of children on fertility, which are often termed substitution effects. Moreover, our own data points to the need to distinguish the assumption that children are treated as substitutes for other goods from the assumption that decisions about fertility are a question of balancing preferences against resource constraints.

The third and fourth premises are standard assumptions of utilitarian theories and relate to the 'rationality' of the individual. The third is that individuals have perfect knowledge of the costs and utilities of children as well as other goods. Willis, for instance, assumes that couples 'possess perfect foresight concerning all the relevant demographic and economic variables'.[14] The fourth posits that choice is made according to the principle of maximising utility. Interestingly this principle is not specifically mentioned by Becker, although it is entailed by his adoption of the utilitarian theory of consumer choice. Easterlin and Willis do, however, talk of the maximisation of utility when decisions about having children are made. Willis assumes 'that the family behaves as if it is attempting to maximise a utility function' (of the type he specifies).[15]

A fifth and final premise should be mentioned, though it is not made in all theories. The premise, which is again specific to the application of utilitarian ideas to childbearing, attempts to cope with the fact that family size is not merely a matter of how many children one chooses or desires, but also of one's success, or lack of it, in controlling one's childbearing, by assuming that the individual has complete power to control childbearing. Becker, for instance, says 'I assume initially that each family has perfect control over both the number and spacing of births',[16] and Willis similarly asserts 'the couples will be assumed to have perfect and costless control over their fertility'.[17] In consequence, the 'rationality' that is assumed of the decision making process itself, is extended, at least initially, to the control of fertility.

II: Testing the predictions

The exact status and value of utilitarian theories has long been a matter of debate. At the centre of the controversy is a disagreement about the supposed nature of the premises on which the theories are founded; more precisely both whether they are unrealistic and whether any lack of realism, which has often been attested, matters.[18] These issues have given rise to a number of more specific questions. Are the axioms intended to embody psychological or social truths? To have an empirical or an *a priori* basis? To what extent and in what ways are the assumptions unrealistic? To what extent does any lack of realism in theoretical premises matter? Are utilitarian theories supposed to have normative or explanatory value? Such questions touch on epistemological and philosophical issues and do not admit of any easy answer. Nevertheless for those, like ourselves, who are interested in the value of utilitarian theories for explanatory purposes there is a standard and reputable (though far from uncontentious) response to such debates that avoids many of the questions: to argue that the proper test of a scientific theory is to be found in the extent to which its predictions fit the facts, and that any lack of realism in the premises which yield the predictions is acceptable, indeed it may even be advantageous.[19] According to this argument what matters is 'the concordance of the theory's logical consequences with the phenomena the theory was designed to explain',[20] theoretical prediction and explanation are held to be two sides of the same coin, and '"realism" is unimportant, abstraction must take place and a model can abstract from anything as long as it performs well'.[21] Let us consider, therefore, whether utilitarian theories of fertility do yield predictions that fit the facts, thereby justifying any abstraction, and allowing us to avoid any more direct judgement of their central premises, and the way in which they are constructed.

In our view it is impossible to test the predictions of utilitarian theories of fertility at all satisfactorily. The reasons for this are apparent if we consider two basic procedures necessary to test any one of the theoretical models against empirical observations. First, the model has to be developed in a sufficiently precise way in order to produce specific empirical predictions. This means not only defining the variables included in the model in such a way that they will yield conceptually and empirically satisfactory measures, but also specifying the relations that hold between variables. Both can only be done by making numerous assumptions in addition to the basic premises: making assumptions such as Becker's that the quantity income elasticity of children is small and the quality elasticity larger, or the later popular one that price of children includes the costs of the wife's time (not the husband's) and that this should be measured in terms of the cost of the income she forgoes.[22] However, as the authors themselves recognise, deciding on the precise nature of assumptions like this, which are necessary to produce determinate predictions from the models, is far from easy.[23] Not only is the relevant empirical data on which they might be based lacking (what is the 'elasticity' of children?) so that assumptions often have to be made on a highly intuitive basis, but in order to produce models that are not excessively complex the assumptions very often have to be over-simple (the cost to the husband of time spent with children has for instance to be ignored, a fixed set of costs have to be included, and so forth).

Now these problems might seem to be problems of theory *construction* rather than of *testing* the theoretical predictions. Yet they relate to the latter as well as the former. For the difficulties of producing sufficiently complex models whose assumptions have a sound empirical basis means that in practice the models are irrefutable, for any discrepancy between observations and predictions may always be due to factors that could not be included, or to the precise nature of certain assumptions. In consequence discrepancies between predictions and observations are regarded as providing grounds for further modifications and developments of the model rather than for its rejection. The point can be readily illustrated by considering Becker's original model. His concern was with the effects of differences in income on fertility and his simple model predicted that those with higher income should have somewhat more children on average than those with lower incomes. However, he recognised that this prediction was not commensurate with most of the observed correlations between income and fertility which the model was designed to explain, since these have only rarely been positive.[24] Hence, he argued, other factors must be affecting the relationship. Being modest in this respect (Easterlin discussing the same relationship lists far more) he discusses two possibilities: that tastes or preference may vary systematically with income and that contraceptive knowledge may also differ.[25] He gave most attention to the latter and suggested that were contraceptive knowledge adequately distributed throughout a population the positive correlation between income and fertility would emerge. But these qualifications make it impossible to test the predictions of his model. Not only is it unclear what Becker counts as an adequate distribution of contraceptive knowledge, and therefore what observations do constitute a test of the theory, but also, since he fails to specify how tastes vary with income, we do not know under what circumstances we should expect a positive relationship between income and fertility.[26] In order to test his model we need far more precise statements about how the qualifying factors affect the relationship between income and fertility than those he provides.

It is true, of course, that later models are far more complex and precise, yet they do not, by their authors' own admissions, either include all the relevant factors or make assumptions about them that are based on sound empirical observations, so that the inevitable temptation is to see any discrepancy as either due to the exclusion of some variable or to the precise form of certain assumptions rather than to question the underlying premises and approach. Hence, as Ben-Porath points out; 'Much of the economic treatment of fertility has been concerned with the relation between income and fertility, largely in an attempt to discover the expected positive association behind the "mask" of the observed negative association.'[27] Yet if this is the strategy adopted it is difficult to see what evidence would ever be sufficient to be regarded as grounds for modifying the central premises of the theories or the approach adopted. Under the circumstances can we treat any consistency between predictions and observations as of any significance either?

A similar difficulty arises when attempts are made to obtain empirical measures of the theoretical variables in order to test the theories. None of the variables are easy to measure empirically. Take, for instance, the task of establishing the costs of children in order to decide whether or not difference in cost affects childbearing. How for instance do we measure the opportunity cost of a wife's time? Is her level of education, which has been used by some, a good enough indication?[28] Equally, establishing the direct monetary costs of children is far from easy though measurement is easier in principle, since assessing the full extent of the costs over the complete period of dependency is very difficult.[29] Inevitably numerous assumptions have to be made to produce any specific figure. Moreover, if you substitute subjective costs for objective ones in the theoretical model the task of measurement is not made much easier, since the expected costs either need to be assessed directly in advance of childbearing, so the relevant data is of course lacking for those whose childbearing is already underway or completed (who are usually the object of study), or else some estimate has to be made on the basis of actual costs.

The same is true of the measurement of resource factors such as income. As Willis argues 'the income variable relevant to childbearing decisions presumably involves the shape and height of the husband's life cycle income as he expects it to be at the time these decisions are taken' so that any single measure of current income is likely to provide a poor estimate of the variable.[30] He therefore attempts to produce a superior measure of husbands' life-time income by using estimates (based on Census data for 1960 and the Survey and Economic Opportunity for 1967), of the life-cycle earnings functions of males by occupation to predict 'the income of husbands as a function of their education, labour market experience, cohort, weeks worked, size of place, and whether or not they reside in the South'.[31] But this 'improved' measure of income is not only an estimate that involves numerous assumptions, but since it is based on data of actual income can only be said to be a good measure of *expected* income over the life cycle by virtue of Willis' initial assumption that the individual has 'perfect foresight concerning all the relevant demographic and economic variables'.

It is even more difficult to measure tastes or preferences for children vis-à-vis other goods or commodities, and they are very often treated as a constant in the model, both for that reason and on the grounds that differences in income and costs are enough to explain differences in fertility.[32] Yet if we do not measure tastes we cannot be certain that they are uniform and that differences in taste are not affecting the relationship we observe. Expressed desires about family size and spacing are a poor measure since tastes and preferences are supposed to *underlie* family size desires and to help to explain them. Fertility, itself, for obvious reasons, is an even less precise measure.

Such difficulties raise, once more, very forcibly, the question of whether the predictions from the theories can be tested at all satisfactorily. Suppose we tackle the problems and produce measures of all the variables using existing empirical data as a basis for estimation, making numerous additional assumptions in the process, and find in the end, that the model's predictions do not fit the observations, then the inevitable tendency is to blame the measures rather than to accept the theory itself is mistaken. Yet if we cannot ever say that the discrepancy between predictions and observations call the basic premises of the model into question, what value has any consistency between predictions and observations?[33]

It is not, therefore, possible to test the predictions of utilitarian theories of fertility in a satisfactory manner. Not only is it difficult to formulate the models in such a way that all the salient factors are included and their relationships specified on a sound empirical basis, but it is also difficult to obtain satisfactory operational measures of the variables. In consequence there is always a good excuse for trying to improved the model or the measure of the variables rather than for rejecting that type of model altogether. We cannot, therefore, justify any abstraction the premises involve by claims about the success of their theoretical predictions. Moreover our examination shows that the theorists have continually to make additional assumptions of an empirical nature in order to yield specific predictions from their models.[34] Both arguments point to the need to evaluate the basic premises and approach of the theories more directly. A claim that can be backed up by another argument: that the test of a good theory, if by this we mean a good explanation, is not just that its predictions should fit the observations it is designed to explain but that it should give us an account of *how* the phenomena in question occurred—an account which must itself correspond with empirical observations.[35] Even if we can establish in a satisfactory manner the correspondence of the theories predictions with empirical observations (i.e. the theory is in practice refutable) this is not enough: for it still leaves open the question of whether the account of the mechanism by which the phenomena were supposed to be generated is satisfactory.

III: Castles in the air

Our discussion of the problems of testing the predictions of utilitarian theories of fertility has touched upon certain inherent weaknesses of this type of theorising. These weaknesses are illustrated very clearly if we examine in detail the basic premises on which the theories are founded.

Direct examination of the basic premises of utilitarian theories of fertility points to a number of reasons why they cannot provide a good basis for a satisfactory theory of fertility when judged by a number of different criteria. First, and most obviously, their scope is narrow as they only attempt to explain a narrow range of phenomena. Not only do many of the models fail to provide any explanation of variations in contraceptive efficiency, but more importantly, much is taken as given within the context of the theory and is not explained. In particular the tastes and skills of individuals are treated as given: a point that has long been recognised. Lionel Robbins talking about utilitarian theory generally has this to say 'in our analysis we take the scale of valuation as given' and later, 'as economists we cannot go behind changes in valuations'.[36] Edward Nell puts the point like this 'households and firms are considered only as market agents, never as parts of the social structure. Their initial endowments, wealth, skills and property are taken as given'.[37] Hence there is no attempt in the theories of fertility to examine the factors that generate 'tastes' for children, nor is there any attempt to examine the factors that generate the skills and technology to realise those 'tastes'. Yet if tastes for children or for other goods vary over time and between groups, as is likely (the assumptions of many economists notwithstanding), then their explanation is an important matter. Against this it could be argued that a theory should be judged by what it tries to explain and not by what it does not. Yet is it merely churlish to feel that a theory of fertility that does not tackle key questions like this can only have limited value? The defence that the theories do not preclude such explanations, perhaps in normative terms, is hardly satisfactory, since they do not provide the explanation. Besides, it is doubtful whether the two types of approach are compatible.[38]

Second, there is good reason to believe that the nature of certain premises is such that the theories could only have, at most a limited range of application and could not provide a *general* theory of fertility in the way the authors assume. The premises are essentially individualistic and ignore the influence of social factors on the individual. By so doing they make assumptions that hold only in certain circumstances, failing to consider how individual tastes and skills might themselves be explained. Take for instance the first assumption that we mentioned above that 'fertility behaviour reflects a balancing of preferences against certain resource constraints'. It is easy to point to many differences between children and the things conventionally regarded as economic goods.[39] One difference is that conception costs nothing and payment only comes later. Another is that the costs of a child are generally more variable and have to be met over a longer period than those of most other goods. Furthermore as far as conventional economic goods are concerned a decision has to be made if a good is to be acquired, whereas children may be born unless some action is taken. Yet such points of difference are not necessarily fatal to the utilitarian approach and are often recognised by those who adopt it.[40] Far more important is the fact that by ignoring the social and cultural context of childbearing the premise is based on assumptions that only apply in certain instances. On the one hand the premise assumes that having children is a matter of *individual* or *familial* choice: that it is legally and socially acceptable for couples to have specific preferences about the number and quantity and children they will have, and to act on the basis of those preferences. This ignores the extent to which there is social and historical variation in such rights. Whilst it is true that in England and other capitalist industrial societies issues of family size and spacing are felt to be a matter for individual choice, though that choice may be influenced by government policies and social norms (the ideology of family planning is to provide couples with the knowledge and skills to have only as many children as they choose, and no more), in many societies there is far less room for personal choice.[41] In countries that adopt explicit and restrictive government population policies and attempt to control fertility very directly, or in societies where family size is felt to be a matter of God's will not man's, this assumption does not apply.

On the other hand even where issues about family size and spacing are taken to be a matter of individual or familial choice, the extent to which the choice is governed by resources, however narrowly or broadly defined, is variable, and an issue for empirical investigation. If we take the example of England in the post-war period, our own work shows that although family size is felt to be a matter for individual couples to decide, and although most couples do take resources such as income and time into consideration in deciding how many children to have and when to have them, the extent to which the level of resources may influence the level of childbearing is culturally restricted just as the concern for resources itself is influenced by social norms. It is generally expected that all 'normal' adults will marry and have *some* children, and this prescription has little to do with resources however defined, although resources may influence the timing of these events to some extent. Nor is the cultural prescription limited to the issue of having some children; it also specifies the acceptable minimum on grounds that likewise do not relate to resources. In contrast, the normative maximum is culturally linked to resources, though in a far from simple way. Now it might be argued, that this is only a matter of cultural and historical variation in tastes and does not reflect on the assumption that fertility behaviour involves a balancing of tastes against resources. Yet if having *some* children is normatively prescribed, irrespective of the level of resources, and this explains why a particular individual does have some, then we cannot claim that in this case the fertility did involve a balancing of tastes against resources. We may say it involved 'tastes', but resources did not come into the matter. Hence on the evidence of our study alone there is good reason to suppose that the utilitarian analysis of childbearing could only have restricted application: it might help to explain choices above the normative minimum, and may in some cases help to explain and legitimate choices outside those norms, but it would be wrong to say that in having two children most couples were balancing tastes against resources. Moreover, as yet the models have only attempted to incorporate time and income as resources, whereas our data suggests that the 'resources' that influence childbearing are broader than this.[42]

The same lack of concern for social and cultural influences on fertility is manifest in other premises of the theories and has the same effect of narrowing their potential range of application. It is manifest, for instance, in the second premise of utilitarian theories listed above: that children and other economic goods are at least to some extent considered to be substitutes for one another. A standard objection to utilitarian theories of consumer choice is that utilities are not comparable: an objection that produces the counter-argument that though comparisons may be difficult in theory, since it is hard to locate the utility from different goods on a common scale, nevertheless in practice people must make and do make such comparisons in the market place.[43] However, this pragmatic defence is not necessarily so readily available when the utility of children is in question. Our own evidence showed that most people did not locate question about whether to have children, how many to have, and when to have them in the context of alternative sources of utility. Even where they were explicitly concerned about the adequacy of their resources and about the cost of children when making decisions about having children, they did not generally regard the issues as one of choice between using up resources on children and using them up on other goods. Though some people may have put children and other goods in the same calculus, most did not. They did not regard the consumption of resources on children as an alternative to their consumption elsewhere, and to have suggested that buying a television might have been an alternative to having another child would have been regarded by them as not only materialistic and selfish, but probably somewhat bizarre.

Moreover there is a further belief in this society that discourages comparisons between satisfactions from children and those from other things. This is the belief that children bring satisfaction that cannot be gained from anything else. Our culture stresses the uniqueness of the pleasures to be derived from having children: we tend to believe they have no adequate substitutes. Becker seems to admit this possibility when he asserts 'There are no good substitutes for children', but then he adds 'but there may be many poor ones', which ignores the fact that other things are only regarded as substitutes for those who have no children *faute de mieux*.[44]

The restriction on the comparisons of satisfaction to be derived from having children and that for acquiring other goods is not true of all cultures. In Hungary, for instance, in recent years the phrase 'kicsi vagy kocsi' ('a child or a car') has been a common one, and indicates that children and certain other material goods (presumably highly prized ones) have at least at certain times been placed within the same comparative framework. Nor does it necessarily extend to other demographic events in this country. Zweig reporting on a study of English workers in the 1950s commented that getting a wife was considered an alternative to getting a car. The question was:

What is better, a car or a wife? I was courting confided one, 'and I should have been married by now, but instead I bought a car'. At first (comments Zweig) I treated this as a joke, but I heard it so many times in so many versions (I can't afford both a car and a wife, so I drifted from my girl') that I had to regard it as a major issue for youth at present.[45]

Here as elsewhere utilitarian theories, by ignoring cultural influences on behaviour, ignore important differences that affect childbearing. Our own study suggested that those who did compare the satisfaction they might derive from having children with that to be gained elsewhere were more likely to think that it was desirable to have no children at all, or only one, than those who made decisions about family size in isolation. Such evidence again suggests that if utilitarian theories have any application it is strictly limited. The same is true of the assumption, made by some of the authors, that individuals have perfect control over their fertility, which automatically restricts the application of the theories (perfect control of childbearing, if by that is meant only having births when intended, is relatively rare even in societies where use of birth control is widespread), as well as making it more difficult to identify the relevant data against which the models can be tested.

Much of the lack of concern for social and cultural processes stems from the abstract nature of utilitarian theorising, and the willingness to make assumptions that have little basis in empirical observation. The poverty of the empirical foundation of utilitarian theorising has been noted elsewhere. Discussing the use of utilitarian ideas in Oligopoly theory, Simon comments:

Oligopoly theory today is embarrassed by its inability to choose among the rich assortment of alternative assumptions that are available to it. It is unable to choose because the alternatives represent conflicting *empirical* statements about the psychological characteristics of economic man, and economic theory is not accustomed to deriving his characteristics from empirical observation.[46]

Talking more generally Eversley suggests that the classical economists 'were not particularly interested in behaviour'.[47] This willingness to make theoretical assumptions that have little basis in empirical observation is especially and notoriously apparent in the conventional 'rationality' assumptions, with the result that the assumptions probably do not apply in any known instance. It has been pointed out many times that people do not and cannot act in a rational utilitarian way even when in the market place. Each person cannot and does not make decisions on the basis of perfect information about the available alternatives, their different costs, or with a clear idea of their different utilities. The assumption that those who have children can know the costs of children is, as we have already pointed out, highly dubious and has been modified in some of the theories, as is the assumption that they can know in advance what satisfaction they will derive from them. The same applies to the premise that individuals or families maximise their utility when making decisions about having children.[48] Even if people had the relevant knowledge about the costs and utilities at issue, and had consistent orderings of their preferences, it is most unlikely that they would be capable of carrying out the sort of calculation necessary to identify what choice would maximise their utility. Yet if we modify these assumptions and adopt more realistic ones about rationality (as, for instance, Herbert Simon's notion of 'bounded rationality', which admits the imperfections of human knowledge, does not require consistent preference orderings, and recognises the limitations of human calculative capacity) we must perforce examine in detail the way in which people do make calculations and choices; on this topic as on other matters we cannot assume uniformity.[49]

Our analysis of the premises of utilitarian theories indicates, therefore, three types of defect. First, that the premises, by treating the values of certain variables as given, fail to provide an explanation of important phenomena that influence childbearing and need to be explained. Second, that certain premises have only a narrow historical and cultural application thereby narrowing the potential range of application of the theories. And third, that other premises make assumptions that would seem to have no empirical application whatever and could therefore only be justified by the results that they produce: a justification which their performance has failed to provide.[50]

The defects themselves have a common origin that can, on the one hand be described as a reluctance to collect empirical data in order to provide a sound empirical basis for the theoretical premises together with a willingness to theorise in their absence, and on the other hand as a lack of interest in the influence of social factors on behaviour. Whilst it is fashionable to decry empiricism and whilst we ourselves accept that any empirical observation incorporates and reflects theoretical presuppositions, the force of this point is surely that our concepts and ideas influence our observations, and not that we can manage to theorise satisfactorily without them. Utilitarian theorising tends to treat empirical phenomena as a painful necessity, as irritating complications to what might otherwise be a neatly ordered world, not as the essential part, the substance, of theorising. The specific failure to consider the influence of social factors on behaviour and the detrimental effect this gives rise to has again been noted elsewhere. This is what Norman Ryder has to say about the failure of some writers to recognise the distinction between tastes and norms:

Norms are not just another discipline's jargon for tastes and preferences; the distinction is crucial between them, because the terms point in entirely different research directions. When tastes and preferences are employed for some purpose more elevating than circular reasoning, they promote research into the properties of individuals, whereas norms are properties of organised groups which individuals pay heed to in their actions to the extent that they have been successfully socialised into membership in the groups . . . Were these norms fixed in time and space one could readily take them as given (meaning essentially to forget them), but they vary from culture to culture, from subculture to subculture, from class to class, and they vary throughout time.[51]

Utilitarian theories have no place for social processes such as the operation of social norms. They are asocial. It is surely somewhat ironic that the ideas of classic utilitarian economics, which reflect the *laissez-faire* individualism that reached its zenith in the eighteenth and nineteenth centuries, should be produced as a general theory of fertility when their adequacy as a basis for the discipline of economics is frequently called into question, and when they have long been rejected as a suitable foundation for sociology.[52]

Utilitarian theories of fertility do not, therefore, provide us with a satisfactory explanation of variations in childbearing, or even the prospect of one. On the one hand, their predictions cannot be properly tested against observations of the phenomena they are designed to explain so they do not, therefore, perform well in that sense. Nor is it likely that they will do much better in this respect in the future, since there are always likely to be loopholes – factors not included in the model, assumptions that could be improved, measures that are not perfect – that are likely to provide excuses for not rejecting the models *tout court,* especially as the abstract nature of the theorising means that the authors tend to eschew the collection of relevant empirical data themselves. On the other hand the theories do not fare well in other respects. Not only do they do poorly judged in terms of comprehensiveness, since they make no attempt to explain variations in tastes for children or other goods, but they also offer a theory that could only apply in certain limited social and historical circumstances over certain ranges of decision making, if any. In addition the account of the mechanism that is supposed to link resource factors to fertility does not itself stand the test of empirical accuracy, and does not, in that respect, provide a satisfactory account of *how* resources influence childbearing, if and when they do. Finally, and related to this, utilitarian theories fail to provide us with an explanation that pays attention to the way in which the actors themselves perceive and interpret their situation, or one that might be either recognisable or acceptable to them.[53] We can only conclude that utilitarian theories of fertility have little or nothing to offer.

4. The foundations for a theory

Neither Malthusian nor utilitarian theories provide a satisfactory explanation of variations in childbearing. The former, because it is based on a model that is imprecise and untestable, confounds the explanation of human action with that of physical events and, in fact, tells us very little about the conditions in which either populations grow or changes in childbearing occur. The latter, because it makes assumptions about how people act when deciding issues about having children, some of which apply only in a limited range of circumstances, and others of which bear little or no relation to the processes involved.

Is there an alternative?[1] The common thread of our criticism of those theories is their failure to take proper cognisance of the nature and complexity of human action; our problem is how to approach the study of fertility in a way that avoids this fundamental error. Rather than describe in detail the different approaches sociologists have adopted to the study of human action our principal task here is to outline those features of human action that, in our view, must be recognised and taken into account in any study of social phenomena, and therefore, in any explanation of childbearing. Such a straightforward list cannot itself constitute a theory: rather it displays what we take to be the 'domain assumptions' that will underlie any satisfactory theorising about fertility.[2] In any case, as our arguments in this chapter and elsewhere indicate, we are sceptical of the possibility of producing the sort of general theory of either population or fertility that the Malthusian and utilitarian traditions attempt; any theory of fertility or population must take account of temporal and cultural boundaries, yet as Eversley rightly points out, 'in the field of population theory, the traditions of the inspired guess and the search for the universal law dies hard', and 'the more painful method of piecemeal investigation still seems to many writers to be as unnecessary as to Malthus' earliest opponents'.[3]

Our starting point must be the recognition that the study of human fertility is the study of human action. Though a birth is, from one point of view, a biological event, something that happens 'naturally', it is at the same time, an event that is inextricably fused, to a greater or lesser degree, with elements of an intrinsically social character. At the very least the natural process of pregnancy and birth is modified and affected by a context of social decisions and actions to do with intercourse, contraception, abortion and so forth. This brings us to what we regard as the first

47

defining characteristic of human action. People are the *agents* of their actions and they have some choice over what they do.[4] To say this is not to say that people are completely free or unconstrained by circumstances and conditions. It is, rather, to say that the notion of action requires the *possibility* of choice. Hence we should normally talk of circumstances and condition *influencing* rather than *determining* what people do. Clearly, though many sociologists ignore the fact, the degree of choice people have is socially, historically and situationally variable, as is the importance that is attached to having *individual* choice. As far as fertility is concerned, some of the difference in the degree of control which people feel they have over pregnancy and birth is at times revealed in the language that they use when talking about them. Our own language has both active and passive terms and phrases in which we may discuss pregnancy and birth; people talk, for instance, of '*having* a child', or of '*childbearing*', of '*going in for*' a child or of '*falling*'.

The second defining characteristic of action, which cannot be ignored by the student of human behaviour, is that it is indissociable from meaning. People inevitably and continually structure, interpret and give meaning to what they do, to the actions of others, and to the circumstances of their lives, and these meanings not only identify their actions but guide and influence what they do.[5] The fact that reality is interpreted and constructed, not given and absolute, has become a commonplace amongst sociologists in recent years, though it is still too often ignored by them just as it is in Malthusian and utilitarian theorising; its implications are more problematic.

We take it to imply both that meanings vary in time and place, and also that we cannot ignore the differences in the way situations and conditions are interpreted if we are to produce satisfactory explanations in the social sciences. Hence we cannot, when studying fertility, ignore the fact that children have a different meaning to different individuals. To some people in our study a child symbolised the love and solidarity of the family unit and was valuable on those grounds alone. To others the meaning of a child was bound up with the things and objects of the material world and was valued in a very different way.[6] Moreover, by virtue of this situational variation in meaning, we regard the notion of 'rationality' as considerably more problematic than do many social scientists who have used it in accounts of demographic and other phenomena.[7] To predicate or deny rationality to an action demands at least that we know the meanings that people themselves attribute to the elements in their calculations, not merely those arbitrarily assigned by an observer.

It is because the interpretations and perceptions of social and economic conditions vary in time and place, as well as the conditions themselves, that the production of generalisations in sociology is far from easy. One cannot simply assume, as all too often happens in studies of fertility as well as in other topics, that a relation existing at one time and place will exist elsewhere. Consider, for example, the common idea that social mobility is connected to fertility. The idea has its origins, according to Eversley, in the conditions of late eighteenth-century European society, in which revolutionary changes were occurring.[8] These changes not only gave individuals a greater chance of social advancement, but a greater belief in the possibility of advancement. Moreover, in this context the desire for individual advancement was conjoined with a belief that this was to be achieved by individual effort in one's job, by hard work, long hours, and the husbanding of one's assets - all of which made marriage and childbearing seem an obstacle to personal advancement. In consequence, ambition and social mobility itself came to be connected with the postponement of marriage and childbearing and were recognised to be so. Yet this association was the result of a specific conjunction of social and economic conditions and beliefs, many of which no longer exist. Not only do far more people have relatively small families which *could* destroy the association, but the dominant modes of social mobility in society have changed since then. We cannot, in consequence, simply assume that a negative association between family size and social mobility is now likely, as all too many authors have done.[9]

Nor can we assume, on the other hand, that some similarity of demographic or other behaviour is good evidence in itself either that the phenomena in question have common origins, or that cultural factors need not be examined in order to produce satisfactory explanations. In the first place, similarity in demographic behaviour may not stem from common causes. Our own study shows, for example, the way in which the reasons for having small families vary considerably, and no single account fits all the couples who show this uniformity in family size. Similarity of explanation needs to be established not assumed. Second, though a common demographic pattern, even one that extends across national and cultural boundaries, may stem from common causes this does not mean that we can ignore the role of meanings, some of which are themselves common to more than one nation or culture. Advanced capitalist societies share certain beliefs and ideas, and these beliefs and ideas are likely to play a crucial role in any explanation of the level of fertility, since they give meaning to the social and economic conditions to which they relate. So-called 'cultural' factors are an essential part of the explanation of patterns of childbearing, as of other social phenomena. Sociologists must, therefore, continually examine specific conjunctions of conditions and ideas; hence the gap between history and sociology is not as large as many have suggested (though there are marked differences in terms of traditions of approach and subject matter).

Any explanation of human behaviour must recognise its active and meaningful nature. It must also recognise its social character. People are *par excellence* social beings who act upon and are acted upon by others.[10] The way in which people interpret and give sense to their world is not random and idiosyncratic, but derives from ideas and beliefs that are socially transmitted and shared. The construction of reality is simultaneously the work of society and individuals: in the sociologists phrase, a 'social construction'.[11] Yet again the implications of this fact are far from clear-cut. Take, for instance, the way in which terms like norm and value are used by sociologists. One school of thought, associated with, but by no means restricted to the structural-functionalism of Talcott Parsons and others, sees some common core of norms and values as a thing-like entity exerting an almost mechanical determinacy on the actions of individuals who go up to make the society that these ideas represent.[12] The objections to and weaknesses of this approach have been noted by various authors.[13] The idea of a 'central value system' is in principle highly dubious and flies in the face of much available empirical evidence about our own and similar societies. Furthermore, to assume that actors are integrated into society through common values, which thereby ensure the smooth functioning of the social order, is also problematic; on the one hand common values tend to be sufficiently vague to legitimate a variety of institutional arrangements and activities, on the other hand, the existence of common norms and values does not ensure conformity. Indeed, the paradox of the approach is that the emphasis on a 'central value system' deprives the actors of their capacity to act, supposedly the starting point of the exercise; the actors become totally bound by their membership of social institutions, the roles prescribed for him within these institutions, and their socialisation into these roles, a process in which they completely internalise the normative framework. This is 'homo sociologicus' in the extreme, whose actions are constrained from above by the elements of the social system.[14]

Sociological theorising like this not only deprives individuals of their capacity to act, it also ignores the fact that meanings, though shared, are potentially negotiable. This is the point made with such force by the phenomenologists and is the common thread uniting the spectrum of sociologists sometimes labelled 'interpretative'. Schutz, for example, is emphatic that for the actors themselves 'meanings are not fixed and irreducible, but are continually in flux, and in the process of being constructed and dissolved in active fashion'.[15] Yet this position, too, presents its difficulties. If the empirical observation of social life undermines the hypothesis of a reified central value system, it equally fails to sustain the picture of permanent and ubiquitous fluidity that ideas like those of Schutz at times imply. There are undoubtedly forces and processes at work in the social world which tend to freeze meanings and the construction of reality in such a way that to many people, much of the time, they and it appear as given and immutable.[16] For us it is crucial not that meanings are in practice constantly subject to negotiation but rather that they are universally potentially subject to it in principle. Hence one part of our account will be concerned to elucidate when and how the potential for negotiation is realised.[17]

Just as there is radical disagreement over the way in which norms, values and meanings are shared in society and 'constrain' the individual, so there is disagreement over the nature of, and the relationship between, the elements of which meaning is composed. On the one hand ideas, beliefs, and understandings of all kinds can be conceived atomistically, as relatively discrete and autonomous entities. Such, for example, is the assumption underlying the long tradition of attitude studies. On the other hand, more properly we believe, they can be conceived more holistically, as meshed into almost complete interdependence. In a weak sense this is the position adopted by symbolic interactionists when they assert that meanings come in clusters not in isolation; that one idea makes sense of another and relates to another.[18] In a strong sense it is the fundamental assumption of structuralists; that the meaning of an element is wholly and exclusively defined in terms of its relations with other members of the set.[19] Not wishing to explore further this theoretical battlefield, which has already claimed many victims, we would simply say that in studying meaning we regard it as crucial to examine whole constellations of ideas, not simply ideas circumscribed in an atomistic fashion. The importance of this approach emerges very forcibly in our own study as the following examples illustrate. A number of parents gave the difficulty of coping with children as a reason for limiting family size, and might, in consequence, be defined as belonging to a common category for purposes of explanation. Yet what, in fact, they meant by 'coping with children' could only be understood when we examined a much broader range of their ideas about having children. Thus for some the problem of coping with children was a question of attaining high standards over a wide range of activities – high standards of daily care, attention, guidance, companionship and control. For others coping with children was a question of meeting some minimal standards of care and provision for their children.[20] In the first case the minimal standards were essentially unproblematic, but not the high ones, in the second even the minimal standards presented problems. Likewise, though it was a common enough idea in the pilot sample that parents should make sacrifices for their children, what making sacrifices for one's children meant varied, and its implications for parents depended again on the whole complex of ideas about having children. For some making sacrifices was a question of foregoing material possessions, for some it was a question of giving up a job to spend more time at home, and so forth; hence, what one would regard as a sacrifice another would not.

It is further a characteristic of meanings that they vary in the degree to which they are salient or even visible to the individual.[21] In some instances a person may be highly aware of them and their status, as, for example, in the case of explicitly held political or ethical beliefs. Often, though, in this study we will be dealing with the attribution of meanings and ideas so 'taken for granted' as to be, under normal circumstances, invisible: the web of meanings which define and establish order and reality in everyday life, which are ordinarily expressed in practice rather than in words. Certainly some of the central meanings in our account of childbearing are of precisely this kind – the meanings of such key notions as child, family, marriage, and so on, are scarcely ever explicitly formulated but must be dug out by the investigator from the mass of empirical details of all kinds which they permeate and inform.

Finally, since we do not accept the idea of some 'central value system' we do not believe that most people's lives are lived within a world made intelligible by a single, integral and consistent system of meanings. On the contrary we consider that in our own and many similar cultures most people encounter a wide range of ideologies. The individual may, thus, be presented with the possibility or the fact of adherence to ideas from more than one system of meaning, systems that may not be consistent with one another.[22] This may mean that the individual holds contradictory beliefs; nevertheless, though an individual's ideas may be incompatible if taken as a whole, beliefs from different ideologies need not encroach on one another, or tend to adjust themselves towards consistency. It may be true as social psychologists claim that the 'mind abhors inconsistency', but only, as some of them point out, if the inconsistency is apparent to the individual.[23] This may often mean that an individual's ideas do not constitute a coherent and consistent set as sampled by an observer; partly because the observer may cut across more than one set of ideas, which have remained distinct and separate, partly because the individual may have incorporated only parts of a familiar constellation of ideas, and partly because certain connecting and unifying components of the individual's ideas may not be readily visible to the observer.

The need to resolve incompatible ideas (incompatible that is, in their implications for action) in favour of one set of ideas will depend on situational exigencies. If action requires some decision between alternatives then negotiation and resolution may be effected, but this resolution does not necessarily crystallise one set of ideas to the exclusion of others in future situations. If it did, then the notion of ongoing individual conflict in ideas would have little meaning. We shall argue in Chapter 11, for example, that though individuals may have to come to some decision about whether to have a child or not at a particular moment in time, this will not necessarily eradicate the conflict about what to do about having more children in the longer term, though it may have implications for future decisions. If, for instance, someone is undecided about whether to have another child, and decides not to for the time being, though this may well not eradicate the original grounds for the indecision it may weight the case against having another one, by adding, say, the argument that it is 'a bit late' to have another because of age, the gap since the last birth, and so on.

The emphasis we have given to meaning in this listing of our domain assumptions might suggest that we are adopting a purely idealist interpretation of human behaviour. In one sense we are, since we think that it is not possible to understand and explain human behaviour without examining ideas and beliefs. On the other hand, not only do ideas and beliefs refer to, as well as define, material conditions and behaviour, but they are also often influenced by changes in material conditions. Hence, in our view, the ideal and the material are inextricably linked and there can be, for instance, no tight distinction between social structure and culture. If we seem in this book to emphasise ideas and beliefs at the expense of material conditions it is both because we think that they have been neglected far too long in studies of fertility, and also because we believe it is essential to examine ideas and beliefs in order both to identify the material conditions that influence fertility and also to establish the way in which they do so.

It is, of course, an inescapable consequence of the emphasis we have placed here upon action and the meanings that individuals attribute to their situations, that it is highly questionable whether the methods of collecting data and the procedures for interpreting them employed in the natural sciences are of any relevance. Certainly some of those authors in this wide ranging debate with whom we are sympathetic, have concluded that the fundamental difference between the natural and social sciences in subject matter and in the way in which knowledge is produced preclude any direct borrowing techniques or means of theory construction.[24] The question is by no means easily resolved and is beyond our scope here. Our own position is that a simple use of techniques based on the epistemology of the natural sciences (and here, as we elaborate in Chapter 7, we would include survey research) is not merely inappropriate, but also misleading.

Our approach does, however, raise two problems which cannot be ignored. The first relates to the nature of any explanation that emphasises interpretations and meanings and the use of methods and theories from the natural sciences. It has been argued that a focus on meaning is incompatible with the production of *causal* explanations.[25] The attribution of causality, in the Humean interpretation, requires that cause and effect be distinguished as separate and contingent phenomena. In so far as an actor's meanings not only explain but identify his actions, then the two are logically and inherently, not contingently related. When the two are not separately identifiable then it is inappropriate to talk of causality in the familiar Humean sense. There is no doubt, too, that we have excluded certain natural scientific interpretations of the notion of causality both by arguing that a set of antecedent conditions cannot be said to *determine* specific effects, and also by asserting that statements of relationship between phenomena will invariably be socially and temporally delimited. But this is not the same as excluding any type of causal statement, and as far as we are concerned, the term cause still has an important heuristic value. In particular, since there is no simple singular relationship between meanings and action and the former do not always logically imply the latter, then some notion of causality is defensible, and the relationships between meanings, rules and actions is a matter for empirical investigation.[26]

The second problem is how to deal with interpretations of situations and actions that differ from those offered by the actors themselves. If reality is defined or constructed by the application of systems of meaning there would appear to be no basis for comparing these interpretations with an empirical reality by which they can be judged correct or incorrect.[27] Scientific knowledge is but one of an infinite series of possible symbolic universes which can make no prior claims to validity or objectivity. At its extreme this interpretation is obviously untenable; not only can it be argued that scientific knowledge differs from other systems of meaning by its concern for logical consistency and by the nature of its theoretical constructions, but it is also the case that all societies must employ some mechanisms for deciding between competing interpretations since, inevitably, interpretations must at times come into conflict.[28] This may mean that our criteria for evaluating 'scientific' explanations have no absolute status or value, but this, in our view, is no cause for great concern.[29] Our argument is not that one cannot go beyond actor's interpretations of their situations and actions – even to the point of saying that actors have misinterpreted situations in terms of the ideas they profess to hold: it is that these interpretations should provide the starting point of our analysis. Hence our objection to the use of natural scientific procedures in sociology does not extend to the desire to test theories or choose between explanatory accounts; it does apply to the narrow and inappropriate conception of the sort of data that can provide a good test of a theory.

Such an approach does not, as might seem at first sight, herald a return to empiricism. Our commitment to looking at the way in which people interpret and give meaning to their situations and to the way in which their actions relate to their beliefs and ideas involves a commitment to empirical study not to empiricism. We do not believe that scientific knowledge can be derived inductively from observation and inheres in some objective external reality. Any observation must involve selection and interpretation: selection and interpretation that are generated by the ideas, interests and presuppositions of the observer.[30] Hence in outlining a set of images of family life in Chapter 10 we have imposed an order on people's ideas about family life, an order that is influenced by our beliefs and values, and by our desire to link general ideas about family life to questions of family size and spacing. It is for this reason that we have attempted in this chapter and else-where to inform the reader of some of our preconceptions, and in the subsequent one have described the way in which our ideas changed and developed. But recognition that science can not and does not proceed inductively should not, we believe, stop us making observations, producing explanatory accounts, or trying to demonstrate their relative adequacy or inadequacy.

Part II

Research design

5.   A natural history of the research

Much of this book sets out the ideas we have now. However, it is important to record the fact that our ideas have changed considerably during the course of a programme of research which has extended over a decade. In this chapter we want, therefore, to describe their development over that period. Without such an account it is difficult to understand both why so much of the data that we collected is of little relevance to our current theoretical position, and why we failed to collect much data that we would now like to have. This chapter is, then, a record of the ideas and decisions of those who designed the research at its various stages, whilst in the two following chapters we, the authors of this book, give our present comments and evaluation of what we did. A research account in this form, though not unique, is unusual.[1] We believe it is necessary for two reasons. First, it provides an essential context for understanding the work we have done and the conclusions to which we have come and thereby for evaluating the research. Second, our experience has made us acutely aware that social research is itself a social construction that demands the sociologist's attention. Hence we have tried to provide an account of the research process itself, in particular the constraints and influences that affect the form it takes.

Any account we give of the development of our ideas has to be not only partial, in both senses, but also inescapably retrospective: we cannot but describe our ideas and decisions at earlier stages of the research in the light of our current interests and understandings. We have attempted, however, to make the record in this chapter a factual one, restricting ourselves, wherever possible, to contemporary documents. As far as we have been able we have reserved our present judgements for the following chapters. We have, moreover, inevitably had to give an account of the ideas, interests and actions of others who participated in the research, or in some way affected its course, but did not participate in the construction of this account. This is our account and they would not give the same one. Notwithstanding such limitations we believe the historical account in this chapter, as well as our appreciation of our mistakes that follows it, are essential to an adequate understanding and appraisal of the research we carried out.

I: The context and origins of the research

Geoffrey Hawthorn initiated the research in the academic year 1964-5. As a graduate in sociology he had recently been appointed as one of the first lecturers in the Department of Sociology in the newly established University of Essex. The University had had its first students in October 1964 and was at that time a small community full of new enthusiasms, new ideas and high expectations, partly stimulated by the Vice-Chancellor's Reith Lectures in 1963.[2] These lectures not only envisaged a democratic University in which students were to be treated as adults with equal status in the community but also emphasised that the University would put great stress on high standards of scholarship and research, and would distribute its resources accordingly. There was never any question but that all members of staff were expected to make an independent and original contribution to the development of their discipline and to give a high, if not the highest, priority to research amongst their day to day activities.[3]

One strategy adopted in the attempt to ensure that the University would be distinguished for the contributions made by staff to their respective disciplines was the concentration of resources on the rapid development of a small number of large departments rather than their diffusion over the full range of academic disciplines as was elsewhere the case. Only in this way, it was believed, was it possible to build up departments with an international reputation. In 1964-5 the policy had not, of course, been realised and there were only four teaching staff in the Department of Sociology, though it was to expend very substantially over the next few years. Initially Peter Townsend was the only Professor and was head of Department. A second Professor, Alasdair MacIntyre, was appointed in 1966 (he left in 1970) and a third, David Lockwood in 1968. As these names suggest the Department's policy in making appointments during the 1960s was decidedly eclectic: the consensus view gave overwhelming weight to the selection of the 'best' people (or perhaps more accurately in the case of junior appointments the 'most promising' people) rather than focussing upon specific interests, areas or skills. In consequence the Department from very early on included on the one hand not only those who labelled themselves sociologists, but also social historians, philosophers and social psychologists, and on the other hand sociologists of a variety of persuasions from – in the recognised terms of abuse of the time – sociographers to Parsonians. It meant, furthermore, that there were always in those years marked and serious lacunae in the coverage of sub-disciplinary specialisms, with a tendency for what one might call the peripheral to be strongly over-represented. Only with the appointment of David Lockwood did the department begin to develop something of a definite core of staff whose interests lay in conventional, 'mainstream' sociology. Moreover the speed with which the Department was expanding in step with the expansion of sociology departments elsewhere made it inevitable that many new staff members of the department were young, had little experience in either teaching or research, and very often had academic backgrounds in other subjects. All this combined to produce a departmental ethos that, though open and often productive, was also at times competitive and cliquish. There were too many young members of staff attempting to establish their reputations as sociologists and too few senior members with the time, energy or appropriate skills to guide research endeavours: it was an atmosphere both stimulating and guaranteed to produce mistakes.

This, summarily, was the institutional and intellectual context in which the fertility research was initiated and it was a context that could not but leave its mark upon the research that ensued. Its immediate effect was to provide the occasion for the research. As part of the policy to encourage research within the University the department had available from October 1965 money for research assistant posts. Hence there was not only the motive to do research but also the opportunity. It was an opportunity that Geoffrey Hawthorn, rightly, felt was too good to miss. It was a chance to do some research, but not necessarily to do research on fertility. Why fertility? At the time Geoffrey Hawthorn described the topic as of potential sociological interest for a number of reasons. It was a field that had, till then, attracted all too little sociological (as opposed to narrowly demographic) attention. Furthermore it raised, rather forcefully, a number of problems that were of especial interest to sociologists. One was, as he put it then, 'the methodological problem of relating one variable that can be handled easily on a ratio scale (family size, births intervals, etc.) to others which, to date, can hardly be fitted into an ordinal scale, let alone anything more precise such as an interval or ratio scale (expectations of the future, family relationships)'.[4] The concern to apply sophisticated types of measurement to sociological data was growing rapidly in the mid-1960s and the type of data provided by a study of fertility was likely to be of especial interest in this respect. The interest was to become particularly strong at Essex where the impact of Peter Abell and various colleagues helped to make Mathematical Sociology an important component of the Department's intellectual identity in the 1960s, and had a marked effect on our research. It was but one example of how the particular configuration of sub-disciplinary specialisation in the department helped to shape the course of the research. But the potential of a study of fertility went beyond the narrowly methodological. Another crucial problem it would raise, he argued, was 'the necessity and nature of motivational propositions in sociological theory in general and demography in particular': an interesting comment in the light of our subsequent disagreement on the matter, and one which indicates that all along the study was to be explicitly concerned with theory as well as method.[5]

These, however, were the potential general interests of the research to sociologists. Underlying the specific choice of topic were other factors: First, a long-standing interest in both population and the family. This is how Geoffrey Hawthorn recalls in 1975 the development of that interest while reading geography as an undergraduate at Oxford.[6]

My original interest in population came (i) from an interest that I had in research that friends registered for degrees, research degrees, in animal behaviour were doing in Oxford (this was represented in my buying and reading while an undergraduate David Lack's *The Natural Regulation of Animal Numbers*), and (ii) from having to read Kinglsey Davis's *The Population of India* for a tutorial essay in my third year. I had also as a result of reading Sociology in my spare time at Oxford become interested in the family (the book that affected me was Neil Smelser's *Social Change in the Industrial Revolution*).

Second he believed that a survey rather than a historical study would yield the most useful data. He continues:

Historical materials on the family, I had been persuaded by Glass, were difficult to come by (no-one had then thought of exploiting the enumerator's handbooks, but that would anyway have only got me to 1861). Historical research on fertility seemed equally difficult, and anyway not urgent. Meanwhile I had become very interested in methodology, the result of teaching the MA course, and since 'methodology' then meant survey analysis, and since 'every proper sociologist' should know about methodology (remember that at that time the subject was defined theoretically among cognoscenti, by Parsons and Smelser in theory and Lazarsfeld *et al* in methods), I decided that I had to do a survey. So, the obvious course was to do a survey on fertility.

Added to these two factors was the realisation that the steady rise in the birth rate in Britain since 1956 was an important and interesting phenomenon. As he explains:

the final solution was crystallised by a remark of Michael Young's reported to me (and he was one of my heroes), that 'the most interesting question' for anyone to look at in 1964-5 (when the birth rate looked, of course, as though they were going to go through the roof) was precisely the rise in the birth rate in the decade 1955-64.

The outcome was a plan for a study of fertility whose initial expressed aim was 'to explain the rise in fertility in Britain since 1956'.[7] If interpreted narrowly this question, with its focus on short-term trends in fertility, could probably have been handled adequately using aggregate time-series data from secondary sources, but the intention all along was to study in detail the casual mechanisms that linked social and economic factors to fertility, and to do so by means of a survey. The assumption that a survey was the best method of data collection in this instance is one we question in Chapter 7. It had a number of immediate implications. It meant, firstly, that much of the data we would collect would relate to intra-societal differentials in childbearing rather than to temporal trends, and though we did not lose our interest in the latter (indeed, we tried to design the survey to allow us to examine trends in fertility) we soon extended the scope of our interest to include differential fertility, and there remained some tension between the two aims throughout. Secondly, it meant that since we intended to survey individual families we concentrated our attention on the operation of factors at that level, examining for instance the influence of the individual's income, education, accommodation, and so forth on fertility, rather than studying changes at the macro level: for instance, changes in the provision of medical services, in government policies that affect the cost of children and so forth. We have tried to redress this balance in our substantive discussion in Part III of this book, but it remains a bias of the study.

The original conception of the research combined, therefore, a number of strands. A belief that surveys were likely to prove the most appropriate method for collecting sociological data (a view reinforced by the quality of the data collected in the studies carried out by the Institute of Community Studies which Geoffrey Hawthorn admired), combined with a belief in the importance and value of theory, and an implicit Popperian epistemology in which explanations were to be produced by testing theories, as hypotheses, against data. It was a conception of research that was exemplified in British sociology by the Affluent Worker study then in progress at Cambridge and the object of much professional interest.[8] To this was added an especial interest in and concern to use sophisticated measurements and statistical techniques.

With the appointment of Joan Busfield as research assistant (with a background in Psychology and Economics) the research was under way.

II: Preliminaries

Given a general subject area there is one essential preliminary to any survey, deciding exactly what to study. To this end we did three things; we attempted some demographic analysis of the recent changes in fertility in order to establish which demographic variables had produced the rise in the birth rate; we reviewed the relevant literature; and we carried out a pilot study.

Statisics of recent demographic changes in England and Wales showed us that all the obvious factors had been changing in ways that increased the birth rate. Age at marriage had been declining, marital fertility had been increasing as had illegitimacy, and so forth. Our concern was to establish the relative contribution of the different factors to the change in the crude birth rate. But here our desire for methodological sophistication led us astray. Believing that sophisticated statistical techniques could provide the answer, we attempted to use regression analysis on the time series data that we had for the separate variables, realising only too late, as we later coolly put it, that 'when measures of association between factors that vary over the same period of time are made, one finds an unduly high coefficient. This, together with the problem of interdependence or co-linearity makes it impossible to say how much of the change in any one variable over time is due to changes in each of the others.'[9] Like other sociologists, both then and later, we fell foul of the desire to use statistical techniques which our training had not given us the proper competence to evaluate. We therefore abandoned this attempt and remained content with the information that the published data provided. Since we had already decided on a survey of individual families we were already most interested in variations and changes in family size and spacing, and both the pilot study and the survey itself were designed with these as the main focus.

Reading the 'relevant' literature, whilst probably necessary, is not without its dangers; it can exert a powerful influence over one's research activity. We found the literature disappointing. Most of the surveys that had been carried out, almost all American, did not seem to have produced findings of much significance, however judged.[10] The work was largely atheoretical based on 'the conventional assumptions of the accounting model in which an array of independent variables are brought to bear on a dependent one until a satisfactory amount of the variance in the latter is accounted for'.[11] It did not concern itself with how the independent variables might relate to one another, or precisely how they might affect childbearing. Having children was not treated as a process occurring over time, and the underlying model was a static one that left out much that was of potential explanatory value. The literature, therefore, reinforced the conviction that a theoretical framework was necessary, and we were anxious to remedy the defect in our own study.

Our early theoretical ideas were simple. Though we recognised deficiencies in the survey work that had been carried out, the theoretical deficiencies in particular did not seem easy to remedy. In our initial summary of the literature we complained of the lack of theory but barely discussed the theories of fertility we had encountered or suggested any alternatives, thereby accepting the general divorce in the field between theoretical and empirical work (though we did discuss sociological theories which incorporated population change as an independent variable as part of our attempt to locate the study of fertility within the mainstream of sociology).[12] Instead we produced a rough classification of factors to study which we described as a 'crude model' that we said 'corresponds to the process of causality lying behind fertility, although it does not specify it'.[13] We asserted that certain environmental variables, which we classified as either material or cultural, influenced what we called fertility behaviour (fertility itself, contraceptive use, preferences about family size and so forth) through intervening variables that we termed dispositions. We further distinguished two levels, the macro- and the micro-aggregate. The framework nowhere approaches a theory of fertility and even as a way of classifying factors that might be studied it was not especially helpful.[14]

We did not, however, ignore existing theories of fertility and in a separate paper Geoffrey Hawthorn discussed both theoretical and empirical work on fertility.[15] In it he advocated the adoption of a Malthusian 'self-regulating' model of population change that paid far more attention to the causal mechanisms involved than previous exponents had: a model that would combine the best of Wynne-Edwards' account of the dynamics of animal populations with the best of J. A. Banks' account of family limitation in Victorian England, a synthesis the explanatory model that we developed for the pilot study failed, not surprisingly, to achieve.[16]

The theoretical literature left us a double heritage. On the one hand a concern with the influence of material resources and standards of living and on the other hand a very narrow conception of the cultural. Not only did we focus almost exclusively on ideas about material conditions, but we tended to interpret the cultural solely in terms of individual variations of meaning rather than looking for the social patterning of ideas and beliefs. We were interested in how individuals perceive the social system, where they locate themselves, what they think of their housing, income and so forth, rather than with the systems of ideas and beliefs about the benefits to be derived from having children, or the common assumptions about the possibility of mobility and how it can be achieved. This bias cannot be fully explained by the bias of survey methodology towards an individualistic approach. It was a bias not only present in the literature on fertility at the time but common to much empirically based sociological research, and reflected an atomistic and asocial conception of human thought and action.

III: The pilot study

The explanatory model on which the pilot study and its initial interpretation was founded, emerged from these attempts to synthesise the literature. When writing the report of the pilot study to submit both to the Nuffield Foundation, which had provided us with a small grant to help finance the pilot study, and to the S.S.R.C., from whom we were seeking money for the survey, we portrayed the explanatory model in the way shown in Figure 5:1.[17] The figure shows the variables only at one point of time.

The model has a number of significant features. First, it included as so-called intermediate variables, intervening between the explanatory variables and fertility itself, only contraceptive efficiency and intentions about family size and spacing. It thereby reflected the usual survey strategy of studying only contraceptive use and ideas about family size and spacing as intermediate variables, with one difference: we talked of intentions about family size and spacing rather than desires or preferences. We envisaged

66

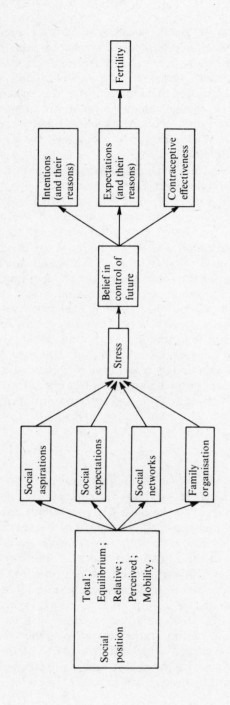

Figure 5:1

that by studying intentions not preferences we would be getting at ideas about having children that would be more closely linked to what people did, since in the everyday mapping of concepts intentions are closer to actions than wants, desires and so forth.

Second, the model was based on the notion of family building to allow us to examine the process of childbearing over time. As such, it was designed primarily to cover the 'normal' situation in which a man and a woman marry, then have children. Those who had children outside marriage, or those who neither married nor had children did not readily fit our explanatory framework, and we did not intend to study these 'deviants', believing that we could not cope with them adequately within the scope of our research.

Third, in selecting explanatory variables we accepted the standard socio-logical idea that various components of what we called social position constitute the underlying influence on social behaviour in general, and hence on fertility in particular. In so doing we did not abandon our interest in the influence of material resources on fertility, but, accepting that the distribution of material resources and perceptions about them were at least in part a question of social position, we put that interest in a more sociological context. Indeed, since our conception of social position tended to be multidimensional, material resources were a significant feature of it. When analysing the pilot data we considered the different components of social position both separately and together. Moreover influenced by ideas that were reinforced by the arrival of Johan Galtung as an occasional Visiting Professor in the Department in the Autumn of 1967, we also studied the 'equilibrium' of the individual's social rankings.[18]

We assumed furthermore, in line with recent sociological work, that it was not just absolute social position that influenced childbearing, but even more importantly, relative social position, which we tended to interpret subjectively. As we said in the pilot report:

the work by Banks, Rainwater and Easterlin in particular all point to the crucial importance of one or more aspects of couple's *relative* social position (whether this be assessed by age, income, wealth, education, status or whatever) in determining their fertility behaviour . . . To put it very simply, it is not only where you *are* in the society that determines these things, but also where you *see* yourself to be relative to others.[19]

Hence it follows, we continued, 'that where one also wants and expects to be, both absolutely and relative to others, is very likely to influence behaviour in the present'.[20] A small family might be planned, we thought, not only by couples with a low income (on some objective scale), but also by those who felt their income to be low and inadequate, even if by some objective standard it was not. This would account, we felt, for the low fertility of the lower middle class who, whilst not having the lowest incomes, might because of middle class aspirations regard them as very inadequate.

Social position was our *ne plus ultra*. In between that and our chosen intermediate variables we introduced a range of variables of a decidedly eclectic nature, in addition to social aspirations and social expectations, which we related to one another on a rather arbitrary and ad hoc basis. Their origins were numerous and would be difficult to document in full. It is enough to say that many of the remaining variables were included in an attempt to explain contraceptive use. 'Belief in control of the future' was fatalism under another guise, and was an obvious factor to consider when trying to explain contraceptive efficiency. Stress had its origins in our interest in the study of animal populations (particularly in this case the work of J. B. Calhoun) backed up by dynamic psychology.[21] Our interest in family organisation stemmed in part from the work of Lee Rainwater and that of Hill, Stycos and Back, who had argued that the nature of the relationship between husband and wife had a significant impact on contraceptive use as well as on ideas about family size.[22] It was Elisabeth Bott's study *Family and Social Network* that made examination of social networks an obvious corollary of any study of relations between spouses.[23]

Finally, the model included two types of factors which did not form part of our explanation of fertility but were of interest nonetheless. On the one hand it included expectations about family size and spacing (which we thought would depend on fertility intentions as well as the assessment of likely contraceptive efficiency) since recent work had suggested that these might be of value in predicting fertility.[24] On the other hand it included the reasons offered for fertility intentions and expectations. Although we did not regard reasons as necessarily the causes of action, or indeed as adequate explanations of the intentions and expectations, we felt they would provide useful information. As we put it in the pilot report

we have emphasised the importance of looking at people's reasons for taking the course of action that they do. Not only are there good *a priori* reasons for doing so, but Allport's practical injunction to the effect that 'if you want to know why people do what they do, why not ask them' seems unanswerable.[25]

Our interest in the status of reasons in explanations of human behaviour was undoubtedly enhanced by Alasdair MacIntyre's presence in the Department, another instance of the personal and institutional influences the research reflects.[26]

This was the rough model underlying the execution and analysis of the pilot study. The interview schedule (see Appendix B) itself did not, as one might expect, correspond perfectly with it. Translation of theoretical concepts into questions on interview schedule is not an easy task. Can we study intentions adequately by simply asking what was intended at a particular time? Can we study aspirations just by asking what things out of a restricted and standard list are wanted for the future? Such questions are at the heart of debates about the validity of survey data which we shall consider in detail in Chapter 7. Our approach in designing the interview schedule for the pilot study was essentially a commonsense one, based on everyday conventions. If we wanted to know about something we asked directly about it; if we wanted to assess material standards we asked if and when certain 'obvious' material goods had been acquired; if we wanted to know how much a couple discussed something we simply asked them. This meant that we did not regard many features of our questionnaire design as especially problematic, something we might otherwise have done.

New to the field we looked at other survey questionnaires for ideas and questions for our own study, and many of the questions we used were taken from other studies on similar topics. We used a number of questions from the questionnaire for Lee Rainwater's study of fertility – which was one of the better empirical studies – published in *Family Design*, both because of the apparent significance and interest of his results, and with a view to obtaining comparable data.[27] This led us to include questions on a further range of items that were never fully incorporated into our explanatory framework. We asked, for instance, a number of questions about satisfaction with family life. Initially, too, because of Rainwater's concern with the spouses' sexual relationship and knowledge of reproduction we began to ask questions on these topics. However, after one or two interviews, it seemed unlikely that we would obtain good information about either without rather lengthy questioning, and since there was so much else we wanted to cover, the factors did not seem of greater explanatory importance, and the topics seemed to provoke some awkwardness in the interviewing, we dropped them.[28]

The inevitable gap between the questionnaire and our theoretical ideas was, therefore, heightened not only by our 'naive' aproach to the task of questionnaire construction but also by our 'open-mindedness'. We wanted to include both questions and variables that others had studied, either because they had found them to be insignificant and we wanted to check their conclusions, or because they had found them significant and we did not think we should ignore them. Hence as well as additional questions that we never properly tied into our explanatory framework (a good example of this were our questions on images of the social structure, which though they could be said to fit into the category perceptions of social position, had not in fact been properly incorporated into our theoretical ideas), we also included questions to cover additional variables that we had specifically excluded from our explanatory model (believing them to be of little importance) just in case they turned out to be significant. Religion is an example of this. On the basis of the evidence we thought that religion was not likely to be a significant factor in explaining variation in levels of fertility in England (and perhaps even more generally – how else could one explain the fact that low fertility was common in several Roman Catholic countries?); we nevertheless included several questions on the topic in the pilot questionnaire.[29]

Our theoretical model demanded information about family building over time to provide an adequate explanation of fertility. How could we obtain it? We ruled out either a longitudinal or a panel study which would have followed a single cohort of identical or similar persons through the life cycle with periodic interviews, on a number of grounds. It would have meant a long wait for useful results and would not have allowed us to cover the childbearing in which we were specifically interested (the rise from 1955 to 1964). More importantly, the time elapsing between each interview makes it difficult to track down the original cohort in a longitudinal study and the further research progresses the greater is the problem of recontacting respondents. Though this problem does not apply to a panel study the additional assumptions that need to be made if the data is to yield the sort of dynamic information about changes in family building of particular individuals over time, make their value for such purposes highly questionable. Both types of study moreover involve an especially large investment of time and money. Hence our only solution seemed to be to obtain retrospective data. The interviews were, therefore, structured, after the first few, around the family-building events in which we were interested. We attempted to take 'a case history' of family building, and of the events and circumstances that influenced it, starting with the period before marriage and leading up to the present. We hoped that the chronological design would increase the reliability of the data we obtained by enhancing recall; that recall of one event would strike off memories of other salient, and roughly contemporary events.

The result was a rather lengthy interview schedule. It had both a definite structure and set questions, yet the questions were open-ended and often general in nature. We never envisaged completely rigid adherence to the schedule, but intended the interviewer to follow up any points of interest that emerged, to probe where answers to questions seemed inadequate and to alter the sequence of questions if appropriate. We also hoped that our plan to tape-record the interviews would allow the respondent to talk more freely. The goal of standardisation was therefore modified by the desire for sufficient flexibility commensurate with an exploratory study.

We decided that the size of the pilot sample should be 50; enough we then thought, to explore and clarify our ideas and do some cross tabulations. but also manageable within the constraints of money and time with which we were operating. (In fact data analysis took much longer than we anticipated since the unstructured interviews had produced a large amount of data that was difficult to quantify.) Since our aim was primarily exploratory we did not feel the need to be highly selective in drawing a sample. However, we thought it appropriate to interview women, accepting the conventional view that since childbearing and childrearing are primarily 'women's work' it is women who can provide most information about the influences on child-bearing. We also decided to interview women who had had children.

The sample was drawn from people who were then living in Ipswich, which we chose for two reasons. First, we had to interview people who lived relatively close to the University of Essex as we had no funds available to pay costly travelling expenses or hire interviewers. Second, Ipswich appeared to have distinct advantages over other possible places close at hand. It had been shown by Moser and Scott in their analysis of the 1951 Census data on British towns to be the town that approximated most closely to the national norms for towns of 100,000 inhabitants on a number of social, economic and demographic dimensions.[30] Though advantageous the issue of representativeness was not a matter of great importance for the pilot study. The exact selection and the characteristics of the sample are described in Appendix A.

Joan Busfield carried out the interviewing which took place between November 1966 and March 1967. By this time an extension of the research assistantship for a further six months on departmental funds had been obtained, and the research was also supported for a further six months by a small grant from the Nuffield Foundation.

Analysis of the interviews turned out to be a laborious process since our main aim was to produce simple two-variable cross-tabulations, the simplest standard procedure for examining the association between variables. This was no easy task as each interview had been transcribed (the grant from the Nuffield Foundation had covered this major cost). What we did was to transfer the transcribed interview to cards which could be punched according a simple coding system to indicate the nature of the information on the card. The system at this stage consisted of broad descriptive categories referring to the variables we had studied. The final coding, devised on a combined inductive-deductive basis, coded the values on the respective variables. The details of our measures of the different variables are given in the initial report of the pilot study and will not be described here since we make little use of the resultant cross-tabulations in this book.[31]

IV: The survey

Financing the survey did not prove easy. However, after a series of applications to the S.S.R.C., with responses ranging from outright rejection to requests for resubmission, a grant for them, initially for two years, enabled our plans for the survey to go forward in October 1968. At this stage Geoffrey Hawthorn and Joan Busfield both had teaching posts in the

Sociology Department, so the provision in the grant for the appointment of one research assistant increased the research team to three. After a number of short-term occupants of the post (we experienced some difficulty in filling the post to our satisfaction, which produced delays in our research plans) Michael Paddon, who had just completed a first degree in Economics and Sociology, was appointed in October 1969. An extension of the original grant for a further year allowed him to stay with the research (full-time) for two years.

Our difficulties in obtaining finance for the survey affected both the scale and the nature of our intentions. The original application to the S.S.R.C. envisaged a survey that extended over the South East of England using two instruments on a total sample of 2,000: the administration of 1,700 questionnaires and 300 depth interviews. As we were unable to obtain support for this large-scale endeavour we decided to carry out a smaller survey and to concentrate on only one town. Hence we proposed in our later applications a sample size of 300, designed both to be adequate for a simple type of data analysis, essentially cross-tabulations with two or three variables, and also, hopefully, to permit more sophisticated computations as well. We had calculated that allowing three values per variable and a norm of ten cases per call (a figure that Galtung, whose methodological ideas had influenced us, regarded as a minimum for any meaningful quantative analysis), we needed a sample size of 270.[32] Since in practice there is always some wastage within any sample, either because certain cases cannot be aggregated, or because information is missing on certain questions, we decided to add a further 30 to this, giving a sample size of 300.

Such a sample would, we recognised, be far from ideal. What we wanted was a larger sample to provide a sounder statistical foundation for any generalisations, although as the original application had demonstrated we recognised that there were certain sorts of information that could better, or only, be obtained in depth interviewing (did we work out very carefully what they were?). The S.S.R.C., too, thought the intended sample was far from ideal but were divided about how the study could be improved. Geoffrey Hawthorn recalls that when a resubmission of the second application was requested there was 'a disagreement between the sociology committee and statistics committee, the one wanting more variables and a smaller sample, the other (the sticky one, given what we *did* ask for) wanting fewer variables and a larger sample'.[33] Neither apparently wanted fewer variables *and* a smaller sample. In the event the sample of 300 was finally approved.

Our sample was drawn, once again, from Ipswich for exactly the same reasons as previously; the town's proximity to the University and its apparent representativeness. The question of how typical a town Ipswich was some 18 years after the 1951 Census was of course more important than in the pilot study since our aim was no longer exploratory but that of producing generalisations, and we shall examine it in the next chapter. However, for a number of reasons it was necessary for us to design the survey sample with considerably more sophistication than we had the pilot. First, we wanted to make comparisons between two different marriage cohorts to allow us to examine changes in fertility over time. Second, we wanted, as far as possible, to be able to make comparisons both with Census data and the data from the Family Intentions Study, one of the few major studies of fertility in Britain which was by then in progress.[34] Third we wanted to avoid the complications of divorce, separation and remarriage in the woman's pregnancy history. We had decided, furthermore, to interview husbands as well as wives where possible for two reasons: first, because we had found that when they had been present during the pilot interviews they had provided important and valuable information; second, because our theoretical emphasis on economic factors, including income, had forced us to realise the husband's influence on patterns of childbearing. Since our resources would not allow us to interview husband and wife separately we planned to interview the couple together, but to accept an interview with one spouse if a joint interview could not be arranged.

The result was a sample of couples from two marriage cohorts, those who had been married between three and seven years when interviewed, and those married between 13 and 17 years, where the wives had not been divorced, had not been separated for more than three months from their husbands, and were under 45 when interviewed: the last three restrictions were ones that had been imposed in the Family Intentions study. The way in which we obtained the sample and its characteristics are described in Appendix A.

The first task of the survey, once we had obtained finance to support it, was to finalise the questionnaire. We retained the basic structure and substance of the pilot schedule, but attempted to standardise the questions and precode as many as possible. This meant that many of them had to be modified either to allow a standard range of items to be covered or to ensure that answers fell within a pre-coded set. For example, rather general questions about accommodation were now focussed specifically on type of house, tenure, number of rooms and so forth. In other instances the tightening up was more in the interests of ensuring a standard format to the responses. More open questions like 'How did you feel you were doing at this time, financially, can you remember?; asked as one of a number of questions about perceptions of their financial situation, became more specific. In the survey respondents were asked 'Were you satisfied with your husband's income at this time?' and shown a flash card with five possible responses ranging from 'very satisfied' to 'not at all satisfied'. We also modified some questions to increase the comparability of our findings with those from the Family Intentions study.

Our difficulties in financing the project also affected the organisation of interviewing. We had hoped to use some survey or market research organisation to carry out the interviewing (preferably the former), since we did not feel that we had either the facilities or the necessary experience to recruit and train interviewers adequately. However, the S.S.R.C. said this would be too expensive so we had to recruit and train our own. We recruited potential interviewers who lived in the vicinity of Ipswich through newspaper advertisements and gave them a brief training. The interviewers tended to have other part-time jobs and their rate of interviewing, begun in July 1969, was very slow. By February 1970 the lack of progress in carrying out the interviews led us to request permission from the S.S.R.C., as part of an application for additional support for a further year, to hand over interviewing to a market research organisation. (To have used a non-commercial survey organisation would have meant further delay at this stage because of waiting lists.) The S.S.R.C. agreed to cover the additional cost and we hired a market research firm (again with cost very much in mind) to complete the interviewing. This second phase of interviewing began in May 1970 and was completed within two months.

Our changing fortunes in the day-to-day organisation of the research were paralleled by changes in our ideas about how best to explain levels of childbearing. Indeed one of the most serious problems that we encountered in carrying out and writing up the survey was that our ideas continued to change throughout its different stages, so that the ideas that we had when we drew up the final questionnaire were not identical to those on which the code book, for instance, was based. Moreover, as the survey progressed we began to experience greater difficulty in reaching agreement about our explanatory ideas and spent longer and longer trying to secure it. Here the delays in carrying out the research (getting the initial finance, getting a satisfactory research assistant, getting the interviews completed and getting further assistance to prepare the data for the computer), made the development of divergent ideas within the research team more likely (all of us had other interests outside the fertility research which exposed us to different ways of thinking), and at the same time provided a further source of delay, since the pressure to try and come to some agreement seemed strong. Moreover the situation was exacerbated both by the practical constraints of attempting to combine research and teaching and by the fact that, in October 1970, Geoffrey Hawthorn left Essex to take up an appointment at Cambridge.

The final form of the questionnaire had been drafted in the Autumn of 1968 and had sealed the content of the survey; it had not settled its interpretation. Geoffrey Hawthorn's own theoretical development is documented in a detailed discussion of the literature on the sociology of fertility in a book that he wrote over the academic year 1968-9, the first year of the survey.[35] In this he developed and used the ideas of the utilitarian theories of fertility that had been the predominant theoretical development of the past decade, adopting a somewhat modified version of the 'utility model', and arguing that fertility could best be explained by applying the classic ideas of utilitarian economics.[36] Specifically, the modification came from dropping some of the extreme (more implausible) assumptions about rationality and introducing a distinctively sociological element by emphasising that norms contribute to the development of tastes, although the two are not equivalent.

We have already outlined our objections to utilitarian theories of fertility in Chapter 3. They emerged gradually in the course of a series of discussions amongst the research team over the period 1969 to 1971. The aim of these discussions was to clarify our theoretical ideas prior to data analysis, which we knew would require us to make numerous important decisions about what aspects of the vast quantity of material we would study in detail. (Given the number of questions we had asked, the number of cross-tabulations that we could generate was far more than we could possibly cope with.) What emerged was a theoretical disagreement that initially focussed on the value of utilitarian models but became more widespread. The immediate problem was whether we either could or should attempt to use our own survey data to test utilitarian theories of fertility and thereby give them a dominant focus in our account of the research. The authors of this book argued that not only had we few questions in the survey that could provide any test of the *predictions* of utilitarian theories, but that such an enterprise was unnecessary and mistaken since the basic assumptions and approach of the theories were unsatisfactory. The broader differences in approach that were beginning to emerge are apparent in two papers written in 1970, 'Work, Family and Fertility', and 'Ideologies and Reproduction'.[37] The former by Geoffrey Hawthorn and Michael Paddon, extended and applied the ideas on which the research had been based up to that time, and adopted a 'positive science' approach to data collection and theory testing. The latter, by Joan Busfield, attempted to examine contemporary English beliefs about having children and adopted a more 'interpretative' approach. The preparation of this paper was influenced on the one hand by an explicit desire for some fresh thinking about the influences on childbearing, and on the other hand by an interest in phenomenological and interpretative sociology and social psychology. Once again the influence of personal and institutional factors can be seen. The presence in the Department from 1966 to 1968 of Dorothy Smith who had previously taught at Berkeley, taught Social Psychology at Essex, amongst other things, and was familiar with the work of Garfinkel and various ethnomethodologists well before they attracted more widespread attention in this country, ensured that more phenomenological ideas did not go unnoticed at Essex. The different approaches sketched out in these two papers is even more marked in the two final accounts of the research programmes: this book and *Having Children*.

It is not possible, therefore, to point to a single explanatory model and say that it alone provided the framework on which the design of the questionnaire, the coding and the computer analysis of the data were based. A simplified scheme of our changing and diverging ideas would fall into three stages. The first covers the period during which the final questionnaire was drafted. Our explanatory ideas then differed little from those on which the pilot study was based, although we had a somewhat greater interest in utilitarian theories of fertility which is only marginally reflected in the questionnaire. (We added one or two questions about whether the couple would have more children if they had more money, whether they felt that it was the time taken up by children that stopped them having more, and so forth.) The second embraces the period when we planned our analysis of the data, attempted to produce a final and comprehensive explanatory model, and drew up the code book. The final stage, when our theoretical disagreements could no longer be resolved, covers the time during which the two reports of the research were prepared.

The explanatory model of the second stage represents our final joint attempt (and from the point of view of this book the final attempt) to synthesise the ideas which we had incorporated in the survey questionnaire with the ideas that had emerged since that time into a single explanatory model, which would provide a basis for data analysis. It is of interest both as the basis of the code book, and because it indicates the way in which we attempted to improve on the explanatory model we had formulated for the pilot study. It is significant, in retrospect, that our reworking of the specification and linking of the intermediate variables, about which we agreed, appears to have been more thorough and successful than our attempt to rework the specification and interrelationships of the explanatory variables about which we had begun to disagree.

In attempting to improve our model of the role of the intermediate variables we moved away from the rather ad hoc approach of simply selecting certain key intermediate variables, which we reckoned had the most impact on fertility, and tried to construct a more or less exhaustive list of intermediate variables and to examine their interrelationships more carefully (our pilot model had merely portrayed intentions and contraceptive efficiency as parallel variables). In this our work was influenced by the approach of Kingsley Davis and Judith Blake who, in a well-known paper, specify an exhaustive set of variables 'through which any social factors influencing the level of fertility must operate'.[38] Their approach has a number of advantages. Not only does it attempt to include all factors that immediately affect patterns of childbearing but it attempts to restrict itself to such factors. It excludes from the list of intermediate variables either contraceptive efficiency or contraceptive effectiveness, which cannot be measured independently of fertility preferring instead the variable of 'use or non-use of contraception'. It also excludes any references to preferences or intentions, which must be mediated via one or more of the variables they specify.

Our list of intermediate variables for our new explanatory model was a modified version of that of Davis and Blake. On the one hand we reduced the variables they list by regrouping some and excluding others. The most important consequence of this was that our model now included the variables of fecundity and patterns of sexual intercourse which it needed to make it more complete, even though we had not changed our earlier decision that we could not hope to study patterns of sexual intercourse.[39] We had, however, included all along some questions relevant to fecundity, such as those about delays in conception, spontaneous miscarriages and known impairments of fecundity. On the other hand we still included a variable referring to ideas about family size and spacing as we had done in the earlier model, with two differences. First, we made it clear that intentions affected contraceptive use and patterns of intercourse rather than fertility directly. Second, we introduced a variable of motivation vis-à-vis family size and spacing since we felt it was necessary to consider not just the content of intentions but their relative strength vis-à-vis other desires; we wanted to have some measure of motivation: a notion that is even harder to measure than it is to conceptualise. In formulating this model we continued, however, to talk of intentions even though we had in the survey asked about the size of family and spacing of children that was *wanted* rather than *intended*. Here as elsewhere our explanatory ideas did not perfectly correspond to our questionnaire design. (It is interesting in this context that the Family Intentions study with which some of our data was intended to be comparable had also worded questions in terms of wants rather than intentions, the title of the book notwithstanding.)[40]

Retaining our firmly accepted idea that childbearing must be studied over time we represented the intermediate variables and their relationships over time as in Figure 5:2.

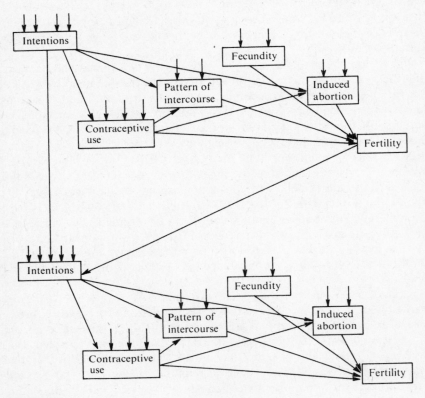

Figure 5:2

The modifications to our ideas about the explanatory variables at this stage primarily focussed on sorting out the interrelationships between them and the intermediate variables. We did, however, incorporate one or two factors like norms about family size that we had covered in the pilot interview, but had not included in the pilot model, and omitted some others, the most obvious being stress (though we had several questions about physical and psychological illness that arose out of that interest). The apparent exclusion of aspirations and belief in the control of the future is accounted for by the fact that we now argued that expectations were a direct product of these two factors. Figure 5:3 sets out the way in which we thought the explanatory variables influenced childbearing but again relates only to one point of time.

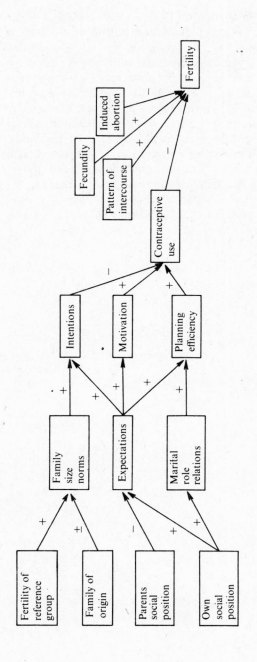

Figure 5:3

In the event this theoretical model influenced our coding decisions but did not provide the basis for the interpretation of patterns of childbearing in post-war England that we offer here. By the time the data had been fully prepared for computer analysis and some initial runs and cross-tabulations of basic variables produced (with the help of a part-time research assistant, again financed by the Department of Sociology at the University of Essex) two things had happened. First, the research team had agreed to produce separate accounts of the research. Second, the authors of this book had grown increasingly sceptical of the value of survey data, initially through increasing recognition of the particular limitations of our own survey, and later through a gradual realisation (partly forced upon us by attempts to make sense of the survey data), that many of the limitations of our own survey, though at times manifested in more extreme form, reflected more fundamental limitations of survey design. It is the flaws, both in our own survey and in surveys generally, that we now intend to examine.

6. A chapter of errors

No piece of research is without its flaws and ours, like that of others, was less than perfect. However, just as it is the customary practice in reporting research to dwell upon one's positive conclusions rather than to discuss at length those relations that lack significance, so it is also usual to outline the technically correct features of one's research design rather than to dwell upon its inevitable imperfections. By contrast, our emphasis in this chapter and the next is at least as much on the flaws and weakness of our procedures as it is upon their conformity to the conventional canons of scientific research. This is not because we believe that nothing of value emerged from research. On the contrary the pilot study in particular generated a large amount of interesting material, as we have attempted to demonstrate in the third part of this book. Nevertheless we believe that some detailed attention to the mistakes of the research is desirable for a number of reasons.

On the one hand it is important to explain why we regard much of the survey data as of little value and have used it only occasionally in our substantive discussion. On the other hand we believe that the errors and flaws of our research were in many cases the result of certain inherent weaknesses in academic sociology (and at times in academic life more generally) in the 1960s, both in its substance and its institutional organisation. Our mistakes were numerous but we do not think they were much more numerous than those made by other researchers working at the time, and though they may be an indictment of ourselves they are no less an indictment of academic sociology, at least as it was practised and interpreted in England in the 1960s. There is little doubt in our mind that the sort of sociology on which our research design was founded was bad sociology based on a spurious and mistaken scientism. It seems proper, under the circumstances, that we should analyse certain aspects of that sociology by way of the marks it set upon our own work, thereby not only providing a record of the errors and limitations of one piece of sociological research in a particular socio-historical context, but also, hopefully, encouraging and helping others to avoid some of the same problems and pitfalls.

The decision to carry out a sample survey was central to our research design, and in retrospect it is this decision about which we are least happy. Yet there was never much doubt when the research was planned that a survey, as conventionally understood, would be the most appropriate and practicable means of collecting data about the topics in which we were interested. In the next chapter we shall question the assumption, prevalent in English sociology at that time, and still too widely accepted, that the survey is generally the best and the most suitable method of data collection for the sociologist. Our own conclusion is that whilst surveys have some (albeit narrow) uses, the ways in which they are commonly used and the epistemological foundations on which they are based are far from satisfactory. In this chapter we want to document the particular flaws of our research since they highlight the problems that any research centred on a survey may encounter, as well as pointing to some of the inherent weaknesses of surveys.

I: Exploring the problem

A survey is normally preceded by a pilot study. Galtung, using the term 'instrument' to refer both to the variables to be studied and the method of data collection, says of pilot studies:

The construction of the instrument obviously derives from a Problem,. however vague, which has normally been further developed by some kind of pilot project. Only the inexperienced or very experienced social scientist will sit down and devote much work to an instrument before he has acquainted himself with the units, the individuals, by means of field work. He must know at least something about how the Problem (or commonsense counterpart of the research problem) appears to the individuals he will be sampling.[1]

According to Galtung good research has, therefore, two essential preliminaries: the development of the 'Problem' and the construction of the research instrument. What he does not discuss is the fact that though a pilot study is generally regarded as vital to *both* tasks, they make very incompatible, if not absolutely contradictory demands. Certainly it was our view that the pilot study should help us to settle issues both about exactly what to study (whether for instance to include questions about sexual intercourse) and about how to study it (the precise wording of questions, for example). Our own research was, for a variety of reasons, defective in achieving both these goals.

The dilemma of any researcher faced with a new research problem is always that of selecting exactly what to study and how to interpret the problem that interests him or her. In focussing and directing our interest in change and variation in childbearing we were open and ready to be influenced, though not uncritically, by the ideas and findings of those who had already done some work on the same topic. Fortunately the material and economic bias of many theories we studied was counterbalanced by the more eclectic and cultural, if often atheoretical, approach of some of the sociological writing in the field. This, in combination with the open-endedness of the pilot schedule, was sufficient to ensure that we obtained some interesting and valuable material in the interviews on some of the areas that, with hindsight, we still regard as important. What was wrong with the pilot study as an exploratory study was not so much the substance of the interviews (though there were unfortunate gaps such as our lack of interest in voluntary childlessness) but the way that we proceeded to treat the material that we obtained. Here our conception of the pilot as a 'dry run' for the survey and our belief in the importance of quantification had a major influence on what we did.

Our aim when analysing the data was to see if we could identify significant relationships between the factors we had chosen to study. Unfortunately the procedure we adopted was to treat the pilot as if it had been a small scale sample survey and to attempt to quantify the different factors we had studied. Hence our ideal of significance was statistical, and our approach to the interpretation and analysis of the pilot data was primarily atomistic and reductive. Though we had each interview transcribed as a whole and read them through with interest, by far the greatest part of our analytic effort was spent in attempting to reduce the material we had collected into a quantifiable form. Instead of examining the detail of what each woman had said, concerning ourselves with each interview in turn as a whole, and studying the complexity of conditions in individual cases and the constellations and variety of ideas, we looked at answers to each question across all the interviews in turn, often out of context of the whole interview, and tried to reduce the complex substance of the material to a narrow range of values on a limited set of variables. We therefore ignored the richness and fullness of the material, and the chance of achieving some understanding both of how each woman thought and felt and of the complex interaction of events and circumstances that had influenced her childbearing, attempting, instead, to reduce the material to a uniform minimum, erroneously destroying quality and meaning in favour of quantity. The result was that the value of the pilot study as an exploratory study was vitiated, and we forced ourselves into the constraints of aggregation and measurement long before it was necessary by any standard. The irony was that we well knew that with a pilot sample of 50 even the most ardent supporters of statistics could hardly claim that such quantification could produce results of any value. Indeed they would be the first to point out the inadequacies of our sample size for such purposes. Yet believing that some quantification must be better than none, we spent long hours on the soul-destroying task of turning lengthy answers into quantifiable data.

Moreover, as we realised we could not 'trust' our quantitative results with such a small sample, our intention of using the pilot to select out certain areas for more detailed study and to refine our theoretical ideas, could not be carried out, since we had adopted a statistical criterion of significance. Hence the quantitative analysis, when it finally stopped (it was never completed), did not produce the benefits it was supposed to. We did drop a few questions but our span remained broad: too broad. Because we attempted to cover so many topics in the survey we were unable to ask sufficient questions to cover any one of them adequately. This is particularly apparent in our questions on income, where our information is insufficiently detailed to give us a good measure of income or income change. We would have done better to concentrate on a far narrower range of topics in more detail, even though this would have meant presenting a more partial picture. It is interesting, in this connection, that it was mainly statistical ideas that made us think that we should attempt to study all those factors that we believed to be of explanatory importance, on the ground that this would facilitate causal generalisation by reducing the unexplained variance (to use the statisticians terminology).

What is striking about the impact of the pilot study on the research as a whole is how little it influenced our theoretical ideas at the time. This does not mean that our theoretical ideas were static then, or that the pilot was not important in other ways: it was. But we learnt all too little from it.

II: Developing the questionnaire

When we planned the survey questionnaire and interviews we took the pilot schedule as a direct model, assuming that the pilot (as it is supposed to do) had served to test out the questionnaire as well as to explore what should be studied. The problem is that such an aim runs counter to the exploratory goal. The virtue of the pilot, though we did not make full use of it at the time, was the open-endedness and the relatively unstructured nature of our approach. The interviewer, though working to a schedule, could follow up areas of interest with supplementary questions, ask the questions in a different order and so forth. But a schedule designed to guide relatively unstructured interviews (with its obvious advantages as far as exploration is concerned) cannot be transposed directly to a survey context. To some extent, of course, we realised this and did change the wording and order of questions to produce a more standard format for the survey questionnaire. Yet the full extent of the difference between the two types of interview, and hence the consequences of making such changes, escaped us. Where we did standardise their format we omitted to pilot the new questions systematically, assuming this to have been adequately covered by the pilot study. As a result we did not foresee some of the difficulties that were to arise with a questionnaire that did not allow for the same flexibility as the pilot interviews had done. For instance, we reworded and rearranged some of the questions on the use of birth control. From comments from our interviewers and from reading through some of the completed questionnaires we realised that they had been so worded that people not using birth control when they became pregnant, perhaps because they wanted a child, were not always being asked what method, if any, they had used before then. Although we then sent new instructions to our interviewers this increased the complexity of that section of the interview, and we are sure that the reliability of our information on contraceptive use is poor.

On the other hand certain features of the organisation of questions that were relatively unproblematic in a study in depth generated substantial difficulties in the survey. In particular, our concern, (still we believe correct), to study the dynamics of childbearing over time had led us to structure the pilot interviews around the sequence of childbearing events in a couple's marriage. This not only gave us information about changes that had occurred over time, but also provided an intuitively logical structure for the interview. As a framework for the survey questionnaire it was far less satisfactory. First, in a structured and lengthy interview that did not encourage detailed answers or the sense of some genuine exchange it became highly repetitive, and this cannot but have reduced the quality of data we obtained. It must have been tempting for the respondent to give the same answer to each question as it reappeared in order to hasten the completion of the questionnaire, though the questions specifically referred to different periods of time. Indeed, the uniformity of the answers in some questionnaires suggest that boredom and irritation may well have encouraged a stereotyping of responses.

Second, it led us to use a questionnaire for the survey that relied heavily on retrospective data. Like many of the important decisions, that to obtain retrospective data was taken when we planned the pilot study and was not seriously reviewed thereafter. The rationale combined our desire for a picture of the dynamics of family building with our belief that there were no viable alternative methods of obtaining such data. Whether we were right in collecting retrospective data in the survey rather than contenting ourselves with examining only events and conditions at the time of interview is debateable. The objections to retrospective data are familiar and powerful. Memory, like perception, is selective, and numerous studies have shown not only how much information cannot be recalled even after very short periods of time, but, more importantly, the extent to which information comes to be modified and reinterpreted in the light of subsequent events and ideas.[2] It is true that few of those we interviewed in the pilot study had complained that they could not remember what they had done or thought at different times, yet how accurately they recalled the past is open to question. Moreover, it is arguable that the selective biasses of memory, as well as a straightforward failure to recall information, are likely to be greater in a survey interview than in a depth one, since if a person is encouraged to reply at length he or she is more likely to be able to get back into the ways of thinking appropriate to the period of time being recalled. Such detail provides, furthermore, some possibility of disentangling older feelings and ideas from more recent ones. We know, however, of no study that has attempted to compare recall in different types of interview. At all events we now have little doubt that our decision to collect retrospective data in a *survey* interview was mistaken.

One other consequence of structuring the survey questionnaire around the events of childbearing was especially unfortunate. The frequency of our observations of the different conditions in which we were interested, such as the nature of the couple's accommodation, their income and so forth, depended on the particular pattern of childbearing they had experienced, and this gave rise to fundamental problems in comparing cases. Those, for instance, who had numerous pregnancies were asked to give information about their jobs, income and so on, at many different points in time, whereas those who had no pregnancies were only asked to tell us in detail about their circumstances at marriage and at the time of interview. As a result we have much less information for those who had fewer pregnancies after marriage than for those who had more. We cannot therefore be certain that the conditions of, for instance, those who did not have a second pregnancy differed from those who did. Because of this, when examining the survey data for the purpose of this book, we decided not to analyse the survey data for each pregnancy, but to concentrate on the background data, the data relating to marriage, and the data relating to the time of the interview, since this is the only data we have requested from every couple in the sample. Of course if we had continued our quantitative analysis and writing up of the pilot to include more material on later pregnancies (we concentrated on the interval between marriage and the first birth in the pilot report) we would probably have noticed this flaw in the design sooner. Yet this is no excuse for our failure to do so. From the point of view of conventional survey design it is the survey's greatest flaw.

In effect, our experience suggests that a pilot survey may be used either for the purpose of exploration, or to fix the terms of the instruments of data collection. It may not be used for both. If the former is necessary then a quite separate phase of pilot work is required for the latter.

III: Sampling

If we are to know what value to give to our survey one question that must be asked is whether the sample was representative. But representative of whom or of what? What was the supposed universe from which we were sampling? Was ours a study of childbearing in England and Wales, in south-east England, or Ipswich? Was it a study of all social groups or only some? Here, as in other surveys, there is a marked degree of ambiguity. Our specific interest was in the trends and variations in childbearing in England and Wales since 1950, and our original intention had been to study a sample of some 2,000 persons drawn from different parts of south-east England. Even a sample of that size, restricted to one region, would have been a dubious basis for making generalisations about the population of England and Wales as a whole. The eventual sample design had two distinct limitations: it was to consist of only 300 couples, and all were to come from a single town, Ipswich. Was our sample then a sample from the universe of England or was it a sample from the universe of Ipswich? We never really decided. On the one hand since we used the Ipswich electoral register as our sample frame it appeared that our universe was only that of Ipswich and those social groups to be found in Ipswich. On the other hand we chose Ipswich because of its supposed typicality of other towns in Britain of a similar size.[3] In effect we were also attempting to sample from the universe of towns of a particular size in Britain: we hoped to counterbalance the limitation of sampling a single unit by selecting one that was, on the available evidence, statistically representative of its class.

It is necessary to ask, therefore, both whether Ipswich at the time of the survey could be regarded as typical of other British towns of a similar size, and whether a sample of 300 was viable.

The idea that the County Borough of Ipswich in any way typifies other towns in Britain of a similar size, let alone other communities more generally, would undoubtedly surprise many of its inhabitants. Like other middle-sized county towns with historical roots, Ipswich is prone to regard itself in the light of its obviously distinctive features. Historically it has derived its importance from its combined position as the commercial and administrative centre of a large agricultural area (it is the county town of East Suffolk), and as a port of some significance at the mouth of the River Orwell. The town has had frequent periods of expansion; the period of most rapid population increase from 11,277 inhabitants in 1801 to 33,980 in 1861 coincided with the integration of Ipswich into the expanding transport network (the Eastern Union Railway arrived and the port was enlarged), and also with the introduction of the engineering industry based on the demands of agriculture.

By 1971 the County Borough of Ipswich had some 122,000 inhabitants and continued to be dominated economically by its role as a commercial and administrtative centre, by the activities of the port, as well as by its agricultural engineering, though the service sector was far the most important in terms of employment.[4] The port has remained a viable and important element in the local economy handling some 2.25m tons of cargo. Though its importance does not equal that of other East Anglian ports such as Harwich or the container port at Felixstowe, the expansion of trade with the E.E.C. and Europe generally has ensured its survival along with other East Coast ports. The fortunes of the engineering firms, all of which operate on a relatively small scale, that furnish the agricultural machinery, as well as construction equipment and so forth, have been more varied. Nevertheless, though the overall level of unemployment in Ipswich has fluctuated since 1950, usually in line with national trends, it has been somewhat lower than that for England and Wales as a whole.[5]

The distribution of the economically active *male* population of Ipswich does not differ very greatly from that of England and Wales as Table 6:1 shows. As we would expect, given its urban nature, there are proportionately fewer farmers and agricultural workers. Less predictably employers and managers and professional workers (socio-economic groups 1-4) are somewhat underrepresented. The industrial base of the community in agricultural engineering and dockwork is reflected in the relatively higher proportions of skilled, semi-skilled and unskilled manual workers than the norm, and its commercial and administrative activity by the higher proportions of junior non-manual workers. Members of the armed forces are also found in higher proportions than in England and Wales as a whole (Ipswich is close to a number of air bases).

TABLE 6:1   *Economically active males by socio-economic group, 1966, Ipswich County Borough and England and Wales*

Socio-economic group		Ipswich C. B. (%)	England and Wales (%)
1	Employers and managers (large establishments)	3.0	3.9
2	Employers and managers (small establishments)	5.9	6.2
3	Professional – self-employed	0.4	0.7
4	Profesional – employees	2.4	3.9
5	Intermediate non-manual	4.4	4.5
6	Junior non-manual	14.1	12.7
7	Personal service	0.8	1.0
8	Foreman and supervisors	3.7	3.6
9	Skilled manual	34.6	31.4
10	Semi-skilled manual	15.5	14.9
11	Unskilled manual	8.7	8.1
12	Own Account (non-professional)	2.8	3.6
13	Farmers—employers and managers	0.1	0.7
14	Farmers—own account	0.1	0.9
15	Agricultural workers	0.4	1.9
16	Members of armed forces	2.5	1.5
17	Indefinite	0.5	0.6
	Total	100.1	100.1

Source: General Register Office, *Sample Census 1966, Economic Activity Tables*, Part IV, Table 37, London: H.M.S.O. 1969.

Residents of Ipswich in 1966 were somewhat more likely than those in England and Wales as a whole to be housed in local authority accommodation. They were also somewhat more likely to live in owner-occupied dwellings, and consequently less likely to live in private rented accommodation, as Table 6:2 shows. However, the ratio of local authority building to that of the private sector has declined sharply over the period 1951 to 1970 so that the proportion of those housed in local authority accommodation is almost certainly declining.[6] As in many other parts of the country the local authority accommodation is concentrated in a few areas of the town and is of varying age. The council houses of the 1930s now look somewhat decayed and gloomy and contrast markedly with the new council estates of the 1950s and 1960s in which those we interviewed, at least in the pilot sample, were more likely to be found.

TABLE 6:2 *Dwellings by tenure, 1966, Ipswich County Borough and England and Wales*

Tenure	Ipswich C. B. (%)	England and Wales (%)
Owner occupied	53	49
Rented – local authority	29	27
Rented – private	16	19
Other tenures	2	5
Total	100	100

Source: Ipswich County Borough Council, East Suffolk County Council, *Structure Plan for the Ipswich Sub-Region, Housing,* Table 5, Ipswich, 1972.

The picture indicates certain divergences between the local and the national patern. Can we maintain therefore that Ipswich is representative of a broader social universe? Not only is there the perennial problem of the extent to which it is possible to claim that any single region, which inevitably has a unique combination of characteristics, is typical of other places, but there is also the problem that Moser and Scott's analysis was based on the 1951 Census, so that at the time of our survey Ipswich may have been less typical than it had been then.[7] Certainly its rate of population growth has diverged from that of England and Wales. In the period 1951-61 it was significantly higher: the annual rate of increase for Ipswich was 0.89%, that for England and Wales was 0.52%.[8] Much of Ipswich's higher growth in this period was due to migration into the County Borough, which accounted for almost a third of the increase over the period: a migration arising both from the general movement to the South East and from the movement out of central London.[9] However, the level of births was also generally higher than that of England and Wales as a whole as can be seen in Table 6:3. The decade 1961-71 saw a marked decline in the rate of growth of Ipswich County Borough to 0.49% per annum, a somewhat lower rate of growth than the 0.56% reached in the same period by England and Wales.[10] Whilst the level of births continued at a slightly higher level than that for England and Wales, there was a reversal from net inward to net outward migration, and between 1961 and 1969 close on 2,000 persons left the Borough.[11]

TABLE 6:3   *Crude Birth Rate, 1951-1972, Ipswich County Borough and England and Wales*

Year	Ipswich C. B.	England and Wales	Year	Ipswich C. B.	England and Wales
1951	17.0	15.5	1962	17.9	18.00
1952	17.0	15.3	1963	18.7	18.2
1953	17.7	15.5	1964	19.3	18.5
1954	18.0	15.2	1965	18.7	18.1
1955	16.6	15.0	1966	17.7	17.7
1956	17.2	15.7	1967	17.0	17.2
1957	17.9	16.1	1968	17.3	16.9
1958	17.3	16.4	1969	17.2	16.3
1959	17.1	16.5	1970	16.6	16.0
1960	18.3	17.1	1971	17.2	16.0
1961	18.0	17.6	1972	15.6	14.8

Source: *The Registrar General's Statistical Review of England and Wales, Part II,* Table E, 1951-1973; H.M.S.O.

Such data, however, offer comparison only with national figures, and not with towns of a similar size to Ipswich. Only a thorough analysis of later Census data of the type carried out by Moser and Scott on the 1951 Census would show how typical, in a statistical sense, Ipswich was of towns of a similar size at the time when we carried out our survey. And only much more knowledge on other dimensions as well would show how typical Ipswich was in a broader sense. The problem, as always, is that in order to decide how representative the unit we studied was, we would need to know much more about those units we did not and could not study. This is always the 'Catch 22' of generalisation. To know whether a generalisation is valid or not you need to have the sort of information about the universe to which you wish to generalise that your original smaller scale study was designed to provide. We can only generalise where similarity exists and to establish similarity usually requires the sort of information we do not have, or there would have been little reason to attempt the study from which we wish to generalise. Sampling conventions do of course provide rules which allow us to establish the likelihood that our particular sample is indeed similar to those units of the same universe (but not others) that we did not study, but they do not apply in this case. Whether the assumptions behind the rules can in practice be met is a question we discuss in the following chapter.

There is, moreover, a further crucial problem with regard to the identification and labelling of the universe and the units of the sample which rarely receives attention. The universe we studied was the set of households listed on the Ipswich electoral register for 1969 and those we interviewed had not necessarily lived in Ipswich for any length of time, or for that matter even been 'born and bred' in England. Our sample did not include only Ipswich people if by that we mean people who were born in the locality or had lived in it any length of time: it almost certainly included people from a great variety of regions (since we did not ask them where they had lived previously, we do not know). It was only a sample of Ipswich people therefore in a rather narrow and contingent sense and we could not use it to make claims about the local culture or about the impact of the locality on childbearing. It is by virtue of this fact – that we do not know anything about the geographical origins of our sample – that, in presenting and considering the material from either the survey or the pilot in this book, we have talked of England rather than of Ipswich.'[2]

Finally, our decision to interview both spouses undoubtedly introduces further uncertainties where inference is concerned. Whilst we remain convinced that it was much preferable to interviewing the wife alone, it turned out, as we expected, to be a difficult goal to achieve, and one in five interviews was not carried out with both spouses present throughout. As a result there is a marked discrepancy in the units of our sample, which raises problems both about the extent to which data from different interviews is comparable, and the nature of the units to which generalisation might be made.

Equally problematic was our sample size. The main limitation of a sample of 300 from a statistical point of view is the restriction that it imposes on the number of variables and the number of values for each variable that can be handled simultaneously, particularly when non-parametric techniques are used. We had justified the size by calculating that it would allow us to handle a maximum of three variables each with three values simultaneously. The trouble was that if we attempted to use our data for any more complex analysis than this, a sample of this size was far too small. Yet it is clear on the one hand that some variables must be given more than three values if they are to yield significant results. We know that there are important variations in childbearing within the blue- and white-collar occupational groupings, and it is difficult to carry out a further subdivision of any use without creating four or five categories. Once one goes beyond a basic manual-/non-manual dichotomy the usual minimum number of categories in 'social class' scales is five. In fact we used two occupational scales, both of which had eight basic values.[13] Although, if we had continued our analysis, we could have combined some of the categories further to have done so would have involved considerable loss of information. On the other hand with presently fashionable techniques such as path analysis or least-square regression, which we had hoped to use, computations with three variables would have been likely to produce an unacceptably high error term, since we know that a large number of factors can influence childbearing.

The limitation of our sample from the point of view of size is further compounded by our high refusal rate (31%). Though we can explain this (as we attempt to do in Appendix A) explanation does not get rid of the problem. Can we regard differences as significant when almost one in three people who were eligible for interview refused to be interviewed? If they differed systematically from those who were interviewed then the statistical findings might have looked very different. And we know that they did differ at least in some respects. Though our information on the refusals is limited (it is given in Appendix A) we know that members of the early cohort were more likely to refuse than those of the more recent one, and it is also likely that manual workers did so more often than non-manual ones. A refusal rate of this order must call into question any conclusions derived on a statistical basis from our survey.

IV: Interviewing and data analysis

It is generally agreed that a good survey depends not only on a carefully formulated and adequately tested questionnaire but also on the skill and expertise of the interviewers. It is the interviewers who transform a series of formal, structured questions into some sort of social exchange, and the manner in which they do so quite obviously influences the form that the exchange takes. For the most part the methodology textbooks tell us that the interviewer should participate in the conversation sufficiently to keep it going but not in such a way as to predetermine the actual responses. Whether such neutrality and uniformity in an interview situation are desirable or not is a matter we discuss in the next chapter; it is clear, however, that in practice they are far from easy to achieve. The interviewer's characteristics, mannerisms, appearance and responses inevitably influence the way in which the subject answers and how he or she expresses him or herself. The competence necessary to manage such factors is obviously crucial if any semblance of standardisation is to be attained.

Unfortunately, however, because of the size of the sample involved survey interviewing normally has to be delegated to those who have not been directly involved with the design of the research. Such delegation is an important feature of survey research not only because it is one reason for the standardisation of the questionnaire, but also because it introduces the possibility of great variations in the quality of the interviews, by virtue of the different skills, and attributes of the interviewers. In our own survey the delegation produced a number of important problems that affected our chances of standardising the interviewing and must have affected the nature of the data that we obtained. In the first place we could not obtain adequate finance to use the services of a specialist organisation so we had to hire and train our own interviewers. This was a mistake. Not only did we lack the necessary time, skill and experience to train and supervise them adequately, but the ad hoc nature of their employment and relatively low level of payment did not encourage them to spend much of their time on the interviewing. Although we obtained information about the training of the Government Social Survey interviewers (whom we would have liked to use to carry out our own interviews), we had neither the skills not the resources to match this training. Our interviewers had two afternoon briefing sessions, and were given written material on interviewing techniques, as well as information about the survey. They also had to carry out a trial interview by themselves. Those who were still interested and had carried out the trial interview to our satisfaction were then employed on the survey interviewing. In effect they had been given a detailed briefing rather than a proper training. With one exception, who did little interviewing, the interviewers were women, predominantly middle aged and middle class, with little or no interviewing experience. Though we attempted to supervise them in the field and encouraged them to carry out several interviews each week the quality of the material they collected was disappointing. They were reluctant to return to gain information they had forgotten to collect or had obtained incorrectly, and their rate of interviewing was extremely low.

Approximately half the sample had been interviewed when, because of all these problems, we managed to gain permission to hire a market research company to take over the interviewing. The company we chose (strongly influenced by considerations of cost) had little experience of social science surveys, though it claimed to be anxious to extend this side of its activities. Though the rate of interviewing improved, we are less certain that the quality did. Our impression was that the firm in question took a very instrumental attitude towards the interviewing and showed little awareness of, or interest in the quality of the data obtained. As a result we doubt whether the quality of either the first or the second half of the interviewing was high, yet the deficiencies of the two halves are almost certainly rather different.

Good analysis of survey data, like a good interview, depends both on the design of the analysis and its execution. Again we find it all too easy to point to deficiencies in our own survey in both respects. Careful selection of coding categories is crucial to the effective analysis of survey data. Many of our questions were pre-coded with coding categories based on a mixture of commonsense and theory. The coding categories for the remainder were based on a combined inductive–deductive procedure. We examined answers for a large number of questionnaires, not only looking for obvious group-ings of responses, but also picking out and categorising distinctions that we thought to be theoretically important, even if they did not differentiate the range of answers as tidily as others. Since by then the research team did not agree theoretically, the weakness of the combined inductive-deductive approach was increased by the lack of consensus about what features of the data were likely to prove significant and should be studied. As a result many of our coding categories were based on compromise. This meant that they were far from ideal for any one of us, and even where information relevant to a particular idea was collected it was often lost in the coding. A good example of the sort of compromise we made is shown in our coding of the reasons offered for ideal and preferred family size. On the one hand we created a category for 'economic' reasons. On the other hand, having excluded this set of reasons, we divided the remainder into those that emphasised the intersts of the children and those that emphasised the interests of the parents. Yet the same set of codes could not hope to high-light satisfactorily both the economic-non-economic dimension and the parent-childcentred one. Though in theory data could be recoded this would be a very costly procedure. Compromise, indeed, proved to be the worst of all worlds.

This problem highlights the way in which a survey demands not only agreement amongst those responsible for its design, if there is more than one person involved, but equally importantly an unchanging theoretical perspective between the construction of the coding categories (if not before) and the final attempt to make sense of the data and to write it up. If your ideas change the chances are, as we painfully found, that the data will have been coded inappropriately. In that sense the conventional procedures of survey analysis are an unfortunately inflexible instrument for the analysis of social phenomena, since one's ideas are likely to change during the course of data analysis, if only because the analysis itself is likely to suggest new ways of thinking.

The actual task of coding survey data, as opposed to devising the coding categories is, like that of interviewing, normally delegated, with similar consequences. We hired women looking for part-time work, who mostly had no experience of coding, and tended to dislike it. This meant that we had on several occasions to look for new coders, attempt to explain the nature of the survey, and teach them how to code: a procedure that was costly in time and must have produced a variable but generally low quality of coding.[14] Certainly the number of questions that had to be recoded when we used the computer to detect obvious errors was high, though this seems common enough. Moreover it is difficult, if not impossible, to ensure that a large number of coders settle the inevitable points of uncertainty in a uniform manner. In theory one devises coding categories and instructions for coding that obviate ambiguity and uncertainty; in practice one cannot.

V: Laying the blame

It is tempting to lay the blame for many of the flaws and errors of our research on certain features of the institutional organisation of academic research that we encountered when the research was designed and carried out. Certainly it is difficult to avoid the conclusion that many of our errors were the result of defects in the organisations that funded the survey and provided the institutional context of our research. In the first place there was the expectation (we would call it pressure) that academics in their first teaching posts would carry out independent research, which though it may have been especially strong at Essex existed elsewhere both then and now.

Not only does this produce the obvious problem of trying to do good research whilst learning how to teach (on the job, of course), but it also meant in the 1960s when academic sociology was expanding so rapidly in England, that many young academics with little research experience were expected and encouraged to carry out independent research in order to establish their merit both as academics and as sociologists, and to enhance the reputation of their departments and Universities. The contradiction was that holding a teaching post was apparently sufficient to establish one's competence in the eyes of colleagues and funding agencies to carry out survey research, yet the successful execution of that research (or at least its completion) was deemed necessary to establish academic competence. Of course, with the current competition for academic posts new entrants to teaching are far more likely to have considerable research experience. Yet this change has only temporarily eliminated the anomaly that a teaching post is taken as a sign of competence to be responsible for independent research, but that independent research is necessary to establish one's reputation as an academic sociologist; an anomaly that can mean, as it did with us, that academics have to undertake independent research without necessarily having sufficient experience to do so.

A further defect of the institutional context in which we carried out our research was the relative thinness and poverty of the advice that we could draw upon to prevent us making the sort of errors that we did. Again the conditions that we encountered were particularly bad. The rapid growth of academic sociology in the mid-1960s meant that there were too few people around with much experience of empirical sociological research, and this was especially true in new departments like Essex. But the rapid growth of the teaching of sociology in Universities cannot take all the blame for the lack of experienced advice we could draw upon. Another factor was, and still is, the pressure on senior academics to work on their own research rather than to take an interest in the work of others and transmit their experience. It is the corollary of the pressure on younger academics to do independent research. In this respect academic life in England tends to be individualistic; it encourages academics to put their *own* research first, and it encourages competition rather than collaboration. (It also all too often tends to favour the quick publication rather than the work of scholarship.) The situation is further exacerbated by the way in which research is usually reported in sociology (and presumably other academic disciplines) where, as we have said, the reader is presented with accounts of research that emphasise what went right and not what went wrong, so that the aspiring sociologist cannot learn from books what is often not available through more informal channels.

The funding body that vetted our plan for the survey must also take some of the blame. It was the funding body which finally approved our research plan, which allowed us, for instance, to proceed with a sample size that was the worst compromise between quantity and quality: it could not yield sound statistical conclusions and it could not yield good qualitative information. If the approval of the sample size was itself the result of the need for compromise between two committees one should, perhaps, question the policy that required the research to be vetted by two different committees representing different disciplinary traditions. Equally importantly the funding body accepted our estimates for the costing of the research. Yet it should have been clear right from the start, to those with any experience of survey research, that the research was grossly under-budgetted. Good survey research by conventional standards cannot be carried out with interviewers who are not properly trained; and it usually takes a longer time than we had allowed, given that there was only to be one full-time junior member of the research team, and would have done so whether or not we had our difficulties in filling that post.[15]

Nevertheless our mistakes and errors not only reflect contradictions and flaws in the way in which sociological research was organised and supported when we carried out our research (and in some respects still is), they also raise the question of whether a survey is indeed the best strategy for studying the sorts of empirical and theoretical questions that many sociologists attempt to answer. Viewed in this light the fundamental problem with our research was not so much our lack of experience, or indeed our lack of funds, but that we accepted the widely held belief that doing a survey was the appropriate way to set about answering our questions. It is this belief that touches on the substance as well as the organisation of academic sociology which we shall question in the following chapter.

7. Survey research

In the previous chapter we indicated some of the deficiencies of our own survey when measured against the methodological criteria of survey text-books. These revelations will not be particularly startling to any sociologist who has carried out a survey and, faced with the practical difficulties they involve, has been forced to make compromises. What is interesting is how few researchers are of the opinion that the deficiencies of their own research invalidate or put into question their conclusions. But sociological surveys have more fundamental flaws than the ones we have considered so far, relating both to the nature of the data they produce and the inferences that can be drawn from them. To demonstrate these flaws and the limitations they impose on the conclusions that can be drawn from survey data, we need to consider surveys in a broader context and examine the assumptions on which they are founded.

Though surveys in sociology vary in scale and scope, they incorporate some or all of a standard set of procedures: procedures designed to yield empirical generalisations by producing aggregate data to which more or less sophisticated statistical techniques can be applied. As such, they are based on a series of ideas and assumptions about what sort of data needs to be collected, how best to collect it and how best to make inferences from it. These ideas and assumptions are not uniform and different standard procedures are based on epistemologies that vary in detail; however, they might all be described by that fashionable term of opprobrium 'positivist' by which is generally meant a belief that 'the concepts and methods employed in natural sciences can be applied to form a "science of man" or a "natural science of society"'.[1]

Of course those who carry out surveys have different epistemologies, different ideas about the role of surveys in developing sociological knowledge, and different ideas about their virtues and limitations. Hence their reasons for doing a survey differ considerably as do the qualifications they place on the data they obtain and the uses to which they put them. At one extreme are those who see surveys as useful only for obtaining 'facts' of a certain limited type (those that readily lend themselves to aggregation), who see them as valid only for those persons studied in the survey, and who do not regard them as a basis for generalisation. At the other extreme are those who regard surveys as the major, if not the sole way, in which the sociologist can produce the causal generalisations which they hold to be the core of the sociologist's scientific knowledge about society. The range is, therefore, enormous; sociologists vary in their ideas about the sort of observations that can be made through surveys, in their ideas about the value of applying statistical procedures to the data that is obtained, in their ideas about whether survey data facilitates causal generalisation and so forth.

We want to ask, here, two questions about survey procedures. First, to what extent are they a valid and useful method of making observations of social phenomena. Do they, in fact, offer the sociologist one of the best ways of obtaining the sort of observations that are needed for descriptive or explanatory purposes or whatever? Second, do survey procedures provide, in addition, a good means of producing empirical generalisations and inferences well beyond the immediate observations and the cases studied. The issue is not whether surveys are perfect (for their most fervent exponents recognise certain problems and imperfections) but whether they provide a good means of facilitating either observations or generalisations about social phenomena.[2]

We shall argue that on the one hand survey procedures tend to be a hindrance rather than a help in making observations of many types of social phenomena, doing little justice to the phenomena they purport to observe; and that on the other hand the standard survey procedures are of little help in making inferences from the initial observations.

We are not, of course, the first to claim that surveys rarely yield the information the sociologist needs; nevertheless despite some lip-service to certain limitations the criticisms all too often go unheeded. We hope that our critique, stemming as it does from a direct attempt to utilise survey procedures, will increase sociologists' scepticism about the value of such procedures and help to weaken the belief that surveys usually offer the best way of doing empirical sociology.

I: Survey procedures and empirical generalisation

Let us start by considering whether survey procedures facilitate empirical generalisations, either of a descriptive or of a causal kind, and let us assume for the moment that the initial observations are valid and useful. The production of empirical generalisations from survey data commonly involves some or all of a number of different procedures: it involves aggregating the data that is collected, measuring one's variables appropriately, drawing a suitable sample of cases to be studied, applying statistical techniques to establish the association of variables, and employing techniques to establish the nature and extent of the association between variables. Do these procedures facilitate empirical generalisation?

The desire to produce aggregate data is central to survey procedures, many of which are designed to facilitate that end. Aggregation is important because it is held to be the principal basis of a generalisation in the social sciences; only if we know how many people do or think something, only if we know how typical the phenomena is that we observe, only if we quantify our associations and establish how constant are the conjunctions between variables, can we produce descriptive or causal generalisations. We do not want to argue here that aggregation (or generalisation, for that matter) has no place in the development of sociological knowledge: indeed, it would be mistaken to do so. The problem with aggregation in surveys is less the desire to produce aggregate data than the means of aggregation that are adopted, and the overriding importance that is given to this goal.

Survey procedures are, as we have already pointed out, based on a positivist epistemology. The particular form this takes as far as the aggregation of data is concerned is the assumption that data can be treated in a simple, reductive, and atomistic manner. The 'facts' are taken to consist of discrete, relatively clear-cut and readily identifiable elements which can be meaningfully aggregated in isolation from their context, and the verbal representation of those facts, to be precise and unambiguous. In particular the approach assumes that meaning is unproblematic: that words have uniform, agreed meanings which are not contingent on their context. We would argue, on the contrary, that a far more holistic and phenomenal approach is needed and that sociologists are virtually guaranteed both to misunderstand and misinterpret what they study and what the respondents say and to cover up relations of significance and interest if they adopt the conventional survey approach to aggregation.

The standard procedure is to treat responses separately, out of the context provided by other responses, and to analyse responses to each variable across all cases in turn as a prelude to examining the relations between variables. This strategy has a number of defects. The first, and most obvious, is that it fails to do justice to the meaning of responses. The need to consider responses in the context of a wider set of ideas to establish their meaning has already been argued (see Chapter 4) and can be readily illustrated by other material from our own study. The reason 'that's all we can afford' was frequently offered to account for a particular family size, and it would have been tempting to categorise all such responses in one group. Nevertheless, the analysis of individual interviews as a whole showed that the meaning of the response differed considerably. For some people it was a comment made only when serious financial difficulties were encountered, for others it was made when no financial problems were in sight, either from a desire to maximise material standards of living, or to plan for a better future or whatever. Only when the remark was examined in the light of many other remarks did this become apparent.

The importance of context to meaning and the problems this engenders have been asserted very forcefully by Cicourel, who points to the difficult task of interpretation faced by an interviewer when entering the everyday world of the respondent.[3] This everyday world will consist of a number of situational aspects, the family, work and so on, within which the actors communicate and interact using commonly understood, often inarticulated assumptions and concepts. The interviewer steps into this world with no understanding of the conceptual vocabulary employed by the respondents in their everyday life and attempting to impose upon it a picture of the respondents' social world as depicted by the research designer. The outcome, the interview itself, is a complex process of negotiation between the scientific conceptualisation and the everyday world where the nature of the responses depends on how questions are interpreted by participants. Nor is this negotiation merely contained within the statements made. The meaning of the statements will depend on what Austin has called the 'illocutionary act', that includes the role of the participants, the tone and manner in which the statement is made, and the purpose in stating it.[4] Furthermore, meaning may be communicated by physical actions such as raising eyebrows, movement of the hands and so forth. Cicourel concludes, therefore, that without understanding the totality of the interviewing context in which a statement is made, one cannot attribute it any meaning.

This analysis contains two elements, one of which we accept, the other reject. We accept the proposition that statements made by respondents should be understood in terms of the nexus of their ideas, the context in which they were given, and in the light of the individual's own perceptions about what is and what is not important. But, second, Cicourel seems to propose that the meaning of a statement made within an interview has meaning only within that context: it is specific to that conversation and cannot be assumed to have implications outside it. This extreme position implies a relativism for which Cicourel has rightly been taken to task.[5] It entails accepting the notion that no statement has meaning outside its immediate context. The first point is about how meanings can be known; the second is about their range of application. But the latter does not accord with the way in which actors themselves behave: we have to assume that statements made in one context have implications and meaning outside that context. The research on fertility which Cicourel himself has carried out indicates the consequences of denying this. His own study shows a preoccupation with the interviewing process itself and a quasi psychoanalytic interpretation of respondents' family lives.[6] That the approach is inadequate is suggested by Cicourel's recourse to precisely the sort of demographic and structural information of which he is critical.

Cicourel argues for the necessity of allowing the individual's own concerns and perceptions of what is and what is not important to emerge. This brings us to the second flaw of aggregation procedures in surveys: they are based on over simple assumptions about the interaction of variables. Each variable is assumed to be equally salient in every case. Rather than examining the pattern and structure of different variables in different cases, the same variables are studied separately, by isolating and analysing them in turn across cases and only then (possibly) considering their interaction. Hence the approach rules out the possibility of establishing that different sets of variables may be salient in different cases and that different patterns of interaction amongst them may occur. In effect, it assumes a uniformity across individual cases that it never establishes. The approach is almost completely 'nomothetic', paying little if no lip service to a more 'ideographic' approach to social phenomena'.[7] Instead of studying the patterning and interplay of variables in different cases, a specific and unchanging set of variables are isolated, are assumed to have some impact in all cases, and assumed to interact everywhere in a similar fashion. We are not proposing the adoption of a completely ideographic approach, but rather, that far greater attention to the variation in the structure and constellation of factors in different cases is necessary before aggregation takes place. In other words, we assume not that every case is so unique in structure and pattern that generalisation is impossible, but that more attention to uniqueness and variation is required before aggregation is attempted. Whilst the nomothetic approach might seem to be the obvious way to be scientific, its success has not been very great, and this is because it excludes so much. Education is not equally important for all, yet when included as a variable in a survey it is assumed to be uniformly salient. Nor is the variation simply that the effect that it exerts may be a threshold one. The point is that it may only have an effect in some cases when combined with certain variables and not others. Survey analysis rules out such complexities.

Aggregation is one component of the quantification that is standard feature of survey procedures; another is the measurement of variables. The statistical procedures that are normally applied to survey data make varying demands upon the level of measurement of the variables to which they are applied. Many require more than nominal categorisation of data with measurement on some ordinal or even ratio or interval scale. Use of scales like this requires the sociologist to make a number of assumptions. First the data must be ranked. This involves a linear ordering of the data, and for ratio or interval scales, the assumption of equal intervals. The problems of ranking, let alone producing an interval scale, for almost all social variables are innumerable. Consider, for instance, a standard sociological variable that appears to present few problems of measurement: length of full time education. It seems easy enough to rank terminal education age and to treat the values as an interval scale since the values are alsready expressed in a numerical form. Yet is one further year's education at 16 equal to one further year's education at 18, or leaving school at 15 in 1933 the same as leaving school at 15 in 1953. The use of an interval scale requires that we make such assumptions.

When it comes to variables to which a numerical value is not already attached the problems, as most sociologists recognise, are far greater.[8] Indeed, much effort is devoted to producing scales of occupation, social mobility and so forth which provide ordinal or interval levels of measurement. The extent to which such activity is worthwhile is debatable. The customary defence is pragmatic. The aim is to enable more sophisticated statistical procedures to be applied to the data, and the results yielded by such procedures justify the assumptions that have been made. If we produce statistically significant results then we need not worry about our assumptions, even if they appeared arbitrary; if we do not produce significant results, then we start again with different assumptions. But do we learn much if we apply more sophisticated statistical procedures to our data? Do the ends justify the means? We shall argue in a moment that many statistical techniques are not and cannot be especially helpful in producing inferences from data.

Before considering the value of sophisticated statistical analysis of survey data there is one further procedure incorporated into the design of surveys that needs to be considered – sampling. The aim of sampling is to select cases in such a way, and in sufficient quantity, that it is legitimate to infer that any observations hold for a wider range of cases than those studied. It is an integral feature of survey design and it raises a number of problems, almost all of the practical sort that we ourselves encountered and have described in the previous chapter. But they are difficult to surmount and when they cannot be, as they usually cannot, then the basis for inference beyond the cases studied is undermined. Obtaining sufficient finance for a large enough sample is a common difficulty, for the size of sample that is necessary to justify inferences to the population from which the sample is drawn is far larger than it is in an experiment, and a large sample is also necessary to permit the use of some statistical techniques which require variables to be handled simultaneously (though it is true that some techniques make fewer demands on sample size than others). Moreover, as we found ourselves if you want to have a reasonable number of values for each variable this too pushes up the necessary sample size. To obtain a sample of an adequate size also raises problems of organisation as well as finance. A common problem is ensuring a high response rate. This is probably more difficult to achieve in surveys where interviewing is delegated than in smaller scale studies. Here as elsewhere the problem is usually recognised, attempts are made to keep the refusal rate as low as possible and to establish the characteristics of the refusals. Nevertheless, in the event the findings tend to be presented as if this problem did not invalidate them. The same is true of the problem of obtaining a comprehensive and up to date sampling frame which permits a high contact rate for the intended sample; this is usually recognised but not held to invalidate the conclusions of the study. Then there is the problem of defining the universe to be sampled and the units it contains. Textbooks characteristically assume that both the universe and its units can be defined with precision and certainty. Sometimes this assumption is correct; more often than not it is highly dubious in which case even a rigorous and successful application of the rules can only provide a sample whose technical status is quite unclear. Many such difficulties pervaded our study: our sample was too small, our refusal rate too high, and the nature of our universe and our units of analysis were ambiguous. In our case, as in others, the impact of such factors must not only call into question any extension of our findings to a wider population but also preclude the possibility of our applying many statistical techniques in a legitimate and meaningful way.

Let us now consider the value of applying statistical techniques to survey data in more detail, making a distinction between techniques designed to establish association between variables (tests of significance, such as chi-square) and techniques designed to establish the nature and extent of the relation between variables (tests of relation, such as correlation). The value of applying tests of significance to survey data is doubly problematic. On the one hand tests of significance, when they can be correctly applied, give us very little idea of whether the variables we believe to be associated are in fact associated.[9] The test of significance does not tell us as is often supposed whether the *association* in question is likely to be due to chance or not and hence whether we can take the findings as evidence for the association, but only whether the *difference* between the results we are comparing could have been due to chance. The so-called null hypothesis, correctly stated, refers only to the randomness of data, not of the association which, in fact, is what primarily interests us.

An example illustrates the point. Suppose we find a difference in the time at which contraception was first used between those with different levels of education. The test of significance applied to these observations only tells us whether the differences in the first use of contraception are likely to have been random or not, it does not tell us the apparent association between education and contraceptive use was random or not. Hence as Willer and Willer point out, discussing the use of significance tests with experimental data.

Any inference made of an association between variables in such an experiment cannot result from the test of the null hypothesis itself but must come from elsewhere, principally from the intent of the experimenter in designing his experiment and consequently determining his controls. The test of significance is no more than a legitimization for an association either already evident by inspection or intended by the researcher.[10]

Of course it is true that Willer and Willer's aim is to demonstrate that we cannot derive generalisations *inductively* from empirical data (their book is an attack on what they call 'systematic empiricism'). Nevertheless, the point remains, even if we try to use surveys in a more hypothetical-deductive manner (a dubious procedure given their inductive foundations), the test of significance tells us little.[11] Can we therefore reasonably claim that it provides either support or refutation of our hypotheses?

Moreover, since it is very doubtful whether tests of significance can normally be meaningfully applied to survey data, they can be hardly said to provide a good basis for empirical generalisation whether the latter are supposed to be inductively or theoretically derived. As Selvin has pointed out, tests of significance are based on the assumption that individuals have been randomly assigned to the groups which are being compared in the way that individuals are assigned to experimental and control groups in a laboratory experiment. Yet this condition is not met in surveys (and cannot be for that is the very reason for doing a survey rather than an experiment), and, 'Where two groups are sampled without randomisation there is no statistical procedure for assessing the possible effects of the uncontrolled variables.'[12] In theory, when such variables cannot be controlled by randomisation they can be controlled by cross-tabulation once the data are gathered. 'But only when all important correlated biases have been controlled is it legitimate to measure the possible influence of random errors by statistical tests of significance' and this is an almost impossible task.[13] Hence Selvin concludes, 'In principle, the tests of significance have a place in non-experimental research. But in practice, conditions are rarely suitable for the tests.'[14]

In the light of these objections it is unreasonable to regard the test of significance as more important in establishing the association between factors than, for instance, a detailed analysis of individuals cases, or indeed, the accounts individuals give of what has influenced them (though the latter are likely to be insufficient in themselves).

What, however, of the techniques designed to establish the nature of the relationship between variables? How valid or useful is the information they provide? We believe their value is limited. Let us concentrate on correlational techniques, since they are most widely used. It is commonly remarked that 'a correlation is not a cause' but the full extent of the limitations of correlation coefficients and the more sophisticated techniques, such as path analysis, based upon them, tend largely to be ignored outside the better methodology textbooks.

First, all variables must be continuous, so the difficulties of scaling and measurement to which we have already alluded are encountered in their most extreme form.[15] Second, the concept of cause generally implies temporal sequence whilst survey data is usually collected at a single point in time. Though this has obviously, in part, to do with the question of data collection, it introduces both technical and conceptual uncertainties into the task of analysis itself. Third, it is necessary in principle to control for all possible influences on the relation in question if one is to infer a causal relation from correlation data. In practice, this is almost always impossible since the number of potential variables that might influence the relationship is almost always large.

These issues apart, there remain further objections. One of the greatest limitations of correlation analysis is that it is capable of detecting only those relations between variables taking a linear form. If there is a relationship but it takes another form – if for instance it is curvilinear – then it may well not be evident from the correlations coefficients. Further the analysis is based on the assumption that variables make an independent, additive contribution to the observed effect. This is not only unrealistic since, where social phenomena are concerned, most supposedly 'independent' variables in a correlation matrix are themselves correlated, but also rules out the possibility of detecting significant features of the relationship between variables. Certain factors may exert a threshold effect; that is, they may only be important when they reach a particular level. Correlational analysis cannot detect such possibilities.

On these grounds, the construction of simple contingency tables and the calculation of percentage differences, which are the simplest procedures for establishing relationships between variables, are far less problematic since fewer assumptions about the nature of the relationship between variables are made. Nevertheless even the simplest descriptive crosstabulations involve the sorts of aggregation procedures to which we have already objected.

II: Survey data

Our discussion of survey procedures up to this point has assumed that it is possible by means of surveys to obtain observations of social phenomena that will provide a valid and useful foundation for making empirical generalisations. We now want to question this assumption.

Quantification – aggregation, scaling of variables, the use of statistical techniques and so forth – is fundamental to survey design. The problem with quantification is not just that it is, as we have argued above, doubtful whether it provides the sort of scientific knowledge of social phenomena that it is supposed to, but also that it affects the quality of the observations that can be made in surveys. Hence, surveys are a poor basis for making empirical generalisations both because the procedures specifically designed to facilitate the production of inferences do not do so, but also because standard survey procedures have a detrimental effect on the quality of the observations on which the inferences are to be based. In most cases, surveys do not, and cannot, provide good data. Our argument is not against the collection of empirical data, though as we have said we eschew empiricism as it is conventionally understood, but an argument about the sort of observations that sociologists need and how best to obtain them.[16]

In what way does the priority given to the goal of quantification interfere with the task of obtaining valid observations of social phenomena? Let us consider two key features of data collection in surveys: first the collection of data on a large number of individual cases: second, the standardisation of the process of data collection.

The immediate consequence of the need to study a large or reasonable number of cases (say a minimum of a hundred, though there is no clear dividing line between a survey and any other type of empirical study if we consider the issues of size alone) is that delegation of data collection is almost inevitable. Our own survey of 300 was far too small for most purposes, yet even with that number and a team of three research workers responsible for the research, delegation of interviewing and coding was necessary.

At first sight, the problems of delegation, like those of sampling, appear to be practical and therefore surmountable. Adequate training of interviewers, adequate briefing about the substance of the interviews and so forth ought to ensure reasonable standards. Certainly too our own experience was especially difficult and should not be regarded as typical. Nevertheless, we believe that the quality of data is almost always likely to be adversely affected by delegation. This is not to malign the skills and competence of survey interviewers. Interviewers, however well trained and briefed they might be, who are not directly involved in the planning of the research and the specification of the problem the survey is designed to elucidate, inevitably have far less idea of the sort of information that the interview as a whole and specific questions are designed to collect. They are in no position to decide whether and when to probe further into answers the respondents give. The more open-ended the question the more disadvantageous this is. By virtue of this and the practical difficulty of recording lengthy answers accurately, textbooks on the subject advise the researcher to maximise pre-coding of answers and to eschew non-standardised questions.

But, if anything, standardisation raises even more objections than delegation. An underlying assumption of survey procedures is that aggregation demands standardisation: standard questionnaires, standard interviewing techniques and standard coding procedures. The belief is that only if all data are adequately standardised can they be legitimately compared to permit aggregation. The question must be the same or you may not get information about the same thing; the nature of the interviewing situation must be the same or the substance of the responses may be variably affected; the coding must be the same or you will be unable to aggregate.

Standardisation is, however, doubly problematic. On the one hand perfect standardisation is impossible to achieve; on the other hand, standardisation procedures adversely affect the quality of the data that is collected. Standardisation assumes that there is a common universe of meaning between the researcher and those he interviews; it assumes that questions can and do invariably have the same meaning for all those interviewed and that the meaning of what is said is readily understood by the sociologists. We do not want to argue here that intersubjectivity is not possible and that there can be no agreed meanings. Nonetheless to regard intersubjectivity as possible does not mean that it should be treated as unproblematic. The sources of variation in meaning that can affect the data that is yielded in a survey are numerous and standardisation does not circumvent them.

In the first place there is the impact of the interviewer. Interviewers may influence the way in which the question is interpreted in a number of ways, by their appearance, manner, tone of voice and so forth.[17] It is a commonplace that these factors may influence the response given.[18] Survey interviewers like those in our own study tend to be middle class, middle-aged women, who (even if they can articulate their own biasses and predilections) may very well influence the responses they obtain because of the respondent's assumptions about their social position, opinions and so forth. The methods conventionally advocated for eradicating any such bias are either to assume that the bias itself is random and that over the range of cases it will cancel itself out, or else to suggest that any systematic bias can be estimated and removed during analysis, but there is no good reason for believing this to be so.

Second, even if the interviewers do not themselves affect how questions are interpreted and the responses that are given, which is most unlikely, we can be certain that the questions would still not be interpreted uniformly. Whilst words may very well denote the same thing for different individuals, they undoubtedly have different connotations, which affect the meaning the question has to any individual and the reply that is given. To take a simple point, it may be true, though we are far from certain, that the word 'planning' has a similar denotation amongst those we interviewed. It was certainly true, however, that the connotations of the word varied considerably, and that questions about planning were interpreted differently. Some people, for instance, denied that they planned although they made a number of decisions in advance that others (including the researchers) would have called plans. A similar problem occurred with the word 'discuss' though here the immediate discrepancy was between our interpretation of the word and that of our respondents. As we point out in Chapter 12, we asked couples in the survey whether they 'discussed' birth control at various periods in their married life with anyone else, hoping to find out more about informal networks for the communication of ideas and beliefs about birth control. We found, however, that our respondents seemed to be interpreting the word 'discuss' as referring only to rather thorough and perhaps more formal conversations about birth control (perhaps situations in which they asked for advice) and not to *any* conversation that included the topic of birth control.[19] Hence most people denied *discussing* birth control with anyone, (and those who said they had some discussion commonly said it was with a doctor), yet in response to another question they frequently mentioned friends, as well as other people as sources of information about birth control. There was undoubtedly considerable variation in the interpretation of the term 'discuss' amongst the sample itself, which only more thorough investigation of the respondents' ideas and concepts, which is impossible in a survey, could have revealed. The problem of the varying connotations of words offers, indeed, a major obstacle to the standardisation of questions and a fundamental objection to the use of surveys. Of course the problem exists whatever type of data collection is used, but the weakness of surveys is that they provide very little opportunity to establish the way in which words are interpreted (other than by circuitous inferential procedures when misinterpretation – by the researchers' standards—is blatant). Moreover surveys offer a poor vehicle in this respect not just because they standardise questions but because they usually seek to keep open-ended questions to a minimum. It is far easier to work out how concepts are being used if you have a good 'sample' of material to examine than if you have only a brief response. It is virtually impossible if the only response you have categorised is the interviewer's ring around a pre-established code.

This raises the second problem with standardisation: not that it is unattainable, but that pursuing it as an objective precludes sociologists from making the sort of observations they often must have if they are to adequately describe or explain social phenomena. It is not just that standard questions will not be interpreted in a standard manner so that the data yielded is not in fact comparable in the way that is intended, but that in many cases (not all) sociologists need to study just those variations and complexities in events, actions, concepts and ideas that the attempt at standardisation ignores.[20]

In what way does standardisation militate against the study of the ideas and meanings that frame human action? It requires, in the first place, that researchers specify certain clearly defined issues for study and formulate questions on these issues relevant to administer to all those they study. This has numerous problems. On the one hand the specific questions chosen are liable, as survey researchers recognise, to structure the responses given. Indeed this is one reason for the concern to ask the *same* question of each individual. But this response ignores the issue of the importance of examining the individual's own concepts and way of structuring the topic in question, which is important information in its own right.

To some extent, of course, survey researchers are aware of the value of finding out about the individual's own concepts and ideas. However, neither of the usual strategies for doing so as part of a survey are very satisfactory. The first, exemplified by the attempt to examine perceptions of social class in The Affluent Worker study, is to have unstructured sections of the interview with no set questions but only a list of topics to be covered.[21] The weakness of this strategy is two-fold. On the one hand when unstructured questions are presented in the context of an interview that is mainly structured, then the 'set' of the respondent is to a more rigid question and answer situation, which does not encourage him or her to talk, freely openly and at length. This happened in our own interviews with the open-ended questions. The identical question asked in the context of a more structured interview with many pre-coded questions provided far less material than when it was part of a less rigid, and far more open-ended interview. On the other hand, in the context of a survey such questioning would invariably have to be delegated leading not only to problems of ensuring that the interviewers have a good idea of what sort of questions to ask, what to follow up and so forth, but is likely to preclude verbatim recording of the discussion since tape recording and transcription becomes impracticable on that scale.

The second customary strategy for either allowing for, or studying the variation in concepts and ideas within the context of survey design, is to attempt to establish the range and variety of ideas on a topic by means of exploratory pilot interviews and to use these as a basis for devising survey questions which allow for the range and variety of ideas. The main weakness of this procedure is that, though the aim is to incorporate the range of ideas into a survey questionnaire, the approach to the study of ideas is invariably atomistic. Attitude studies invariably fall into this atomistic trap and as a result rarely yield much data of value.

Equally importantly, however, the need to select standard issues to study by way of standard questions means that inconsistencies and variations in people's ideas tend to get lost. We have to assume that the individual has a clear-cut set of ideas which the researcher can tap in a relatively straightforward and simple way. Yet people's ideas may very much depend on the context, may not be consistent or at all precisely formulated. Direct questioning may not only lead individuals to accept or express opinions that they do not have, but prevent much of the complexity of their ideas emerging. In the Affluent Worker study, though individuals were questioned about their perceptions of social class in a relatively unstructured way, the questioning here did not even then provide a full picture.[22] Asked about their image of society in this manner, the dominant model was a pecuniary one. In contrast, when asked elsewhere to rank occupations differentiated both in terms of income and prestige, status rankings were common. This finding has been interpreted in a number of different ways, but it illustrates the danger of having too simple a view of how individuals perceive and interpret the social world. Again, the danger exists with any observational technique in sociology. With surveys, nonetheless, it is especially difficult to escape.

Our objections to surveys, both for inferential and observational purposes stem, therefore, from a common weakness of survey procedures: they are based on an oversimple view of social phenomena. On the one hand they assume a uniformity and simplicity in the interaction of social phenomena (variables) which ignores their variety and complex structure. On the other hand they assume a uniformity of ideas and ways of thinking. This means not only that surveys are bad instruments for any study that attempts to examine ideas but that they are also bad instruments for studying what people do, since they still assume that questions can be standardised and will be interpreted similarly, and that the structuring and interaction of phenomena is simple. Surveys are satisfactory only when questions do have a uniform meaning and the aim of the study is to collect a narrow range of 'factual' information. Indeed, surveys are least objectionable when used to collect the sort of data that is very often already collected by governmental agencies and institutions: to ask questions like how many children do you have, what was your date of birth, and so forth. Extremely factual questions like this, whilst they do not guarantee reliable and valid information that can be legitimately aggregated and compared, are far more likely to produce satisfactory answers than those about planing, decision making, or discussion, where concepts are more variable. When sociologists move beyond such clear-cut questions and when they attempt to use survey procedures for explanatory rather than descriptive purposes, then the value of survey data diminishes almost totally. Nor is the pragmatic defence acceptable here. Surveys are not the best tool out of a poor set, but often the worst tool out of a kit whose potentiality has hardly begun to be explored.

The conviction that a good sociological study means a survey, and preferably a survey that incorporates the application of sophisticated statistical procedures originates from a particular view about scientific knowledge: a view that is not only positivistic but believes in particular that it is not merely facts, but quantifiable facts that are the basis of scientific knowledge. It originates moreover from a desire to make sociology a respectable science, to give it the *appearance* of a science. It is hard to believe that outsiders will long remain impressed (if they ever were) with the knowledge that is yielded by this pseudo-science. Sociologists would be more successful if they concerned themselves with trying to understand and explain social phenomena than with trying to make their subject appear scientific.

Part III

Marriage and childbearing in post-war England

8. Marriage

Some consideration of marriage is an essential part of any study of childbearing in England. This is because, as in many other places, there has been and still is, a strong normative connection between getting married and having children, a connection which means that in practice patterns of marriage and patterns of childbearing are closely linked.[1] On the one hand since marriage is generally thought to be a necessary step for those who have children, marriage generally heralds the beginning of childbearing for both men and women. In consequence there is a close connection between the timing of marriage and the timing of childbearing. Women who marry early also tend to start having children when they are younger, and conversely those who marry late have children when they are older. The point is obvious, yet it is of immense demographic significance, since even if family size did not differ according to age at marriage, when age at marriage declines overall, the gap between generations is considerably reduced, and population growth is correspondingly faster than when it rises. Moreover, women who marry early in England do have more children than those who marry when they are older, and are continuing to do so, albeit to a lesser extent, even though their numbers have been increasing steadily over the post war period until very recently. As Table 8:1 shows, there is a significant difference in the family sizes of those who marry under 20 and those who marry when they are between 25 and 29.

The precise reason for the association between age at marriage and family size, which has persisted in the face of overall reduction in family size during the century, is not entirely clear, though we know it is not simply a question of differences in the length of exposure to the chance of conception (women who marry young have more children after five years of marriage than those who marry at older ages after the corresponding length of time).[2] Nevertheless, the persistence and strength of the association is an important reason for studying the influences on marriage as well as childbearing itself, despite the fact that with the increasing use of contraception in marriage variation in the age at marriage is no longer as important a mechanism for controlling fertility as it has been in the past.

On the other hand, those who get married, for whatever reason, are in turn expected and encouraged to have children, for the normative connection between marriage and childbearing is a symmetrical one and just as marriage is deemed necessary for those who have children, so having

TABLE 8:1 *Age at marriage and family size after 10 years duration of marriage, marriage cohorts 1925-1960, England and Wales*

Date of marriage	All marriages	No. of births per woman marrying at the age specified					
		Under 20	20-24	25-29	30-34	35-9	40-4
(a) Absolute figures							
1925	1.72	2.38	1.93	1.48	1.28	0.79	0.39
1930	1.64	2.38	1.81	1.44	1.10	0.67	0.27
1935	1.60	2.31	1.76	1.42	1.10	0.54	0.27
1940	1.63	2.08	1.73	1.50	1.16	0.61	0.24
1945	1.79	2.22	1.85	1.69	1.33	0.73	0.25
1950	1.84	2.41	1.89	1.66	1.32	0.68	0.22
1955	1.99	2.45	2.00	1.83	1.40	0.74	0.23
1960	2.13	2.50	2.11	1.99	1.57	0.80	0.28
(B) Ratios (family size of those married at 20-4 as standard)							
1925	89	123	100	77	66	41	12
1930	91	131	100	80	61	37	15
1935	91	131	100	81	63	31	15
1940	94	120	100	87	67	35	14
1945	97	120	100	91	72	39	14
1950	97	131	100	90	72	37	12
1955	100	122	100	92	70	37	12
1960	101	118	100	94	74	38	13

Source: (absolute figures) Registrar General's *Statistical Review of England and Wales* 1972, Part II, Table QQb; London, H.M.S.O. 1974.

children is deemed necessary for those who marry. This means that conditions that facilitate marriage tend to facilitate childbearing (other things being equal) as well as vice versa, and the proportions marrying and the proportions becoming parents are closely (though not perfectly) associated.

The close connection that exists between marriage and childbearing in England is common elsewhere, and may be even stronger. Indeed the importance of children to marriage in most societies has been such that those who have attempted to produce cross-cultural definitions of marriage have often done so by reference to childbearing. The most recent edition of *Notes and Queries,* the standard terminological guide for anthropologists, defines marriage as 'a union between a man and a woman such that children born to the women are legitimate offspring to both partners'.[3] Here marriage is held to be the social arrangement that creates legitimate offspring: i.e. offspring who stand in clearly defined relationships to existing groups, which is important not only for the transmission of property, but also for the social location and identification of offspring. Definitions like this one, however, ignore other activities which are often arranged and regulated through marriage, such as sexual, household and economic ones.

Nevertheless, though having children is not the only component of marriage, the arrangement of childbearing and other related activities such as the transmission of property are very often central to it.

We have already described in the introductory chapter the major variations that have occurred in patterns of marriage in England during this century. The significant features have been the continuing tendency for those of higher social status to marry later than those of lower status, the increase in the proportions marrying, and the decline in the age at marriage during the century, a trend which became especially marked in the 1930s and continued until very recently. The present pattern of almost universal marriage often before the age of 25 constitutes a significant departure from the pattern of marriage that had been long established in England. That pattern, termed 'European' by Hajnal, was characterised by relatively low proportions marrying and a high average age at marriage for both men and women.[4] Hajnal shows that this pattern has been geographically and historically restricted: it was typical of many western European societies from the early eighteenth century, and may date back even further. Far more common has been a pattern of virtually universal marriage at an age close on puberty, although some societies have manifested an intermediate pattern with quite large proportions marrying at relatively early ages, but not necessarily as early as a year or two after puberty. The recent pattern of marriage in England might be termed intermediate in this sense. Although the proportions now marrying and the current age at marriage have not reached the levels that characterise the common 'non-European' pattern, nevertheless they can no longer be regarded as no more than fluctuations within the European pattern that Hajnal outlines. How long they will be sustained is uncertain. Our own analysis suggests, for example, that the conditions in England in the 1970s are generally less favourable to early marriage.

Hajnal's analysis, by showing that age at marriage and the proportions marrying are characteristically associated, might be taken to imply that the two factors are generally influenced by the same conditions: that some circumstances facilitate marriage and in consequence more people marry and marry at younger ages, whilst other circumstances hinder marriage and thereby lower the proportions marrying and raise the age of marriage. Our own analysis, however, indicates that this is an oversimplification, at least for twentieth century England.

It suggests that certain facets of marriage primarily encourage men and women to marry at *some* time in their lives, whilst others primarily affect *when* they can marry, and that the two may change independently of one another. Nevertheless, the features of marriage that encourage people to marry also tend to encourage them to marry as soon as they can, and those that directly affect the timing of marriage are also likely to ultimately affect the total proportions marrying. Hence, the frequent statistical connection between the two.

Trends in marriage are, of course, influenced by the relative proportions of males and females in the population, and a relative scarcity of females is likely (where monogamy is the norm) to push down the age at marriage of women, as well as to increase the difference in the average age at marriage of men and women. However, there is little evidence that changes in the sex and age structure of the population of England and Wales can account to any great extent, for the 'revolution' in patterns of marriage with which we are concerned in this chapter.[5] We need, therefore, to consider non-demographic influences on patterns of marriage.

I: The pressure to marry

Put simply we could say that most people have married in post-war England, and have married at relatively early ages when they could, because they felt it was desirable or necessary to do so; marriage has seemed an almost inevitable step in the transition to adult life. But put like that the assertion does not explain very much. It does not explain *why* marriage has seemed an inevitable step in life, nor does it help us to explain the variation and change that has occurred in the patterns of marriage in post-war England and before. To help us to answer such questions it is necessary to examine the circumstances that have made marriage seem necessary, if not desirable, and to consider possible changes and variations in these circumstances that have related to differential patterns of marriage.

Marriage has seemed inevitable and often attractive to most people in post-war England because of the way in which marriage has come to be connected (in terms of both ideas and practice) to the attainment of various rights and status advantages which are themselves highly valued in the society. Hence people have married because marriage has seemed the obvious and natural step in the achievement of these other objectives. Take, for instance, to illustrate the general point, the connection that exists between getting married and having children, to which we have already referred. Most people want to have, or get themselves into situations where they are going to have, children; since they also take it for granted or accept it as inevitable that if they want to have or are going to have children they should or will get married, many of them do marry; hence, because marriage confers the right to have children, having children becomes a major reason for and legitimation of marriage. The logic of the connection was apparent in many of the comments made by the pilot sample when asked why they had married when they did.

This is how one woman responded to the question:

Well, I don't know really, that's apart from that you wanted to, you know, you wanted to have a family and a life of your own. It was something that – I'd always looked after other people's children, you know, and I sort of wanted children you know, and I sort of wanted children of my own and a life of my own.

As she makes clear, for her the desire to have children is such an obvious reason for getting married that it needs no comment. She might well have been surprised if she had then been asked, 'But why did you marry if you wanted children?' For other women, having children seemed to be the only good reason for getting married. As one woman said, 'I would never have got married, and I don't think he would've either if we hadn't've wanted wanted children. Well, whats the sense in getting married if you're not gonna have children really.'

The crucial connection here is the assumption that only married people have a proper right to have children and if you want to have children then you should get married. Presumably underlying this is the belief that marriage provides the right environment for having children and bringing them up: a belief that is primarily visible from the stigmatisation of and arguments against illegitimacy than from any more direct justification and support. It is the arguments against having a child outside marriage that get mentioned, not more positive arguments for having a child within marriage. People commonly argue that the illegitimate child is disadvantaged in a number of respects, in particular because of the prejudice and discrimination that it will have to face.[6]

The way in which marriage confers the right to have children is one factor that has made marriage inevitable for the majority in the post-war period. It is not, however, the only one. Marriage has also seemed either desirable or necessary because of its association with independence, or, to be more precise, with the degree and type of independence that is held to be appropriate to being an adult (which clearly varies for men and women). Marriage is both ideologically and practically associated with the social right to be treated as a full adult and an independent member of the society, a right that cannot be gained very easily by other means. It is true, of course, that many legal rights that we associate with being an adult are a question of age; nevertheless, in many contexts it is marriage rather than age *per se* that automatically gives people the right to the full independence of adulthood. It confers the right to adult sexual relations (on a regular basis); the right, if not always the possibility, to live away from the parental home; the right to give first place to bonds with persons other than one's parents; and it confers the right to a general independence of belief and action from one's parents. Many of the pilot sample highlighted this connection between marriage and independence when they talked, as did the woman quoted earlier, of marriage giving 'a life of one's own', and accounted for their own desire to marry in these terms. At times the pressure was the obvious unpleasantness of the home environment: one woman said she had married 'mainly because I wasn't very happy at home and I wanted to get married and lead my own life', and another, when asked why she had married when she did (she was 19) commented:

It was just that I couldn't wait to get away from home really; although I was very fond of my husband, he was – you know – I wanted really an opening in the outside world. It turned out all right, it could have been grotty really.

More often it was not; for many marriage offered the attractions of an independent life even without the obvious stimulus of an especially unhappy or constrained home life. Some, not surprisingly, found the supposed independence did not materialise. A wife asked what she had thought marriage would be like replied:

Well, I thought you could please yourself. Which you can't. I think you – I think all people seem to think that once you get married – you can come and go as you please and things like that, but it's not true. You're tied more so than when you are single.

Independence from her parents did not mean complete independence.

Marriage provides an opportunity for a life of one's own (albeit with spouse and then children, with all that this involves) because it creates a social unit that has been and still is considered viable and legitimate domestically, economically, sexually and emotionally both in the short and long term. This introduces a third important connection that makes marriage seem so inevitable and often desirable to most people: the connection between marriage and the assumption of a legitimate and clearly defined social roles and identities. The way in which marriage simultaneously organises a variety of activities in a legitimate manner is significant not just because it offers a means of attaining independence from parental ties, but also because it allocates people to what are held to be their proper and rightful roles in society. Much of the pressure to marry comes from the simple fact that being married and having a family are regarded as proper and normal conditions. The argument might sound circular, as if we are back to simply asserting that people marry because they are expected to do so: yet the point has more force than this. It is not that people marry because they are expected to marry, but that by marrying they come to occupy roles that are socially acceptable and legitimate. Marriage slots people into their rightful places as adults in society, and this makes it seem necessary to marry for a number of reasons. In the first place, as we have already pointed out, society is designed to a large extent for the nuclear-family unit of parents and children, so that marriage combines in one institution the organisation of a range of activities, which it is more difficult to arrange independently outside marriage. Hence those who do not marry face various practical obstacles. They either have to remain living with their parents with the attendant cost in autonomy and status, or else they have to attempt some other domestic arrangement with the isolation and expense this often involves (the housing market is organised for families) or some sort of communal living arrangement with the problems of working out a viable division of labur with little normative guidance.[7] Marriage appears to offer an attractive solution (though it may not work out in practice) by providing a means of organising a range of activities at one stroke. Second, and more important, is the fact that by marrying people take up roles that are governed by a range of norms that are more or less clearly defined which reduces uncertainty and makes social interaction easier to manage. There are, for instance, definite expectations about the length of the relationship (permanent), which not only increases emotional security and reduces uncertainty, but allows people to plan ahead. It also means that other people have a better idea of what to do – of what to expect in terms of behaviour and of what to do themselves. We all know how to treat a married couple or even an engaged couple, we are less clear about how, for instance, to treat an unmarried couple who live together. Third and finally, by taking up roles that are legitimate and proper, people also establish that they are normal and competent members of the society. Marriage, therefore, is a way of establishing personal and sexual adequacy and those who do not marry run the risk of being regarded as deviant – of being thought to be somehow less competent and less successful in their social relationships, and of being thought to be less desirable, less attractive and less mature.

These advantages apply to both men and women. Undoubtedly, however, in this society, it is women rather than men who are exposed to the greatest pressure to marry on these grounds. This is because the female role and identity are defined almost exclusively in terms of marriage and motherhood, to the extent that those who do not marry and have children tend to be seen as not properly female. This is so despite the fact that nowadays such a small portion of women's lives are spent in caring for young children. In contrast, the roles of husband and father are not offered as the sole or even the most important roles for men though they are generally held to be an essential part of their adult life. Whilst men can establish their social worth through work as well as through familial roles, and are encouraged to seek success in their occupations, a woman's social identity, her status as a person, depends almost entirely on her performance in familial roles. Women may, of course, be successful in, and derive some status from a job outside the home (a job and marriage are generally held to be compatible, at least at certain points in the family cycle), but work outside the home is allowed to the extent that it is used to reinforce familial roles, by, for instance, increasing the family income. Those who put a career before marriage (whether married or not) are generally given the derogatory stereotype of 'career women' and tend either to be denied the identity of 'real women' or are forced to emphasise and manipulate that identity to achieve success.

A man's position is similar to a woman's in some respects. On the one hand a job and marriage are generally thought to be compatible. Indeed the 'support' of a wife is often regarded as important, if not essential, for stability and success at work.[8] On the other hand, men's work is often seen as a way of providing for the family, and extra work is often legitimated in these terms. Nevertheless, the relative importance attached to occupational and familial roles is markedly different. Men are expected and encouraged to do well in their social roles outside the home, whilst women must do well first and foremost in their familial roles.

That women rather than men should be especially anxious to marry is not inevitable. Lucy Mair has argued that women are most concerned to marry where the husband is the economic provider in the family.[9] When marriage brings the man especial advantages, such as providing him with a source of labour (in a non-domestic sense) in his wife and children, or making him a member of a particular lineage, then it is the men who are most motivated for marriage.

There are, therefore, a number of pressures on both men and women to get married that stem from the connections between marriage and other social rights and statuses. Marriage is not only held to be necessary to, and confers the right to have children, but also provides the right to independence from parental ties, as well as being necessary if one is to assume the legitimate and social acceptable social identities of spouse and parent, identities that not only confer some status in themselves but can be manipulated to enhance one's own status.

In view of all this, it is hardly surprising that most men and women have married in the post-war period, often at relatively early ages. But why have more of them done so and at younger ages than before, up till very recently? Have our ideas about marriage changed? Has marriage come to occupy a rather different position in society than it did in the past, connected to and satisfying rather different objectives than formerly? Or have more people become anxious to achieve conditions whose connections with marriage have not changed?

A superficial glance might suggest that the necessity of, and desirability of marrying is now somewhat less than it was formerly: that if anything marriage is somewhat less of an ideal than it once was. It is often argued, for instance, that the 'permissive' society is undermining the morality that requires people to marry before engaging in sexual relations and having children. And there may be some truth in the argument. Certainly it is arguable that there has been some change in the norms about sexual relations outside marriage that is evidenced in the increasing proportions of extra-marital conceptions over the post-war period (though whether we should see the change as one of increasing permissiveness is doubtful).[10] And it is also true that the automatic association of women with the roles of wife and mother has been under direct attack over the past decade. On the other hand, there is little systematic evidence of much change in the norm that children should be born within marriage. Though illegitimacy increased from the early 1950s up to 1968, since then it has fluctuated (measured both by the rate per 1,000 unmarried women and the proportion of illegitimate births per 1,000 live births).[11] Likewise (as we might expect from the figures for illegitimacy) though the proportion of extra-marital conceptions legitimated before the birth of a child did decline from 60.2% in 1950 to 51.3% in 1967 the figures have fluctuated since then.[12] Moreover such changes do not provide clear evidence of normative change. Much of the increase in illegitimacy paralleled the overall increase in fertility suggesting that some of the factors that produced that rise may have also produced a greater number of illegitimate births. Moreover, the cessation of the steady rise in England, though it did not coincide with the first reduction of the birth rate in 1966 paralleled some of the other demographic changes that occurred soon after.

Far more important in its impact on patterns of marriage than a possible change in the belief that those who have children should marry has been the fact that since there have been far more extra-marital conceptions at younger ages, more people must have been getting married simply because the woman was pregnant.[13] This could contribute both to a higher incidence of marriage at younger ages than formerly and, possibly, an overall increase in the proportion marrying. The proportion of pre-maritally conceived legitimate maternities has increased over the post-war period and it is much higher amongst those who marry at younger ages than amongst the older marriage groups. The 1967 Abortion Act, which came into force in April 1968, by increasing the possibility of legal termination of extra-marital conceptions may have produced an important change in this respect, and may have facilitated the decline in the proportions marrying at the youngest ages first manifest in 1967.[14] Likewise the incidence of pre-marital conception almost certainly varies between social groups: those in low status occupations probably have a higher proportion of pre-marital conceptions, and this is likely to be one reason why they marry at younger ages.[15] The reason for the varying incidence of pre-marital conceptions is itself a complex matter which we cannot discuss here.

Over the recent post-war period there is little evidence of a reduction in the pressure to marry in order to gain a legitimate and socially acceptable place in society. Though there have been changes in patterns of marriage and childbearing over the last decade and a recent reversal in the trend towards earlier and more common marriage, there is little evidence that this is because most men or women have been changing their ideas about their legitimate and appropriate social role in life, despite the feminist revival. Indeed it is interesting that one strong theme in certain sectors of the new wave of feminism has been that familial roles should be more highly valued, rather than that women should only be able to gain status in a world defined and evaluated by men.

On the other hand, if we consider the longer term, there is evidence that the pressure to marry in order to establish a worthwhile and reputable social identity has increased rather than decreased. This is primarily because the relation between work and marriage has changed. Marriage is now generally held to be compatible with most occupations outside the home to a far greater extent than previously, and this change, by making work and marriage less alternatives than complements to one another, has almost certainly made it more necessary to marry in order to gain a legitimate and socially acceptable place in society.

In Victorian England men, and to an even greater extent women, in a wide range of occupations were not permitted to marry. There were, for instance, a number of occupations for women that were held to be suitable for, and were only open to unmarried women. They were both jobs that tended then, and still are, to be termed vocational (like teaching and nursing) and those of lower social status like domestic service. This meant that having such an occupation was not only an obstacle to marriage, but was a legitimate and institutionalised alternative to it (albeit less ideal), a social role that precluded marriage, at least for the time being. In fact most paid employment for women was employment for spinsters. During this century not only have more women entered paid employment, both full and part-time, but the proportion of single women in employment has rapidly declined, with the two wars producing the greatest changes.[16] Nowadays most jobs for women, even the vocational ones, may be held either for a short period prior to marriage or alongside it. There is, undoubtedly, still prejudice and discrimination against married women in the employment market, particularly against married women with young children, and references to this were not infrequent amongst the pilot sample. One husband's comment about his wife's work situation was by no means unique: 'she didn't go back to work any more when we got married. She went – tried to go back but they more or less said "well, we're sorry but we don't want married women"'. Nonetheless employment does not rule out marriage to the extent that it formerly did, so that a job has become less of an obstacle to marriage and less of a good reason for not marrying.

Of course work has sometimes, though less often, been an alternative to marriage for men, and here again the changes in this century have made work less of an obstacle to marriage than it once was, and less of an alternative to marriage (in some instances, as we have said, it is positively encouraged). On the one hand, there are now very few occupations that require or expect celibacy. Only Roman Catholic priests and monks have to remain celibate throughout their lives (and even this restriction is now under pressure). On the other hand, some occupations that restricted marriage during training no longer do so. At one time apprentices could not marry until their apprenticeship was completed, a restriction that has now been lifted. Again, however, the conventions have not changed completely. Although most establishments for further education permit students to marry it is often felt to be undesirable and discouraged and some of the changes here have been very recent. The possibility and likelihood of having a job that is an obstacle to or a justification for not marrying likewise varies between social groups. Those who are higher up the social scale and reach higher educational levels are probably more likely both now and in the past to have either training or occupations that make marriage more difficult and so can more readily justify not marrying.

To some extent changes and difference in the relation between work and marriage, and hence in the possibility of having a legitimate place in society without marrying, themselves reflect changes and difference in the patterns of marriage in the society. We would expect that where marriage was less common and occurred at later ages, there would be more institutionalised alternatives to marriage, and that growing pressure to marry would bring about changes in the rules that prevented people from marrying in certain occupational situations. On the other hand, other factors must have contributed to the change in conventions and practices about the employment of married people. When labour has been scarce, employers have had to accept more female employees, whether married or not, and have been less able to impose conditions on any employee.[17] Indeed, there seems to have been a general change in the rights of an employer to control aspects of an employee's life which do not directly relate to work, that have given workers somewhat more independence outside the work situation. The declining importance of particular occupations, such as the decline in domestic service, have also played their part. In particular the decline in the custom of having resident domestic servants, which resulted from a variety of different forces, reduced an important sector of the employment market for women that discouraged marriage.[18]

Such changes in the relation between work and marriage must have had an especially marked impact on women's conceptions of their roles, and have reinforced the association of the female identity with the roles of wife and mother. If work was no longer an alternative to marriage for women then it was likely to be viewed as more subordinate to marriage and family life, since those were already regarded as the ideal roles. Hence, ironically, an improvement in the employment position of married women may have enhanced women's tie to marriage and the family.

Furthermore, if a woman's place is increasingly in the home, in the sense that her job horizon must be subordinate to family life, a woman's place is supposed increasingly to be her *own* (or more accurately her husband's) home rather than that of her parents or other kin. There is less and less of a domestic and familial role for women within the wider family. The figure of the maiden aunt, either benevolent or shrewish has been a common one in literature about the last century or the beginning of this.[19] For a woman never to marry or have children was not considered ideal, but it was by no means unusual, and those who did not marry had a well-defined role within the broader family which would offer them economic, social and emotional support. Here, the very reduction in the frequency of remaining single, has contributed to a change in norms and practices that make it more difficult for women to remain unmarried.

Change and variation in the patterns of marriage may also have resulted from changes in the association between marriage and independence. Though marriage is still the most important way in which children can achieve independence from their parents and be granted adult status, the opportunity to achieve the latter, if not the former, is now more readily available by other means. In the first place more people now have the chance to achieve at least temporary independence from their parents by engaging in further education.[20] It is, however, a far from perfect method. It may not mean moving away from home; if it does, pressure may be exerted for a return home when the training is completed; and those who move away are not usually regarded, at least by their parents, as really living away from home or fully independent (they are likely to be financially dependent on their parents). Though this is not likely to have had much effect on the trends in marriage since the increase in further education has been relatively small (and it would have encouraged people to defer marriage rather than to marry younger), it may account for some of the variation in age at marriage that is found amongst different social groups, since the proportions receiving further education varies considerably.

Second, the fact that various legal rights are now given at younger ages than formerly (of which the right to vote at 18 instead of 21 is a recent example), though it may itself have been influenced by the recognition that many people were marrying at younger ages and were thereby already achieving certain features of adult status, may also have weakened the link between marriage and independence. The interaction of different factors is, however, very complex and intricate. For example, more liberal childrearing practices and increased recognition of the rights of children and adolescents might suggest that marriage would become less attractive and less necessary as a means of establishing independence. Yet by heightening the desire for independence, it may make marriage seem more attractive in that respect. Clearly our information is inadequate to enable us to judge between these alternatives.

Examination of the ideas and beliefs about the circumstances in which marriage seems desirable and the rights and status advantages to be gained from marriage helps us to pinpoint some sources of change and variation in patterns of marriage. They do not, however, provide the complete picture.

II: The material and financial demands of marriage

Just as certain characteristics of marriage in contemporary English society make it seem either desirable or necessary to marry, so certain of its characteristics may make it seem either desirable or necessary to delay marriage for a shorter or longer time. It is the rights and status advantages of marriage that generally make it seem inevitable to many people. It is the material and financial demands it imposes that may provide grounds for delay, and may at times preclude it altogether.

Many of the material and financial demands of marriage stem from two characteristics of marriage that we have already mentioned, its association with independence and its association with having children. Though marriage may seem attractive because it confers the right to a life of one's own and is held to be the appropriate condition for having children such advantages, nonetheless, make demands of those who marry. The fact that a married person is expected to live an independent life and to have a family has very definite material and financial implications, which may constitute obstacles to marriage. Indeed, the obligation on a married couple to constitute a distinct family unit independent of parents or other kin, is frequently mentioned in attempts to explain the typical 'European' marriage pattern of a late age at marriage and relatively low proportions marrying. Different explanations of the pattern stress different aspects of independence: at times it is economic independence, at others domestic or residential, though very often they are assumed to coincide. Hajnal in his original description of the 'European' pattern suggested economic independence: 'In Europe it has been necessary for a man to defer marriage until he could establish an independent livelihood adequate to support a family; in other societies the young couples could be incorporated in a larger economic unit such as a joint family.'[21] Habakkuk, in contrast, proposes domestic and residential independence as the 'proximate' cause of the pattern. 'Europeans married late because in Western Europe the responsibility for the care of the children rested on the husband and wife as opposed to some wider family group – and marriage was therefore tied to the setting up of a separate household.[22] The obvious problem with either explanation is that the expectation on couples to constitute an independent family unit has remained despite considerable change in patterns of marriage in Europe over the century. Nevertheless, though such explanations are not adequate in themselves they point to the importance of the convention that a married couple should act as an independent family unit, which gives rise to many of the material and financial obligations of marriage.

When we turn to consider the financial and material demands of marriage more directly we encounter the problem of lack of information. Although material standards (that is what people regard as desirable as opposed to what they have) are often mentioned as an important influence on patterns of marriage and childbearing, they have been given remarkably little detailed study, and it is not easy to establish whether they have changed in ways that could account for trends in marriage over this century. One of the few attempts to specify the material standards, in an ideal sense, of married life, is J. A. Banks' study of middle-class family life in Victorian England, *Prosperity and Parenthood*.[23] Unfortunately our own study was not designed to provide the sort of detailed information about material standards that Banks discusses, which would allow comparison between his data and contemporary standards of family life. We also lack any comparable analysis of working-class standards in Victorian England as well as studies of the standards at any point of time in between. Of course, it is not too difficult to suggest certain changes and argue that these may be responsible for some of the trends in marriage, and it would be possible, as Banks did, to build up a picture of the standards now and earlier from secondary sources.[22] However, this would require much more detailed investigation than we can hope to attempt in this study, especially since our own research suggests that there is considerable variation in what are held to be the financial and material standards of family life. As we show in Chapter 10, couples view their family life and their roles as parents in a variety of different ways, and this affects their material and financial standards. Nevertheless, even if we cannot hope to consider changes in standards in any detail here, it is possible to indicate ways in which the ease of meeting some of the financial and material demands of marriage has changed over time and also vary for different sectors of the community at any one time, that must account for some of the variation in patterns of marriage that we observe.

Take the case of housing. Conventional wisdom has it that 'a life of one's own' requires 'a place of one's own', and the couples we interviewed invariably mentioned the importance of having a place of their own when they married.[25] One husband, discussing whether he was satisfied with the two rooms and shared kitchen he and his wife rented when they married, said they were:

Not satisfied, but it was a place of our own. Definitely it was a place of our own, rooms of our own. We could close – shut the door behind us and that was our home. We weren't living with anybody, we had rooms of our own.

A woman who lived in 'a couple of rooms' when she first married said of her plans at the time, 'We were always looking forward to having a place of our own. That was our biggest dream, to get our own somewhere.' Another discussing the things that had been important to her before marriage said:

I think the most important things these days is trying to find somewhere to live before you can get married. If you can't find anywhere to live, well its no good getting married. I think that was the hardest thing we found to do, was looking for somewhere to live.

Moreover, the pilot sample's comments showed how the timing of marriage was for some directly and explicitly tied to the issue of housing. A wife asked why they had married when they did, replied:

Well, I can answer that question now; well, we got engaged and then we said we'd save a deposit for the house, and then we had the chance of this one, and that was in the nice part of town, you know, the part of town we wanted to be, so we sort of saved a bit extra like, and just decided to get married, we thought that would be cheaper in the long run.

For this couple marriage was made possible, apparently somewhat earlier than expected, because suitable accommodation became available. More often housing was mentioned as a reason for some delay in marrying, and very often it was those who were trying to buy their own houses who mentioned it. (If a condition permits you to do something there is normally less reason to mention it than if it does not. Hence we would not expect those who married relatively early to mention housing as a reason for this.)

Of course, as the remarks above show, what couples regard as a place of their own varies as does their willingness to live in accommodation that does not satisfy those standards, and no doubt these standards have changed during the century. Nevertheless, without detailed examination of such standards, and the values and beliefs that underly them, it is easy to see how differential access to types of accommodation, either at a particular time or at different periods of time, must help to produce some of the variation and change in patterns of marriage we observe.

In England in the 1950s and 1960s a middle-class man could, from quite early in his career, typically expect to be able to purchase by means of a mortgage his own house either detached or, more usually, semi-detached. In contrast, the working-class man would not be likely to have both a sufficiently secure job and a sufficiently high income to enable him to obtain mortgage finance to buy his own house. Instead, he would usually expect to have to rent either from a private landlord or a local authority. This meant that for the middle-class man it made sense not to marry until the mortgage deposit (usually 10% of the house price) had been accumulated, and a sufficiently secure job with an adequate minimum income had been obtained. Since buying a house of one's own was possible in the near future there was little point in not waiting to marry until the objective could be achieved. For the working-class man who had little chance of purchasing a house of his own, there was no point in postponing marriage to accumulate a deposit. Nor, since his income would be unlikely to increase much after the age of 21 (except by working longer hours), was there much point in deferring marriage to be in a better position to pay the rent more easily. Indeed, since local-authority housing is primarily designed for families (married couples with children) getting married and starting a family as soon as possible was a sensible thing to do. With the reduction in private rented accommodation over the century this strategy has become more essential since getting council accommodation may be the only way of getting a place of one's own.[26] Getting married and having a child, or preferably two, while living with one's parents is doubly effective in comparison with the apparently more prudent strategy of waiting to marry until some separate accommodation is available, since it not only creates the family unit for which most council accommodation is designed, but it also often produces overcrowding which itself usually improves one's chances of a council house. It is true that local authorities vary in the precise system they operate for allocating accommodation just as they vary in the amount of housing they provide and their policies for making it available for sale to tenants. In general, however, the criterion of need assessed in terms of current accommodation, and size of the potential domestic unit are important, though not the only consideration: length of residence in the district and length of time on the housing list are often also taken into account.

The difficulty of obtaining a place of one's own also varies over time, for the housing situation changes markedly, occasionally very rapidly. Those marrying in the 1960s were probably uniquely advantaged in the post-war period in the availability of housing, particularly in the form of newly-built houses available for purchase through the building societies. The figures in Table 8:2 show very clearly the marked differences in the tenure of accommodation occupied at marriage by the two cohorts of the survey sample, with far more of the 1960s cohort buying houses on

TABLE 8:2   *Tenure of accommodation in survey sample at marriage by marriage cohort*

| | Marriage cohort | | | |
| | 1951-7 | | 1961-7 | |
Tenure of accommodation	No.	%	No.	%
Private landlord	57	45	64	39
Local authority	4	3	4	2
Relative	20	16	18	11
Firm	5	4	8	5
Owner-occupier (no mortgage)	4	3	7	4
Owner-occupier (mortgage)	12	10	47	29
Other	24	19	16	10
Total	126	100	164	100

mortgage at marriage, despite the fact that they were marrying on average at younger ages. The superiority of the more recent cohort's accommodation is reflected in the fact that according to our figures 60% of the couples had their own lavatory, bathroom and kitchen when they married, whilst 25% had to share all these facilities, in contrast to the earlier cohort in which only 36% had their own lavatory, bathroom and kitchen whilst 46% of them had had to share all these facilities. Not surprisingly expectations about future accommodation for those who planned to move within the next ten years had also increased. Whilst 32% of the 1950s cohort had expected that they would live in their next accommodation as owner-occupiers, 48% of the 1960s cohort expected to do so. Proportionately fewer of the later cohort expected to be in some sort of local authority accommodation when they next moved (20% against 50%).

But the improvement in accommodation, either in terms of the size of the housing stock or the availability of mortgages, has not been a steady and consistent one. The improvement in the 1960s combined a boom in the construction of houses for private sale (see Table 8:3) with readily available mortgages, low interest rates and house prices low enough to be within the range of most of the middle class. In the immediate post-war period housing was especially difficult because of damage and deterioration to housing stock during the war. There was some improvement in the 1950s especially in the

TABLE 8:3 *Permanent houses built in five-year periods 1919-68, England and Wales*

Year ending 30 September	Local authority	Private builders (a)	Total
1919-24	176,914	221,543	398,457
1925-9	326,353	673,344	999,697
1930-4	286,350	804,251	1,090,601
1935-9	346,840	1,269,912	1,616,752
1940-4	—	—	151,000 (b)
1945-9	432,098 (c)	126,317	588,415
1950-4	912,805	228,616	1,141,421
1955-9	688,585	623,024	1,311,609
1960-4	545,729	878,756	1,424,485
1965-8	621,324	809,961	1,431,285

Notes:
(a) Including 431,669 built between 1919 and 1939 with the aid of a subsidy.
(b) This figure is for the period September 1939 to March 1944. There was an embargo on the building of new houses for the rest of 1944.
(c) From 1945 onwards figures in this column include houses by New Town Development Corporations and by Housing Associations and Government Departments, but exclude temporary houses built by local authorities.
Source: Rollett (1972), Table 10:24, p. 311.

public sector but it was not until the economic boom of the late 1950s that the private development of housing began to increase rapidly. Those who have married in the 1970s have not, however, been nearly as advantaged as those in the 1960s; fewer houses have been built, their prices have risen, even allowing for inflation, interest rates have increased steeply and mortgages have not always been very easy to obtain. These difficulties cannot but have played a part in the trends in marriage that have been visible since 1967. It is interesting too that the previous boom in house building, both by local authorities and the private sector, in the mid-1930s, coincided with the acceleration of the reductions in age at marriage.

The important implication of the varying ease with which it is possible to obtain a place of one's own for one's married life, is that in some cases it makes sense to delay marriage in order to improve one's chances of obtaining the sort of accommodation one desires whilst in others it does not. As a result, there is likely to be a varying willingness to marry *before* the assets considered necessary to married life have been acquired according both to the state of the housing market and the couple's prospective income. The point is equally, if not more important when it comes to other material and financial demands of married life. We want to argue that one of the major changes during this century has been in the ease with which the material goods and services that people feel are desirable for married life can be obtained, so that the advantages to be gained from accumulating assets before one marries have been reduced. One of the striking features of the comments made by the men and women is the lack of concern they showed for making much provision for the financial and material demands of marriage before they married, as well as the general lack of anxiety and concern about how they would meet the demands once they married. The one point of concern that couples said they had before marriage, if any, was about housing, but apart from that the only things mentioned at all frequently were the need to furnish one's accommodation, and a rather general reference to the need to try and save some money before marriage. Moreover, further questioning almost always revealed that the savings were intended either for housing or furnishings (including, of course, consumer durables). There was little reference to the cost of children, job prospects, economic uncertainty, and so on. It is true that our sample contained few members of the professional middle classes, (though there were quite a few white-collar workers), yet the absence of concern for the future income of the husband, or his general 'prospects' was very marked.[27] One woman who said her parents had been pleased because her future husband had a 'steady job' struck a note that was hardly sounded elsewhere. Of course it could be argued that most sectors of the community, other than professional middle-class groups, have all along been little concerned about their prospects of meeting the obligations of marriage. We would argue that the change is less in the importance that is attached to meeting the demands or even (probably) in the demands themselves, than in the ease with which this can be done.

There have been several obvious ways in which it has become easier to obtain the goods and services that people feel are desirable for family life. First, the state now provides a number of services for most (though it should be all) members of the society that previously had to be paid for directly by individuals if they had them at all. State education and the National Health Service have made individual provision for education and medical care less necessary. One consequence of this, no doubt, has been to raise the standards that people expect for themselves and their families, but for those who already made such provision privately (to a greater or lesser extent) or were concerned to do so, the introduction of state services has almost certainly eased the burden of making such provision. The change is not just a question of overall cost, but in the forethought, planning and saving that is necessary to provide one's family with education and medical care.

However, state provision of education and medical services are not the only aspects of the so-called welfare state that affect the prospects of married life and the need to plan for them. The welfare state also reduces, at least to some extent, economic hazards and uncertainties. The contingencies of illness are reduced not only by state health services but also by compulsory sickness insurance, the financial consequences of unemployment are reduced by unemployment benefit, and so forth. This is not to say that there are no gaps and inadequacies in the state provision. There are. But concern with existing, or past shortcomings should not blind us to the extent to which the present provisions have cushioned the material hazards a family may encounter, especially since the war.[28] In brief, the state now intervenes to compel almost all workers, from the very start of their careers, to make provision for many of those contingencies that, previously, only the prospect or the intention of marriage may have elicited, and has, therefore, in that respect, made marriage less of a hurdle.

Furthermore, the 1950s and 1960s have been periods of relative economic security and affluence for much of the population, so that in comparison with the 1930s or even the early 1970s individuals were less likely to have been worried about their job prospects. For a number of reasons, therefore, individuals during that period were less likely to have been worried about their future material circumstances and about the potential financial burdens of married life, and for that reason, must have been less likely to defer marriage.

If the individual's financial future over a lifetime looks somewhat less uncertain and hazardous in some respects than it did, there has also been less need to wait for one's gratification. One major change of this century has been the development of ways in which future income can be converted into current assets, through the growth of credit financing of various types, not only of mortgages (a seventeenth century development, but first widely used in the 1930s), but also of banking with overdraft facilities and more recently credit cards, as well as hire purchase (which spread rapidly in the post-war period to replace the various credit clubs). All this has meant that the individual does not always have to wait to purchase goods and services but can use his prospective income to gain immediate credit. Indeed in times of inflation there is an added reason for doing so, and the prudent may well be those who increase their debt rather than save.

When it comes to analysing cross-sectional differences in marriage the situation is rather different. Though it is true that the financial situation is more favourable to the middle-class on dimensions of security, ease of obtaining credit and so forth, which according to the argument above, would suggest that the middle classes should marry earlier, the differences in life chances in terms of overall income prospects, stability of income and so on, is such that there is less advantage in delaying marriage for the working classes.[29] As with housing, the person whose income will rise in the future has reason for delaying marriage that the other does not.

In sum, therefore, a number of changes during the century have facilitated early marriage – changes which, in conjunction with the probably increasing pressure to marry, have increased the proportions marrying and pushed down the age at marriage. Nevertheless, though there is little evidence as yet that the pressure to marry has been any less during the 1970s, a number of conditions, such as the state of the housing market and the general financial and economic climate, have become less favourable to early marriage, and this has halted the previous trends in patterns of marriage. We cannot, however, hope to predict whether the recent reversal will continue.

9.   Thinking about children

In the last chapter we attempted to explain the variation in patterns of marriage in post-war England and earlier by examining some salient and widely accepted ideas about marriage in that period, and we tried to identify certain points of change and difference in these ideas and the circumstances and practices to which they relate. We shall start by adopting the same strategy in order to explain differential patterns of childbearing and consider some of the common ideas about having children, but our examination can be far more thorough and detailed since the material from the pilot study on this topic is far more comprehensive.

I: Becoming a parent

Perhaps the most significant aspect of childbearing in contemporary industrial societies, yet one that tends to be taken for granted and little mentioned, is that most married people usually have children. The majority become parents just as they always have in non-industrial societies, even though new techniques of birth control make it much easier for individuals to choose otherwise. In most societies, of course, having children must have seemed an inevitable consequence of getting married, for the degree to which it has been customary to control childbearing within marriage, whilst by no means always insignificant, has generally been limited. There can rarely have been much prospect of having intercourse with any degree of regularity and remaining childless. Only the recent and growing use of effective and reliable methods of contraception has made possible the separation of marriage from childbearing, by facilitating the separation of intercourse from conception. Yet so far there is little evidence that many are choosing to remain childless throughout marriage.[1]

It is difficult to calculate the total proportion of adults who do become parents in this country, whether or not they marry, but it has probably been around 80% in the post-war period.[2] In comparison about nine out of every ten women who have married over the same period have had at least one child.[3] How do we account for these high proportions? Why do most people have children? What makes children seem such an integral part of marriage? Is it that children are thought to be essential for one's future material well-being? Is it that children are thought to be intrinsically enjoyable? Is it that children are thought to be essential to the continuity of society, or what?

What people say about having children indicates that there are a number of related ideas that have contributed to the sense that children are essential to married life, if not life more generally.[4] We have already pointed in the previous chapter to the way in which getting married may seem essential because it is necessary to allow the individual to take up the clearly defined and legitimate social roles of spouse and parent. Likewise one reason why it may seem important to have children is that doing so makes one into a mother or a father. As in the case of marriage the point is almost definitional: you cannot be a wife or husband without getting married, and you cannot be a mother or father without having children. Yet the implications go beyond this: it may be the occupation of the role that is important rather than having children *per se*. Certainly a number of comments made in the pilot interviews suggested that for some women having children was important because it made them into *mothers*; it was the *idea* of being a mother that was significant. The comments of one woman after the birth of the first child illustrate the point; she reported: 'The funny thing was when I'd finished giving birth I said "Oh, I'm a mother" and that made the doctor and the midwife laugh.' Another described her feelings when she had had her second child like this:

I was pleased, I felt I was somebody important. I'd really got something. I had a family. I was a mother and I was going to decide and tell these what to do and what not to do. I felt really important. You feel fulfilled in a way.

We would of course expect women to make such comments more often than men since, as we have said, the female identity is more closely tied to the familial roles of spouse and parent than the male identity. In consequence it is not surprising to find one woman asserting, 'I don't think a woman is a woman until she has had children'.

A second salient idea is that since having children is a major, if not the sole reason for getting married it seems to make little sense to marry and not have children. To do so would not only be unthinkable, it would also be illogical. Hence the connection between marriage and having children is self-reinforcing. It makes those who want to have children marry, and it makes those who marry feel they should have children. The way in which having children is seen as the essential purpose of marriage, and the way in which this idea makes it difficult to think of not having any children if you marry, was brought out in a number of comments made in the pilot interviews. A wife expressed the argument particularly succinctly when, asked about having children, she said 'I'm married to my husband to have children'. Another, talking about the importance of having children, said:

Well, I think it's important if you're married. If you're single you make a life for yourself, don't you, a different life altogether. But if you're married, well, I should think that's the whole point of marriage really.

A third put the argument even more forcefully, though with more difficulty, when asked whether having children was a burden but worth the trouble.

Well, I think that's worth – well, I always say, that's what you get married for isn't it. I mean, I mean those that, those that – if they don't want children they should – they want a good time, well they shouldn't get married, should they? They should go out and have a good time, and that's that. That's like – often my argument, I mean, I say, if they don't want children why get married. I mean that's a fact, isn't it? I mean that's what marriage is. Marriage is a home and family and a husband and family. Marriage isn't to keep going out and keep – is it?

Nor was she alone in suggesting that if you didn't want to have children it was better not to marry. Another woman remarked:

I think marriage without children is a very empty life, and I think there's absolutely no point at all in marriage without children; if one gets married it should be for the purpose of creating children, otherwise I think if a man and a woman just desire to live together I think they may as well do just that, because if they don't want it to be a permanent union and have children there really is no point in joining together for life.

For her, as for many others, marriage made little sense if you did not have children.

One familiar variant of this idea is that children are important, if not essential, to the survival and success of marriage. As one woman commented 'they do make a marriage, they definitely do'. Another said of having children 'Well, I do think it makes marriage a success. I don't think it would be much of a success without.' Another woman remarked more forcefully when asked 'What if you'd had no children, what difference do you think that would have made?' 'I think that would have been almost, probably fatal to our marriage.' A husband replying to the question conveyed the same idea in a vivid and telling way:

If you don't 'ave any children, if you have any difference of opinion you're inclined just to sort of pack up your gear and get going. But if you've got children, I mean, we're like everybody else, we've 'ad violent rows and one of us 'as been going, you know, but if you just look into the bedroom where the two children are sleeping in bed, you know, you couldn't possibly go. And I think it tends to hold the family together in a crisis. I mean, if we struck bad times I should think the family would keep you together more.

What is interesting, given the frequency with which such ideas were expressed is that, in this country at least, there is little evidence that the marriages of those who have children are more likely to last, though such statistical findings tell us little about the role children may play in maintaining a marriage.[5]

A further salient belief is that just as children 'make a marriage', they also 'make a family'. When asked about having children most people draw upon a set of ideas that links getting married, having children and having a family to one another, making all seem mutually interdependent. Underlying this set of ideas is the belief that a married couple with children constitute a natural, normal and complete family. Without children a married couple are not a proper family. Indeed in the context of a married couple it is the children who are the family. In expressions such as 'they haven't got a family' and 'their family has left home' the family simply means children. Indeed, when we asked questions phrased in terms of 'children' our respondents often talked of the 'family'. Marriage by itself is apparently not enough to create a family: a couple must have children to make one. One woman discussing the importance of children conveyed the idea of how children make a family like this 'I think that children make a family and I think that if you get married it is important to have a family'. She later described the difference having children made in these terms 'I think it brought us a bit more together—made us a family.' Another said 'I don't think you can have a family life without children.' Yet another talking about life without children commented 'But that's not a family when there's no children. Children make a family.'

That children are the *sine qua non* of family life is obvious enough; what is important is that given the desire to have a family life, this becomes a reason for having children. It means that those pressures that encourage an individual to engage in family life are likely to become pressures to have children. It is this equation between having children and having a family that presumably underlies one familiar argument for having children that they will be someone to 'turn to' when one is older. In that sense children provide an investment against future loneliness and uncertainty. Here is how one woman described what her husband said when discussing why he wanted two children (she herself wanted only one):

Well, he said two or more, because he thinks that, that it's when you're older you need the children. He said like his mother, he pointed out to me his mother, for instance, the children go and see her you know, and my mother the same. Whereas if you're married and you've got no children and then anything happens and you're left on your own, you'd wish then you'd got children to come round and see you.

Another, asked whether having children was one of the most important things in life, had this to say:

I personally, we both personally do. I think it must be terrible when you get sort of older and you got nobody, say your parents are dead, you got nobody to come and see you, you know, and I think it must be awful if you – you must be alone really, you know; but everybody can't have the same opinion of course.

A similar argument was put by a woman who had delayed having children till she was 30. When asked what had influenced her ideas and those of her husband about having children, she replied:

I don't know. All me family had got one, I was the only one out of my family what hadn't got any, you know. I used to think when theirs are all grown up, when they get older, you know, they'll want to see their children and I shan't have nobody, if I might be left on my own, and I thought well, that'll be something to look after and that, won't it. That's how we come, you see, how we come to talk about it.

Others, too, though they did not offer this as an argument for having children, showed they were concerned that their children should keep up contact when they left home. Here, for instance, is one description of a good son:

Well, I suppose good to his parents. I don't expect him to support them, but if they're old and that, but I think if a son comes home and sees his Mum and Dad when he's married and that, bring his wife and children—sort of keep in the family.

As these comments illustrate, people do not like to talk of children as a material investment for themselves, and, when discussing the relations they anticipate with their children after they have left home, they tend to stress companionship rather than any material support they may receive, though in practice a large proportion do receive some sort of transfer of income from their children.[6] Asked about the relationship they expected to have with their child in the future (with the explicit suggestion that the child might be a source of financial or emotional support), 70% of both men and women in the survey sample gave an answer indicating that they expected their children to be a source only of emotional support.

Most people, however, probably think less of the distant future than of the situation when they have their children at home and are looking after them, and for that period there can be no doubt that it is the emotional satisfaction they provide that counts. Having children is an attractive idea because children are thought to be intrinsically satisfying. They are thought to offer an important and unique range of satisfactions. Many people believe that having children and bringing them up will give and does give them a great deal of pleasure; they think that having children is emotionally and even intellectually satisfying; they think life with children is richer, more interesting and more enjoyable than life without.

Many of our pilot sample described the feelings they have about children in very positive terms. As one woman remarked: 'I adore my children and I don't know what I'd do without them.' Another commented of her husband 'Oh, he loves his children very much, he just lives for his children, you know, in every way.' Yet another said 'He adores them, he wouldn't change them for anything.' Of course not everyone feels so positively, but the idea that children could provide no intrinsic satisfaction was very rare. People differ, too, in the precise nature of the satisfaction they think is provided by children. Many emphasise the satisfaction they get simply from having the children at home, from watching them grow up, from teaching them things and so on. For some, usually the wives, it is having a baby that is especially satisfying. 'Babies are lovely' said one woman 'they're all soft and cuddly, and they're yours then, aren't they when they're tiny.'

Among the accounts of the sources of emotional satisfaction that of doing things for one's children, especially providing them with opportunities that parents have not had for themselves, is prominent. Again what things or opportunities are provided depends on situational extingencies. For some it is satisfying simply to provide for children's basic needs. It was a pleasure, one woman said 'to know that I can feed and clothe them as I would like'. Another said 'I think it's a pleasure to you and everybody else to have children, to look after them nice, and dress them nice, you know.' For others, the pleasure comes from having a second chance to have or attain what one did not have or get oneself. The cry 'I wouldn't want mine to have what we had to have' was common. Or a parent may feel pleased to give to their children those things that they had to strive for themselves. Moreover, in their concern for what they can do for their children parents frequently assert that children make effort and sacrifices worthwhile. Many men, when questioned about their jobs, stress that children are an important motivating factor for hard work and long hours, and 'I do it for my children' or 'I do it for my family' is a frequent claim. Whether this is always true or not, beliefs of this type seem to provide one way of making everyday activities meaningful and contribute to the satisfaction that comes from having children. Having children provides a sense of purpose, a 'reason for living', that is at times explicitly recognised. One woman asked what things had been important for her husband since the birth of their last (sixth) child commented:

Well, I think he feels the same as I do about it, you know, at least we've got something now that the others are pulling away from us, we've got something to live for and sort of have around us sort of thing.

More often it is apparent in comments such as 'he lives for his children'.

Satisfaction is also thought to derive from one's children's successes: from what they do as well as from what one does for them, though the two are by no means clearly differentiated, and the satisfaction from doing things for one's children clearly originates in part from the fact that they are a reflection of one's own endeavour. One woman asked 'What are the main pleasures that you get from your children?' replied 'Well, any success obviously gives me pleasure.' How a child appears to others on the matters held important by the parents is crucial. Children in this way offer a chance of enhancing status. Dennis and his colleagues have described how this operated for women in a traditional mining community in the early 1950s:

Women are denied participation in those activities whereby men achieve success or reprobation. They definitely try to assert their individual worth among other women by doing the job of motherhood as well as or better than their neighbours. In fact this means showing the outward signs – new clothes, new toys, well-fed children. It is by these standards that a mother is immediately judged. The child is in the dangerous position of being a status object for the mother.[7]

But children are not only satisfying because they are interesting to care for and bring up; they are satisfying because they ensure a continuity of individual characteristics and give a sense of keeping part of oneself alive.

Having a child is one way of ensuring some sort of indirect immortality for oneself. This is a frequent theme of Shakespeare's sonnets:

> Thou are thy mother's glass, and she in thee
> Calls back the lovely April of her prime;
> So though through windows of thine age shall see,
> Despite of wrinkles, this thy golden time.
> But if thou live, remember'd not to be,
> Die single, and thine image dies with thee.

Or,

> And nothing 'gainst time's scythe can make defence
> Save breed, to brave him when he takes thee hence.

Such ideas are still evidenced in the interest in familial and personal similarities, from the initial searching for likenesses of facial and other bodily characteristics of a new born baby, to the later marking of similarities of personality and ability, and may be particularly important now that many people no longer believe in either bodily or spiritual immortality. It is, however, the least clearly articulated aspect of the satisfaction that may be gained from having children, though it was occasionally mentioned in our interviews. One woman expressed the ideas like this:

I think children are pretty important because well, I think that's the instinct to survive in all of us, sort of thing. The children survive us, its the only thing left behind from us. And I think all of us, in some way or other, love to impose our opinions and our ways of life in some way or another, and children is the only way you can do it, 'cos nobody else just wants to know.

Though children are believed to offer a unique range and variety of satisfactions, this does not mean that they are regarded in a wholly positive light, either in anticipation or once they arrive. Our data does not allow us to distinguish prospective and retrospective judgements of this type in any precise way. Nevertheless, amongst those we interviewed many people spontaneously mentioned certain consequences of having children making it clear for them they were disadvantages, and it is unlikely that at least some of these disadvantageous implications were not anticipated, since they too are part of widely known and widely accepted ideas about having children.[8] There was however little evidence that the disadvantages and advantages of having children were regarded as commensurate and weighed up against each other in a single calculus, either before or after a couple had children. Given as a starting point the belief that it is important to have children for one or more of a number of reasons, a weighing up of the merits and demerits of having children is inappropriate and irrelevant to whether one has children or not. If there is any tendency directly to juxtapose possible advantages and disadvantages, the belief that it is desirable, if not essential to have children, is likely to encourage the view expressed by one woman: 'If you have a little trouble with children that's forgotten, but the joy and the pleasure is never forgotten.'

Beliefs like this produce a situation where both men and women often think that having children is one of, if not the most important thing in life, and feel that having children is essential to a full and complete life. They are an experience not to be missed. One woman commented:

Well, I don't think that family life could possibly be complete without children. I don't think that life is complete unless you have a child really. Because I think if you haven't you just don't know what life is. I think it – well it brings you down to earth and you see life from the beginning and I think it really does broaden your outlook.

Others spoke of life without children as an empty life, of the need to have children to have a full life, and of children giving them a new interest in life. In the survey sample when asked 'What difference would it make if you had no children?' the majority of those who gave a definite answer to the question said that life would be worse without children (64% of the husbands and 68% of the wives). Almost all of them felt it would be worse in ways which we categorised as emotional. However it is interesting that 22% of the men and 20% of the women said that life would actually be better without children (in some cases, no doubt, because the reality has not matched up to their expectations). Many people, too, made it clear that they expected they would find it unpleasant and difficult when their children left home. One woman remarked 'I shall be very sad in all ways'. Another commented 'I reckon I'll break my heart'.

The importance attached to having children is also reflected in the way in which those who want to have children, yet cannot, suffer from their situation; they are pitied by others and feel frustrated and inadequate in themselves. This is especially true of women because of the way in which having children and looking after them are customarily designated as women's activities. Of course in some societies having children may be even more important for women. Infertility in a woman may, for instance, be sufficient grounds for divorce or be the greatest humiliation.[9] The misery and disappointment that attaches to childlessness is a common feature of the values surrounding reproduction and is evidence of the almost universal emphasis on the importance and desirability of becoming a parent. Many women who have children would echo one who said 'If we couldn't have had any of our own we probably would have adopted some', though for most adopting children is very much a second best to having children of one's own.

The belief that children are essential to married life also produces a situation where it is generally assumed, both by the couples themselves and those they encounter, that as they are married they will have, and must want to have children. This itself is an additional pressure to have children, and for those who are married childbearing tends to be taken for granted. The question tends to be not 'Are you going to have children?' but 'When are you going to have children?' The logic here seems to be that if those who want to have children get married, then those who get married must want children. The automatic assumption that married people will want children has its counterpart in the assumption that women who are not married cannot want children.[10] Doctors tend to assume that if a woman is single any pregnancy is unintended and act accordingly. The continuing assumption that those who marry will have children often has a marked impact on the couples. As one woman remarked:

That's about the only thing I ever did get was – 'Do you want any children?' The same with my husband, you know – 'Don't you, don't you have any family yet? Don't you have any family yet?.

Another found it difficult to talk to her doctor and to the family planning clinic about contraception when she had no children partly because she felt that as she was married she was supposed to have children. As she commented 'It would never occur to us to say let's get married, we don't want children.'[11]

This analysis of some of the salient ideas underlying the belief that it is essential to have children, especially if one is married, brings out a number of important points. It shows, in the first place, the strength of the normative pressure to have children. It is hardly surprising that most people have children since in their eyes not to have children may be simultaneously to deny oneself a legitimate and valued social identity, to make a 'nonsense' of marriage, to put one's marriage in danger of failure, to reject the benefits of family life and to deprive oneself of a major and unique source of satisfaction which helps to give life both purpose and meaning. It shows, secondly, that for most people the belief that it is essential to have children is so integral to their way of thinking that when they marry they cannot be said to calculate and weigh up against each other the respective advantages and disadvantages they may gain from having children. Rather once they marry they tend to assume that they will have children and plan their lives accordingly. As one woman said when asked about her ideas about having children when she first married 'Well, I didn't consider not having children I don't think.' In that respect alone the idea of some utilitarian calculus is totally inappropriate for describing the cognitions involved in having *some* children. Finally, it shows that in post-war English society children have been valued for their role in constituting and maintaining marriage and family life as well as for the intrinsic satisfaction and sense of purpose they provide, and not because they are, for instance, regarded as a financial investment, or as a means of maintaining society, or as a sign of the providence of God. Without radical changes in these beliefs it will continue to be normative to have children if you marry, whatever the developments in contraceptive technology.

II: Family size

For most people the only question about having children is not whether to have any, but how many to have and when to have them. Nevertheless just as there is a strong belief that when you marry you should have children, which is based on widely-held ideas about the importance of having children, so there are clear-cut beliefs about the desirable number and, to a lesser extent, the desirable spacing of births within a family, which are themselves based on a number of more specific beliefs about what having children involves, with the result that in practice decisions about family size and spacing are made within a fairly narrow range, and tend to take a standard range of issues into account.

What are the common ideas about the size of family that is to be preferred? What are the ideas on which these preferences are founded? What social and economic conditions do people consider when they have children?

In post-war England a family of two to four children has been regarded as desirable, a norm that emerges repeatedly from a variety of sources. It emerges on the one hand from studies that have questioned men and women directly about the size of family that they regard as 'ideal' or that they say they actually want. Though the data from such questions is not easy to interpret (it is not very clear how people interpret questions about ideals and preferences and what sort of distinction, if any, they make between the two), nevertheless the uniform way in which most people give an answer in the range of two to four, whatever the study and whatever question, indicates that this is the normatively acceptable range of family sizes. The variation comes in the distribution of answers within this range and this depends, at least in part, on how the question is framed. Some questions specify certain conditions to be assumed in making a judgement of one's ideal, others do not, thereby allowing more variation between individuals in the conditions they infer. Not surprisingly, what size of family is regarded as ideal usually depends on the circumstances to be assumed and questions that hypothesise the presence of favourable circumstances generally produce somewhat higher ideals than those that mention more 'realistic' conditions or make no mention of them at all (when presumably the individual tends to assume that this actual or similar circumstances apply).[12] As commentators have pointed out the size of family considered ideal has in this and other advanced industrial societies been higher on average than the number actually desired by couples or even the number they end up with.[13] It would appear, therefore, that when specifying 'ideals' men and women do apparently assume circumstances more favourable for having children than the ones they experience, whilst when asked about the size of family they currently *desire* they do appear to take more account of the constraints and realities of the circumstances they face.

Our own data on ideals and preferences are generally consistent with the findings of other researchers. The question about ideal family size in the survey asked for the number the respondents considered ideal for themselves 'assuming that there were no worries about housing and money and things like that'. Forty-six per cent of both husbands and wives said that they now regarded two children as the ideal number, proportions quite similar to those who said they had regarded two as ideal when they married, when 45% of husbands and 40% of wives regarded two as ideal in those circumstances.[14] However only 9% of the husbands and 8% of the wives said they now thought that less than two children or more than four was ideal and the proportions falling outside the range of two to four for ideals at marriage were only marginally higher (10% for both groups).[15] In line with other studies the size of family *desired* at marriage and at the time of the interview was on average somewhat lower than the ideal, with 51% of husbands and 50% of wives saying that they wanted two children when interviewed, whilst 62% of husbands and 54% of wives said they had wanted two children at marriage.[16] But the proportions wanting less than two children or more than four were little greater (11% of husbands and 14% of wives had preferences outside this range when interviewed, whilst 11% and 12% respectively did at marriage). The precise distribution of ideal and desired family sizes for the survey sample is given in Table 9:1.

TABLE 9:1   *Ideal and desired family size in the survey sample*

| No. of children | Ideal family size | | | | Desired family size | | | |
| | At marriage | | When interviewed | | At marriage | | When interviewed | |
	H %	W %	H %	W %	H %	W %	H %	W %
0	3.6	3.8	1.6	1.0	5.0	5.2	1.6	2.5
1	2.0	1.0	2.4	2.4	4.2	3.8	4.9	5.6
2	45.2	40.3	46.4	45.9	62.4	54.0	50.5	49.6
2 or 3	6.0	7.1	7.2	8.7	5.0	6.6	3.2	4.6
3	10.8	10.3	16.0	14.6	7.5	7.3	19.8	16.9
3 or 4	3.6	5.2	4.8	6.3	2.1	2.1	0.8	1.8
4	13.2	11.6	12.0	13.9	9.6	11.4	10.9	10.9
5 and over	4.2	4.8	5.2	4.5	2.1	2.8	4.5	5.6
D.K./ no idea	10.4	9.0	4.0	2.4	5.4	6.3	3.2	2.5
No. of cases	250	288	250	288	248	287	247	284

H—Husbands   W—Wives

Note: These questions were only asked if the husband or wife was present.

Interestingly, our data suggests that the relative popularity of family sizes of three and four children changes as marriage progresses. At marriage a family of four is more popular than a family of three, though there are quite a few people who are undecided either between two or three children or between three or four; by the time of the interview more of the sample had made up their minds about family size and overall a family of three was a more popular preference than one of four.[17]

The desirability of having a family within the range of two to four children also emerges from the comments that people made about different sizes of family, and from the accounts they gave of their own preferences and ideals about family size in the pilot study. Indeed it is the comments and accounts that not only reinforce the statistical findings we have considered so far, but also help us to make sense of them. The statistics show us that many people prefer to have two children; it is their comments that make it clear that having only one child is generally regarded as highly undesirable. Likewise, though people rarely choose a family of more than four children the detailed comments about having children tell us that the distinction between four and five children does not have as great a significance as that between one and two children. People choose to have four children rather than five because they do not want to have too large a family, but they do not appear to draw as sharp a boundary between families of four and five children as they do between families of one and two.

For some people justifying ideas about family size is apparently not easy: questioned about their ideals and preferences they fall back on reassertions of the inherent desirability of the size they have chosen, which provide no additional information about why that size is considered desirable. Here is a comment of this sort from one of the women in the pilot sample:

To my idea it was a family, a mother and a father, two children. I don't know where I got the idea from, and I think probably if I asked my children they probably think the same, two children, you know.

Like others she reiterates the norm but offers no explanation of it, such reiteration asserting simply that a particular number of children is 'nice'. If we relied solely on the data from the survey, accounts of family size that merely repeat the norm would appear to be relatively common. Of those who attempted to offer some account of their ideal or desired family size either at marriage or when interviewed, about one in five gave an answer that fell in our coding category 'nice number – unspecified', and gave no other reason for their choice. It was clear from the pilot study, however, that even those who tended to rely on such justifications when directly asked to explain their choice of family size, made comments elsewhere that not only attempted to account for their own preferences about family size, but also showed that they were familiar with the range of ideas that people commonly draw when discussing family size. We would argue that on this issue, as on the question of having children at all, there are certain common ideas with which everyone is likely to be familiar (if not to accept): ideas that influence decisions about family size, and are invoked when the individual has to justify his own preferences or explain those of others.

What are these common ideas? What arguments underly the typical preference for a family of two to four children? In the main the ideas focus on what parents want to do for and provide for their children, and on their ability and capacity to make such provision, with an emphasis at times on the former, at times on the latter and at times not very clearly on either.[18]

Such ideas structure the usual accounts of why it is important to have at least two children: a standard norm that is backed up by accounts that are equally standard. In this case they emphasise the importance of meeting certain conditions when bringing up one's children. Time and time again people argue that a child must have a brother or sister either because they believe an only child is sure to be lonely or else because they believe an only child is sure to be spoilt. Here is the theme of loneliness as expressed by one women, backed up as often with this idea, by reference to personal experience:

I think one is, well, I think that it's lonely just to have one. I am sure it must be lonely for them. My mother was an only child, and she's been lonely. She always said how lonely it was just to be an only child. I think you grow up lonely when you're just, you know, when there's just the one.

Another put the belief like this 'I think one child is a very lonely child. I don't think that's at all fair just to have one.' Yet another gave a more detailed account of what she thought loneliness involved:

Well, I'd definitely say that I'd sooner have two than one, I shouldn't think it's nice having one. As you see, we have a family here with just one child, and he looks so lonely and lost half of the time, and my sister one day, she could have cried when he said 'why haven't I got brothers and sisters to play with'. That make you think. That's a lot more work but they've always got someone to turn to and they help defend for each other.

The underlying concerns here are to provide a child with social support and to prevent the possibility of loneliness. As one woman put it 'two's company aren't they?'

Almost as frequent was the argument that a child ought to have a brother or sister for fear he or she would be spoilt. One man said 'Well, my idea was that I thought one would be spoilt and get the best of everything, whereas two can learn off each other.' Another said 'We didn't want to have one so that he would have everything, you know, and we thought he would grow up to be greedy and have his way all his life, sort of thing.' A wife with two children said that she would have rather ended up with three than one, commenting 'Well, they always say that one tends to get spoilt, so I imagine I should prefer three. You do tend to put all the attention to the one I expect, whereas three would be better for the child I am sure.'

In our pilot sample the rejection of the one child family was strong, and most people did not consider the idea of having only one child by choice a serious possibility, just as they did not seriously consider the idea of having no children, and they made some of the same comments about it. They talked of one child not being a family, and they talked of how they would have wanted to adopt a child if they could have had only one. One woman reflected the contradictory position of the one child family in an ideological context that makes one child a family and yet not fully a family, when asked what size of family she thought of as small. She replied 'Oh, one. I don't think of two children being a small family because I think it is a family, but to me one is not a family at all.' So strong is the norm that an only child is undesirable that many people believe that parents who choose to stop at one must be selfish. In the words of one woman: 'I wouldn't have wanted one. It's selfish. If I had any I should want two at least.' The characterisation of women with only children as selfish was also common in Rainwater's sample of women from parts of the United States in the 1960s.[19]

The concern to have enough children to 'make a family' which was present in some of the comments about having an only child, is for some people not a reason for having two children, but a reason for having three, four or even more children. As one woman commented when asked whether she thought that the fewer the children a family has the happier it is 'Yes, as long as it's enough to make a family: three or four.' When, however, people talked of needing three or four or even more children to make a family it was not just preventing loneliness or spoiling at some minimal level that was at issue, but having enough children to provide support, co-operation and companionship in the family and to encourage the give and take that they regarded as important characteristics of family life. When one woman was asked whether she thought her family size of six was a good number she said:

I think that really to know there are other people in the world, and they must probably let Tommy have a new pair of shoes without having any, you've got to have about four, you've got to see the other person's point of view. You must have at least four.

Another woman with three children conveyed a similar idea like this:

Doctor said to me once, doctor said 'If you have three it knocks – knocks – knock the edges off each one.' I think that's true. They do, I mean, you, you're not torn between the two, I mean, whatever you've got, when you're fetching anything, it's got to go between the three of them, I mean.

The idea that a family beyond the minimum of two is likely to provide a good atmosphere for bringing up children, may make for a happier family, and can have a beneficial effect on the children because it demands more give and take within the family, stops the children being spoilt, and brings the family closer, was not restricted to those who chose to have more than two children. Many people mentioned that they thought larger families could have advantages of this sort. One woman who had decided to have two children but had had a third unplanned pregnancy had this to say about large families:

I think a large family is a happier family. I come from one of fourteen, and we're very close, and well we didn't have a lot when we were younger but I don't think it's done us any harm. We didn't have lots of toys or sweets or those sort of things, but we're no worse off for it. I think today that children get far too much where toys and sweets and that is concerned. Probably if you got more, so they can't have it, so they'd probably grow up a better child, I suppose.

Another who had eventually decided to have two children commented, when asked whether she thought that the more children a family has the happier it is:

Oh quite so. I quite believe it. Now next door they've got eight, and I think their children are far more happier than my two are. They seem far more contented than my two. I think you find that all the way along, where there's a big family of children, I think you find they're far more happier, than they are when there's just two. They seem to look after each other, and help each other more. When you've just got two, they seem to be squabbling all the time. But where there's a big family, you've got the older children can help with the younger one.

On the other hand a variety of ideas underlie the preference for a 'smaller' family, which in the period of our study has meant two, three or at most four children, that are apparent in the accounts of such preferences. These ideas also focus on what parents want to do and provide for their children and on their ability to do so, but in this case they result in a desire for less rather than more children. Unlike, however, the beliefs that a child should not be lonely or spoilt which require a definite minimum of two, though they may be used as arguments for having more than that, the concerns that are used to legitimate the restriction of childbearing do not set any maximum level to family size, and in that sense are more flexible. In most cases they can and do equally serve as arguments for keeping family size down to six children as for keeping it down to two.

At the most general level the idea is simply that there are difficulties in looking after and coping with a family and that children involve various responsibilities which justify some restriction of family size, but the responsibilities and difficulties are left unspecified or are only implicit. One woman explained her choice of family size like this 'I shouldn't have minded any more but thought that three was just a number you could look after properly.' Another said 'I love babies, but you've got to think of bringing them up I'd have no end of babies if there hadn't have been the responsibility.' In a similar vein a husband who had decided to have two children said 'Mind you, I was prepared to have ten children if there was ways and means of providing for them and looking after them.'

By talking of providing for children the husband here appeared to have had had in mind a common and more specific idea that acts as a reason for curtailing childbearing: that children cost money. 'That's all we can afford' is a common idea behind the limitation of family size in England in the post-war period just as it was in the parts of the United States that Rainwater studied.[20] Many of the things that parents want to do for their children require money and many people emphasise the costs of having children and think this is a good reason for limiting family size. As one woman said 'I thought two's just enough. We could afford to keep two.' Another justified her choice of two or three children as the ideal family like this 'Well, I don't think many people can afford more than three. Well, a lot do, but they seem very hard up to me. So those I see walking around, they seem very poor, if they got more than three or four children.' Yet another, explaining her choice of three children, said 'I don't know, I suppose as time went on, we found that two were quite enough to support and look after, as our financial situation is, I mean, it's not so great, I suppose.'

When we originally attempted to quantify the pilot study data finance seemed to us the commonest reason for restricting childbearing, and we calculated that in 31 out of the 50 cases finance was offered as the main reason for the family size that had been intended.[21] In contrast in the survey sample only 41% of husbands and 31% of wives who attempted to give some reason for their preferred family size at marriage offered either their their first or second reason one that according to our coding was classified as 'economic'. Even fewer offered an economic reason for their ideal family size. Nineteen per cent of husbands and 14% of wives mentioned economic factors as either their first or second reason for the size of family they said they had considered ideal when they married, and 15% and 14% respectively mentioned economic reasons for the size of family they considered ideal when interviewed. (Couples were not asked to give the reasons for the size of family they thought preferable at the time of interview.)

However, the discrepancy between the data from the pilot and the survey is readily explained. Not only were the pilot interviews more likely to have provided an occasion in which much more would be said about the reasons for choosing a particular family size, so that there was more chance that finance would be mentioned as one contributing factor at some point in the interview, but our belief at that stage that finance was the most important influence on family size, probably meant that our analysis was biassed in favour of selecting that as the main reason for the family size that had been chosen. The figure of 31 out of 50 probably gives us a better idea of the proportion who made some mention of finance in accounting for their choice of family size, than of the proportion for whom it was the most important factor.

A concern for the costs of children might seem to suggest that parents were primarily thinking about their limited capacity to provide for their children. However in many cases where finance was mentioned it was clear that much of the concern about finance stemmed from parents' desire to be able to do things and provide things for their children at a good enough level, and that the emphasis was on the standards they wanted to satisfy. What they wanted was to be able to meet certain standards in bringing up their children: not just to feed and clothe them but to feed and clothe them well; not just to provide them with the obvious essentials but also to provide them with other less essential items. In the following passage one wife shows the concern to maintain satisfactory standards in providing essentials like food and clothing for her children.

I wouldn't like a large family that had to go without and I don't mean without everything, but I like to feed my children well and if I felt that I hadn't got enough money to feed them I should be committing a crime and I feel that way still. If I couldn't clothe them, like at the time we had two children and we had to go round jumble sales, it broke my heart to have to go and buy second-hand clothes for sixpence.

In other cases the desire is to provide a good education for one's children which is often felt to have financial implications. One woman said that she and her husband could not afford more children and commented 'I mean, if we need to help them with their education, you just can't afford it, if you've got lots of children.' Another, who was sending her sons to private school, said they could not afford more than three children and explained:

Well, of course, they don't cost anything when they are babies, it's when they are old enough to go to school they cost money. When things like school fees, and of course, when they start eating like horses which mine really do. When they are babies you can keep them very cheaply. It's when they get a bit older that they are expensive, so you have to look ahead from that point of view.

In many cases, however, parents talk rather more generally and imprecisely than this; what they say they want to do is to 'do better' or 'the best' that they can for their children. They imply that only doing better or the best is adequate. Such a desire almost always has financial implications even though the aims may not be material. Here is the theme of doing better in response to the question of whether having many children is a lot of trouble and not worth it.

I don't think you can afford it today, not really do you. Not a lot of children. It's alright if you've got the income, lets put it that way, if you earn the money that's alright but – well, look at us, we're only 'er you know, just like labourers, no skill attached to 'em, and therefore I don't think you'll – you've got the money to have a lot, because if you did, they've got to go without things, and we had to go without things when we were small, so my mother had a lot, and his father has a lot of children, and you have to – you know you don't want the same for yours that you had yourself, I don't think you do anyway. I wouldn't want mine to have what we had to have.

One man expressed his desire to do the best for his children like this 'I mean you owe them something and you have to do your best for them and really two is about as much as we can manage at the moment.' Later he justified his choice of two children with the comment 'It's not sort of too many to give as much as you possibly can.' A woman explained why she did not want three children like this 'Obviously you can't afford to give them everything if there's more.' Another, however, made it clear that her concern to do her best for her children was not just a matter of money 'Well, I'd like them to have the best of everything. No, that's not quite true I don't think, I don't mean moneywise.'

With so many parents wanting to do well by their children and provide them with better or the best, it is not, perhaps, surprising that many feel that they cannot afford a large family and that there are definite advantages in a relatively small one. But the issue is not only one of finance. Though many things that parents want to do for their children cost money and may be more readily met by those who have money, they involve other things as well, often ones that cannot readily be bought with money. Children require love, day to day care and attention, as well as advice and guidance and invariably parents feel that they themselves should largely provide these. The concerns and problems in providing day to day care for one's children feature in many accounts of family size preferences. At times the focus is on the desire to provide children with the adequate or even the best care. One woman, asked why she thought two was a good number of children to have, said:

Well, I think you can give more attention to just two, but if you've got a lot, you haven't got the time to give attention to any of them have you, and then some of them must feel pushed out, because automatically the youngest comes the first, that's got to have everything done for it, and then the oldest felt more pushed out of it, and I think that cause a lot of jealousy sometimes.

Another said 'They don't get so much attention individually if you've got a lot.' Yet another claimed a smaller family was happier because 'You can spend more time with the children if you haven't got so many.'

At other times the focus is on the problems of providing such care. Many people point out that having children involves quite a lot of work for parents and this is sometimes mentioned as a reason for curtailing family size. A woman who had wanted three children decided to have no more after her second, and explained her change of mind like this (she later changed her mind again and had a third):

Well, it was a case of I'd had enough seeing after two, and by the time they went to bed, you're quite worn out quite honestly. I mean you are continually doing housework, you get up in the morning and you've got to do all what you've done the day before, whereas, I mean, once they start school, I mean you can do a room out one day, the next day it only needs a dust, doesn't it? I mean, I thought if you've got this to go on and on and on, I mean, no thank you.

This comment however, suggests that this woman's concern was not just a question of the problems and difficulties of putting in the necessary hard work in terms of capacities and abilities but of whether she was *willing* to do so, and in this respect she was unusual. Accounts of family size preferences, if they concerned themselves with meeting one or other of the demands made by children, usually implied the problem was one of capacity and not of willingness.

While the substance of these accounts is not the same as those that stress finance, the structure of the argument is: that as a parent you want, or feel you have to provide and do certain things for your children, whether material or non-material (those who are concerned about their capacity to cope with and provide for their children seem more often to talk of what they *have* to do for them, those who talk of the importance of doing things for their children talk more in terms of what they *want* to do for them); that parents want or have to satisfy certain standards in what they do for their children; and that having children therefore makes demands upon capacities and resources both monetary and otherwise that are not unlimited. From this they conclude that there are definite advantages in curtailing family size, either because it allows you to do better for your children, or because your capacities and resources are less pressed. A number of parents made the first point. One husband said 'Every one extra is going to lower the standard for the others isn't it, their standards of living and what they have and what they can't have, the advantages they might have.' A wife made the same point about possessions.

They probably have more things when you've only got two or three. You can probably give them a lot more. I mean, like when Christmas comes and birthdays come, if they've set their hearts on anything like my little girl set her heart on a doll's pram for Christmas. Well, if I had a lot of children, she wouldn't have been able to afford it. And I think that is one of the many things. I mean, she'd set her heart on a doll's pram and my little boy had set his heart on a train set, which they were both expensive. But if I'd have had more than two children, they wouldn't have been able to have had them. Because, I think, you know, that would have just been too much. So therefore I think if you've got a large family, they probably wouldn't have you know, get the things they want.

The second point was often made in financial terms. A wife said 'If you've got a large family you've got to scrape and scrounge a bit more than what you have if you've only got two.' Another said 'I mean, if we had a large family, still on the same wage, well I don't suppose we'd be quite so happy, because we should have to sort of skrimp and save, and do this and that, you know and make things go.'

But the ideas used to explain choices of family size do not all focus on either the desire or the ability to do and provide things for one's children. One idea that features in accounts of family size is that the pleasures of children simply make one want more children. On the one hand people referred to the pleasures of children when explaining why they had more than the normative minimum. Asked, for instance, why she had a third rather than stopping at two one woman had this to say:

I really don't know, but it's rather a more-ish business having children. They are all entirely different from each other. It's awfully interesting to see what they turn out like. It seems a ridiculous idea for going on having them because you're getting a different one each time, but it's a very compulsive business, you know.

Another asked why she wanted children said 'I don't know maybe I always was passionately fond of children.' On the other hand the pleasures of children featured in many other accounts of family size, not as an explanation of the family size that had been chosen, but as a qualifying preliminary to the justification of limiting family size. Many accounts of why a family size of two, three or even four children had been chosen were prefaced by comments like 'I would still like to have more, but . . .' or 'I love babies, but . . .' or 'Mind you I was prepared to have ten children if . . .'

It is important to note, however, that not everyone expressed an underlying desire for more children, and by no means all attempted to qualify their accounts of why they limited their family size in this manner. We cannot assume, therefore, that all parents would want to have more children even if it were easier to provide for and look after them adequately. (It is interesting to note, in this connection, that only 21% of husbands and 25% of wives in the survey sample, who gave a definite answer to the question, said they would like more children if they were twice as rich.)[22] People who do not express an underlying desire for more children do not deny that having children gives them pleasure, but they do not claim that having more children would give them more pleasure. In contrast. no one in our pilot sample attempted to justify having a small family by asserting that they did not like children, though one woman who wanted two children did say at one point that she did not like babies. Presumably it is all too easy to think in terms of how one cannot provide for more children without having to think (even privately) that you do not like children very much.

One further idea that features in some explanations of family size, which also relates to the pleasures to be derived from having children, is the desire to have a child of a specific sex. Some parents feel sufficiently strongly that they would like a daughter or a son, and regard the pleasure that they would get from having one a sufficient reason for having another child, even if they would not otherwise have wanted one. As one husband said of the decision to have a third child: 'If the second one, or the first one had been a boy there wouldn't have been a third.'[23]

Finally some accounts of family size differ both from those that focus on providing for and doing things for one's children and one's ability to do this, and from those that relate to the pleasure for parents from having another child or more children, by placing the issue of having children in the context of other activities. The concern is the standard one of providing for children, but the novelty comes from the explicit concern with alternative sources of pleasure or satisfaction than having children. It is interesting, nevertheless, that just as there are few accounts of becoming a parent that put that event in the context of alternatives, so that are few accounts of family size that explicitly consider alternatives to having more children.

One of the most common complaints about having children is that they tie you down.[24] Here is how one woman described the consequences of having a baby:

Well, it ties you, I mean it ties you in when you've got a baby. You can't sort of, not that we went out a lot, but you can't go out much with a young baby, times for feeding and all sorts of things, well, it just tie you up quite a bit. But once you get used to it it's all right. I think I'm more tied now with their going to school, because I sort of have to have clock watches on all the time.

Like many other women she made it clear that she accepted the tie that children involved. Others sounded more discontented and reluctant. 'I think you know for a girl to be sort of tied to the house is ridiculous really. This is how I feel really. I think it's awful being just a housewife.' Yet few of these women said that the tie of children was a reason why they did not have any more, perhaps because they do not like to admit, in view of the conventional definitions of their social role, that they would get more pleasure from some other activity than from caring for children. In the pilot sample one woman who did link the tie of children to her ideas about family size was an exception. Asked why she had wanted two children when she married she said:

'cos at that time I wasn't awfully keen on housework and looking after children, I didn't like to be tied to the home a lot, so I didn't think that would be an awfully good idea to have more than two, because then, I thought, I could get them off my hands and go out to work, you know.

Occasionally others, like the woman earlier who talked about the hard work children involved when explaining why she had not wanted a third, made comments that suggested that their willingness to work and provide for their children was at issue, and they were thinking of other sources of pleasure. A woman said three children was definitely enough for her because:

I think you are inclined to make yourself, a woman is inclined to make herself a drudge, and you know, you are never finished doing this, and you are never finished doing that, and if you look after them properly, and you know, I like to bake and that sort of thing, and, when you got more than three children you always seem to be on the go, you know, you never seem to stop having to work. I think you need some leisure time.

In addition the tie of children and the attraction of alternatives featured quite commonly in the explanations that were offered of why *other* people might choose to have small families, especially in the explanations that were offered of the trend toward smaller families that people observed. According to one woman people have smaller families:

Because there are other things, other attractions; years ago father went to work and mother brought up, washing and cooking, there was nothing else, but now there's holidays abroad to be looked at and all sorts of social life – bingo, I suppose, and dancing and all sorts of things.

Another explained the change like this: 'They can get out and about and it's far easier to do it with a smaller family.' A third said 'I think people go out much more and I think they think if they have a big family they can't go out so much.'

We would argue, therefore, that it is not normative to decide the question of one's own family size by considering children directly in the context of alternative sources of satisfaction. It is true, of course, that some people who talk about whether they can afford more children or talk about the problem of giving children enough attention may at times have in mind alternative ways of spending their time and money, but if they do there is little evidence that they directly compare the sources of satisfaction. They invariably talk of family size, as we have shown, in terms of their desires for their children, the problems of realising these desires and the pleasures to be gained from having children. The question of alternative sources of pleasure is usually left out of the equation. The texture of the argument is different from that of a husband who put his concern for the cost of children in the context of other things that he wanted. When he and his wife were asked whether they thought having children was a lot of trouble and not worth it his wife made a standard comment 'The trouble is if you have lots of children, you can't afford to keep them or bring them up.' The husband however said:

We like the good things in life so we try to limit ours a bit. I mean we wouldn't overburden ourselves with children for the sake of children, anyway, I think everybody should limit the size of family to their means.

II: The timing of childbearing

Recent wisdom amongst demographers has it that even if family size is not (any longer) especially sensitive to economic factors, the timing of child-bearing is.[25] Couples may not, the argument goes, choose their family size according to their level of financial resources, but they do choose when to have children according to them: when times are hard they will postpone conception, when times are good they will not. Our own data suggests that this generalisation is at best an over-simplification.

If we examine the ideas people have about the timing of childbearing within marriage we find that though there is some similarity in ideas about the desirable interval between marriage and the first birth and for the interval between births (two years is the wives' most frequent preference in each case), the considerations that couples have in mind when planning the timing of the first birth and when planning the timing of subsequent births differ radically; economic considerations are only of direct importance in the timing of the first birth, and then not in all cases. The timing of the first birth does, however, influence the timing of the second since, as we shall see, the first birth acts as the benchmark for the next.

The most commonly preferred interval between marriage and the first birth amongst those wives in the survey sample who had an explicit preference was about two years, but only just, and the husbands preferred that interval, and one from more than 2 to 4 years, about equally.[26] Quite a few wives also wanted, as Table 9:2 shows, to have a longer interval before having their first child, and a significant proportion of both husbands and wives wanted to have their first child straight away, despite the fact that this question was not asked of couples where the wives were pregnant at marriage or within the first three months.

TABLE 9:2   *Desired interval between marriage and the first birth, at marriage, in the survey sample*

Length of desired interval	Husbands %	Wives %
Less than one year	4.0	4.3
1 year to 18 months	10.0	9.6
19 months to 2 years	26.0	26.8
More than 2 years to 4 years	26.6	23.0
More than 4 years	6.0	4.3
D.K./no idea	34.2	32.1
No. of cases	165	187

Note: This question was only asked of husbands and wives present in the interview; it was not asked where the wife was either pregnant at marriage or within the first three months.

This lack of consensus about the preferred interval between marriage and the first birth, was matched by a lack of consensus in the ideas on which those preferences were based, though people found little difficulty in giving some reason for their preference, if they had one (only 3% of husbands and 6% of wives in the survey sample said the preferred interval was just 'nice'). The data did however suggest that economic considerations, rather broadly defined, were quite often of importance in planning the interval between marriage and the first birth *if* some delay was planned. The accumulation of assets (material goods or savings) was a common theme in the accounts of those who did not want to have their first child immediately after marriage. The following remarks about the planning of the first child were typical.

Well, we decided definitely that we would go to work to start with; I'd carry on with my good safe job, and help to save up for a home; that was one thing we were quite decided on, we didn't want children right away, and I did actually work for three years after I married, because neither of us had much money in the bank, or to set up the future with, and we did actually start in two rooms that we rented and we bought some bits of furniture and furnished them, but we weren't happy there and we soon went into a mortgage and started buying a house.

Another said:

Well, I didn't want one right away, but we did fall for one right away so we just had to make the best of it. I think it is better if you can save for a couple of years to get some money behind you.

Often deferring the first child in order to accumulate assets was said to be the only important plan for the first years of marriage. One woman asked about their plans for life after marriage, said 'Well, I think the only plans were to be – not to have a family as soon as we married.' Questioned further she added 'Till we'd got enough money to have one.' Another responded to the same question like this 'Well, the only plans we had to carry out was not to have any family as soon as we got married, because I wanted to work for a while, but apart from that we just let things turn out as they would.' They wanted to wait before having the first child because 'money was tight and we didn't want to get into any more debt than what we were, so we was hoping just to wait a few years before we had any and we was lucky enough to go along without having a family I think'.

As the comments above indicate, much of the concern to conserve and accumulate assets in the early years of marriage was motivated by a desire to consolidate one's material and financial position before having children, and was a preparation for family life. Occasionally, however, the money was wanted for other things as well. A woman who had waited two years before having the first child said 'Well, we thought we could get all the bits and pieces we wanted then have a really good holiday.' The idea that delaying the first birth gave you a chance to do things that you could not do once you had children occurred elsewhere. Another, who said at one point that she and her husband had wanted 'a place to live in, and a decent home' before they got married because 'If you don't get it before you have children, you never get it after do you?' later said they had wanted the first child two or three years after they married and commented 'When you're first married you can go out together, well when you've got a child that stops all that doesn't it.'

More often, however, if the reason for delaying the first birth was not to accumulate assets in preparation for family life, it was still related to marriage and family life. One woman talked of having time to adjust to married life. Asked when she had wanted her first child she said.

I always said I didn't want one until after I had been married – didn't want to start one until after I had been married for a year, at least a year. Having a little time to get adjusted you see. Of course I went a lot longer than that.

Another who had married in 1942 had wanted to wait to have her children till her husband came out of the army because she 'didn't want to bring a child up during the war time'.

The most common reason for wanting a child straightaway was simply that a family was wanted. As one woman said when asked when she wanted her first child 'Oh, straightaway, I didn't mind, I wanted to start a family as soon as we could.' Pressed on the point she did, however, add 'Well, if you're young you grow up with them.' She wanted a family and could see no good reason for not having one as soon as possible. At times the fact that having a child could be an advantage in getting a house from the local authority was a reason for starting a family relatively quickly. One woman, asked if she had talked about using birth control with her husband when they first married, said:

No, he did say to me when we were first married 'what do you think, should we wait ahead before we have a family?' and we were living with my mother then, and I said 'what's the point, if we have a family we can get a house' and that's how we sort of didn't bother.

Occasionally there were other reasons for deciding to have a child soon after marriage. One woman said she and her husband 'weren't at all sure that we were going to have any children actually because John, he was about 20 and had this mumps thing, you know, and he thought he'd never be able to have any children', 'so we had a go straightaway'. Another who was 30 when she married, asked when she wanted her first child said: 'I didn't want to wait too long, you know, as I say, because of my age, you know.'[27]

Consensus over ideas about the timing of the subsequent births was greater. It was not that people totally agreed about the best interval to have between births, for although the most commonly preferred interval of two years was more popular than it had been as the interval between marriage and the the first birth, there was still some variation in the range of preferences as Table 9:3 shows.[28] The consensus came in the ideas people mentioned when justifying their preferences for the spacing of the births.[29] Two ideas dominated the accounts of the preferences about the spacing of births: one that encouraged a relatively close spacing of births, the other a more distant one. Neither show any concern with economic considerations. On the one hand with what they think is good for children in mind, people argue that births should be relatively close so that the children can grow up together; on the other hand with their ability to look after and care for their children in view, they argue that the births should not be too close to make it easier for the parents to cope with the work that a baby involves. Many people mentioned both points and were clearly attempting some balance between them.

TABLE 9:3   *Desired spacing between births at marriage in the survey sample*

Length of desired interval	Husbands %	Wives %
One year or less	3.0	2.6
About 18 months	9.5	11.0
About 2 years	40.5	47.1
About 2½ years	15.5	15.2
3 to 4 years	10.1	13.1
More than 4 years	0.6	0.5
D.K./No idea	20.7	10.5
No. of cases	168	191

Note: This question was only asked of husbands and wives present in the interview; it was not asked where the wife was pregnant at marriage or within the first three months, or of those who regarded a family size of less than two as ideal and also desired a family of less than two.

The desire that births should be relatively close, so that children could grow up together and be companions for one another, was expressed in a variety of ways. A woman, who had hoped for an interval of about eighteen months, said she had not wanted the births 'too far apart, so that they could grow up together'. Another woman put her ideas about the timing of the second birth (she wanted three children) like this 'Well, I said I'd like another before she got too old, so she'd have a little playmate, and she was two when my other was born.' A third wanted to have her second child after about two years because 'they would be able to play with each other, wouldn't be too old'. Yet another said she wanted her later births 'within two years, as soon as possible' and her husband offered this explanation, showing that for him the idea of growing up together was part of his idea of family life, 'That is a family, to bring, to come up together, to bring them up together'.

But the desire not to have births too close was mentioned equally often. Parents wanted one child to have established some independence before the next child came along. One woman who had thought she would wait at least two years before having the second child offered the following explanation:

Oh well, I think you get – by the time they are two they are more or less off your hands. I mean they eat by themselves, and run round on their own and let you know what they want. I mean you haven't sort of got to be behind them all the time.

Another woman wanted her second child after two or three years and explained the preference like this:

I thought the little girl would be sufficiently grown up, just out of the baby stage and she could do little things for herself and that I wouldn't be coping with tiny babies, I felt that as she was older I'd be able to cope better.

Getting the earlier child out of nappies was often mentioned as a decisive factor. A woman who wanted to have two years between the births said 'Well, that one is getting off your hands a bit then, getting out of the nappy stage.' Another commented 'We said we didn't want any more until she could walk and things like that, till I'd got her out of nappies a bit, and then go in for another one.'

Occasionally other ideas were mentioned in accounting for the choice of spacing of births. A woman who had wanted her first two children reason- ably close together, and had then mentioned both companionship and the issue of coping, felt rather differently about the timing of the third birth:

Well, we thought we'd wait a little while after we had the second before we had any more, and we'd enjoy ourselves a bit, and have a better life, and we used to go out a little bit more then, we used to walk after tea, never used to join anything, no social clubs or anything; used to go out with my people, or as I said, we had a caravan down at Felixstowe, took the children down there, let them run down there.

Sometimes, though a particular spacing was preferred, circumstances made it difficult to realise. One woman had planned to have the second child fairly soon after the first, but delayed getting pregnant till she and her husband had moved into their new house, a move that took longer than expected. Another, who had her second child less than two years after her first, also indicated that housing had been an influence, but this time to have a second child quickly. She explained: 'Well, things gradually got worse with this old man we was living with, and we kept going down the council, and they kept telling us we couldn't have a house with only one child, so we went in for our second one.' The experience was supported by the remarks of others. A husband commenting on the birth of the first child said:

Well, the important thing was when we had the child, we were on the council housing list for a house, and with a child, of course, our priority advanced and we did manage to get half a house, 'cos there was sharing at those times, so we did get half a council house. So that was one foot towards getting a full council house as we have now.

No couple, however, mentioned the problem of finance as a reason for the chosen spacing of their births, even as an undesirable or unexpected contingency.

IV: The nature of the calculations

What conclusions emerge from this analysis of the ideas that people put forward to justify their preferences about family size and spacing? It shows, in the first place, that people ordinarily thought about family size and the spacing of births rather differently from the way they thought about the possibility of becoming parents. People tended to take the idea of having children for granted when they married and invariably the issue was hardly an open question. Family size and spacing tended, in contrast, to be matters that were thought to require decision and calculation. They were, however, calculations that typically had certain special characteristics. On the one hand the calculus for family size usually only included some combination of the following components: first, what parents wanted or felt they had to do and provide for their children, second, their capacity and ability to make such a provision, and third the positive satisfactions they expected to derive from having (more) children. It did not normally include any direct consideration of either negative feelings about children *per se*, or one's willingness to cope with the demands of children, or (which is not the same) any consideration of alternatives to having children as sources of satisfaction and as ways of spending one's time, money and energy. Usually the issue was whether having more children was compatible with bringing them up properly, not whether it was compatible with other activities altogether. The typical calculus for the timing of children was similarly constrained. As far as the decisions about the spacing between births was concerned, the calculation was primarily a question of balancing up what was good for the children against what was practicable for the parents (which usually was a matter of coping with more than one young child, but occasionally brought in the question of housing). The decision about the timing of the first birth usually involved more elements, which not only often included the pleasures of children, but also, at times, alternative sources of pleasure. Indeed, our sample seemed most willing to consider alternative sources of satisfaction when planning to have their first child, though most were primarily concerned to delay having a family in order to make more adequate preparations for that event.

On the other hand the calculations about family size and spacing were usually influenced by a limited set of ideas about what it was important to provide for and do for one's children, and about how difficult or easy it was to meet these demands. In many cases, though these ideas were not directly contradictory (with the possible exception of the anxiety about not spoiling children with the desire to do one's best for them which often included giving them the best) they had contradictory implications in terms of size and spacing. This raises the question of the extent to which they are a source of conflict and ambivalence, and of whether and how they are reconciled, points that we touch upon in Chapters 10 and 11.

When making decisions about family size and spacing many people were concerned about the cost of children, and this was often one important issue in deciding how many children to have.[30] Though it was rarely mentioned in connection with deciding the spacing between births, financial and material issues were important to many of those who decided not to have their first child as soon as they married. The aim was, as we have said, to get oneself on a reasonable material and financial footing before starting a family. In practice such a concern is enough to link the timing of births of different parities to economic conditions in many cases since people normally time second and subsequent births in relation to previous ones and not to some other benchmark.

Nevertheless, despite the fairly widespread concern with the cost of having children, it was by no means the only consideration, and our data, like that of Rainwater's, only supports the contention that 'one should not have more children than one can support' only if the notion of supporting is interpreted very broadly.[31] Often parents were concerned to provide things for their children where money was of little relevance and in some cases having more children was an advantage: though they were concerned that they should be able to give their children enough attention, and they were concerned that they should be able to cope with the daily routine of children and babies, they also considered companionship, learning to co-operate, and having to give and take important.

Nor do our data indicate that there has been a norm in post-war England 'that one should have as many children as one can afford'.[32] It is true that many people felt that those who decided to have only *one* child were not being fair to the child and must be selfish people, but there was little evidence that above the minimum of two children there was any sense that parents should have as many children as they could afford. Our pilot sample could usually see good reasons for having families of any size within the normative range of two to four and did not express concern that people should have more than they wanted, or felt they could afford. Nor, indeed, did all of them imply that they would have more children if they themselves could afford more. Though some of them did, others did not, and neither group suggested there was anything particularly admirable about having *more*.

It would be tempting to conclude from this analysis, nevertheless, that given the ideological climate we have described, variations in family size within certain normative boundaries are merely a matter of varying resource or capacity constraints: that those with greater access to resources and capabilities both material and non-material will tend to have more children and may be encouraged to start childbearing earlier than those whose resources and capabilities are inferior. Our data indicates however that such a view is too simple. As the careful reader of this and the previous chapter will have noticed, though people draw upon a standard and well-known set of ideas in making decisions about having children, they do not attach equal importance to the different ideas, and though they may make the same comments they do not always mean the same thing by them. What parents meant, for example by doing their best for their children varied considerably as did the situations in which they would say that they could not afford any more. Nor do all regard a large family as some more or less distant ideal which they are varyingly constrained by circumstances from achieving. We need, therefore, to examine the varying constellations of the different beliefs about having children in order to explain the differences in preferences about family size and spacing that we found. How else can we explain how people in apparently similar circumstances nevertheless plan their childbearing very differently? The issue is not just one of the differences in resources and capacities, but of the differences in what people want and regard as important, which cannot be simply tied to immediate differences in resources and capabilities. In the next chapter, therefore, we take our analysis further and attempt to identify some of the important constellations of beliefs that influence ideas about family size and spacing, and in the subsequent chapter we look at how individuals attempt to build a family from these foundations.

10. Images of family life

It is commonplace that people differ in their ideas about what is important in life and what gives them satisfaction, and that these differences affect what they do; we want to make the equally obvious point that such differences in consciousness are reflected in the sort of family life people envisage, and affect both their ideas about the number and spacing of children they consider desirable, and their efforts to realise those preferences. Nevertheless, whilst there has been some attempt to examine the influence of cultural factors on fertility in certain societies, there has been little attempt to document the variation in ideas and values that may affect patterns of childbearing within any one industrial society.[1] Indeed, the possibility that such differences in values affect childbearing, though sometimes admitted has had little influence on studies of fertility in industrial societies.[2] This chapter attempts to remedy that defect.

Of course the variety of ideas and beliefs elicited by our research was immense, and we could not hope to document it all, nor indeed would it be especially useful to do so. What we have done is to differentiate certain constellations of ideas – ideas that seemed to be interrelated and to constitute distinctive patterns – which appeared to have an important influence on ideas about family life, and especially on ideas and decisions about family size and spacing. We have identified the ideological perspectives by what was regarded as of especial importance in family life, as well as in life more generally: by whether, for instance, the pursuit of possessions, or the desire for a quiet life, or the desire for a better future was the dominant concern. But it is the set of ideas as a whole and the relations between them that are salient, not single elements, many of which are not unique to one ideological perspective. Furthermore, as we shall show in the following chapter, any one individual may at times adopt the crucial elements of more than one ideology.

Our delineation of these different ideologies can only be tentative, since the pilot study, which provides much of the substantive material for this chapter, was not designed to elucidate such differences. We regret in particular that relatively few men were interviewed since we suspect not only that we might then have identified some further ideological perspectives, but also that the operation of the ones we have outlined may be rather different for men than for women, given that having children usually has very different implications for the two sexes. We regret, too, that our pilot sample included only those who had had at least one child, and therefore

163

those whose ideas were more likely to be conventional. This meant that we did not have as many points of contrast when delineating the different ways of thinking as we would have liked, and had little chance to examine the ideas of those who decide to have no children.

Within the sector of English life that we studied, five different ideologies, with their respective images of family life, appeared to have an especial impact on ideas about family size and spacing.

I: The collective life

It is widely accepted in this society that family life should be based on, and encourage certain characteristics amongst its members: love and affection, companionship and support, tolerance and understanding, generosity and altruism.[3] Those who attach particular importance to these qualities in human relations are likely, if they have a family, to be especially concerned to enhance those features of family life. They are likely to think that a 'real' family should foster solidarity and support amongst its family members above all else, and be anxious to display these virtues as parents. For them the quality of familial relations is more important than its material circumstances or the worldly success of its individual members. Indeed, the social order is likely to be seen as relatively fixed and stable as is the individual's place within it, and perhaps, as a consequence, consideration of one's place within the social order does not seem to be as salient to ideas about family life as it is in some of the other perspectives we outline.[4] It was noticeable, too, that women adhering to this particular image of family life often denied that there were class or other differences by which people could be grouped.[5]

This ideological perspective has distinct implications for the importance that is attached to family life and having children, and to what is done about having them. In the first place, given some initial commitment to family life, such as the decision to marry or have children, family life itself is likely to be highly valued and considerable priority given to it, both because children provide an opportunity for parents to give love and support to others, but also because putting the family first is necessary to create the close-knit family that is considered desirable. Indeed, the opportunities that family life provides for the realisation of this particular set of beliefs and values may well be an incentive to marry and have children. Furthermore, having a baby in the family may also seem particularly satisfying, especially to women, since an infant's dependence provides conspicuous opportunity to give love, care and support. Caring for the very young may dramatise both a woman's importance in the role of a mother and the unity and solidarity of the family.

Second, a larger family (at the top of the normative range), born reasonably close together is likely to be considered desirable. It provides, on the one hand, more opportunity for the parents to give care and support, as well as a broader set of persons for them to turn to, and be close to both now and later; on the other hand, it provides the necessary family conditions for bringing children up. More children means opportunity for companionship, solidarity and understanding among the children, and is likely to foster the atmosphere of give and take that will ensure that they in turn are generous, tolerant persons who give love and affection to others. Third, not only is a larger family likely to be considered desirable, but the pressure to control childbearing beyond the intended level will not be especially strong. Since children are highly valued, an extra one, even if it brings some problems, is also likely to bring satisfaction by enhancing the potential solidarity and support of the family unit. In consequence, though an extra birth may not be actively desired or planned, there may well be less reason to do anything about avoiding one.

This image of family life is of fundamental importance for two reasons. First, many of the ideas that are involved form part of the familiar stock of knowledge about having and rearing children that we have already outlined – the belief that children should not be spoilt and learn to give and take, the belief that they should be provided with companionship within the family, the belief that children should be given love and affection (though more importance is attached to some of them from this ideological perspective than in others). Second, a common image of the 'good mother', and of what she has to do in the family, which is not only found amongst those of this ideological persuasion, is based on these ideas. The 'good mother' is very often thought of as someone who gives love, affection and support to her children, and to the family as a whole; she is someone who puts her children and family before herself.

Though we did not ask the pilot sample to describe a 'good mother', we did ask what they thought were the main things a wife had to do in the family, and caring for and looking after the family in a selfless manner was, not surprisingly, a common theme of the replies. One wife said, 'Clean and cook, make sure that her husband is happy, and children are happy'; another remarked, 'Well, I think a woman has to keep the home tidy, but more than that I think its her place to keep the home together'; a third said, 'look after her children and look after her husband'. A similar emphasis on the importance of the mother's role in generating support and solidarity in the family was apparent in the answers to the question, 'What do you think are the important things in keeping a family ticking over?' One woman replied, 'Well, sort of, well sort of being kind to them, and, you know, and that, and looking after them, and doing what you can for them. You can't do more than that can you?' Another commented in a somewhat different vein, 'I think that you discuss things together with the children, you don't sort of try to lead a private life apart from your children, I think you must all live sort of interwoven together.' To the extent, therefore, that such ideas are an essential part of the image of what it is to be an ideal or good mother, and of her role in family life, most women will be socialised into this way of thinking as part of their knowledge of the maternal role. In consequence it is likely to the backdrop behind other ideas about family life and about being a wife and mother.

This belief that a 'real' mother is someone who devotes herself to the care and support of her children and her family, and that a 'real' family is a close-knit, cohesive unit, almost certainly lies behind the comments of those who qualify their explanations of why they are limiting their childbearing, with assertions that they would really like more children. A larger family is part of this salient and often idealised image of family life which, though many people feel circumstances do not permit, cannot be completely relinquished. Hence four children often remains the ideal even if reality does not seem to make it possible.

It is this ideological perspective that Mrs Abbott conveyed when she talked about the sort of family she wanted and about her ideas about having children.[6] She had been married when she was 19 and her husband was 18, some 18 years before, and had six children. Her husband had been an agricultural worker when they married but by the time of the interview was working as a self-employed plasterer. Their family of six children was by no means a planned one. One reason for this was Mrs Abbott's original ignorance about contraception, and her later hostility to it, partly produced by a sense that birth control was something alien and somehow wrong (reasons that we shall discuss in more detail in Chapter 12). But another important factor was her way of thinking about family life. Though she was by no means unaware of what she might be missing because of her commitment to family life (she had attended a Grammar School until she was 16), having committed herself to it, she had very definite ideas about what it should be like and what was important about it. Her concern was to enhance solidarity and understanding within the family, to encourage her children to be tolerant, generous and loving towards others, and to provide care and support for her family in a selfless manner: concerns which reinforced one another so that the outcome of a large family was, to some extent, overdetermined.

Mrs Abbott's ideas about family life and the influence that they have had on her childbearing are manifest in a variety of ways. In the first place a number of her comments about having children show how they are valuable to her because they contribute to the cohesion and solidarity of the family and allow her to realise her ideas about her role as a wife and mother. She described the family as 'close-knit' and her reaction to the birth of their sixth child (she had been very distressed to learn she was pregnant again after an interval of nine years) brings out the importance she attaches to closeness in the family. When asked what she felt when the baby was born, she said, 'Oh I wanted to have my picture put on the front of the Sunday papers, I was thrilled to bits.' Questioned further, she added:

I wouldn't have missed having this baby, nearly ten years after the family, for anything. The whole family came closer together, and more love, more understanding; it moved everything and everybody. You see, I haven't got many friends, and I wouldn't have missed it for anything, and it does something now, its made a change familywise.

The same emphasis on the role of children in bringing family members together, this time herself and her husband, as well as an illustration of her concern for closeness and solidarity are visible in her response to the question of what difference it would have made if she had had no children. She replied, as we have quoted elsewhere, 'I think that would have been almost, probably fatal to our marriage', and continued:

Knowing my husband, and knowing what the children and family itself mean to him, I don't think he would have been, I think the children are something that brought us together more. I think it has brought us together more. I think it has made what he and I are to each other, probably the children, because having no social life, not many friends, the sort of link between us is the children, and the great kicks we get out of things, probably the children, and disappointment, that's the only thing we have, you see, we haven't anything much else, we don't want anything much else, I mean that is the lot.[7]

On the other hand, children are important to her because there is the satisfaction of looking after, caring for and giving love to them.[8] Being a mother, she said, made her feel fulfilled. Asked what she liked doing she replied:

Well, I don't have time for anything except home now, but I enjoy everything at home. I'm not passionately fond of housework, But I enjoy the doing part of it because it means we have comfort for the family. I like cooking a nice big meal because the family will enjoy it when they come home. I'm not desperately fond of washing up either, you make a terrible mess when you cook, but the fact that you cook it, and they all come in and enjoy it, sit down and have a really good meal, that part I enjoy. There is a time when the money has run out, and I just get what I can that has worried me, but when I can really get something going, and they all come in, I really enjoy it.

Her role in the family was, she felt, crucial. Talking of what kept the family ticking over, she said, 'I think the mother can make the house either very miserable or very happy, I'm sure she can.' However, despite the importance of caring for and supporting her family she did not think babies, pleasurable though they were, were more satisfying than the older children. (Perhaps because she did not like to have more affection for one member of the family than another.) Asked at what stage in their lives she liked children best, she commented:

The boys, I mean, John, now coming on in his eighteenth year. I'm as thrilled of things that he does as I was when he was eighteen months. I don't think they look at it that I'm proud of them, and I get the feel, you know, that he's ours, and what he does matters. They're fascinating really, like a cat or a dog, when they're tiny, they're absolutely fascinating but other things come along when they get older, really just as much.[9]

Mrs Abbott's ideas about family life, and the importance she attached to the quality of personal relations, were also manifest in her ideas about what she wanted her children to be like – ideas which had a very direct influence on her views about the ideal size of family. She wanted her children above all to be tolerant and understanding; asked how she wanted to bring up her children she said:

Well, in one way I'm glad that they like to go to school. I don't have any great ambitions for them, they must grow up – the main thing is I want them to be people who always see the other person's point of view, and to take things seriously, and getting up and being responsible for oneself, not all the time to rely on someone else, and to always look a little bit higher than what you are at the moment. This is a little bit difficult, but to want something a little bit more than what you've got, not to hanker after it, always have a bit more, aim, you know, to be a bit better than what you are at the moment. It's difficult, but I haven't got any real ambitions for them.

Though she does not seem to eschew social advancement altogether it is personal qualities that come first; even doing better seems to be more a question of showing certain moral and personal qualities than achieving worldly success.[10] Likewise, asked what she thought a good son would be like, she had this to say:

I would say they've got to be thoughtful; I'm not saying that they've got to be ever grateful, I don't think that you've got to expect them to be ever grateful for bringing them into the world, and bringing them up. They must be thoughtful and have respect.

Notice too that the giver and provider should not expect any return. Elsewhere, similar concerns were specifically linked to the issue of family size. Four children are necessary to produce the conditions that would teach children the desired give and take as she argues here, not always very coherently:

I don't think that six is a good number, but I think actually to get a real family, or a decision in size, you must have at least four. I think that to be a family there must be four. You can't have two having a good argument without two or three; with two you can separate them you see, then you'll probably find that one's got more leaning towards the father or the mother, and vice versa. I think that really to know that there are other people in the world, and they must probably let Tommy have a new pair of shoes without having any, you've got to have at least four. You've got to see the other person's point of view, you must have at least four.

But the grounds for having a larger family are not just that it is better for the children. It is also that children should come before other things. And the logic of this, given her lack of interest in improving the family's material standards or status, is to have *more* children. Improving material standards might be all-important to some; she made it clear that she would choose to use the money on another child.[11] When asked why she thought that families with the same amount of money had different numbers of children, she said:

You ask about comparing families, you just can't. Comparing a family – well, the family next door have two, and next to that they have two, and next door they have five; well, probably Mr and Mrs Jones have got a different attitude, they have a different way of looking at things. I won't say they don't worry quite so much, but they just have a different way; they're probably – well, the importance is not on whether they've had new dining room curtains every five years; they'd probably let them hang up ten years and have another baby, and be much happier than those next door, who are happy in their way. Because you see, its a done thing to have new curtains, if you see what I mean, its their way of living, their whole life, so you can't really, probably they're getting the same amount of money but they're using it in a different way.

Here Mrs Abbott's reluctance to be critical of those who are concerned, unlike herself, to put material things before babies, itself reflects the value she places on tolerance and seeing the other person's point of view. However, the low priority she gives to increasing their material possessions, which she mentioned at other points in the interview, does not mean that money was never mentioned as a reason for curtailing childbearing. It was. She described how they used birth control periodically after the third child was born, 'If something happened', 'if we were terribly short of money, we can't afford one, but that was just periodical, it wasn't all the time'. And after the fifth child was born she had 'thought we had enough, and didn't want any more children, we couldn't afford it'. She then added, 'but we didn't decide anything'. For her, however, the issue of not being able to afford more children only arose when the financial pressures were already very great; they were not the starting point of her ideas about family size.

One of the most important consequences of Mrs Abbott's ideas about family life was that, whilst she did not plan to have a large family (she accepted that having children was part of married life and that she would have children, though she started to feel after two or three children she had probably had 'enough'), she did not feel very strongly about this. Part of the problem was her hostility to contraception; just as important were her ideas about family life which encouraged her not to take any firm action about birth control. On the one hand there was always the potential satisfaction to be gained from having another child. Hence, as she said, when asked what she felt after the fourth child was born: 'I was always pleased, I was never just sort of flat, I was always thrilled when I had a baby. I think if I had twenty I would still be excited and pleased'; and after the fifth, having described how the pregnancy was not planned, she had to add, 'but I can't say that I wanted not to have the child'. On the other hand, her desire to put the interests of the others before her own, appeared to lead her to subordinate her own wishes to those of her husband, as far as the question of having children is concerned, if not more widely. Although she said she felt she had certainly had enough children after the fourth and fifth were born, she clearly did not press her views very strongly. Asked if she and her husband talked about birth control after the fourth child was born, she commented:

Not really get down to it, not really, no. I think it might have been my fault, if I'd turned round and said that I object to being pregnant and I don't want any more, we probably wouldn't have had them, but I just went along with it, and he could see I was healthy and cosy, it just didn't matter, so it was probably my fault.

Even allowing for any tendency to avoid blaming others, this remark indicates that Mrs Abbott was reluctant to impose her views on her husband.

Mrs Abbott's remarks about family life and having children show how a particular set of ideas about what is important in family life are closely associated with, and influence what is done about having children. It suggests too, that women who marry and have this particular set of ideas are unlikely to choose not to have children, or to attempt to combine any other sort of life with having children. This is not true, of course, of men, who are normally required to combine a family life with a job. Nevertheless, we would expect that men who share this ideological perspective and have a family would attach considerable importance to family life and regard their job primarily in terms of providing for the family, though perhaps maintaining a marked differentiation of roles within the family.[12] Certainly there was considerable segregation of roles within the Abbott family. This is what Mrs Abbott said when describing how they decided how to spend the money:

If an occasion should happen, then we would, well, from the time my husband leaves the house, till the time he comes home with the money, I take care of the money. He finishes there, I don't expect him to do anything actually, because he's not the type, because there are types. When he sets foot in the house he is hopeless, he couldn't even carry a cup and saucer straight, I don't think. He will cope if I'm ill, he will struggle through with the help of the girls, but otherwise when he comes inside he is hopeless.

One would expect, too, that segregation of roles between spouses would enhance, as well as reflect, women's sense that it is their job to devote themselves completely to family life.

We also had the impression that where segregation in the division of roles within the family was combined with a sense of isolation, for one reason or another, the pressure to have large families could be even greater. This was particularly visible in the two couples in the pilot sample where the husband had worked as fishermen in the early years of the marriage. In both cases the wives reported the husbands were very keen on family life, loved the children and were happy to have a large number; and in both cases the wives made comments suggesting children helped to fill the gap created by the husband's frequent absence. Talking about the period after the birth of the first child one remarked, 'of course, we spoilt her terribly and, well, my whole life was her. And I took her everywhere I went and in a way she was closer to me than any of them, really, because he was away a lot and I only had her.' The other, who had eleven children when interviewed, questioned about the difference having the second child made, said, 'For me that was sort of company, because he was still on the water then.'

The factors underlying Mrs Abbott's image of family are interesting in this connection, for she seemed to be attempting to compensate for the lack of closeness and solidarity she found both within her own family and in other social relations as a child and later (she remarked several times, 'we haven't got many friends'). Her father had worked at the gas company, but she did not know exactly what he had done. When asked, she said, 'I don't know really, that's the amount of communication that used to go on between our parents and us. I couldn't really tell you what he did.' She had not, she said, been particularly happy as a child, her parents had been 'terribly pessimistic', and her life had been very restricted: 'We weren't allowed out, we used to take part in church functions, etc., but our life was very dull, and it was all school and housework and church Sundays.' When she met her future husband, the middle child of a family of seven, whose father was a postal worker, she was clearly attracted by the more spontaneous, close, outgoing and generous family, that she contrasted, unfavourably, with her own controlled, privatised and Puritanical family life. In consequence she felt marriage provided a chance to get 'an opening in the outside world'. Given her hostility to many of the values into which she had been socialised, her husband and his family offered an alternative set of ideas and values which she was happy to accept, and to which she became very strongly committed.

Hence though from what we have said so far, it is clear that we would expect this collective image of family life to be more common amongst women than amongst men and more dominant amongst those brought up in the 'traditional' working class than amongst other social groups, other factors such as hostility to existing values, isolation, and so forth, must also play a part. Furthermore, it is a way of thinking about family life that we would expect to be more dominant amongst those strongly committed to certain religious ideologies such as Catholicism.

II: The material life

All parents are aware that satisfying the material needs of a family costs money. Children, as well as parents, have to be clothed and fed and provided with somewhere to live, and most parents express a desire to make adequate material provision for their children. Some people, however, give particular prominence to the material conditions of their life: they have high material aspirations and derive great satisfaction from improving their financial and material circumstances. Such concerns have important implications for the sort of family life that is envisaged, for the significance that is attached to having children, for ideas about the desirable size and spacing of the family and, not least, for the effort that is made to realise those preferences.

The pursuit of material possessions is a familiar-enough phenomenon in our own society, as is the image of family life with which it is associated, and we found that those who did not accept the ideas and values that it involves, very often used it as a point of contrast with their own way of thinking just as Mrs Abbott did (see page 169). Indeed, those who thought that other things were more important than money and material possessions were often at pains to point this out, and complete indifference to the question of one's material standard of living was rare. Certain general features of this ideological perspective, and the image of society with which it tends to be associated, have been described in some detail elsewhere. Lockwood, for instance, has outlined what he calls the 'pecuniary model' of society as follows:

The single overwhelmingly important and the most spontaneously conceived criterion of class division is money and the possessions both material and immaterial that money can buy. From this point of view, for example education is not thought of as a status-conferring characteristic but rather simply as a good that money can buy and as a possession that enables one to earn money. In general power and status are not regarded as significant sources of class division or social hierarchy . . . Status is not seen in terms of the association of status equals sharing a similar style of life. If status is thought of at all it is in terms of a standard of living, which all who have the means can readily acquire. It may not be easy to acquire the income requisite to a certain standard of living and hence qualify for membership in a more affluent class; but given the income there are no other barriers to mobility.[13]

As he points out, such a consciousness tends to lead to a wage orientation to work, and jobs are likely to be evaluated in terms of money: a good job is one that pays more money. The way of thinking was frequently illustrated in the pilot sample. One wife's comments about her husband's job are typical: 'He just didn't want to be a shop assistant all his life, because of the money. I mean the higher you are the more money you get.'

When given a domestic focus the ideological perspective is consumption oriented and has definite implication for ideas about having children. First and foremost, its adherents invariably want a 'nice' home, and a nice home means one's own house, nicely furnished, with some children but not too many. It is important to have children as they are an essential part of the home and family which together constitute the standard unit of consumption within our society. Furthermore, they provide a means whereby the achievement of high material standards may be demonstrated. Last, but not least, having children constitutes a defence against charges of selfishness and hedonism to which those who emphasise material concerns feel liable. Since the important thing as a parent is the material provision one makes for one's children, which may well include giving them a good education as the means to a good income, two or three are usually the desired number: enough to meet the minimal normative requirement of two, and to justify and legitimate the material concern, but not too many to stop the individual realising high material standards within the family, or to preclude giving children 'the best' (or 'better than one had oneself') materially.[14]

Nevertheless, though children are a crucial part of this image of family life, the comfortable material standards are also an essential prerequisite. Hence although possessions may not be said to be *more* important than children (to say that would be non-normative), establishing a high material standard *before* one has children may be considered essential: a way of thinking the following extract clearly reflects.

Well, I think really, we didn't want to get much before we had a child. All we wanted was a house to put it in. We wouldn't have a child in rooms. So we said we want our own home, and we want it furnished adequately, so that we could have a child, you see. We didn't have anything else we wanted, before we had the child.

At times, however, the image of family life is less home-centred than this, and a nice home is not the only thing; having a car, getting out and about to spend money, having good holidays, sailing, and so forth, both with and without the family, are also very salient to the good life.[15] In this case children are, perhaps, less essential, though still desirable, since they create the normal unit for participating in many of these activities, and two rather than three children are the obvious ideal, since that permits the greater mobility that is involved. As one woman said, when asked why she thought two children was a good number: 'Well, you can fit two into a car can't you.' The role that the couple envisage for themselves as parents is, however, little different.

Those especially concerned to provide a good material standard of living for themselves and their children almost always want to defer having a family till they get themselves onto a reasonable financial footing (though as we have already indicated this desire is common and not restricted to those who espouse a material life), and they may well believe, as we have said, that getting oneself established materially is an essential preliminary to having children. Once childbearing begins there is, however, no particular reason for spacing births far apart, since a longer spacing will not improve the standard of living that can be achieved within the family. Indeed, a shorter space between births has the advantage that it enables the wife to return to work sooner and increase the household income. The strength of the pressure to keep within the intended two or three children will vary according to the couple's current financial circumstances. If, for instance, these improve then there may be little reason for not having another child.

If the couple's focus is the home there may well seem to be not that much difference between two and three children; the extra expenditure may not seem to be very great and implications for the family's standard of living rather slight. Hence if two children are planned the couple may not feel especially hostile to the idea of a third, particularly if they do not get one of the preferred sex. However, they would feel very differently about a fourth, which would create a 'large' family and be seen as generating much greater financial and material strain, and might no longer permit them to do the best for their children.

Mr Carter, who was interviewed with his wife, illustrates this aspiration for high material standards, the impact that it has on ideas about family life, and the implications for what is done about having children. When interviewed he had been married eight and a half years, and had two children, both boys, of five years and twenty months respectively. Mr Carter had started off as an apprentice on day-release with a local engineering firm, had returned to the same company after National Service and worked in various clerical jobs there around the time he married. After a period as a salesman for the same group of companies, he had recently gone back to administrative work.

From the first Mr Carter's concern for the material and financial circumstances of his life dominated his marriage. Like many couples, he explained the length of his engagement (eighteen months) in terms of his financial situation 'We didn't have, well, we didn't have sufficient money, did we dear? I mean I was just surviving on mine, and you were saving yours, to try and get enough.' Once married their first object was to get more possessions. Talking of the period between marriage and having the first child, he described his principal interest as 'establishing ourselves and setting up a home. Getting it as we wanted it, you see.' When asked how he wanted it, he added:

We wanted – we didn't want the best of everything, because we obviously couldn't afford it then. We wanted the best we could afford, and we worked very hard to those ends, I would say. We both worked hard and saved like mad, for the first time in our lives, or for the first time in my life anyway.

How to spend their money was the only thing they discussed at all seriously at the time; when asked how much they talked about things when they were first married, he replied:

Well, seriously, we didn't talk about anything seriously – well, that's a lie, because we planned or we tried to plan ahead, our home and how we would want to have things. But how we were going to spend our money, and how we were going to map it all out, I think that's about the only thing we discussed, wasn't it?

But life at that time was not completely dominated by saving money; they were also spending it. Talking of their activities in the period after marriage Mr Carter commented:

Scrambling we did. I think we had a dab at practically every sport you could have, without much success in any of them. It was a good time, really, in our lives that, wasn't it, because we had, we had the money and we had the time to enjoy ourselves, and we just did everything we could. We used to cram in a very full week, really, didn't we?

At that time he judged jobs primarily in terms of money.[16] He was very unhappy with the job he had when he married because of the low pay, and he had changed his job within the firm after about a year of marriage in order to get more. Mrs Carter's job was, therefore, initially very important to them because of the money it brought in. When asked how important working was to her at the time, she said 'very important, really, because I was earning the money'. And her husband added the illuminating comment, 'Don't think our life was completely governed by money but it was very important'. Elsewhere, he remarked, 'You have to adapt your whole life round what you can afford and what you can manage.' In this situation of two incomes and no children they felt quite well off, particularly once Mr Carter had changed his job. Describing their financial situation, he said, they were doing 'very well, because we seemed to have just saved a few weeks, a few months, and well, we soon furnished the home, so we thought we were doing quite well'.

Both Mr and Mrs Carter had wanted to have a family when they married, though Mr Carter did not regard having children as the most important thing for him. He remarked:

More important than having children? Yes, I think perhaps to be – the material side of life I think perhaps is more important than to have children. To be well off, well, not well off, but to be comfortably off, and able to enjoy life to the full, I would say.

Though he now liked to think of himself as a 'family man' he also said, 'Children are nice, I mean, I wouldn't be without mine, there's no doubt about that, but if I hadn't had any I don't suppose I would attach that much importance to it.' By saying explicitly that material things were more important to him than children he was unusual.[17] Those who attached great importance to the material standards, usually claimed that having children was one of the most important things in life, but qualified the statement by saying that perhaps it was not for some (such as those who were not married, or those who had strong career commitments, like doctors) but that it was for them, or as Mr Carter did in the second statement, by saying that it had not seemed especially important until they had children. However, in the impact of his concern for a high material standard of living on his decision about family size and spacing Mr Carter was typical.

His ideas about how many children to have and when to have them were directly guided by his desire to maintain and enhance material standards whilst having a family. He and his wife did not want any children when they first married because 'there were so many things we wanted you see.

We furnished – we had the furniture, and we wanted a car, and we wanted this, and we wanted that.' As a result, 'we forget completely about children until we got settled, more or less'. But like other couples concerned about their material standard of living, the plan was not just to postpone the start of childbearing, but also to keep their family size small. Mr Carter wanted two children for, as he said, 'I think everybody should limit the size of family to their means.' And later, 'we like to live well, and if you've got three, four, five children, then well, you can afford it, but you have more of a job than we're having at the moment'. On another occasion he remarked:

And when the second one came along, we decided we would still get, go on more or less in the same way as we had been going on, with the two, and if we had three or four then we wouldn't be able to afford little things that we were getting, the things we like now.

Affording 'little things' for the children, as well as for themselves, was essential, for he wanted to be 'able to give the children, you know, the things they want, and keep everybody happy'. As he makes clear, he regards his children's comforts and his own as closely associated. When the first child was born he remarked, 'we tried to get, you know, everything for him that we could. I mean to make his life easy; to make your life easy.'

As these extracts show, when Mr Carter says that two children is all he can afford, he does not mean that he could not provide for more children, but that none of the family could have quite as much if they did have more. It is not that he does not have enough money to provide for more, for as he said (perhaps with some exaggeration, in view of his earlier comments about his dissatisfaction with his income very early on in marriage) 'money has never worried us . . . we've always had enough'. and if it were not for the likely impact on his standard of living he would be happy to have more children. When the couple were asked what difference it would have made if they had had four children, Mrs Carter said, 'Well, we wouldn't be so comfortably off' and her husband added, 'I think that is the thing. I mean, it makes no difference to your lives, I suppose, socially or anything else, but in the years, financially it makes quite a difference.'

It is significant, however, that Mr Carter does not have 'great ambition' for his children and views his parental role almost entirely as making a good enough material provision for them. Doing 'the best' was not a matter of attempting to ensure their advancement up the social ladder, or even that they would get a good job, though he would like it if they happened to 'do well'. Asked if he had any particular ideas about how he wanted to bring his children up, he replied:

Well, of course, we want the best for them, but provided we can give them a home background, I suppose, and keep them out of trouble, we've no great ambition for them. Naturally I want them to get on as well as they can, but I would never force them I don't think to greater heights than they seemed able to attain.

Though a good son would work hard at school, how well they would do there and later, was not a matter which he seemed to feel depended either on his own or the children's endeavour. Asked if he had any ideas about what jobs he would like to do he commented:

No, not really. I should like them to have a decent position, but of course you can't really tell how your child is going to turn out. You hope he's going to be bright, and you hope he's going to do well at school. But some children don't.

As the full answer to the question of what a good son would be like also suggests, whether his children try hard at school is not something he feels he can influence, and he does not seem to have any great hopes that they will. A good son, he thought, was 'just a lad, I suppose who tries hard at school, and behaves himself. Well, just a friendly good-natured lad, I suppose.' The contrast with Mrs Abbott who also disclaimed much ambition for her children is noticeable. Though she was not much concerned with social advancement either, she had more positive ideas about what she wanted her children to be like and expected far more of them in terms of personal qualities than Mr Carter did.

Mr and Mrs Carter had managed to plan their childbearing successfully up to that time (though Mrs Carter had not become pregnant as quickly the second time as they had wanted). They had used the sheath, without taking chances, but were thinking of changing to the pill on their doctor's recommendations. Nevertheless, the possibility of an unplanned pregnancy could not be ruled out as the following exchange indicates:

INTERVIEWER: And how have you felt since the second one about families and having children? You still – its still two?

MRS C.: Yes.

MR C.: Well, we would like to keep it to two, but I don't think we'd be terribly disappointed if a third one came along. We certainly shouldn't be annoyed.

I: Do you think there is any chance at all of your deciding to have a third?

MR C.: Not at the moment, I don't think. I think we're – we – I don't think we shall. We possibly may have a third, but I think it will be more by accident than by trying.

A number of factors could influence whether they do have another child: whether Mrs Carter does shift to the pill thereby reducing the risk of an unplanned pregnancy (though not completely since the pill can easily be forgotten); how well off Mr Carter feels in his new job in comparison to the previous one; whether economic circumstances affect their financial position and the standard of living they can realise favourably or adversely; whether Mrs Carter gets bored and lonely with domestic life and finds alternative sources of satisfaction or not, and so on. The outcome is difficult to predict and depends on numerous contingencies. But even if they had a third they would unlikely to have a fourth since, as we have argued, they would almost certainly feel much more strongly about the possibility of a fourth than they do about having one more.

Mr Carter's ideas typify the material orientation that was shown by many of those we interviewed, and the effect that it has on ideas about family life, and on what is done about having children. For such people family life, to be satisfactory, must achieve as high material standards as possible, and it is for this reason that small families are regarded as desirable. Many of them (unlike Mr Carter who only said that a third child would not make much difference to them, except financially) say explicitly that they would like to have more children if it weren't for the question of cost; they also give more emphasis to their children's material comforts, as opposed to their own, than did Mr Carter.

In our sample a material orientation towards family life tended to be associated either with personal experience of privation in childhood, or with financial circumstances that did not compare favourably with those experienced as a child. A number of people who were especially concerned to improve the material conditions of themselves and their children said explicitly that they wanted the best for them because they had not much when they were children. As one woman put it, 'I try to bring him up well, give him everything what we never had.' Though it could be argued, that it was the individual's concern with his material circumstances that made him or her feel that they had been deprived materially in childhood and not vice versa, the descriptions that they gave of their parents' occupations and the number of children in the family indicated the latter. It is arguable, indeed, that the pervasiveness of material concerns in our sample may be partly explained by the fact that many of our sample had spent their childhood either during the depression of the 1930s or the austerity of the 1940s.[18]

Mr Carter illustrates the origins of a heightened material consciousness in a discrepancy between the material conditions that had been expected from experiences in earlier life and the financial situation he himself was able to attain. His father had worked on 'machine maintenance' in a local engineering firm, and he was the only child. In consequence, 'I was – not thoroughly spoilt – but I didn't want for much.' His father was a very 'careful man' and he was sent to a 'private' school from the age of eleven until he was 16½. He did not enjoy the later part of school, 'because all my friends were out working and earning and I wasn't'; later he regretted that he had not worked harder there: 'My only regret is that I didn't try harder. I didn't take it serious enough, I think. I mean I wasted my time at school.' In consequence he feels he would have a better job if he had worked harder at school. Yet as with the children's progress at school, it did not seem to be a matter about which he felt he could have done very much. As well as his overall financial situation housing was an area in which he admitted they had not been able to realise the standards he wanted, and it had been far less than perfect throughout their marriage. When they first decided to marry they found that they could not get the sort of accommodation they wanted:

Housing was difficult then. I mean we tried for several houses to buy ourselves, but were always beaten by the mortgage I'm afraid, or somebody else was there before you. And to rent a place, it's terrifically expensive isn't it?

They ended up living with his parents for the first year of the marriage, which was 'a disastrous year, wasn't it? As I said, all our – our little plans and dreams were shattered.' They then moved into a council flat, 'which saved all the embarrassment of having mortgages keep being refused. People said, "I'm sorry sir, but that's not quite enough for a deposit", and things like that.' After they had the first child they were allocated a full council house and though they still wanted to buy a house they felt 'that's just beyond us'.

In consequence, though our data are not inconsistent with the suggestion elsewhere that a material or pecuniary orientation is likely to be found amongst those social groups often termed the 'new working class' or the 'privatised' workers, it suggests that there is no simple equation between class position and dominance of a material orientation.[19] It suggests, further, contrary to the arguments advanced by others, that personal experience of privation may well directly enhance the desire to achieve a better material standard of living.[20]

III: A better life

Having children always involves some concern for, or commitment to the future, and reference to the future occurs in numerous ideas about having children. On the one hand as Francis Bacon put it, children are our 'hostages to fortune'. More practically, they have to be provided for during the period of their dependence. On the other hand, they offer numerous opportunities and prospects for the future: the opportunity to maintain or enhance one's identity or status or that of the family; the prospect of companionship or material support in later life, as well as a good reason for continuing to live. Amongst parents whose conception of the world is framed by the desire to make a better future and a better life, there is likely to be an especial interest and concern in their children's future, for children provide an ideal opportunity to make a better life; one that may in theory or in practice be unachievable elsewhere.

The concern for a better future either for oneself or one's children is again a familiar one. Its essential characteristics for our purposes are three-fold: first it emphasises and gives prominence to the future rather than the present: second, it postulates not only the possibility, but also the desirability of some degree of progress from, or improvement of one's present position; third, it assumes that this progression or improvement depends upon individuals asserting effort and endeavour on their own part. The full connotations of 'doing better' are provided by other components of the whole ideology in which this desire is commonly located. Underlying the idea of doing better as it has often been observed in post-war English society is the notion that society is organised into ranked groups between which individuals can move on the basis of their own merit. With this image of society as a social ladder the 'doing better' means moving up the rungs, and mobility and success are held to depend on individual effort, hard work and a willingness to sacrifice immediate pleasure for future gains.[21] The ideology, therefore, rests on the assumption that individuals can control their world and by exerting control over themselves will determine their future in it.

Of course, notions like doing better, and making a better life, which have in the past been associated with ideas of progress are abstract ones and, in a society that tends to be preoccupied with material objects, many who espouse this way of thinking are, if pressed, likely to interpret the idea of doing better in a similar way to those whose emphasis is on material matters, and may say, for instance, that a good job is one with more money. But the two orientations can and do need to be distinguished, for they give rise to rather different images of family life and usually have different implications for ideas about having children. Whilst it is true that a concern for a better future does not preclude a concern for one's present material standards, and that the substance of the better life in the future may be given a rather material interpretation, nevertheless, those concerned with the better future will be more willing to sacrifice present comforts for future gains, will be concerned about prestige and status as well as income and possessions, and will place more emphasis on endeavour and sacrifice.

When this individualist and meritocratic ideology is extended to family life the implications are predictable enough, for 'the future in family terms, means the children'.[22] The desire for a better life embraces the children who become the object of some, if not most of the aspirations for the future. In consequence the parents' aim is to give their children the sort of care, attention and guidance that will encourage them to work hard and develop their abilities in order to achieve social success. It usually means a concern that they should be given a good education (not just to get a job with more money, but to acquire the attributes of higher status more generally), and that they should not be indulged or spoilt with material possessions since that could interfere with the development of the sort of self-denying, persistent character necessary to achieve social mobility. It also means an emphasis on the importance of the parental role in providing the right sort of care and guidance: a belief that, though school may be important, the parents can be even more so, and it is up to them to make the necessary sacrifices and put in the necessary endeavour to ensure their children's success. Again some of the ideas of this ideological perspective are very common and are not exclusive to this way of thinking, as for instance the belief that children should not be over-indulged or spoilt, and the idea that parents should make sacrifices for their children. It is, however, the constellation of ideas that is important and, as is almost invariably the case, the meaning and significance of an individual notion can only be understood in the context of the ideology as a whole.

The implications of this perspective for ideas and decisions about having children are also predictable. It is a way of thinking that demands a small family, almost certainly only two children, not too closely spaced, in order that they may be provided with the necessary care, attention and parental guidance. The cost of children may figure in the calculation too: not so much the cost of providing for children's immediate material wants but that of providing them with a good education, enough space, books and whatever else might be necessary to the development of their abilities. Furthermore, it may well be considered desirable not to start a family straightaway in order to accumulate the necessary material assets that will contribute to providing a 'good home background' for one's children. In that respect the implications of the ideology differ little from that of the material one. The implications for contraceptive use are markedly different. On the one hand, if a family size of two is planned there is far more reason for sticking to that plan and avoiding a third pregnancy, since an additional pregnancy will not only increase the monetary expenses of the family, it will also require more investment of time, care, energy, patience and guidance from the parents themselves. On the other hand, given the future orientation of the ideology, which will be reflected in a great belief in planning and on individuals determining what happens to them, a contraceptive accident is far less likely. Carelessness, ignorance and casualness in contraceptive use are anathema to this way of thinking.

Mrs Kowski, who was English, illustrates the desire for a better life in a striking manner. She had met her Polish husband while they were both working in the Forces, she as a clerical worker and he as a toolmaker, a job with which he continued when he left the Forces and settled in Ipswich. They had been married eighteen years when interviewed (she was interviewed by herself) and had three children, a daughter of 15, and two sons, one of 12 and one of 3, the last as a result of an unplanned pregnancy. The importance Mrs Kowski attached to achieving a better life, as well as her sense of frustration when not able to do so, are demonstrated in a number of ways. First, in her ideas about the structure of society and their own (herself and her husband's) place within it. Her ideas were basically meritocratic: she viewed education as an essential element for success, and felt that her husband's lack of the former deprived them of the latter. Her husband she said:

has a good job, he's a toolmaker in one of the local factories, actually its a good job, because the boys that go into it now need G.C.E.s, because of course in those days they didn't do, and he hasn't got G.C.E. But's very good at figures, and he's good at his job, he's had the same job for 18 years now.

Nevertheless, she thought there were other people doing better than them. When asked, she replied, 'Yes, there are, but that depends upon their qualification and education, not on life. If they're doing better, they deserve to do better.' And she was not really satisfied with their position on the social scale. Questioned as to what sort of people were doing better, she added:

Those who have had a better education, they're climbing up the ladder in their jobs, and we sort have got as far as we're going to get, and now we have to keep plodding at this level, and we're not going to go any further.

They could not move up the social ladder because her husband had not got better educational qualifications, which she thought he deserved:

Oh, he did very well at school, he was good at maths, not so good at language, but he was quite a bright boy, if he'd been in this country he would've won the scholarship but they haven't got the scholarship thing, there was no free places to grammar schools. But I think if he was in this country he would have won a scholarship.

But success in her eyes was not just a question of having the right opportunities, as her comments about her own upbringing and that of her children make clear. She was not herself successful, she felt, because she had not used the opportunities provided for her:

I think that I was a bit of a problem to my parents, I wouldn't work at school, and they tried all sorts of openings for me in careers and I just wouldn't bother, I just wouldn't try, I just wouldn't put my shoulder to the wheel. And I could have a marvellous career now, if I'd done almost any of the things my father planned for me, but I wouldn't, and I think now what good parents they were to me, and now that I'm married and I've got children of my own, I appreciate ten times more what my parents did for me.

Not surprisingly she was anxious that her children should do well at school and afterwards, and not make her mistake. Asked what a good son would be like she commented, 'At the moment, the age my son is, I'd expect him to do well at school.' Of a good daughter she said, I'd want her to do well at school and a career as well.' Mrs Kowski believed that hard work was essential to success and a number of other comments bring this out. When asked how her children were getting on at school she said, 'My children? Quite average, they're not brilliant, they've got to work hard if they want to get on, but I think they've got to the age now where they know they've got to work hard and they try.' A moment later she showed her concern that her children should do well, and her belief that they need to work to achieve it, in her comments on the schools they attended.

I'm satisfied with the school they're at now, but the junior schools they went to, I was not satisfied with – I was very dissatisfied with. They just didn't seem to be making any headway or anything at the infants and the junior school. We used to think they were extremely dull and backward children, the teachers were all too kind to them, and didn't give them a prod when they needed it, and then when they went to their senior schools they thought oh what a horrid lot of teachers, driving us all the time. That's the only thing that's got results.

Education, she thought, was not only important but definitely worth considerable sacrifice. Questioned as to the importance of educaton for children she replied:

Well, I think its all important, I think its the only thing worthwhile spending money on, and for parents to deny themselves and educate their children at all, they should definitely give up a lot of comforts in the home and life to educate children.

Mrs Kowski also manifests the characteristics of this ideological perspective in her concern to provide her children with the right sort of help and guidance at home. When asked what sort of things made her anxious or worried, it was not the possibility of her children being ill or having some accident that was mentioned. Instead it was being able to give her children adequate educational help at home.

Little things, like my son's homework, when he brings home subjects which I've never done, and he brings home some maths and perhaps he couldn't work out, and I could cry real tears over these sums 'cos I can't do them, and I think, 'Oh gosh, if only I had the same education as my son I'd be able to help him as other mothers and dads can', and I worry a great deal over this. So much do I take it to heart that I thought at least I'll do English at home, and just before I knew this baby was on the way I sent for a correspondence course in English, and I started doing it, a couple of hours every day, but now, of course, I've got this little one, and I haven't got time at the minute for any studies . . . there must be thousands of parents who can't either, but I know also many who do help their children, and it must be a great asset to have parents to help you with your homework, so that you've got teachers at school and at home. And that's what worries me, if I'm not capable of helping.

The passage also brings out the frustration she experiences if she cannot do what she thinks is necessary. A short while later guidance was the theme. Questioned as to her ideas about how she wanted to bring her children up she commented:

Well, I suppose we had our definite ideas years before about, that we wanted our daughter to be a nurse. We've got nursing in the family, and we sort of brought her up with the idea that nursing would be fine for her, and sort of under our guidance, she actually does want to be a nurse, so that I think guidance has quite a part in what your children want to do, you know. Not exactly pressure, but guidance is a good word, you know. You can try to persuade them into what you want them to do, you can't force them, but you can guide them and persuade them to a great extent about the future.

The link between these ideas and Mrs Kowski's preferences about family size and spacing is complex. Certainly her preference throughout her marriage for two children is consistent with her concern to make a better future for her children and her ideas about what this involved. But the interpretation of her statements about family size and spacing is complicated by her current hostility to family life, a hostility which itself stems from her concern for a better life, which she wanted to include herself as well as her children. She now felt that her family life was far from satisfying and implied that she would have been better off if she had remained single. 'I think', she said, 'I could have made a very good life for myself if I had stayed single.' The sense that she was not achieving a better life for herself within the family had a number of origins. On the one hand there was her sense, to which we have already referred, that she could not make any social progress either through or with her husband.[23] Then there was a sense that domestic life itself was rather dull. Above all, however, there was the accidental pregnancy coming when she thought her family was completed which tied her to the house, when she expected she would be able to go back to work. This event clearly heightened an already existing sense that her family life did not provide her with the opportunities for status and success that she would have liked and that her endeavours were not rewarded, and seems to have symbolised to her the fact that she could not control her world in the way she wanted.[24] In consequence, her accounts of her plans about having children were coloured by her dislike of domestic life and of being tied to the children, which were almost certainly not present to the same degree when the family was originally planned. She emphasised the problems of coping with more than two children, though she did not elaborate on exactly what these problems were in this context. Her original idea was, she said, to have two children, 'We always thought we'd like two children.' Questioned why, she added, 'I never was really ambitious to have a big family because I don't think I'd have been able to cope. I thought two would be about as many children as I could manage to look after.' However, even though this account may be affected by her current feelings of dislike at having to spend all her time looking after the children, much of the problem is that children do need, in her view, a lot of care, attention and guidance, and as previous comments have illustrated, she does not find this easy to provide. Later when asked why they had stopped at two, given that she said at one point that her husband had been undecided between two or three, her answer shows the same tension between the standards she sets herself in bringing up the children, the sense that meeting these standards is not easy, as well as her growing reluctance to do so.

Yes, we weren't so definitely decided, but after we had the two, we realised what life was like with two small children, how mischievous they are, and my husband thought well, they run the home if they're not checked, and of course, we were older probably, we were middle aged people, and we thought two was enough, and for reasons of coping with children, not so much expense.

Hence for her the notion of 'coping' with children now has a double meaning. Can she look after them properly and give them the care and guidance they need? Is she willing any longer to make the effort?

When it comes to the issues of deciding when to have the children and of birth-control practice the implications of Mrs Kowski's concern for a better life are more clear-cut since there is not the same conflict and confusion between her ideas about what would make a better life for *herself* (to have had no children) and what would make a better life for her children (to have a small family to which she devoted herself). Her own and her husband's ideas about when to start a family were dominated by their desire to establish themselves for the future, by saving and sacrificing immediate pleasures for future ones. Her remarks show there was much greater self-denial on their part than in the Carters' case. Talking of starting a family, she said: 'We thought we'd wait about three years, and it was just over three years, and I went out to work, and I stayed in my job.' Elsewhere she commented, 'we said that we wanted to both work and save some money to get a home together, we didn't want children at first'. Questioned about waiting three years, she added:

Well, we thought that in three years we'd manage to save a fair bit, which we in fact did. We used to live most economically, we didn't go out, didn't spend much on pleasure, and in fact we almost paid our house mortgage on our first house, or smaller house. And then of course I was actually 27 when my daughter was born, and everyone said, 'You don't want to wait any more years.'

Coping, predictably, is the reason mentioned for the spacing between births (two to three years) that they planned.

I thought the little girl would be sufficiently grown up, just grown out of the baby stage, and she could do little things for herself and that I wouldn't be coping with two tiny babies. I felt that she was older I'd be able to cope better.

Mrs Kowski's unplanned pregnancy notwithstanding, there can be little doubt either of the strength of the couple's desire to avoid unplanned pregnancies, or of the extent to which they had tried to avoid one. Though both were Roman Catholics (Mrs Kowski a convert before her marriage) they used the sheath, taking no 'chances' during the first three years of their marriage, 'because we were so definitely against having children'. When they had the first child according to plan, part of the pleasure came from the realisation of that plan: 'We felt satisfied in every way that our plans had worked out, we had planned for her and we were happy.' They then decided to use the 'safe period' and continued to do so, apart from the time when they had the second child as planned, in a very controlled and careful way. Mrs Kowski said the 'safe period' was 'at most three to four days after the period finishes, but in actual fact, I think its only two days to be absolutely safe'. She and her husband restricted intercourse to 'two days after – the first or second day'. Their downfall came, as we describe in Chapter 12, with irregularity in Mrs Kowski's periods but provides no evidence, as the extent of her reaction to it indicates, either of any increasing willingness to have another child or of any lack of planning on their part. As these comments illustrate, planning was very important to Mrs Kowski. Not surprisingly, when asked whether she made plans in advance or acted on the spur of the moment, she said, 'I seldom act on the spur of the moment.'

The example of Mrs Kowski not only illustrates the implications a concern for a better life has for ideas about having children, given the commitment to marriage and family life, but also suggests that those women who embrace this ideology may be somewhat more likely than others to become dissatisfied with their domestic role, even if the family is successful, since doing better is dependent on their husband and children's success. When the family is not, then dissatisfaction is even more likely, as it was in Mrs Kowski's case. Indeed this ideology presents married women with a potential contradiction. Their roles as wife and mother require them to devote themselves to the family and to decide issues about family size without thinking of alternative sources of satisfaction, yet the ideology demands some concern for one's *own* success within the social system. And this potential contradiction is true for any parent, male or female, who pins their hopes for a better life solely on their children. To do so requires strong identification with one's child, and this is susceptible to all sorts of threats. It may also be that women dominated by a concern to do better and to make a better life will be somewhat less likely and more reluctant than those of either of the two ideological persuasions that we have outlined so far to get married and have children, since doing better can come to mean for them, as it does for men, achieving status through work and a career.

The concern for a better life for oneself and one's family and the ideology in which it is located are usually held to be typical of the middle rather than the working class. Indeed, the ideology is often held to be paradigmatic of middle class values and ideas. Zweig, discussing the immediate post-war period, had this to say of the consciousness of the English middle classes:

A middle-class man thinks first of all of the betterment of his condition by his own individual efforts, and he does not rely on organisation at all. All the time he is thinking how he can climb up the ladder of social achievement, while the working man is content to stay put as he is.[25]

Lockwood specifically linked the ideology with a desire for a small family and regarded them as typical of the middle class.

A relatively small family and a strong desire for educational success of one's children have been the hall-marks of middle class status since the closing decades of the nineteenth century. Taken together they represent a concern with social mobility through individual achievement and a conscious discounting of the present against the future.[26]

Nevertheless, as these writers would, presumably, recognise, though this way of thinking may be regarded as 'typifying' middle class thinking, it is neither restricted to those in non-manual occupations, nor is it the only way of thinking to be found amongst the middle class. It is an ideology that is to be found amongst the aspirant working class and was typical, for instance, in Jackson and Marsden's sample of working class parents whose children went to Grammar School.[27] Such people may have close ties with members of the middle class and can at times be reasonably described as 'sunken middle class', in the way Jackson and Marsden suggested.[28] But we suspect that there is, as before, no simple equation between this way of thinking and social origins. Again Mrs Kowski illustrates the point. Though by virtue of her own occupation before and early in marriage she might be classified as a non-manual worker (if sociologists classifications of women's social rank were based on their own occupation rather than that of their spouses, which they are usually not) her background was a manual one, for her father had worked as a postman. And it was clear from what she said that her ideological perspective was based on and derived from her parents ideas, and though she had been the 'wayward child' in the family before marriage, she now accepted her parents ideas and values as we have already indicated, and as she herself admitted quite explicitly. Questioned as to the effect that she thought her parents had on the way she ran her life she said:

Probably they have a lot of effect, if I'm – I often find myself saying little idioms and little scoldings that my parents said to me, although I thought they were long since forgotten, but little sayings come to mind, and I just say them the way my mother said them all those years ago, little things come back, so sub-consciously they are with you through all your life really, the effect of your parents, you never really lose it.

It is equally important to note, too, the association between this way of thinking and the 'protestant ethic' which underlies its connecton with the middle class: this may also mean that such a way of thinking is likely to be more common amongst non-conformist sectors of the community.[29]

IV: The active life

The endeavour and activity that are associated with the ideological perspective that we have just outlined are essentially instrumental in two respects. First, they are the means of achieving success: hard work and effort are a way of getting things done and thereby making individual progress in the social system. Second, they are not held to be intrinsically pleasurable: the pleasure is supposed to come from the accomplishment and from the consequences of the activity, and not from the doing *per se*. Indeed any emphasis on the pleasure of the activity in itself might well be held to be incompatible with the sort of personal and moral development requiring self-denial, persistence and sacrifice that are thought to make a person successful. In contrast, in the ideological perspective which shall describe in this section activity is viewed and understood very differently. What matters is the doing and not its end result. It is the doing that gives a sense of fulfillment and pleasure. Activity in itself is held to be intrinsically satisfying, and an active, busy life is all important. Certainly one tries to do the activity well, since that is the logic of engagement with it, but that is not the first concern. In consequence, it seems important both to use one's abilities, energies and talents to the full, and to be free to use them as one likes (which could be in the service of others).[30] Hence though the ideology is individualist and stresses the individual's active, creative capacities and autonomy, it is not concerned with some race up the social ladder, and does not lay the same stress on denial and self-sacrifice or on foregoing present pleasures for the sake of supposed future ones, as does the pursuit of a better life. The ideology seems freer, more open and more confident. It is the zeal of the protestant ethic freed from its acquisitive and meritocratic constraints: an ideology of those who do not have to worry about material matters or social success.

When extended to family life this ideological perspective is likely to be associated with an emphasis on the pleasures that can be gained from family life and on the importance of providing family members with the opportunity to fulfill themselves in the activities that interest and appeal to them. The vision of the family unit stresses not so much the closeness, solidarity and integration of the unit as the need for independence and autonomy of family members. Marriage is seen as more of a partnership of equals, and the children have to be given the necessary facilities and skills to develop their energies and abilities, to realise their autonomy and to discover and pursue their own interest and activities. Education is, moreover, likely to be considered important to this process of self-realisation and development. This is not, however, the 'privatised' family anxious to avoid interference and to be allowed its own life; the meaning of independence differs, it is not freedom *from* constraints that is at issue, but freedom *to* do certain things.

Within the context of family life any child will be valued as an individual and provide a source of pleasure, but it may well not seem very important either to marry or have children in the first place. On the one hand, the belief that pleasure can be obtained in a variety of different ways means that marriage and family life are likely to be regarded as potentially satisfying activities. On the other hand, since there are plenty of alternative sources of satisfaction, the pressure to marry and have children is less great. Furthermore, given the emphasis on individual freedom, those concerned for an active life are less likely to worry about not conforming by remaining single and not becoming a parent than others.

Moreover, the implications for ideas about family size and spacing and contraceptive use, if a family is planned, are not always the same for different individuals. On the one hand, those who espouse this way of thinking are likely to feel confident of their own abilities, to be unworried about the problems of coping with the care of children, to think that having children like many other activities could provide them with pleasure, and to be happy, therefore, if they decide to have a family at all, to have a larger family, say three or four. On the other hand, to the extent that they are also likely to find other activities interesting and satisfying they may decide to limit family size to a low level. Women, for instance, who share this ideology may well attempt to combine a career with having a family and might decide to have only one or two children for that reason, and be less worried about doing so that those aiming for a better life. They will be less concerned to succeed in their jobs, and be more willing to weigh up children against other sources of satisfaction, even though it is not normative. The same applies to the spacing of children. On the one hand, having children close together would be unlikely to present especial problems in terms of 'coping'; on the other hand, it might be considered necessary to fit in with other non-family commitments. Contraceptive performance is equally unpredictable in the absence of greater knowledge about the relation between family life and other activities in each particular case. There would be unlikely to be any problem about using methods efficiently or reliably on grounds of knowledge and competence, but the strength of the concern to avoid an additional pregnancy will vary. For those trying to combine family life with other activities that precluded more children, there would be less chance of an unplanned pregnancy. In other cases, given the pleasures to be gained from any activity including having another child and the few problems it would present, an 'unplanned' pregnancy is possible.

Mrs Butler illustrates this way of thinking and the effect it can have on ideas about family life. She had married at the age of 28 (her husband was then 26) and had been married over 12 years when interviewed. Her husband worked as a successful solicitor and they had three children, all boys, aged eleven, nine and seven. Mrs Butler's concern for an active and busy life was manifest whether she talked of her family life or the life she had before she had children, and the pleasure she derived from being active is very apparent. Before she had the children, her work, running a laboratory with a staff of six girls, engaged much of her time and was very satisfying. Nevertheless, there were numerous other activities that gave her pleasure. When asked what things she had enjoyed doing when she was first married, she expanded on some of them:

Well, I enjoyed my job, I must say, I was very sorry to give that up, even though I had the attraction of having a family instead. I used to play tennis then, which I don't do now. I quite enjoyed doing that. I like swimming. We have always spent a good deal of our time on the beach or swimming in the summer and now sailing, now we've got a boat. That's something we both like doing. Oh something I like doing which I can't do now, I enjoy travelling. I love going abroad, and I haven't done that since I've been married. I'm dying to do that again, but that's something which I had to give up.

Even when she had the children it was very important to her to do other things as well. Domestic life was in that respect somewhat frustrating since, to some extent, it reduced her freedom to engage in other activities. This is how she described herself after the birth of her first child:

I was probably a bit more demanding than I'd been beforehand. Though I love children, I don't love domestic life at all and I probably wanted to get out and do other things, you know, and leave him babysitting in the evenings and at weekends sometimes and he didn't mind.

In fact she felt sufficiently strongly about maintaining an active life that she managed to fit in quite a few activities apart from the immediate care of the children. She started evening classes twice a week after the first child was born because she felt she was 'getting a bit of a cabbage' and managed to look after her father who way dying of cancer when he came home from hospital a month after her third child was born. A year later, having given up her job when she began having children, she started part-time teaching. On top of that she tried to help her children in various ways. As she said, 'I give them all riding lessons from time to time because I'm very keen on riding'; and she coached her eldest son for his public school entrance exam because 'he really hadn't learnt anything at all at the primary school he went to before'.

Hers is a philosophy that regards actions as more important than words. When asked how she and her husband decided things when they were first married she replied, 'Well, anything to do with his job of his activities he decided. We don't discuss things much, we just decide our particular branch of the concern and get on with it.' Likewise, when asked whether she and her husband talked about sex when they were first married, she responded, 'Not much, no I don't think we discuss it, we just do it.' It is also a philosophy that believes, as these remarks suggest, that individuals should be allowed to carry out their own activities, that they choose themselves, without interference. Autonomy is important and applies to children as well as adults, as her remarks about bringing up her children demonstrate.[31] Questioned as to the jobs she would like for her children she said, 'I think one should let them choose for themselves', and when asked whether a child should follow in his father's footsteps she replied, 'Well, I'm not convinced this is a good thing. I think it's better for them to strike out on their own.' Giving children freedom applies to the present as well as to the future. Asked about the important things in keeping a family ticking over Mrs Butler had this to say:

I suppose by that you mean sort of living happily together and not getting on each other's nerves. Well, I think you give them all the freedom so they can enjoy their own pursuits and encourage each one's separate talents so that they can do what they want to do I think. You mustn't try to be too restrictive with a family. You mustn't try to keep them all together. You must let them each go out and encourage individuality in them, and let them pursue their own direction, you know what they want to do, each individual one. Same with husband.

A moment later when talking about the things that make living together difficult she elaborated on the theme of freedom for each child to do what he or she wanted.

I think one needs lots of space. I think its very difficult for children to be cooped up, sort of two or theee to a bedroom or something like that. I think they all need space to have a bedroom to themselves, somewhere where they can work by themselves, where they can keep their own private stuff for their hobbies and so on. I think everyone in a family should have privacy of their own, the freedom to do what they want to do with their own free time, not too much regimentation.

Here we get the positive virtues of privacy described. Not the desire to avoid detection and judgement that seems to underlie the desire for privacy, as described by others, of those of a materialist orientation,[32] or those concerned, above all, for a quiet life, whose ideological perspective we outline in the subsequent section, but the desire for independence to pursue one's own activities, or in the language of a somewhat different, but surely related, ideology 'to do one's own thing'.

Independence, the possibility of doing what one chooses, is vital to Mrs Butler, and it crept into many of her comments. Talking about her feelings when she was pregnant she remarked:

Oh, I don't like being pregnant at all, I absolutely loathe it. I think the worst thing about it is you feel your body is not your own, you have to lead such a healthy life, because you've got to look after this child. No dissipations. I feel ever so guilty if I sort of drink too much, or smoke like a chimney when I'm pregnant, and I think this is the worst thing about it as far as I'm concerned.

Likewise discussing their financial situation since the third child she commented:

I always feel better off when I'm earning a bit of money on my own and spending my own money. I don't like feeling too dependent on my husband. Its rather silly I suppose. I never buy anything frivolous on his money, you know. If I want something that I consider is a bit of a personal frivolity, well I use my own money for it.

An active life also demands openness and flexibility. Mrs Butler's comments about planning illustrate how she tries to remain open to an opportunity that presents itself, and her answer below provides a clear contrast to Mrs Kowski's response to the same question. Asked whether she made plans in advance or took things as they came, Mrs Butler replied:

Well, I think I plan in advance to a certain extent, but I try not to exclude opportunities that come along. I try to make the best of any opportunity that comes along, even if they interfere with the plans, shall I say.

These ideas and beliefs have had very definite implications for Mrs Butler's ideas about having children. In the first place it was not especially important to her to become either a wife or a mother, for she did not particularly like the idea of being tied to the house and, as we have described, she already had a satisfying job and plenty of activities. Asked what she had thought marriage would be like, she remarked:

Well, I didn't like the idea of being a housebound housewife much; I wasn't all that keen on the idea of getting married from the point of view of being a housewife. I got married to John because I wanted to live with him, I think, you know, more than wanting to be a housewife.

Nor did she think that having children can have been all that important to her 'because I suppose I wouldn't have married him otherwise, because there was this question that we might not have been able to'. Elsewhere she commented about this possibility, 'I think he did worry about that, but I didn't. I didn't mind one way or another, you know, I wasn't all this child mad until I had one.' Once she started having children she began to enjoy it a lot, but the prospect of her children leaving home does not appall her, 'I don't think I shall mind, I think I shall be quite pleased.'

In view of her husband's anxiety about whether he was fertile they decided to try and start a family straightaway, and their first child was born a year after they were married. Neither of them had initially any very definite ideas about how many children they would like, though 'I don't think we ever envisaged having more than three or four.' But once they had one they were keen to provide him with a companion, particularly because he had a relatively minor handicap and they felt that 'at least with a brother or sister of his own he will grow up with some playmate who won't notice that he has a handicap and it will give him self-confidence to be the older one'. Though Mrs Butler became pregnant again very quickly, she had a miscarriage; however, she was more successful with the next pregnancy and ended up with a gap of only two years and four months between the first two children. By this time she was getting quite a lot of enjoyment out of having the children, as she did from her other activities, and she wanted to go on and have another: 'I thought let's have plenty and then stop having them.' As she said, 'the more the merrier'. Part of the reason for having another was the interest a new child provided, and it was Mrs Butler who made the remark that we quoted in the previous chapter when accounting for her desire to have a third that:

Its a rather more-ish business having children. They are all entirely different from each other. Its awfully interesting to see what they turn out like. It seems a ridiculous idea for going on having them because you're getting a different one each time, but its very compulsive, you know.

The remark also reflects the importance she attaches to individuality. Equally important, though she does not directly refer to it in her account of her intention to have a third, must have been the fact that she found it easy to cope with the 'demands' of children. Talking of the difference having the third child made to their lives she said:

Well, it didn't change them all that much, actually. If you've got one baby you might as well have half a dozen, you know, all about the same age. It didn't make any difference really at all.

A moment later she added, 'Having two babies is just like having one.' This was one reason why there was no point in having a large gap between the births. Once the activity was started she liked to get on with it till it was done, then she could do something else.

Mrs Butler's sense that babies could be coped with easily, and that the attention and daily care children needed did not tax her competence or capacities was not, however, the result of any lack of concern for their upbringing on her part. As several of her remarks have already suggested she tried to do a lot to develop her children's skills and abilities, and engaged in quite a few of their activities. She also thought having children was quite a responsibility. When she was asked whether she had any anxieties about being a mother she replied:

Yes, I do in a way. I think it's quite a big responsibility. I don't think anxiety is quite the right word, though. I'm not really frightened of failing as a mother because you can't do more than your best, you know. You try and give them everything you've got and if that's not enough, well its not your fault, so I'm not anxious about it. But I do think its a big responsibility. I give quite a lot of thought to the children and their problems.

Indeed it was her concern to do the best for her children that was the reason why she had decided to stop at three. It was not her own capabilities, but finance that was the limiting factor (a restriction that appeared to have been reinforced by her husband). After the third,

I still wanted more, I would still have liked more, but we'd got three boys, and you've got to educate them somehow, and we worked out that with three boys, when they all got to secondary school that would be £1,000 a year, and we thought that's as much as we could cope with for the time being so we stopped. But there was always in the back of our minds the idea that we might have another or some later on, so that there was a bit of a gap in the eventual education expenses, but I don't suppose we shall in fact have any more.

But the reference to finance is not a result of any great concern to enhance the family's material standards. A remark illustrates this, 'I don't spend anything much on clothes, I shop for myself and the family at Marks and Sparks, but its all a matter of relative values. I could spend more if I wanted to.'

Mrs Butler's desire to avoid a further pregnancy was not all that strong, as her comments indicate, because of the pleasure she would get from having another child. However, she was unlikely either to plan another pregnancy, since she felt that at 41 she was getting too old for having more children and her husband did not seem to share her enthusiasm for having more, or to have an accidental one through carelessness or ignorance, given the importance she attached to being capable (a pregnancy due to failure of the method cannot be ruled out since she was using the cap). Her account of contraception when she first married is illuminating in this respect. She consulted her doctor and got herself fixed up with the cap before marriage though this was not really necessary then in view of their plan to try and have children straightaway. So, 'We sort of tried it out', but they never used it much till after the third child was born, since she wanted the children quickly. They then began to use it regularly.

Like the ideological perspective that stresses collective values the concern for an active life is striking for the marked lack of interest either in increasing one's material standard of living or one's position on the social ladder. The point of contrast between the two is the relative emphasis on collective versus individual values: a contrast that suggests that whilst the former ideology is likely to be more common amongst the working class, the latter is likely to be more common amongst the middle class. However, in contrast to the desire for a better future or more possessions, the desire for an active life is likely, as we have already suggested, to be the ideology of those who do not have to worry about material possessions or status, who have in that sense 'made it'. Yet it is not the ideology of the ambitious who themselves succeed, but of those who positions are already well-established, who are accustomed to their position in society, and have been brought up to it. Hence, it is the ideology of the middle and upper reaches of the middle class rather than that of the lower middle class or upper working class.

Though less attention has been paid to this ideological perspective in general terms than to the two previous ones we have described, there have been some studies that have discussed a way of thinking similar to the one that we have outlined here, which tend to portray it as the ideology of the 'traditional' middle class, especially of those in the professions.[33] Mrs Butler was herself the daughter of a successful and established middle-class family, though not a professional one. She was the only child of a farm manager who managed three estates, including the one on which they lived, for a member of the aristocracy, 'and he managed the land that was let out to tenants and farmed the land at home'. As a result of their rural life she felt that she had numerous opportunities that she would not be able to give her children. Her father appears to have had a forceful personality and she was very influenced by his ideas. His character emerges in her account of how he discouraged her from marrying a man almost twice her age who was looking for a wife:

My father was very much against it. He could see what was going on, which I couldn't. He said, 'this bloke's had a look at you, you know, he thinks, well she's got fat legs, but she's very capable, strong and healthy looking, she'll do you know'. I was absolutely outraged 'cos I thought this was all right, but anyway in the end my father convinced me that I shouldn't be in too much of a hurry.

Her comment that she was very pleased, soon after, to have escaped from his 'staid life' sums up succinctly her own ideology.

V: The quiet life

To those who regard an active life as important, the knowledge that children make demands upon their parents' time, energies and attention does not present an intrinsic obstacle to having children (sometimes the reverse), although if the individual has other activities and interests which seem to conflict with having children he or she may, nevertheless, have no children or only a small family. To those, however, who espouse the fifth and final way of thinking that we want to outline that same knowledge makes having children highly problematic. In this way of thinking the concern is to avoid the demands and difficulties that any activity involves: to keep the tasks of living, and in the case of family life, the burdens of having children and caring for them, to a minimum. Life is felt to be too complicated, too demanding, too problematic, and the task of satisfying all that is expected of one seems impossible: all one can do is to try and get through it with as little pain as possible. This desire for a 'quiet life' is not however, simply the antithesis of the desire for an active one, for the underlying ethic of the quiet life is negative, and in that respect it should be counterposed to all the ideological perspectives we have outlined, for they all take a positive form. In contrast satisfaction in the quiet life comes solely from reducing unhappiness or displeasure: it is an ethic of negative utilitarianism.

Those who seek a 'quiet life' expect little from life other than trouble, and feel themselves to have little control over what happens to them. This makes conformity in daily activities vital. Conforming to what is expected is important because it avoids trouble and becomes the only reason for acting at all. Hence an important feature of this way of thinking is the sense of constraint and obligation it involves: a sense that one does something because it is expected and considered necessary, not because one wants to. Life is full of what one *has* to do, not what one *wants* to do. In consequence, a desire for a quiet life breeds certain features of the 'ritualism' that Merton has described, in which the individual 'continues to abide almost compulsively by institutional norms' and is characterised by 'over-conformity' and 'over-compliance'.[34] It also creates a desire to avoid conflict, since conflict means trouble and difficulty and makes demands upon the individual, as well as a concern for independence – a desire to be free of interference, which is very different from the concern for freedom and independence of those who seek an active life.

It might be thought that the logic of this ideology, when applied to family life, would be not to have any children at all on the grounds that having children will inevitably increase the burdens and tribulations the individual has to face, just as its logic elsewhere might seem to be to do nothing. But not having a family is itself liable to provoke trouble and difficulty and engender sanctions for deviance, and would therefore be counter-productive. The solution vis-à-vis family life as in other things, is to conform. To get married, and to have children, and to accept that it is important to do so, but to keep family size to the lowest normative figure, and not to have the births too close to minimise the burdens babies impose. Those who desire a quiet life are also likely to be anxious not to have more children than intended, and to feel strongly about the spacing of births too. On the other hand, dislike of conflict may mean husband and wife do not resolve any differences of opinion about family size, if they exist, and this, together with the reluctance to act, makes the chance of inefficient use of birth control quite high.[35]

Mrs Walker illustrates the salient characteristics of this ideological perspective. Married over eleven years before, she had two children, a girl of 9 and a boy of 4, when interviewed. She was 20 when she married, and her husband was 21. Both had been working as nurses in the local hospital, and her husband had qualified as a S.R.N. some six months before they married. Mrs Walker continued to work part-time once she was married, but stopped when she became pregnant for the first time, a pregnancy that ended in a miscarriage. She had not worked since.

Life for Mrs Walker is dominated on the one hand by a sense of constraint and obligation and a desire to conform, and on the other hand, by strong feelings that life is troublesome and difficult and little can be expected from it. The sense of constraint and need to conform emerged in many of her answers to questions about herself and family life. Asked whether she had any particular ideas about bringing her children up she said: 'Well, you've got to bring them up as best you possibly can, haven't you?' (many people talk of *wanting* to bring up their children as best they can). A moment later, talking of her husband's feeling about the children and family life she conveyed the same sense of constraint: 'Oh, I don't know', she commented, 'I don't really know how to say anything about that, I mean, when you've got children, you've got to do the best you can for them.' But the constraints and obligations extend beyond the children. Questioned about how often she went out with her husband she said:

Oh, well, about every month or so, if we can make it, you know. Or if there's anything special on, we make an effort and go. We try and get out together, and I think you should. I don't think you should stop in all the time.

Later asked whether she and her husband had worried about the cost of being married she said, 'It wasn't any good worrying. We were married, and we had to make a go of it.' Her assessment of her husband's situation at work, though it may be realistic, again emphasises how constrained life seems to her. Talking of whether she had any regrets about her own or her husband's education she remarked, 'No, I don't think we could better ourselves. I think we've done the best as we can. He can't go further than what he is at the moment.' So too do her remarks about how she and her husband got on when they were first married, as well as suggesting her dislike of conflict, 'Oh very well', she commented, 'We never had any rows or anything. We just used to carry on, and plod along the best we could.'[36]

They 'plod along' in the face of what to her seem to be a sea of perpetual troubles and difficulties, as many of her comments about having children bring out. When asked whether she thought having children changed her or her husband as people she replied:

I don't know, I think – I don't think they change – I don't think they change yourself. I think if there's been a lot of worry, I think – well, I've had a lot of worry with my two children, and I think that they – I think that if there's a lot of worry you get sort of tense and nervous and that, but that doesn't change you as a person. I think that they bring their big share of worry with them, and I find if you get worried, you know, perhaps you don't talk together quite so much, you probably just sit, you know, but it doesn't change them altogether apart from that.

Children, she believes, bring their continuing share of anxieties. Asked whether she had any anxieties about being a mother, she had this to say:

Oh, yes, when they're ill sometimes I get worried. I think that does make you anxious. Just ordinary little everyday things, you know, you find you get anxious over. Especially perhaps when the children don't really want to go to school, and then when they set off at nine o'clock, you worry until twelve comes, and wonder if they've been all right. I think that life's always got something to be anxious over when you've got children. I mean when they come out at four o'clock, you never know what's happened between two and four.

To worry when children are ill, is not unusual: the opposite; to have such a continuing and dominating anxiety is far less common. Mrs Walker seemed to expect and even look for trouble. When asked whether she thought that having children was a burden and not worth the trouble, she replied:

Well, I think they're definitely worth the trouble, whatever trouble they bring. They're definitely bound to be worth it, aren't they? I think they are, although you never know what trouble your children are going to be in. But whatever trouble they got into, or are going to get into, I would always stand by them, and I would never, you know, turn them out or anything. I'd always, you know, help them as much as I could. But I wouldn't say that they had been a burden to me.

Not surprisingly, given how burdensome family life seems (though she denies it), if she can avoid any responsibility (which she cannot usually with the children, given the need to conform to what is expected of her as a mother) she is pleased to do so. Asked who paid the bills when they were first married she said, 'Oh, he did. He always has done, and I hope he always will.' And she does not have any high expectations of her life. As she said when asked if she made plans in advance, or took things as they came:

Well, perhaps normal plans, you know, well, just sort of everyday things. I'll say to myself probably next month I'll do this, or something like that, but I never, you know, build high hopes of anything.

When she married, Mrs Walker 'wanted a family' and, like many others in the sample, saw children as an obvious and inevitable part of marriage and family life. She replied, when asked whether she thought having children was one of the most important things in life, 'Well, I think when you're married, everybody wants children. I don't think it would be a home if you didn't have a family. I wouldn't be without my two.' Nevertheless, though having children is essential to her role as a wife and mother, children bring her trouble and difficulty, and this had definite implications for her ideas about how many children she wanted and the spacing of the births she intended. Here is an exchange on the question of how many children she had wanted that brings this out.

INTERVIEWER: Why not more than two, do you think?

MRS W.: Well, I don't think anybody could put up with more than two children. At least I know I couldn't.

I: Why?

MRS W.: I'm not all that keen on babies.

I: I mean, what is it do you think that . . . ?

MRS W.: Oh, there's lots of things that put me off having another one.

I: Well, is it having them, or . . . ?

MRS W.: No, its not actually having them its just, I think, when you've got them, oh dear, you know, getting up in the night, and all those sort of things that puts me off. And when I see other people now, you know, one or two have got grown up, and I see people with babies in prams, that's just you know – and I think to myself, oh I'm glad I haven't got any more, especially when you hear them crying and that, you know. No, we always just wanted two.

Her account of her preference for having a three year gap between the two children makes the same point.

No, well I mean, if you've got one baby, and then you go and have another one, it must be absolutely dreadful, especially when you think you have two screaming babies at once. I couldn't bear that. I just couldn't bear it. I like to get – have one, get that settled and get that organised, get that so it can feed itself, and so on, and dress itself, before I would think of having another one. I couldn't possibly have two babies, not close together.

As she said, she finds it harder to manage two children than others do a larger family. Questioned as to the differences it would have made if she had four children she replied:

I probably wouldn't be sitting here now. I don't know what would have happened to them if I'd had four. I'd probably, oh, I don't know, I reckon that would have drove me mad. I couldn't bear it, to have more than two. As I've said before, I just –I wouldn't have the patience, I don't think for a start. Well, I wouldn't want any more than two. I don't know how people manage, when they have, you know, when they've got several children. But there again they do seem to manage better than probably what I do with two.

Mr and Mrs Walker had not used any contraception until they had had their second child. When they first married, 'it didn't enter into our heads to use anything at all', and they hadn't discussed the matter, despite the fact that they knew about birth control, 'Just tell me who doesn't.' She couldn't really explain why they had not used birth control either then (she was somewhat unclear in what she said about when she wanted the first child), or once the first child was born, when she did not want another child straightaway, though she said at one point 'I don't believe in it.' It may have been that her husband wanted the children relatively quickly and she did not want the bother and trouble of raising the matter and coming to a decision about it, when she regarded birth control as distasteful. (In fact, she had some difficulty getting pregnant again after the first child was born, which explains the gap of nearly four years.) Once the second child was born, however, her husband started using the sheath and has been doing so regularly since then: an appropriate decision from her point of view since it means that she does not have the responsibility for birth control and yet, hopefully, avoids, the unplanned pregnancy she would regard as such a disaster.[37] Certainly she expected that they would be successful with the method.

It is tempting to regard the ideas that Mrs Walker conveys, and her reactions to having children solely in terms of personality: to think of her as a passive, anxious, pessimistic person, (which no doubt she is if we want to think in terms of personality characteristics) and to assume these characteristics are stable and inherent. Yet our interest is in the way of thinking that she manifests, a way of thinking that she shared with other members of our sample, which we have identified and described in terms of the constellation of ideas that it involves, and which is not just a question of isolated, distinct personality traits. Moreover, there is no reason to think that a proclivity to this way of thinking is innate, but is rather a reaction to certain experiences in life, either in childhood or later. Unfortunately, Mrs Walker did not convey a very clear picture of her childhood or of her family background, so we have not outlined it here.[38]

We would suggest, however, that this way of thinking is particularly likely to arise either when avenues of satisfaction that are highly regarded are blocked for some reason or other, or when conflict exists between two different ideological perspectives to which no solution seems possible. Merton, of course, suggested that ritualism has its origins, in 'acute status anxiety' and 'anxiety over the capacity to live up to institutionalised expectations'. 'It is', he says, 'in short the mode of adaptation of individually seeking a private escape from the dangers and frustrations which seem to be inherent in the competition for major cultural goals by abandoning these goals and clinging all the more closely to the safe routines and the institutional norms.'[39] He expected to find it in the lower middle class:

For it is in the lower middle class that parents typically exert continuous pressure upon children to abide by the moral mandates of the society, and where the social climb upward is less likely to meet with success than among the upper middle class.[40]

Nevertheless, his remarks though suggestive, cannot be directly transferred to the ideological perspective of the quiet life. In the first place, though certain features of ritualism, as Merton describes it, bear a striking resemblance to our account of the desire for a quiet life, there are important differences. Not only is Merton describing a 'mode of adaptation' which takes as its starting point behaviour rather than ideas, but he also makes a distinction between cultural goals and institutional means. As a result he puts weight on certain defining characteristics of the mode of adaptation to which we do not attach much importance. Indeed since we would not give much emphasis to that distinction, or assume that there is a value consensus within the society, in anything other than a very narrow sense, we would not want to say that those concerned for a quiet life have completely given up the cultural goals that are accepted by others. The important point is that *priority* is given to avoiding pain and difficulty, in a world that is full of tribulations. And that means that a desire for a quiet life, though it may arise because individuals cannot succeed in what they attempt, can arise when the achievement of *any* 'goal' is frustrated, and can occur at any position in the social structure. To the extent, however, that it can result from ideological conflict it is more likely to occur in periods of rapid social and ideological change.

VI: Contrasting implications

We want to summarise this account of the different ideological perspectives that exert a direct influence on childbearing by contrasting the perspectives in two ways. First, by presenting the different characteristics in summary form in a single table. This we do in the table on the following pages.

Second, by considering briefly whether, and in what way those of differing ideological persuasions are likely to deviate, either intentionally or unintentionally, from the norms that we outlined in the previous chapter, about having children. The most likely form of deviance of those committed to a collective ideology is that of going beyond the limit of four children by having an 'unintended' pregnancy that could well result from half-hearted contraceptive use in the face of low cost and considerable pleasure that would result from having another child. Deviance amongst those of a materialist persuasion, where it occurs, is likely to take the form of having only one child, or none at all, if financial circumstances are especially difficult. Hence the frequency of deviance amongst this group will relate to general economic conditions. Accidental pregnancies that raise family size above the level of four, though not impossible, are unlikely.

Deviance of any type is probably least likely amongst those concerned to make a better life, since they are not only highly unlikely to plan a large family, or to use contraception carelessly or inefficiently, so that family size goes above the level of four (or even three), but are also unlikely to choose to have an only child, since for them the arguments for having at least two are likely to seem cogent. Having no family at all has also been unlikely amongst this group up till now, since those subscribing to this way of thinking are likely to be relatively conformist in their behaviour, because of their desire for status and success. However were norms to change, and the idea of having no family to become more acceptable, then they would be obvious candidates for deciding to remain childless.

In contrast, those committed to an active life are most likely to deviate in their childbearing, and to deviate with definite intent, given their individualist beliefs, and the potential attractiveness to them of a variety of other activities and interests. Deviance amongst this group is most likely to result in families of only one child, or none at all, but it may produce families above the norm either by specific intent, or by a failure to take sufficient care with contraception, since an extra child may seem no great problem. Finally, those anxious for a quiet life, though especially keen to conform, will not necessarily do so, for if they encounter obstacles and difficulties in the process – problems such as getting hold of contraception, persuading a spouse that a small family is desirable and so forth – they are likely to give way to them.

We have made no attempt in this chapter to establish the distribution of the different ideological perspectives within the pilot sample. There are two reasons for this. First, since the research was not designed to obtain ideological information of this type it is not possible to identify the nature of an individual's ideological commitments in a satisfactory manner in all cases. Second, and more importantly, our assumptions about the importance of uncertainty, negotiation and change in ideas about family life make any attempt to establish the proportions expressing commitment to a particular ideology at any one time of little value in itself. It is the dynamics of the process of family building that are crucial, and it is to these that we now turn.

Images of family life

	The collective life	The material life	The better life	The active life	The quiet life
Basic features of ideology	Importance attached to group solidarity and support, and to love and understanding. People are more important than things. Social order is fixed and stable and one's place within it clear.	The aim is to improve one's material standard of living, and therefore to increase income. Jobs are judged in terms of wages, and social differences are seen as a question of income.	Goal is to improve the individual's social status, and to move up the social ladder. Orientation is to future and its planning. Hard work and sacrifice are means to success. Ideology is individualist and meritocratic.	An active, busy life is all important and gives pleasure – a life in which one uses one's abilities to the full. Independence, autonomy, and freedom are crucial. Ideology is individualist but little concern for possessions or status.	The aim is to avoid trouble and pain. The individual tends to conform, to avoid conflict, and to have low expectations of life, except of trouble. Life brings a sense of constraint and obligation.
Parental role	Giving love, support and care, and encouraging give and take, tolerance and understanding in family.	To provide children with the best or better than they had materially and help to ensure a better material life for them. Education may be a means to do this.	To give children a chance to move up the social ladder, by giving them care, attention, guidance and a good education.	To provide children with the opportunity to develop their abilities and interests, and give them freedom and independence for an autonomous, active life.	To satisfy the demands children make and conform to the norms in bringing them up.
The value of children to parents	Crucial to closeness and solidarity of family unit. A chance to give and receive love and support.	Create the home and family life that serves as normal unit of consumption and legitimates materialism.	Provide opportunity for a better life (one parents may not have had themselves).	A source of pleasure as a new/different, and engaging activity.	Allow parents to conform, but essentially a burden.

Ideas about family size	A larger family (4) considered desirable, to generate companionship and give and take in family, and to have more chance to give care and support.	Small family – 2 or 3 at most – to allow family to maintain material standards and give children 'the best'.	Small family (2) to allow children to be given enough care, guidance, attention, and good education.	Either larger, say 3–4, since children are easy to cope with, or small 1–2 to permit other activities.	Small (2) to keep burdens of children to a minimum, but to conform to norm of two.
Starting a family	Little reason for postponing first birth.	Postpone to accumulate possessions and (perhaps) give some chance to enjoy consumption first.	Postpone first birth to husband resources as an adequate preparation for family life.	Little reason for postponing unless to fit in with other activities such as job.	Defer till present less burden – i.e. have accommodation and some money.
Spacing	Close for companionship and solidarity.	Not much reason for long space, and short gap gets wife back to work sooner.	Not too close to give enough care and attention to each child.	Little reason for long spacing except to fit in with other activities.	Long spacing to spread burdens of child care as thinly as possible.
Birth control	Pressure to avoid unplanned births not very great since children bring satisfaction.	Pressure to avoid a third birth, if not planned, not as great as does not make too much difference. Will try to avoid a fourth.	Strong pressure to avoid unplanned births, since planning is important and children need a lot of care, and so forth.	No great pressure to avoid one extra birth, unless interferes with other activities. Can be competent if wish.	Pressure to be efficient, but use involves decisions and activity that are antithetical.

11.   Uncertainty, negotiation and change

I: Uncertainty and change

Deciding how many children to have is often, or even usually, a far from simple matter. It would be wrong to assume on the basis of the argument in the previous chapter that most people have absolutely definite ideas about family size and spacing, or that their ideas never change. On the contrary individuals have to take numerous factors into consideration when making decisions about having children whatever their ideological persuasion, and may often feel uncertain about whether or not to have another child, or when it is best to have one. They may, moreover, change their ideas as their marriage and life cycle progress and they encounter new circumstances. It is, as a consequence, usually difficult to predict the fertility of any particular couple, group or population, and there is considerable potential for significant demographic change over time in the aggregate level of fertility.[1] It requires only a fairly small proportion of a population to be uncertain in their ideas about having children, to make the overall level of fertility potentially quite indeterminate. This does not mean that it is easy to manipulate an individual or a group's fertility, since the influences on decision making are complex: it does make the task of prediction very difficult.

A person may feel uncertain about, or change his or her ideas about having children for a number of different reasons. In the first place, even if he or she has a definite and undivided commitment to a particular ideological perspective, has a definite idea of the sort of family life that he or she wants, and also happens to share both with his or her spouse, the couple have the problem of putting their ideas into practice in the face of the realities of their own skill, vision and capacities, and of a specific set of social and economic circumstances, which may either make issues of when and whether to have a child far from clear-cut, or else may lead them to change their ideas about having children from time to time.

Uncertainty in ideas about having children of this sort is likely to stem from lack of information and knowledge about the likely nature of the various factors that have to be weighed up in coming to any decision. If, for instance, a couple are anxious to maintain a high standard of living but feel that they cannot accurately anticipate the future level of the household income, they may well feel that they cannot decide between having two or three children at the present time and postpone the decision as long as possible. Equally, others may well feel that they do not know how much pleasure they will get from having children or how well they will be able to cope with them, and wait until they have a better idea before coming to a definite decision about family size. In consequence, we would expect that uncertainty arising from such sources would diminish over time. On the other hand, even if a couple feel they can make good enough predictions about the factors they want to include in their calculations and have definite plans about how they will build their family, unexpected circumstances may well make them change their minds: exceptional difficulties in pregnancy, an unexpected decline in income, or loss of employment may all produce change in plans for having children, even though they do not produce change in the ideological objectives the couple is trying to realise.

Uncertainty and change in ideas about family size and spacing, may also stem from the problem of interpreting the implications of particular ideological perspective for family life. This is less common, since for most people the underlying ideological concerns and the image of family life, are closely connected and the implications of the ideological concern for the sort of family life that is desired (though not how it is to be achieved) are little questioned. Nevertheless some people may question the implications of a particular ideology for family life, by, for instance, considering whether it is compatible with having some children, or whether it demands a larger or smaller family, and so may feel undecided, or change their minds about having children. An example illustrates the possibility.

Married almost eleven years when interviewed, with one daughter aged three and a half, Mr Jones was by then a successful business man with his own company, employing his wife in the business. He had had a large number of jobs previously, mainly less successful attempts to establish his own company. His opinions about the sort of life he wanted were forceful and definite; he was strongly committed to the idea of an active life and emphasised the importance of 'experience'. This was reflected in his conception of marriage: 'We decided not to make a stale marriage, to see things, to do things. Whatever we decided we did together; we wanted to enjoy it.' The important thing he felt was to live life to the full: 'We like living, we like life. The average person just lives an existence.' For him living meant the antithesis of the steady or routine life: 'We don't go in for the average idea that steady living is the answer to life. Experience is the answer, and doing things as you feel. The average person is in a rut.'[2]

When Mr Jones and his wife first married they did not regard having children as an important part of their image of a desirable life, so 'we decided to have no children'. Simply to have had children would not, they thought, have been sufficiently interesting. As Mr Jones put it: 'You must have a hobby for a healthy mind, business is a hobby; just to bring up a family, you go to seed, to rot.' And later 'the important thing in life is living rather than having children'. Children were for him, doubly problematic: on the one hand they did not play an important part in his image of a satisfying and full life; on the other hand they would directly interfere with his chance of achieving that life. Asked why he did not want any children when they first married, Mr Jones responded, 'who likes responsibilities?' and his wife added, 'to tie yourselves down straightaway'. Their desire not to have any children was sufficiently powerful to make them obtain more than one abortion when Mrs Jones became pregnant due to irregular contraception. Nor did Mr Jones' views on the secondary importance of children and their practical disadvantages change once they had a child. He described the effect of having a child on their lives like this:

We stopped a lot when we had Joanna. A child comes along and brings your life to a stop unless you can get a baby sitter, and even then we were reluctant to leave her too often. It makes things more difficult. If we want to go abroad we have to think of her education.

Elsewhere he commented, 'You're no longer free, you've got responsibilities. You can make it a joy, a pleasure, but it isn't really.' Later he added, 'We want to start living again and including her, going back to enjoying things. She's big enough to enjoy things now.'

Nevertheless, despite Mr Jones belief that children interfered with an active life he had eventually made a definite decision to have a child, for though that belief did not change, as circumstances changed, the implications of his ideological perspective began to look rather different, and having a child came to seem almost a necessary step in the realisation of his own values and beliefs: an experience that he could not afford to miss. Two factors contributed to this change of interpretation. First, his financial and material circumstances improved as he became more successful in business. This, presumably, gave him more of an opportunity to obviate some of the disadvantages of having a child; it also gave him less excuse for not starting a family. Second, there are strong suggestions that with the passage of time, Mr Jones began to find it more difficult to realise his desire for an active and interesting life, and that, having tried out and done many things, to have a child came to seem a new way of adding interest to his life. Not only did he indicate that their married life before having a child was not completely satisfactory, 'Life wasn't interesting enough; it was a bit dull', but he also suggested that a child offered the possibility of a new source of interest and pleasure. Asked, for instance, what he thought a good daughter would be like he said, 'Sweet and charming, well behaved and an absolute devil.' Having exhausted other possibilities he turned to children. Hence, when he accounted for the decision to have another child by saying that he wanted to give his wife 'a full life', the comment seems to apply to himself.

This change in the way in which Mr Jones interpreted the familial implications of his ideological commitment is of interest because of the change in plans and decisions about having children that it involves; it is also of interest for two other reasons. First, because it shows the way in which the connection of particular ideological perspectives and particular images of family life as a whole are not fixed and unalterable but may be subject to individual variation, and change over time both individually and culturally. We suspect, for instance, that in the past, especially among certain social groups, a material orientation may have been associated with a rather different image of family life, one in which having a large family was considered advantageous.[3] Second, it is a variation of a common process in which the specific implications of a particular ideology are tied to, and seen to be conditional on an individual's social and economic circumstances including age.

It is apparent, for instance, that those who are committed to a materialist orientation usually expect to have a period before they marry in which they enjoy themselves in a relatively indulgent and hedonistic manner, as well as a period immediately before and after marriage in which they accumulate assets before starting a family. Hence individuals are likely to expect that they will feel differently about having a family at different stages of their lives.[4] This was brought out in several interviews, although it was not a topic that we specifically attempted to explore. Mrs Osborn, with three children, had not wanted any when she had married, and all three pregnancies were unintended and a source of bitterness and much resentment. It was clear, however, that part of the reason why she had not wanted any children then was her feeling that neither she nor her husband were 'ready' for a family. They were both 19 when they married, wanted to have a reasonable material standard of living, and did not feel they could afford a family (her husband's pay was low, partly because of his age; she was working and did not want to lose her income; they had not had time to accumulate money for a 'decent' home and the usual furnishings); nor did they feel that they had had the chance to have the enjoyment of youth before settling down to family life. (Mr Osborn liked to spend money on a car; she liked to spend money on clothes; they both liked to go out.) Though Mrs Osborn was far from sure that she would have definitely wanted a family later on, she expected that she would have had one, and undoubtedly would have felt very differently about children if she had not ended up with three unplanned pregnancies before she had been married four years. The main difference between her ideas and those of Mr Jones (apart from their ideological commitment) was that he had initially expected that he would not have children (though he never ruled out the possibility) whereas Mrs Osborn had expected that she would; in that respect not only was Mr Jones more deviant in his ideas, but also his interpretation of the implications of his ideology changed, whereas hers did not.

Third, uncertainty and change in ideas about family size and spacing may also stem from inconsistencies in an individual's ideological commitments, inconsistencies that may be a source of psychological conflict, and are likely, sooner or later, to produce doubts and uncertainties about family size and spacing. Such inconsistencies are most likely to occur when an individual adheres to crucial components of more than one ideological perspective. The point is clearly illustrated by Mrs Edwards whose ideas we describe in the final section of this chapter, who was both anxious to achieve a better life for her family and also adhered to key components of a collective ideology. It is also illustrated by the divided commitment of other members of the pilot sample. A common form amongst women, to which we have already alluded, is adherence to certain elements of a collective ideology in ideas about family life (in more than a notional way) combined with a concern to maintain and enhance the family's material standard of living.

Fourth and finally, uncertainty and change in ideas about family size and spacing may all stem from the need to work out ideas about having children with one's spouse. The sources of potential disagreement between husband and wife, which have implications for childbearing and require negotiation, are numerous. Even if spouses share a common ideological perspective, and have a common image of family life they may not agree about precisely how this is best realised in face of the practical constraints they encounter throughout marriage, since the interests of the two partners will not be identical. Others, though they share a common ideological perspective may interpret its implications for family life somewhat differently, or feel rather differently about them. This is especially likely amongst those seeking an active life who may have different interests and activities and are likely to be unequally affected by having a family. And, of course, those who marry will not necessarily share a common ideological perspective. The different orientations of Mr and Mrs Edwards provide one example of this.

Both inconsistency and conflict in an individual's ideas about having children, as well as any sort of disagreement between spouses about the matter, are especially important for they are likely to have an adverse effect on contraceptive practice, as the Edwards also show. When spouses do not themselves know how many children they want or cannot agree amongst themselves how many they will have, then contraceptive practice is likely to suffer, and this is, of course, important demographically.[5] But there are exceptions. Mrs Marsh, who had two children, could see a number of arguments for having another one: her husband wanted a larger family and she not only admired and respected his image of family life, but also wanted to please him; moreover, though feeling increasingly dissatisfied with her role as wife and mother, she seemed to feel that having another child might make it more interesting. Nevertheless, she could not bring herself to make a definite decision to have one. In many instances such indecision and uncertainty might well have resulted in carelessness and irregularity in contraception, particularly if the individual in question was taking the responsibility for contraception. This had not happened. Mrs Marsh's commitment to a better life, though not undivided, was potent enough to ensure that the prospect of an *unplanned* pregnancy was totally alien to her. The solution was to leave contraception in the hands of her husband, who, whilst he would have liked more children, also liked to please his wife, and would not have stopped using contraception unless she had said explicitly that she wanted another child. He himself would have preferred her to use a female method of contraception but she adamantly refused, being clearly unwilling to allow her own doubts and uncertainty to have their head.

Some idea of the pervasiveness of uncertainty and change in ideas about family size and spacing can be guaged from responses to certain of the survey questions. It is not surprising, for instance, in view of what we have said about the range of sources of uncertainty in ideas about having children, to find that when they first marry many people do not feel very definite in their ideas about how many children to have or when to have them. Though most husbands and wives when asked the size of the family they wanted at that time gave a specific preference (the wording of the question encouraged a specific answer), only about half the husbands and wives claimed to have been *very* definite in their ideas about family size at that time, as table 11:1 shows.[6] By the time of the interview there was more certainty, as we would expect: even fewer did not state a specific preference about family size and, as the same table shows, about three-quarters of both groups said they felt 'very definite' about how many children they wanted.[7]

TABLE 11:1   *How definite spouses in the survey sample felt about the number of children they wanted, when they first married, and at the time of the interview*

	At marriage		When interviewed	
	Husbands %	Wives %	Husbands %	Wives %
Very definite	48.0	50.3	74.5	74.8
Fairly definite	23.0	22.2	14.6	12.9
Not very definite	26.6	25.7	10.1	10.8
Don't know	2.4	1.7	0.8	1.4
Total	100.0	99.9	100.0	99.9
	(N = 248)	(N = 288)	(N = 247)	(N = 286)

Note: This question was only asked of husbands and wives present in the interview.

TABLE 11:2 *How definite spouses in the survey sample felt about when they had children, when they first married, and at the time of the interview*

	At marriage		When interviewed	
	Husbands %	Wives %	Husbands %	Wives %
Very definite	30.9	33.5	61.2	60.2
Fairly definite	26.8	28.2	16.5	19.7
Not very definite	38.2	36.6	20.1	18.1
Don't know	4.1	1.8	2.2	1.9
Total	100.0	100.1	100.0	99.9
	(N = 246)	(N = 284)	(N = 224)	(N = 250)

Note: This question was only asked of husbands and wives present in the interview; it was not always asked if no (more) children were wanted, but the instructions on this point were not clear.

The extent of uncertainty about the timing of births was even greater. Approximately one in three of the sample claimed they had either not known or thought when they would like to have their first child at marriage, and some 15% of husbands and 8% of wives said they either did not know or had not thought about the spacing between births. Moreover, only 31% of husbands and 34% of wives said they had felt very definite when they married about the timing of births (see Table 11:2).

In view of the degree of doubt that a large proportion of the survey sample claim to have felt initially about family size and the timing of births, it is interesting that the proportions with different reported 'ideals' or 'desires' at marriage and at the time of the interview, was not higher. Stability in ideals about family size over this period was quite high, with 73% of husbands and 71% of wives (who stated some ideal for both points of time) reporting the same ideals for when they married as at the time of interview.[8] In comparison, some 62% of husbands and 59% of wives reported the same *desired* family size for the two points of time. However, such figures have a number of limitations; on the one hand they are likely to underestimate the extent of change in ideas about family size and spacing up to that time, since they do not tap intermediate changes in ideas, and those relating to marriage are retrospective, which almost certainly means that past ideas are portrayed as closer to current ones than they actually were. On the other hand, like those relating to definiteness, they tell us nothing about the sources of the changes (or uncertainty) in ideas.

The survey does, however, provide some other fragments of evidence about the relative importance of different sources of uncertainty and change in intentions about having children. First, there is the discrepancy between a person's ideals and preferences about family size. A willingness to admit that ideally one would like a different number of children from the number you now intend suggests at least some division in ideological pressures and some 28% of husbands and 31% of wives (who indicated particular ideals and preferences) did not have the same ideal as desired family size. There was more similarity in ideals and desires at marriage (23% of husbands and 24% of wives did not give the same figure). This could mean that as marriage progressed more of the sample felt they had to compromise their ideals in the face of their own specific circumstances, or it could simply be that in retrospect any divergence between ideals and desires is often forgotten.

Second, there is some evidence about the extent of consensus about family size and spacing between spouses (though not of agreement in overall ideological perspectives). As Table 11:2 shows, although when interviewed only 14% of spouses who indicated a preference for family size were not in agreement with one another some 23% had different stated ideals, and the discrepancy between one spouse's *desired* family size and the other's *ideal* was even greater. Thirty-eight per cent of husbands' ideals at the time of interview differed from their wives desired family size at the same time, and 39% of wives' ideals differed from their husbands desired family size then. The difference in ideas about family size at marriage was probably even larger. Eighteen per cent of couples did not state the same family size preference for marriage, and 27% of them did not state the same ideals. The discrepancies between one spouse's stated ideals and the others preferences at that time were about the same as at the time of interview (37% and 38% respectively). However, these figures are likely to underestimate the divergence in ideas because of the retrospective nature of the material, and the tendency for spouses to present a picture of consensus and agreement amongst themselves (which affects all the figures about agreement). The effect of this was almost certainly heightened by the joint interview situation. Moreover, the figures tell us little about how much negotiation was necessary to produce this consensus of opinion. The fact remains that despite all the factors that may have reduced the figure, something like two couples in five show some divergencies of opinion about what we might call basic numbers. The possibilities this situation contains for negotiation and change, if not conflict and uncertainty, do not need to be emphasised.

II: Negotiation

Ideas, plans and actions about family size and spacing are obviously affected by the negotiation between husband and wife on these matters. Negotiation between spouses will itself influence the extent and degree of their disagreement about having children, the respective uncertainty and change in their ideas, as well as their contraceptive use. It is conventional to argue, for instance, that if plans are to be carried out effectively and if birth control is to be used in a regular and careful manner, then spouses must discuss, and reach agreement on questions of family size and spacing and make 'joint' decisions about having children and birth control.[9] And the assumption tends to be that where the role relationship between spouses is segregated (the couple shares fewer activities, have their own spheres of decision making, and discuss things little) then contraception will be less efficient than where the relationship between spouses is more a 'joint' one. However, the argument raises a number of problems. In the first place, though it is true that some studies have produced correlations between role segregation and contraceptive use, the interpretation of those correlations is a far from simple matter, particularly because family size preferences tend also to be correlated with role segregation. Second, the measurement of role segregation is itself problematic. On the one hand, the degree of 'role sharing' in some activities does not coincide with that in others, or the amount of communication with that on another. On the other hand, as we found ourselves, segregation in decision making does not necessarily coincide with segregation of activities or communication.[10] Third, there is no reason to believe that discussion is always necessary or valuable in securing agreement about family size and spacing or in producing efficient contraceptive use; not only may husbands and wives come to agree without directly discussing the matter, but discussion may even be counter-productive, entrenching positions and increasing conflict and hostility. Moreover, when and if agreement is reached on a particular subject, discussion may be infrequent, yet this cannot be taken as a sign of poor communication or disagreement.

We would suggest, instead, that there are a number of different ways in which issues relating to having children may be negotiated, which may variously help or hinder agreement between spouses on this subject. We can get some clue as to the different modes of negotiation about having children if we consider some common ideas about this process. Four beliefs were either implicit or explicit in the accounts that were given by the pilot sample of how they tried to settle questions of family size and spacing with their spouse. The first belief to which we alluded in the previous section, relates to the outcome of negotiation; it is that spouses should agree about how many children to have and when to have them. The belief seems to be one facet of a more general belief that spouses should agree, or come to some agreement about the salient matters that affect their lives together; it is apparently part of the idea of being a couple or a family unit that you agree on key issues. The idea was manifest in a number of the comments on the negotiation between husband and wife about having children. Where differences existed about family size, for instance, one spouse would invariably point out that they agreed that they would have a particular number of children and then consider the matter again. Its salience was reflected, too, in the consensus between husbands and wives in stated ideals and preferences about family size. However, the precise force and meaning that is given to the belief, as to others, varies. For some couples agreement on almost all matters is clearly all-important, and the very idea that there could be any difference of opinion is unacceptable. For others agreement is necessary about certain matters like how many children to have, for pragmatic reasons, yet this is not held to require that spouses should have similar ideas or opinions, and the existence of consensus in ideas and beliefs is considered unimportant.

The other three beliefs relate to, and affect the way in which negotiation is conducted, as well as the importance that is attached to securing agreement. The second is that having and caring for children is primarily women's work. This belief may make a wife feel that since she has the work of looking after children then she should have much of the say about how many to have and when to have them, and may make her feel resentful if she feels forced by her husband to have more than she feels she can cope with. Equally, it is a belief that may make a husband feel that it is primarily up to his wife how many children they have and when to have them, and certainly that he should not make his wife have a child she does not want. It was noticeable how often the wives in our pilot sample reported that when there was some disagreement about family size, their husbands had said that it was up to them whether they had another child or not. Indeed, if we considered only that evidence alone, it would appear that wives had their way about having children far more often than husbands. Yet the third common belief is one that encourages wives to pay attention to their husbands views about having children and allows his preferences about family size to exert a considerable influence. This is the belief that wives should, on this matter as on others, do what their husbands want. In an extreme form, the idea is that the husband is the sole, power and authority in the family and has the right to make all the main decisions within it. Young and Willmott give an example of such an attitude in relation to having children.

When one husband said to us, 'We wanted the baby' his wife retorted, 'You may have done; I know I didn't'. Asked later if she wanted more children, she said, 'I don't want them but you can't tell. You ought to ask him (pointing to her husband) about that. He's the guvnor.'[11]

In our own sample, the idea was more subtle. It was not that the husband was held, either by himself or his wife, to have the right to make decisions within the context of family life without taking his wife's interests into account; but that the wives (and no doubt some husbands expected this), made it clear that they felt that they wanted to try and please their husbands, and that they should try and do what they knew their husbands wanted. It was this particular belief that appeared to play an important part in Mrs Abbott's willingness to have more children because her husband seemed happy to do so, although she herself had begun to feel that they had had enough.[12] It was also apparent in numerous other comments made in the pilot interviews when wives made it clear that they did not like the idea of going against their husband's wishes about family size and spacing.

The fourth and final belief that influences negotiation about having children is that family size and spacing are a matter for joint decision between spouses: that husband and wife should not only come to agree about what to do about having children but should do so by discussing the matter and sharing the decision making. This belief was manifest in the frequency with which decisions about having children were said to be joint ones (that is either taken by both, or sometimes by one and sometimes by the other; some 68% of all the sample couples fell into this category at marriage and some 64% when interviewed) and in a variety of comments which emphasised how the spouses had discussed questions of family size and spacing and had decided the matter together.

These four different beliefs are not necessarily incompatible in their implications, if couples happen to have the same ideas about having children, and it is possible for a couple to accept all of them.[13] Often, however, one or two of the ideas tend to dominate an individual's approach to the process of negotiation. Hence, for one person the important thing is that women have the right to the final say in any decision making about having children, since they have to care for them (a belief that may be held alongside the belief that husband and wife should come to a joint decision), whilst for another the important thing is that both spouses should decide the matter between them. Where spouses' ideas about the process of negotiation coincide, the process of negotiation itself is facilitated even if they do not have the same ideas about having children, and has a more predictable outcome, with more importance attached to the husband's ideas, the wife's, or both.[14] In some cases, however, spouses' ideas about the process of negotiation themselves differ, and this makes negotiation more difficult and the outcome less certain. A noticeable and interesting combination was one in which the husband felt that family size and spacing was up to his wife, if their views did not coincide, and the wife was anxious to please her husband and realise *his* wishes. The logic of this combination would seem to be that the wife should have the number of children that the husband wants, when he wants them; but his stress on her views in the matter may make the situation far from clear cut. The negotiation between Mr and Mrs Draper, who had four children, illustrate this. When they first married they had similar ideas about having children, both wanting a largish family, and decided to have a child straightaway. However, Mrs Draper found the birth very difficult and despite her dislike of one child families (she had been an only child and had not enjoyed it), she 'decided I wouldn't have any more'. Though her husband wanted more he left the decision up to her, as she said, 'he didn't mind, he left it entirely up to me', explaining a moment later 'he knew I was frightened to have another one, and he wouldn't force me to have another one. It was my own decision to have the next.' It was, she said, her daughter's behaviour that made her change her mind; she became 'bossy and spiteful', so Mrs Draper thought, 'I'd have another brother or sister, you know, and it would show her she's not the only one around.' Her husband was delighted with the second child, 'he was thrilled with him, to think he'd got a boy', but said the decision whether to have another was hers. 'He didn't mind how many I had, or didn't have. He just left it to me.' However, this type of comment is deceptive in two respects. First, it is clear that, although Mr Draper would not have wanted to force his wife to have a child, and felt that she should made the decision to have one, he certainly made his own desire for more children explicit. Second, since Mrs Draper was aware of what he wanted, and apparently liked to please him, his views were a significant factor in her decision making. Her account of the decision to have the fourth child brings out both these points. Mrs Draper had felt she had had enough after the third, 'Well, I didn't want any more, that put me off altogether, and – but he did, he said "yes, let's have another one." And then one day I said, "Oh, all right then".'

The outcome of the process of negotiation will also be uncertain when ideas about negotiation conflict markedly with ideas about family size. If, for instance, a woman is anxious to have a large family because she values solidarity within the family, and also wants to please her husband who himself wants only a small family, being concerned about the family's material standing, then the process of negotiation is likely to be especially difficult, since the woman will feel torn between her desire to please her husband and her own wish to have a large family. The same problem can occur with those anxious for a quiet life, who may be torn between a desire to please their spouse, and their desire to have a small family: a conflict that Mr Edwards had to face as we describe below. This type of conflict is also likely to lead to inefficiency in contraceptive use.

As the examples suggest it is probable that ideas about negotiation between spouses are associated with the ideological perspectives that we outlined in the previous chapter. We would expect, for instance, to find that those adhering to a collective ideology would believe that where differences of opinion on questions of family size and spacing arise, they should either be primarily a matter for the wife to settle, or else that the wife should try to please the husband. This means that even if husband and wife adhere to this particular ideological perspective they may not have the same views about the process of negotiation. On the other hand, those believing in the importance of their material standard of living are likely to think that the husband's opinions in the matter are all-important since it is he who brings in the money and is the economically productive partner. The opposite is probably more often the case amongst those anxious for a better life. Since the role of the parents is to provide the right sort of attention, care and guidance, then the conventional importance attached to the woman's role in bringing up the children may well lead to a sense that the wife's feelings about having children should be especially attended to, though importance is also likely to be attached to joint decision making, as well as achieving some agreement about the matter. The concern for an active life is likely to be associated either with a belief that a woman should have considerable say in decisions about having children, since she is more likely to have to give up other interests because of family life, and/or an emphasis on the importance of coming to a joint decision, given the belief in equality. Pragmatic agreement rather than essential similarity in beliefs would be the aim. Finally, those concerned for a quiet life are likely to be especially anxious to agree about family size and spacing, and also to accept the wishes of the other in order to achieve a quiet life, though, as we have said, if this means having more children this will conflict with the desire to avoid more than the minimum burdens of childbearing and rearing.[15]

III: A case study of the dynamics of family building

The points that we have made in the two previous sections can best be illustrated by considering one couple in detail in order to show the complex interplay of forces in negotiating and attempting to come to some decision about questions of family size and spacing.

Mr and Mrs Edwards had married in 1955 and had two children when interviewed, a girl of nearly ten, and another of nearly eight. Mr Edwards was then working as a maintenance engineer doing bakery maintenance. He was 34 when he married, his wife 20. The couple differed considerably in their ideas about family life and had not found any stable solution to their disagreement. It was difficult to predict with any certainty whether they would have any more children or not.

Mrs Edwards was the oldest of two daughters. Her father had had 'all sorts' of jobs, 'mostly labouring, he wasn't skilled at anything'. He hated work and 'always tried to get off'. Her mother had had a rough life living with him, and her parents were now divorced; her father had remarried and her mother now had a 'small business'. Mrs Edwards regards her own childhood as unhappy 'due to my father, he used to knock us about sometimes'. She went to Grammar school until 16 and then left to work as a comptometer operator. She did a year at night school, 'book-keeping, shorthand and typing', and worked herself up to 'supervisor' and 'trained girls'. She left work when she was six months pregnant.

Mrs Edward's ideas about family life incorporated key elements of more than one ideology and had potentially contradictory implications for having children. In the first place, her education and the parental influence it reflects (presumably maternal) had left their mark: she believed that one should try and make a better life and work hard to that end. Asked whether it was better to make plans for most things in life she said, 'You've got to make a few plans and try and carry them out, and better yourself all the time, but you can't plan far into the future.' 'Life', she said, 'is what you make it.' And she was anxious to make a better life for her children. Asked how she wanted to bring her children up she said:

Well, I'd like them to have the best of everything; no, that's not quite true, I don't think, I don't mean moneywise, but I think its sweeter what they've earned, not to win the pools or anything like that, not money easily earned. I'd like them to get a good education, not that we can afford to send them to a private school, because we can't, and that's out of the question, we've never even considered that, that's never even been discussed, because we know that we can't afford to send them to a private school.

Though this passage suggests she would have liked to be able to afford a private school she was pleased with the schools the children were at; she commented, 'the education that's very good, and we hope they'll do their best'. But what she does for them at home is important too:

I think you can still help them to better themselves. I mean Hilary will sit and read, and I watch her at night, if I give her soap powder, she'll stand and read it, and I help her with things like that – when you get things out of the 'fridge, margarine and butter and all things that she hasn't seen, and when you've got a little spare moment; not that there's ever any.

Nor should the children always get what they want or be indulged too much. It is important she remarked, 'Not to say "yes" to everything they want, because I don't think that's kind.' She felt certain, and was probably accurate in her assessment, that the older daughter who was 'top of the class' would get to a Grammar School; she was less confident about the younger one:

Well, the big one take the 11 plus next year, she's bound to get through and go to my old school. And the young one, we don't really know much at all about. She goes in patches, she'll burst through and fly ahead, and then she'll go down.

Mrs Edwards did not have any high expectations for herself or her husband. She felt that they had had to work hard for what they had got, 'We've always had to work for everything, haven't we? We've never had anything given us', and she had tried to encourage her husband to do better. She described how she had made him leave an earlier job, 'I had to push you into leaving, I kept on and on.' But as these comments suggest, doing better is a very uphill task and she sounds resigned about their position. Of her husband's job she remarked, 'Oh it suits him, he wouldn't be happy doing anything else. Making, that's your life isn't it?', but she is not really satisfied and wishes her husband had had a better education, 'I wish he had a chance to further his, because I think he's got quite an intelligent brain, and he hasn't had the opportunity to use it.' Her hopes are pinned on her children.

Nevertheless, Mrs Edward's desire for a better life for her children was not the only salient feature of her ideas about family life. She had not, as one would expect from those ideas alone (and there is no reason to believe that her concern for a better life developed after having children, and every reason her case for thinking that they were the result of socialisation at home and at school), wanted to have only two children. She had originally wanted four, and had not fully relinquished that desire when interviewed. It was a rather different set of ideas, apparently more emotionally based, more difficult to subject to reason, and not perceived by her as being in any way contradictory with the first, that seems to have made her want four children. For Mrs Edwards the argument for having four children was that she continually experienced a 'terrible craving' for more children, which she found difficult to explain. Having children and babies and being pregnant simply seemed very satisfying and it was this that made her want more. As she said, 'I adore children, if I see a baby I just grab it.'

It was possible, however, to see that much of the source of pleasure from having children was that they satisfied her desire to give love and care to others, and that children and babies had come to have a powerful symbolic significance for her: they symbolised giving love and support to others and being surrounded by an atmosphere of love and care. What was important to her in the family was that family members should love one another and support one another. Hence, in this respect, her ideas manifested a commitment to a collective ideology: though one with strong emotional overtones, and one that gave more attention to the importance for her of giving and receiving love, than on the way in which her children would develop in consequence. The importance she attached to giving and receiving love emerged in numerous comments. Of babies she said, 'Babies I adore, so helpless and that, and you can love them can't you.' Of herself she said, 'I'm very feeling. If anybody's got any troubles they always come and tell me. I'm very soft-hearted, and I love animals. I'm crazy on animals, and I hate cruelty to anything.' Of disciplining the children she said, 'Oh we do smack them when its necessary, but they need a lot of love.' Her eldest daughter's own 'tender-heartedness' is clearly a source of satisfaction. When her husband said the eldest daughter cried easily Mrs Edwards commented:

But you can get round it with a little bit of love. She's very tender-hearted the biggest one; if she knows I don't feel too good she'll go and get a bottle and make me a hot water bottle to put round my back, and pad me round with cushions.

There is, then, a potential contradiction in Mrs Edwards' ideas about having children: both a desire to go on having babies who are helpless and need her love and care, and a desire to make a better life for her children that should, in theory, encourage her to keep her family small. Nevertheless, the contradiction was not visible to Mrs Edwards who found the desire to have more children very powerful. Had it not been for her husband's rather different ideas about family life, and certain unexpected contingencies (her difficulties during pregnancy), the potential conflict in her ideas might have had no consequences for their decisions about having children, (though if she had had a larger family her desire for a better life might have brought dissatisfaction later on). As it was, both these factors strengthened the case for a small family.

Mr Edwards' family background was rather different from that of his wife. His father was a gasworks manager, 'It was only a very small place, only him and two blokes, or him and one bloke, I believe, I forget now, but he used to do the lot . . . charts, and coal, he was up eleven hours, he used to sleep on the couch, I can see him on the couch now.' He was the last of four children, and described his childhood as happy 'on the whole' and added, 'I had a lot of restriction, I had a Victorian mother, like chapel three times on Sunday and things like that, and well, it's a good thing, I don't say it's all wrong, but strict discipline and that.' He was happiest when he was on his own, 'living out in the country with the rivers and fields, and that, well, I was really happy, and I could wander around with the dog and amuse myself'.

Mr Edwards emerged in the interview as a cautious, conservative person whose ideas about family life were a marked contrast to those of his wife. His overriding concern was for a quiet life, free from interference. Getting married and having a family were a necessary part of life, he thought, but did not seem to offer great attractions for him. Being able to escape on his own gave him most pleasure as some of his comments about marriage bring out. Mr Edwards had been slow, and probably reluctant to marry. He had been engaged for six years to another girl before meeting his wife, but eventually decided that the first fiancée, 'didn't suit, there was something wrong anyway' (perhaps his wife was more forceful than she had been). His first concern was to find 'a place of my own', which would allow him the necessary freedom for a quiet married life:

Well, my idea of marriage was that I'd have a place of my own, free and easy. I like to do things my own way, I could work on it, like we have done, and have the children, the children eventually come along. I didn't know for sure at the time, but I hoped they would, and we'd settle down and do all the things I wanted to, and have me shed, and . . .

The shed at the bottom of the garden (like children for his wife) had a strong symbolic value for him, and was his refuge – a refuge that his wife resented, since he spent a lot of time there. She remarked at one point, that he was selfish, 'in the fact that I'd like you in here with me sometime, but you'd work out in the shed. In the first years when we were married, you were out there every evening.'

Mr Edwards was not especially concerned either to enhance the family's material standard of living or their social status. His concern with money was primarily to avoid debt and any financial difficulty rather than to improve their material standard of living, as the following passage brings out:

All our money and things are always accounted for, because its easier. We don't get ahead of ourselves or anything like this. We're always in pocket sort of thing, aren't we? We don't fall behind our way of living sort of thing. We don't really claim big things. We're insured for life, and the house.

Though at times he showed some concern for status, it was not very marked. When his wife said, 'you say sometimes we're a cut above the council houses, don't you, you often say that?' his comment, 'Yes, it's a different way of living isn't it? I like to live off me own back, not half off other people', along with other remarks he made, indicated that it was less moving up the social scale that was at issue, than a concern for independence. Mr Edwards, though content with his own job, did echo his wife's desire that their children should do their best and stressed that they should work hard, 'I don't want them to get anything the easy way, I just want them to work for it or else', but such ideas did not appear to have the same significance as they did for his wife (indeed, at times they mainly seemed to reflect a desire to agree with his wife). Social conformity and avoiding trouble were far more salient as his description of a good daughter brings out:

My idea would be that a good daughter, say, if she's 16 say, she should like all the other things that girls like of her age: dresses and music and all the rest of it, and she could have one or two late nights out, and come home when she's told to come home, and things like that.

Having children was far less important to Mr Edwards than to his wife, though as we have already indicated he saw them as an obvious and integral part of marriage. The idea of having no children does not, however, greatly upset him:

I would've probably compensated for no children by doing, say, doing more fishing. I would've had more time, because things couldn't get so dirty and messed up, because the children wouldn't be about, we'd've had more time for going about.

Here the concern for the way children mess things up reflect his desire for peace and quiet, and the implication that he would like a more *social* life, was quickly picked up and rejected by his wife who commented, 'But you never were a one for going out.' His reply, 'No, but fishing and things I used to do, didn't I?', reinforces the picture of someone who values isolation, privacy, and freedom from interference.

As we would expect, Mr Edwards thought that a small family was desirable. At one point he said, 'two or perhaps three children' were the ideal, at another that 'it's better to have two children'. Apart from his comments about the mess children make, his emphasis was primarily on the financial burdens. Asked what difference it would have made if they had had four children, he replied: 'It would affect the parents and the household, making ends meet, whereas with two children, you've got a fairer chance of making things meet easier.' This remark again brings out the nature of his financial concern: to avoid overburdening himself.

Given these divergent ideas about family life, with a direct disagreement about the size of family they should have, the need for negotiation between Mr and Mrs Edwards was considerable, yet it was likely to prove difficult. On the one hand Mr Edwards was anxious to avoid the burdens of a large family but also wanted to please his wife; on the other hand Mrs Edwards, though thinking she had the right to decide questions of family size and spacing, was likely to experience some conflict in her ideas about having children, given their potentially contradictory nature, when faced with her husband's different views about their desirability. Hence though their views about the process of negotiation complemented one another, both were likely to experience conflict in their ideas about having children, as a result of the contradictory-implications of their own beliefs.

Initially, however, disagreement could be avoided by the negotiation of an agreement that they would have, according to Mr Edwards, 'at least two', which satisfied his general desire to avoid conflict as well as the belief that spouses should come to an agreement about having children. This still left the question of when to have the first child, about which they differed. On this matter, as we would expect, Mr Edwards gave in to his wife, not wanting to face conflict with her, and presumably feeling that the question of the timing of births was less important than the number. In fact, when they had first married they had agreed that they would not have the first child straightaway and Mrs Edwards was happy about this. Mr Edwards reported that 'we said we'd wait three years before the children come'. Soon, however, Mrs Edwards started to change her ideas, and persuaded her husband that they should have one sooner.

In the first six months I couldn't have cared less about having children, but after six months I went nearly mad to have one; you used to talk and say, 'if you want one really as bad as that we'll try', and then we didn't have one; we tried for nine months before I fell for Susan.

The gap between them about when to have the second child was somewhat less, but still demanded negotiation. Mr Edwards remembered 'we said we'd wait two years'; but again his wife came to feel rather differently. This is her account of what happened:

Well, the doctor said we mustn't have one for two years. When the little one was not a year old, and she was a big baby born, and she wasn't a baby very long, well, they were both big babies weren't they, and I wanted another baby right there and then, when Susan was six months old, and we tried again, we tried for eight months, before I fell for Hilary, and Susan was only a year and a month when I did fall for her.

Again Mr Edwards gave into his wife's pressure. As she said, 'you said "no, it's too soon to try" but I crazed you, I used to cry because I wanted another one so badly, and I've had it since, since I had the second one'.

The real issue, however, was whether to have more than two children or not. Their divergent ideas, and the way in which they attempt to agree with each other's, and yet fail to do so, is brought out in an exchange about family size. The exchange begins with both putting their different arguments about family size:

INTERVIEWER: What do you think made you intend to have two at least?

MR E.: Well, my idea was that I thought one would be spoilt and get the best of everything, whereas two can learn off each other.

I: And what did you think?

MRS E.: Oh, I didn't want to have one, I wanted four.

I: How strongly do you think you wanted four at the time?

MRS E.: Oh, very strongly.

I: And what about you?

MR E.: Oh, I was more cagey, I was thinking of the cash side of it.

MRS E.: Well, I didn't care about the cash then, I was so, oh, I definitely wanted four, I had a terrible craving.

It is interesting that here, as elsewhere in the interview, when asked to explain his ideas about family size, Mr Edwards starts by justifying having two children rather than one, as if he would have preferred only one if that were more socially acceptable, and continually had to rehearse the argument for two in order to convince himself. Having put their respective cases they then attempt to show to each other than they are not completely ignoring or rejecting the concerns of the other. Mr Edwards hastens to add that he would like more children if it were not for the question of finance: 'Mind you, I was prepared to have ten children if there was means and ways of providing for them and looking after them.' Mrs Edwards then shows that she, too, is not unconcerned about the financial side of having children with the reply (which we have quoted at greater length elsewhere, see page 149). 'I wouldn't like a large family that had to go without, and I don't mean without everything, but I like to feed my children well, and I felt that if I hadn't got enough money to feed them I should be committing a crime, and I feel that way still.' Yet her financial concern is with meeting adequate standards unlike her husband's.

As the above extract brings out, Mrs Edwards can see arguments for having a small family, and it was she, not her husband, who started to change her plans about family size. The cause, according to her, was the difficult time she had with both pregnancies, which brought a new element into her calculations, and a new weapon for her husband in persuading her to stop after two. She nearly had a miscarriage with her second pregnancy and was ill throughout:

I know after the second one you said 'we can't go through that again', because I was queer the whole nine months, I didn't know if I'd lose it or not, the whole time. I was only five weeks pregnant and I nearly lost her. The whole nine months I couldn't hardly walk, I had all sorts of pains, and the doctor didn't know what it was, she couldn't do anything to help me, could she?

In consequence, she started to feel another pregnancy would be difficult, though at times she wanted another child very much.

Well, I had to keep going to the doctors because of my back, and I thought if I had to go through another nine months with all that weight to carry, what it would do to my back, I don't know how I would've got through the nine months. Sometimes I could hardly walk and we didn't dare try, did we? Although I did get those feelings again and I used to cry for months, for about three months at a time, I used to cry every day, because I wanted another one, from about the time the second one was about a year old, until she was about five; and I haven't had it, I've had it, but not severely, and I haven't cried about it. I've been miserable inside, but I haven't had these outbursts of tears.

It is interesting here that when she talks about having another one she does not (rightly) see her husband as any serious obstacle, and almost implies (wrongly) that he would have liked another child. One wonders, too, to what extent some of her difficulties during pregnancy were a result of conflict and ambivalence about having children.

Although their second child was almost eight when they were interviewed, Mrs Edwards was still not completely decided that she would not have any more children, and the uncertainty that both she and her husband feel about the matter (she because she would like another, her husband because he knows that if she wants to have one he will be forced to give in) is reflected in their comments about their current ideas about having more children. Asked how many children she thought they would end up with, Mrs Edwards replied:

I don't know, we haven't planned on any more. Well, if another one come along, I wouldn't be sorry. But if I had one more I should probably want two because of the age difference between them now, and I think one baby now would be a lone child and you'd want another one to keep it company, because I don't like children by theirselves.

To which her husband responded, 'You'd want two, but I don't think you'd have them – well, you don't know.' And his wife added, 'Well, you don't know do you.' A moment later, Mr Edwards said, 'I think we can safely say that we'll probably stick to the two, as far as I can see, anyway', to which his wife responded: 'Unless, well, it all depends how I feel, because when a woman's in a change of life, as I say, you can fall so easily, I mean it happens in such a lot of cases. I shouldn't like to have a baby then, because we'd be too old.'

Both feel they can get what they want *if* they want it; Mrs Edwards that she can have more children if she wants them, 'Well, if I want another one, I shall try to have another one'; Mr Edwards that he can avoid having another if he wants to, 'I think if I put my mind to not having one, then I could manage all right, but I think I have so far haven't I?' The trouble is that Mrs Edwards does not know what she wants and her husband, though he could exert his authority, is likely to defer to her wishes about having children, as he has done in the past. In consequence, the outcome depends to a considerable extent on her feelings. Certainly Mr Edwards defers to her on other matters apart from questions about having children. Talking about how they decide to spend the money he commented: 'What it amounts to naturally I say, "Oh no, we can do without that", sort of thing, but she gets it and I admit they are decent buys that we've got, you know.'

Mr and Mrs Edwards' uncertainty and their failure to resolve the question of family size is reflected, as we would expect, in their contraceptive practice. When their second child was born, they had 'decided to call it a halt for a little while', and Mrs Edwards got herself fitted with a cap. However, recently she had been taking chances and not using it, commenting, 'It wouldn't worry me if I had another one, not now, because I'm better than I was', and was using the cap less than half the time. But when she did not use the cap, her husband used withdrawal. Hence she affirmed by her frequent failure to use the cap her willingness to become pregnant, as well as her failure to decide whether she definitely wanted to; her husband by withdrawing when she does not, his desire to avoid pregnancy, yet his willingness to risk it by using an unreliable method. Neither side is willing to take a firm stand: Mrs Edwards to decide that she will or will not get pregnant, or Mr Edwards to ensure that she does not. The chances of an accidental pregnancy must have been quite high.

Of course, the uncertainty, conflict and change in this couples' ideas were greater than in many instances, stemming as they did not only from a divergence in ideological perspectives between them, but also from Mrs Edwards' acceptance of crucial elements of more than one ideology. Yet the negotiation process itself was less complex than it might have been (unsatisfactory though it was), since their ideas about negotiation complemented one another. Moreover, though their disagreements and inconsistencies were more extreme than many others face, the couple illustrate, nevertheless, the problems of negotiation that many encounter.

12. Controlling births

In the two previous chapters we have considered the implications of different images of family life for contraceptive use, arguing that the nature and degree of commitment to a particular image of family life, as well as the negotiation between spouses about questions of family size and spacing, are likely to affect the pattern of contraceptive use. In this chapter we want to consider contraception in a broader context by first, examining whether changes in contraceptive technology and in the availability and use of contraception exert an independent influence on patterns of family size and spacing, and second, considering some of the other influences on contraceptive use apart from a couple's intentions about family size and spacing.

I: The role of contraception

Men and women not only differ in their images of family life: in their willingness to invest time and resources in children and in what they regard as the important aspects of family life; they differ too in their ideas about contraception: in the extent to which they believe it is possible and relatively easy to control their childbearing, in their willingness to use contraception, as well as in their beliefs about who should be responsible for its use. Major changes have occurred in the means whereby reproduction is controlled during this century and these have, inevitably, been accompanied by significant changes in ideas about contraception. Though there are few societies where reproduction occurs unchecked, the means that are used to control childbearing and the degree of control that is exercised vary considerably. The revolutionary change of this century has been the development and increasing use of effective methods of contraception: methods of birth control that allow intercourse without conception. It is arguable, indeed, that the developments in contraceptive technology and the vast increase in the use of contraception within marriage constitute one of the most, if not the most radical social change of the century. The revolution in the lives of one half of the population, women, and the potential for further change is incalculable.

The increasing use of contraception during this century has been well documented. As Table 12:1 shows, the proportions of men and women in this country using contraception at some stage in their married lives has increased amongst all social groups. Of the few who still do not, some must be infecund.[1] Figures like this should not blind us, however, to the fact that

225

TABLE 12:1   *Birth-control practice in Britain*

(a) Lewis–Faning study

	Percentages who had used some type of birth control during marriage			
Date of marriage	Social class I	Social class II	Social class III	All social classes
Before 1910	26	18	4	15
1910-19	60	39	33	40
1920-4	56	60	54	58
1925-9	58	60	63	61
1930-4	64	62	63	63
1935-9	73	68	54	66
1940 +	67	53	47	55

(b) Population Investigation Committee study

	Percentages who had used some type of birth control during marriage		
Date of marriage	Non-manual group	Manual group	All socio-economic groups
1941-5	89	77	82
1946-50	88	86	87
1951-5	96	86	90
1956-60	94	89	91
1961-5	93	91	91

(a) In each case the figures for the most recent cohorts are lower because the couple had had a shorter period of married life in which to adopt birth control.

(b) The Lewis–Faning study included women whose first marriage had not terminated before the age of 45. The Population Investigation Committee study included only women with uninterrupted first marriages who had married aged under 35 years.

(c) Glass (1971, p. 191) argues that the Population Investigation Committee data is free from the understatement of earlier studies, which helps to explain the discrepancy in the two series.

Sources: Lewis–Faning (1949): Glass (1971).

by no means all those who do use contraception at some point in their marriage attempt to control all their childbearing or do so with complete success. Regular use of contraception throughout marriage, except when pregnancy is intended or conception impossible, is much less than we might expect from the figures for 'ever use'. Surveys both in this country and the United States show that at any time a fair proportion of men and women are not using contraception, even though they do not wish to get pregnant, especially early on in marriage; and that others, though using contraception, are doing so with less than perfect regularity, a picture that is illustrated by the figures in Table 12:2.[2] Moreover, even those who use a method regularly will not necessarily avoid an unwanted pregnancy, unless the method is 100% efficient in use, which none are. Indeed, though the efficiency rates of several methods are high, (that of the sheath has probably increased during the 1960s),[3] only the pill has a sufficiently low failure rate in use to make the chances of an accidental pregnancy at some point during marriage very low, given the length of time over which pregnancy has typically to be avoided.[4]

TABLE 12:2   *Whether birth control was used, reasons for non-use, and frequency of use, at marriage and at the time of interview, in the survey sample*

	At marriage	When interviewed
(a) Whether birth control was used		
Yes	33.4	17.2
No	66.2	81.7
Don't know/No response	0.3	1.0
	100.0	99.9
	(N = 290)	(N = 290)
(b) Reasons for non-use		
Wanted a baby	25.8	37.9
Ignorant	23.7	0.0
Carefree	28.9	12.1
Religion	8.2	6.9
No need/medical	3.1	32.8
Don't know/No response	10.3	10.3
	100.0	100.0
	(N = 97)	(N = 50)
(c) Frequency of use		
Every time	66.1	78.8
Nearly always	23.4	18.2
About 50%	6.8	1.7
Less than 50%	2.6	1.3
Don't know/No response	1.0	0.4
	99.9	100.0
	(N = 192)	(N = 237)

The shift in the methods of contraception commonly used during this century is again well-documented.[5] The major change has been the shift

TABLE 12:3   *Type of contraception currently used in 1967-8, or last used, marriage cohorts, 1941 to 1965*

	Year of marriage		
Type of contraception	1941-55 %	1956-60 %	1961-5 %
(a) Non-manual group			
Non-appliance only	31	15	18
Appliance only	47	42	40
Pill only	3	16	21
Appliance and chemical	11	20	14
Other combinations	8	7	
Total	100 (N = 118)	100 (N = 111)	100 (N = 123)
(b) Manual group			
Non-appliance only	52	37	35
Appliance only	30	33	33
Pill only	2	21	25
Appliance and chemical	5	4	2
Other combinations	11	5	5
Total	100 (N = 122)	100 (N = 167)	100 (N = 192)

Note: The sample includes only first marriages where the wife's age at marriage was under 35, and the table relates only to those who have used contraception at some time.
(b) The figures for use of the pill in the manual group include a few cases of pill plus appliance.
Source: Glass (1971), Table 4, p. 193.

from 'natural' to mechanical or chemical methods of contraception, which if correctly used reduce the chances of an accidental pregnancy, as the figures in Table 12:3 illustrate. The pill itself was first available in this country in 1961; however as our own study, like others conducted at roughly the same time, shows the pill had only attracted about a quarter of current users by the late 1960s (see Table 12:4) and the condom has been the most frequently used method throughout the post-war period, with a remarkably constant proportion of users up to the time of our study.[6] The same table also indicates that, as we would expect, few of the survey sample had used the pill when they first married (see Table 12:4) since even the 1960s cohort had mostly married when it was not prescribed widely. When interviewed, however, as Table 12:5 makes clear, more of the 1960s than the 1950s cohort were using the pill, a finding which reinforces other observations that the more recent marriage cohorts are more likely to be taking the

TABLE 12:4 *Main method of contraception used when first married, and the method currently or last used in the survey sample*

Method of contraception	When first married		Currently or last used	
	No.	%	No.	%
Abstinence	0	0.0	3	1.2
Withdrawal	14	7.3	13	5.4
Rhythm	7	3.6	7	2.9
Sheath	134	69.8	135	56.0
Cap	17	8.9	17	7.1
I.U.D.	0	0.0	0	0.0
Pill	14	7.3	62	25.7
Other	5	2.6	2	0.8
Don't know/No response	1	0.5	2	0.8
Total	192	99.9	241	100.0

Note: These figures are not directly comparable with those from other studies since they refer only to the main method of contraception used. This is one reason why the proportion using withdrawal is lower than in other studies. We understand that the I.U.D. was not prescribed in the area at the time, which presumably explains why one sample contained no users. Other discrepancies between our data and that from other studies are, we suspect, due to the inadequacies of our data collection.

TABLE 12:5 *Main method of contraception currently or last used, by cohort in the survey sample*

Method of contraception	1951-7 cohort		1961-7 cohort	
	No.	%	No.	%
Abstinence	1	0.9	2	1.5
Withdrawal	7	6.6	4	4.4
Rhythm	7	6.6	0	0.0
Sheath	56	55.7	58	56.3
Cap	9	8.5	6	5.9
I.U.D.	0	0.0	0	0.0
Pill	22	20.8	40	29.6
Other	0	0.0	2	1.5
Don't know/No response	1	0.9	1	0.7
Total	106	100.0	135	99.9

pill than earlier ones.[7] Though use of the pill has apparently increased since those studies were carried out, the long predominance of methods of contraception under the control of the man is striking.[8] Together the condom and withdrawal accounted for between 60% and 75% of current use of birth control, at the end of the 1960s, and the condom was more popular than the pill then, even amongst the more recent marriage cohorts.

In the light of such information about the methods of birth control commonly used, their efficiency and the regularity with which they are used, it should not surprise us to find that, though most people in the pilot sample wanted to limit the number of children they had, and clearly felt that they had some power to do so, most did not feel that they could necessarily avoid an unplanned pregnancy. While they might believe the method of their choice to be reliable, and believe themselves most unlikely to get pregnant (a feeling that seemed to increase as pregnancies continued to be successfully avoided), nevertheless the typical response to a question asking whether any more children were intended was invariably, (if no more children were wanted), something like, 'No, but you never can tell', or 'I don't intend to, but you never know', or 'Not if I can possibly help it.' We would expect, however, an increasing number of those marrying in the 1970s feel somewhat less uncertainty about controlling childbearing successfully.

Beliefs about the possibility and ease of controlling childbearing by contraception are dependent not only on whether the use of contraception within marriage is customary, but also on the nature of contraceptive technology. Methods that are easier to use efficiently enhance a sense of control – of this there can be little doubt. The interesting question, however, is deciding precisely what role changes in contraceptive technology and changing ideas about contraception have in accounting for changes and variations in patterns of childbearing. Is it the increasing capacity to control childbearing, as a result of technological developments, that explains the small families with which we are now familiar? Or is it an increasing public acceptance of contraception of whatever form that is the important factor? Or are both dependent on an increasing desire to control childbearing?

Attractive though the idea appears at first sight, the arguments against any thesis that assigns contraception much of an *independent* role in explaining patterns of childbearing are strong. Take, for instance, the claim that improvements in contraceptive technology, and the gradual diffusion of the new techniques throughout most of the population, have produced some of the significant reductions in the birth rate since 1850. Although the early stages of the reduction in the crude birth rate in the nineteenth century were associated, not only with increasing publicity for contraception generally, but with publicity for mechanical means of contraception in particular (though there were signs of a reduction in the more sophisticated measures of fertility before this), it is clear that the nineteenth century reductions in childbearing, where they were due to an increased use of contraception rather than an even later age at marriage, were primarily due to the use of non-mechanical methods of contraception, and not to the diffusion of new technologies.[9] Likewise, though the first signs of a reduction in the crude birth rate in 1965 seem to conveniently coincide with wider availability and growing use of the pill in this country, in fact the reduction occurred too soon for the pill to have had any significant role in the *initial* lowering of the birth rate since its use then was still very limited.[10] Again, it seems difficult to give contraception much of an independent role in accounting for any increase in childbearing during the century. The rise in the birth rate between 1955 and 1964 did not coincide with any withdrawal or rejection of certain methods of contraception. Arguments like this are further reinforced by the repeated failure of birth control programmes in developing societies. Providing men and women with effective methods of contraception is not enough to guarantee their use. Nor, as is indicated by a number of historical studies, does the absence of technically sophisticated methods prevent effective control of births.[11]

If we put the thesis rather differently, and argue that it is not changes in contraceptive technology *per se* that are crucial, but changes in the knowledge, of and willingness to use contraception, the argument is no more satisfactory as it stands. If, for instance, we consider the nineteenth century transition in fertility this, as we have already pointed out, was effected by the use of methods of contraception that were already widely known. Moreover, in as far as there was an increasing willingness to use contraception, as indeed there clearly was, this change was itself primarily the result of an increasing desire to have smaller families. It is tempting, therefore, to claim that whether contraception is used and the regularity with which it is used, depend almost entirely on intentions about family size and the strength of those intentions, and that developments in contraceptive technology and changing ideas about contraception exert relatively little independent force. Certainly we have assumed in our own study that preferences and desires about family size are a major influence on contraceptive use. It is clear, however, that both ideas about contraception and developments in contraceptive technology should be given a significant part in any explanations of trends in childbearing, especially over the long term.

In the first place, it seems likely that knowledge of, and availability of contraception, as well as the nature of contraceptive technology, can influence ideas about family size, even though they are not sufficient in themselves to produce low fertility. Ignorance, difficulties in obtaining contraception, and poor technology are likely to predispose people to the idea of large families, so that a large family will tend to be taken for granted, whilst the contrary conditions are likely to encourage people to consider the *possibility* of greater control of their childbearing, though they will not ensure the desire for smaller families. Second, developments in contraceptive technology can have a direct effect on patterns of childbearing, independently of desires and intentions about family size and spacing, since if less effective methods are replaced by more effective ones, there will be a reduction in the number of accidental pregnancies, even if there is no change in ideas about having children. Third, our own data shows that a couple's intentions about family size and spacing are not the only influence on contraceptive use. On the one hand, though we take it for granted that those who want to get pregnant will stop using contraception, there were occasional comments in the pilot study indicating that this was not always the case. Sometimes couples who had got used to using contraception found it difficult to stop when they decided to have a child. One woman for instance, who had been using the safe period said it became 'habit forming', and when they decided to have a second child they still tended for some months to have intercourse only in the safe period 'because you feel happier then'. She commented, 'although you want a child somehow you put it off'.

On the other hand, though we also rightly assume that those who do not want to get pregnant are more likely to use contraception and to use it regularly than those who do not, the evidence from our own and many other studies shows, as we have already indicated, that the desire to avoid pregnancy does not ensure regular use. Consider the simple point of whether or not contraception is used at a particular time. When interviewed those members of the survey sample who did not want any more children were certainly more likely to be using contraception than those whose actual family size was below their desired family size, but not all of them were. The change, as Table 12:6 shows, is somewhat greater for women than for men. Likewise those who did not want any more children were somewhat more likely, as the same table shows, to be using contraception 'always' than those whose family size had not yet reached the desired level; though here the change is even smaller.[12]

Of course, we did not have an adequate measure of the 'strength' of intentions and it could be argued that it is this factor that accounts for the discrepancies between intentions and use that we have described.[13] We doubt, however, whether it would entirely, though it is likely that those who feel more strongly about their intentions do more to realise them. We cannot claim, therefore, in our view, that contraceptive use is simply a question of realising intentions about family size and spacing. If it were, the notion of an unplanned pregnancy would have little meaning. There can be no doubt that accidental or unplanned pregnancies occur even to those who are most concerned to prevent a further pregnancy. To resort, for instance, to some concept of unconscious desires or intentions to account for every unplanned pregnancy does not seem a very fruitful exercise.

TABLE 12:6 *The desire for more children, whether contraception was used, and the frequency of use, at the time of the interview*

	Husband		Wife	
	More children wanted	No more children wanted	More children wanted	No more children wanted
(a) Whether using contraception when interviewed				
Not using contraception	30.8	10.4	34.1	9.2
Using contraception	69.2	89.6	65.9	90.8
Total	100.0	100.0	100.0	100.0
	(N = 78)	(N = 163)	(N = 88)	(N = 185)
(b) Frequency of use of contraception when interviewed				
Not always	25.9	19.9	29.3	17.3
Always	74.1	80.1	70.7	82.7
Total	100.0	100.0	100.0	100.0
	(N = 54)	(N = 146)	(N = 58)	(N = 168)

Consider, for example, Mrs Kowski's unplanned pregnancy nine-and-a-half years after the birth of her second child. She and her husband had been using the safe period in a stringent manner (they had intercourse only during the two days after the completion of her period) for some thirteen years believing of the safe period that:

If it's followed, it is quite infallible; it's as good as any other method. But some people don't want to limit themselves to those two days, that's the general reason why they get unwanted children.

By then, perhaps not surprisingly, she and her husband 'were quite certain that our family was complete and we never dreamed we'd have any more children'. Her horror at finding she was pregnant again was considerable and indicates the strength of her desire not to have any more children. Asked whether she ever wished family life was different in any sort of way, she had this to say:

Well, I suppose we were pretty satisfied until the third one came along, and then we can't help wishing that we hadn't gone in for the third baby. And in fact I'd go so far as to say that had we known he was on the way earlier than we did, we might have done something to prevent his coming along, but I was five months pregnant before I knew I was, and I felt so fit and well, and then suddenly the bomb dropped, you know, and one evening we were going out, and I went to put on a skirt that I hadn't worn for ages, and I suddenly realised Gosh, I really must be pregnant, and I thought that at 40, I was already well on with the change, and I realised what a silly fool I am, how could I possibly think so, and of course I'm pregnant, and I was, and I went to my doctor, and he confirmed it within 24 hours, but that I was already five months, and at five months nothing could be done; and within a few weeks I realised how I was swelling, and I just couldn't believe how I hadn't noticed it, and I hadn't and there I was, and we resented it bitterly, and I was terribly depressed, and I had almost suicidal tendencies, but, however, we thought about the other children and we've done the best we could to stay together; we even thought of divorce, it nearly broke us up, but we've settled down a bit now that he's growing up, now that he's three years old, we realise we have to, its a responsibility to be faced and we're doing it, but sometimes we still have flushes of unwillingness coming on and we still resent it. I'm 43 and my husband's 52, and we realise we shouldn't have this thing thrust upon us in our old age, because we feel it was thrust upon us you know . . .

Despite the reference to 'going in' for the baby it is hard to believe from this lengthy outburst or from all Mrs Kowski says elsewhere (her ideas about family life were described in Chapter 10) that this pregnancy was in any way intended, or that she did not want to avoid a further pregnancy. It is unlikely that had she not been using a method of contraception whose efficiency is so dependent on the regularity of the menstrual cycle that she would have become pregnant. The fact that both she and her husband were Roman Catholics explains the choice of method and reinforces the interpretation that it was not some unconscious desire that produced the contraceptive failure. The case, therefore, not only illustrates that unplanned pregnancies can occur even where the desire to avoid a further pregnancy is strong, but also the choice of method, and the reasons for that choice are of great importance.

Mrs Kowski was not alone in the strength of her feeling about an unplanned pregnancy. Another wife, Mrs Williams, described her reaction when she learnt she was pregnant with her fifth child (the second child she had definitely not wanted), like this:

I was broken hearted, I sobbed my heart out, I asked the doctor to try and get rid of it for me, even went to the surgeon at the hospital, we were willing to pay, but they said they couldn't do nothing. The annoying part was, I think really, was that I went to the doctor's when I was only two days late, and I think he could really have done something for me, because it wouldn't have hurt at that time, I think that got me down more, when I think that I just have to have it when it was only a couple of days. And they kept telling me I weren't until I was nearly five months . . . I kept having losses all the time, and discharging, and I was about 4½ months when the specialist at the hospital said I definitely was. He say that wouldn't have mattered anyway, because they wouldn't have taken it away.

Asked how she felt once she'd had the baby, she said:

Well, I've got to speak the truth, and I didn't want her, and I weren't really interested in children any more. I just got so broken hearted I didn't care. I wanted to die while I was carrying, so I wouldn't have no more. But I just got round to thinking, oh well, its better than having a cancer or something. A neighbour kept trying to rally me round, I just had her, and I just thought, well, I've got to make the best of it now, it's not her fault she's here.

It is interesting that in both this and the previous instance there was delay over the definite recognition of pregnancy, though in the latter case the delay was on the medical side rather than the mother's. Mrs Kowski was not the only woman who did not realise or admit she was pregnant until she was relatively late in the pregnancy because she simply could not believe that she was pregnant (presumably because the idea of being pregnant was so unpleasant and unexpected), and we had the impression that problems over the recognition of pregnancy either by the professionals or the women themselves were far more common where the pregnancy was unwanted. In no case where a pregnancy was planned did any woman report that she had not known she was pregnant later than three months.

For other women pregnancy, even when unintended, is less disastrous than it was in these two cases. Mrs Thomas had wanted two children when she married; for her it was the ideal family for a number of reasons, and after they had the second child she started using the cap regularly. Asked whether they ever took chances, she said: 'No, I don't think we ever took chances, it was just a routine thing, you know, I got so used to using it.' She was not especially concerned, however, when she did get pregnant:

I wasn't unduly bothered because, when I fell for Wendy, because I had gone nearly three years and I hadn't got a baby about and it seemed funny without a baby, and I quite looked forward to having her. There's no good saying she was planned because she wasn't.

Mrs Thomas' response to the pregnancy makes it clear that she did not mind getting pregnant as much as the previous two women did, and in that sense she did not want to avoid pregnancy as much as they had. Nevertheless, there is no reason to suppose that the pregnancy was in any way intended or any less of an accident than in the other cases. It is true, of course, that deciding whether a pregnancy was intended or not is not always an easy task, and there is room for debate even in cases like the ones above, where, as far as we know, contraception was being used in a careful manner. Nevertheless, though each case may need to be debated, and though errors of judgement may occur, there are no grounds for extending the concept of intention so far that every pregnancy becomes an intentional one, for this destroys the value of the concept.

We want, therefore, in the rest of this chapter to examine some of the conditions that affect contraceptive use, apart from a couple's desires and intentions about family size and spacing.[14]

II: Knowledge of contraception

The first prerequisite of successful contraceptive use is knowing that it is possible to control conception by such means. It is common to claim that virtually everyone in advanced industrial societies does get to know that it is possible to control births by contraception. It is equally common to draw the conclusion that differences in knowledge cannot adequately explain changes in contraceptive use over the last century, let alone any variation or change in the post-war period, either on the grounds that differences in knowledge are insignificant, or else that their existence is primarily the result of differences in ideas about family size and spacing. We want to argue here that contraceptive knowledge in the post-war period has been far from adequate in a number of ways, and that differences in knowledge are not just a question of the desire to limit childbearing, though that is likely to encourage a person to increase their knowledge.

Let us consider, first, whether there are significant differences in knowledge of contraception that might affect contraceptive use. Though it may be true that virtually everyone gets to know that births can be prevented even if intercourse occurs, such knowledge is not in itself sufficient to ensure successful use of contraception. Unfortunately it is not easy to specify exactly what one needs to know as a precondition for using contraception efficiently. It cannot be enough to know that contraception is possible: one needs to have the knowledge at the right time, and one needs to know *how* to control births by contraception. And knowing how to control births by contraception is itself a complex matter: it requires knowledge of the different methods that can be used to prevent conception (ideally as wide a range as possible, with knowledge of their respective advantages and disadvantages), it requires knowledge of how to obtain the selected methods (in the case of mechanical and chemical methods);[15] and it requires knowledge of how to use the chosen method correctly (as distinct from knowing how it works, though at times the latter may be necessary for the former).[16] Hence people may vary in their knowledge of contraception on a number of different dimensions, and there are many ways in which their knowledge may be inadequate and they may be poorly informed. Knowing how to use a sheath correctly is a different matter from knowing that a sheath can prevent conception; similarly learning about the cap after several unplanned pregnancies is a different matter from learning about it before marriage. These are simple points yet there has been little attempt to study the details of knowledge about contraception in a systematic manner.

The standard survey question asks simply which methods are known using a check list, an exercise that often suffers from the terminological variety that pervades the topic.[17] Using this procedure Ann Cartwright found that almost all mothers knew about the commonly used methods of contraception, but that they were not all familiar with some of the less popular ones:

Nearly all mothers had heard of the pill, 99%; the sheath, 97%; and withdrawal, 97%. One in ten had not heard of the cap, one in five of the I.U.D. so, of the three medically prescribed methods, the I.U.D. was the least well known. One in eight said they had not heard of the safe period, one in four of chemicals on their own, douching or 'going on breast-feeding' as a method of contraception.[18]

She then adds:

But some mothers who heard of the existence of certain methods knew little or nothing about them. Only just over half the mothers knew enough about the I.U.D. to recall any advantages or disadvantages. This proportion was two-thirds for the cap, four-fifths for the safe period, six-sevenths for the sheath and over nine-tenths for the pill.[19]

It is significant, too, that when asked whether they knew as much about different methods of birth control as they would like to, 56% of them felt that they did not.[20] The fathers' knowledge of the different methods of birth control was equally poor, and 52% felt that they did not know as much about different methods as they would like.[21]

That knowledge of contraception has been far from perfect amongst some men and women marrying in the post-war period was confirmed by comments made in the pilot study. Mrs Abbott, married in 1948, had six children by the time she was interviewed. When asked why she had not used birth control in the early years of her marriage she replied:

Well, actually I was really very ignorant; going back there again to home, nothing was ever discussed with my mother, nothing at all, not even the growing up, coming into your teens; having your normal period wasn't ever mentioned, I was just sent along to the lav., my sister came with me, she said 'you wear this', and that was that. My mother never even mentioned it, I can't remember her mentioning anything like that ever. So I don't know, I only had to gather up, and when I came here I think I learnt more from my husband's mother, which in a way wasn't what I should have learned really. She was awfully kind and understanding and informative, but I began to think that when you got married, you just had a lot of children, that was it. You got married and you had children, I didn't know there was such a thing that you could not have them and it just went on and on.

A little later she commented:

I just thought that if you didn't have them you were, not particularly lucky, but more fortunate; if more came along you just had to like them and look after them. It was terrible really, I hope that my girls will never grow up in that ignorance as I did.

Her husband, she thought, had been equally uninformed, 'I'm sure he didn't understand either, I don't think he knew what he should have done.'

Mrs Abbott's ignorance may have been extreme, but it was not unique and it must have contributed to the fact that she did not use any contraception during the early years of marriage. Mrs Thomas, whose later unplanned pregnancy we have already described, also felt that her knowledge when she married (in 1950) was inadequate. Asked whether she expected to end up with the two children she intended, she commented:

Well, yes, I thought that if you decided to have two, then you had two and that was that. I think I was a bit naive when I got married, I knew the facts of life and that was about all I knew I suppose; I don't think parents discussed that sort of thing with you in that age as they do now. I mean girls and boys know so much now that they discuss it as a matter of course, I don't think my daughter would be a bit embarrassed to tell me anything. But I wouldn't tell my mother, even though I thought a lot of her, I wouldn't have dreamt of telling her anything, even after I got married.[22]

Though less clear in describing what she did not know at marriage, Mrs Thomas obviously feels in retrospect that she should have known more. Nor was lack of information about contraception restricted to those who had been married quite soon after the war. A woman married in 1960 said she only knew about the sheath, which they used, when she first married, and commented, when asked if she and her husband had talked about birth control at the time, 'I've never had a thought for birth control, I didn't know such things existed as family planning clinics, and I didn't – we never even thought about that sort of thing, you know until the time came.' We suspect indeed, that in many cases contraceptive knowledge at marriage is still far from adequate.[23]

More common than a sense of general ignorance, is the situation where a person, though knowing a reasonable amount about contraception, lacks certain items of information that would facilitate efficient use of their chosen method. The unplanned pregnancy of Mrs Kowski when using the safe period, which we discussed earlier, might well have been avoided with greater knowledge, though she did not say so. This is how she explained the failure:

When I found I was having this baby my doctor said I had probably started the change, because a year previously I had missed some periods for no reason, no reason at all, I wasn't pregnant, and I thought 'oh here I go', because I was late starting, and I was 18 before I actually started having my periods and I don't have them very regularly, so when the following year, a year later, I started missing again, I thought 'oh here I go', I thought it was just a continuation of the change, and when in fact my doctor found that I was pregnant, he said you probably had started the change, but you haven't gone far enough to tell, and then of course when you start like that, your periods, you miss some and then you have some, then you can't count on the safe period; you're only safe when you have a regularly monthly period.

The implication here is that Mrs Kowski did not know how unreliable the safe period was once her periods had started to become more erratic. In other cases too, unplanned pregnancies occurred because of mistaken impressions about alterations in the chances of conception with age. By the time Mrs Thomas became pregnant for the fifth time she knew far more about contraception than she had at marriage and had used both the cap and the sheath; nevertheless, a sense that pregnancy was no longer very likely seems to have contributed to this last pregnancy. When asked how regularly they had been using the sheath after having the fourth child she said:

Well, I think for a few years anyhow, pretty regularly; I don't know I don't think we ever took any chances; I think perhaps we took chances just before he was born, we sort of got a bit cocksure you know, we thought I was past it more or less, I mean, I was 37 or so when I fell for him.

These cases illustrate a number of points. They show first, that knowledge is not just a question of intentions about family size and spacing and hence reinforce our earlier conclusion that contraceptive use more generally is not merely a matter of the desire to control childbearing. Of course, the circumstances vary in each case. We have already argued that it makes little sense to regard Mrs Williams' final pregnancy as planned, intended or wanted; equally Mrs Thomas' final pregnancy was not planned or intended though it was, like the third, accepted willingly enough when it occurred. With Mrs Abbott the situation is more complex since it was less that her lack of knowledge about contraception hampered the realisation of specific intentions about family size, than that her intitial expectations about having children were, in part, dependent on, and indeed an integral feature of her lack of knowledge about contraception. As she said she 'began to think that when you got married, you just had a lot of children, that was it . . . I didn't know there was such a thing that you could not have them.' Later she began to have a greater sense that fertility could be controlled, but was both reluctant to use contraception and could see good reasons for having a reasonable-sized family. Her ideas here demonstrate very clearly the way in which ignorance of contraception and a belief in the inevitability of large families tend to go hand in hand; a conjunction that itself emphasises the importance of ideas about contraception.

Second, these cases illustrate the way in which knowledge of contraception tends to increase during the course of marriage. Both Mrs Abbott and Mrs Thomas did use contraception later in their marriage, and by then their knowledge was much greater. To some extent, of course, their lack of information at marriage may have been due to marrying relatively young (Mrs Abbott was 19, Mrs Thomas, 22) but it is difficult to disentangle whether their increased knowledge was a function of age, of experience within marriage, or a general increase in information about contraception during the post-war period.

Both Mrs Abbott and Mrs Thomas were unusual because they were both apparently given their first information about methods of contraception by a doctor. Our own data and that from other studies shows that friends are the most common source of information about methods of contraception. As the figures in Table 12:7 show most people claimed to have heard of the method of contraception they used at marriage, if they used one, from friends. Friends, however, apparently only provide information (perhaps listing methods and giving some details about use), for, when asked with whom they *discuss* birth control when they first married, it is medical personnel who were mentioned most often, though most (some 76% of the whole sample) said that they had discussed birth control with no one then (excluding presumably spouses) and the figure was still 63% for the time of the interview. It may be that the apparent discrepancy here means that people do not often *ask* someone else about contraception, but if they do they ask a doctor; nevertheless they often hear about contraception when the topic comes up in conversation with friends.[24] Hence since many doctors do not themselves spontaneously raise the question of birth control and tend to do so only after childbearing has started, and many individuals do not themselves raise the question with a doctor, a large proportion rely on what they hear about contraception through informal channels or the media.[25]

TABLE 12:7 *From whom couples had heard of the birth control method they used at marriage*

Source of information	Number	Per cent
Relatives	11	5.7
Media; TV, press, etc.	19	9.9
Friends	95	49.5
Doctor	15	7.8
Family Planning Clinic	8	4.2
Other	28	14.6
Don't know/No response	16	8.3
Total	192	100.0

The fact that many people hear about methods of contraception (and presumably obtain some of their information about how to use them) through informal channels is important. At first sight it seems to contradict the fact that a great deal of information about contraception is disseminated through formal ones. Not only do schools frequently provide lessons in 'health education' which often include some information about contraception, but couples tend to be bombarded with pamphlets about contraception when they get engaged, marry and have children. The response to survey questions suggests, however, that it is the information that is provided through informal channels that makes its mark and is remembered, and that the provision of information through formal channels (when it is not specifically requested by the individual) may have little impact on contraceptive knowledge.[26] Lessons in schools probably have more impact than the distribution of pamphlets since the lessons provoke the informal talk that, it seems, is all important. This does not mean, however, that the publicity that is given to particular methods of contraception through the media from time to time is completely unimportant; the fact that the pill was the most widely known method towards the end of the 1960s may well be due to the publicity it attracted in the media. Since much of the publicity has now died down (apart from the occasional scare about side effects, of which that which led to the banning of pills with high oestrogen content in 1972 was the most obvious), the proportions knowing of it may have even declined. Furthermore, the reluctance to allow advertising of contraceptives of many types (though there has been some relaxation in recent years) cannot have helped to increase information about contraception, and is undesirable on that ground.[27]

TABLE 12:8 *How often husband and wife talked about birth control: the survey sample*

Frequency of discussion	At marriage		When interviewed	
	No.	%	No.	%
Never	80	27.6	108	37.4
Sometimes	163	56.2	151	52.2
Often	44	15.2	30	10.4
No response/Don't know	3	1.0	0	0.0
Total	290	100.0	289	100.0

Discussion between spouses about birth control can increase knowledge because information is shared. In the survey sample as many as 28% of couples claimed never to have talked about birth control when they first married and some 37 per cent of couples said they now never talked about the subject (see Table 12:8). However, these figures reinforce the point that we made in the previous chapter that not talking about a subject at a particular point in time may simply mean that ideas and information have already been shared, and agreement has been reached. It is also likely that the use of certain methods of contraception provokes more discussion than others, and that once the method has been selected there is little more said about its use. The pill appears to be a method like this, which would account for the fact that when interviewed those who claimed to talk 'often' about birth control were somewhat *less* likely to be using the pill than those who said they never, or only sometimes talked about the subject.[28] Nevertheless some discussion with spouse about birth control, both to share information about methods, especially if one spouse is poorly informed, and also to settle which method is to be used, is likely to be important if birth control is to be used efficiently. Both Mrs Abbott and Mrs Thomas had little discussion with their spouses about birth control and although they felt their husbands were also poorly informed about birth control, discussion might have helped by pooling their information. When Mrs Abbott started using the cap after having her second child, on the advice of her doctor, because she was in a nervous state, there was little discussion with her husband. Asked what her husband thought about her using the cap, she said:

I don't really know, we didn't discuss it. Oh. he thought at the time it was better, if it was going to make me better; he doesn't say very much unless you ask, or there's a discussion comes up, he just doesn't say very much.

Mrs Thomas said that she and her husband had not discussed birth control until they had had their second child, and added a moment later, when asked whether the idea of using birth control had occurred to her when she was first married:

Not a lot: I think perhaps it would have been better if it had; now as you get several more years in your married life, you can discuss things more than you can when you are younger. I mean, I think if I'd gone those four or five years without any children, then we would've been able to discuss it better.

Presumably the association between the degree of communication (overall) between husband and wife and their efficiency of contraceptive use is partly due to the fact that those who score low on measure of communication tend not to talk about birth control and therefore do not share their knowledge or discuss how they can best limit their family size.[29]

III: The acceptability of contraception

Knowledge does not guarantee use. Some may not use contraception because they do not want to limit their childbearing (a reason for non-use that we do not intend to consider here); others may not because for some reason or other they object to the idea either of obtaining or of using contraception.[30] When Mrs Abbott was introduced to contraception by her doctor she did not like the idea. Her initial use was very much under doctor's orders and when that constraint was removed she stopped. Discussing what happened after the birth of her second child she said:

I know that some time after Mark was born, I had a dreadful fear of the atom bomb, terrible it was, I really thought we were all going to go up in smoke, I got in a dreadful state and I thought I could never have any more children to bring them into the world. I know I really did get into a panic over that. I went to a family planning clinic then, through my own doctor, because I really got myself in a nervous state, and he said it wasn't fit that I should have any more children at that time, that was only for that time, it wasn't for ever and ever. The feeling didn't last long, when I got better, I sort of calmed down a bit.

She went to the clinic and started using the cap, but as she added, 'I didn't use it for such a long time, because I didn't like using it, I didn't like the idea of using it.' Her explanation of this is interesting:

Well, I was better, and I didn't like using it at all. Probably because I didn't know much about bodies, and myself, and to me, in a way, it was forbidden, it was more or less a dirty word, it was bad, perhaps you can't understand. I mean all parts of my little girl's body we talk about, but to me it wasn't quite nice, it wasn't done, it wasn't the thing, so it went against my upbringing you see to use it, I didn't like using it.

The link between knowledge and acceptability here is very close: the unkown is forbidden and the forbidden unknown.

The prohibition of knowledge of sexual matters implicit in Mrs Abbott's comments reflect elements of a Puritan ideology: elements that are hostile to sexuality. Other components of Puritanism are, however, far from antithetical – the concern to plan and organise for one. One ideology that is explicitly and hostile to most forms of contraception, if not to contraception generally, is Roman Catholicism. Nevertheless, recent studies show both that many Roman Catholics in England are not hostile to contraception, although they are more likely to favour methods that are explicitly acceptable to their Church's doctrine, and also that many who do disapprove of contraception nevertheless use it.[31] Presumably the desire to control childbearing outweighs the religious scruples in these instances. As a result, the proportions of Catholics who use contraception at some time in marriage differs relatively little from non-Catholics, although there are differences in when contraception is first used, and in the methods that are commonly used.

The relationship between Catholic doctrine and Catholic practice raises the question of whether attitudes hostile to contraception are likely to be outweighed by practical necessities and are therefore of little importance in explaining patterns of contraceptive use. Three points need to be made here using the example of Roman Catholicism. First, much of the evidence suggests that the doctrinal rejection of most forms of contraception is linked with positive attitudes towards large families and that Catholics do often want larger families than non-Catholics. Second, though economic and material considerations (practical necessities) may lead Catholics to choose smaller families than they regard as ideal, those who do not face such constraints do realise their ideological commitment to a larger family. And third, as we have said, negative attitudes towards contraception do affect when contraception is used and which methods are used, and these factors themselves affect the level of success with contraception.

More often hostility to the idea of contraception, or to particular methods of contraception, cannot be tied to any religious ideology in any simple way. Reluctance to use any contraception, irregular use, and avoidance of particular methods seem to be primarily a question of the 'inherent' characteristics different methods are felt to have, though no doubt the way in which particular contraceptive methods are perceived is influenced by religious and other ideological beliefs. For most people there is no perfect method of contraception; there are only one or two that are less objectionable or more attractive than others, and at times the problems and objections to all possible methods seem sufficiently powerful for no method to be used at all even though a pregnancy is not wanted. Consider, for instance, to illustrate some of the common objections and problems of different methods of contraception, the 'reluctance' to use the pill. The pill different methods of contraception, the 'reluctance' to use the pill. This pill is widely and correctly believed to be the most effective method of contraception;[32] it is also the method most commonly prescribed by doctors when they give contraceptive advice,[33] yet the method has, at least until recently, been less popular than either the sheath or withdrawal. Why?

Ann Cartwright's study indicates one reason. One of its most striking findings was the extent to which the pill was perceived by both men and women to involve health risks. Seventy per cent of mothers and 67% of fathers asked to describe the disadvantages of the pill spontaneously gave an answer that could be categorised as 'harmful to health'.[34] Comments of this type were also frequently made in the pilot study. One woman started using the pill after her fifth child at her doctor's suggestion. Asked what she thought about the method she said:

Well, I'm hoping that's going to be all right. The only thing that worries me is if there are illnesses effective from these pills, but my doctor reckon there ain't none proved, and he thinks they're all right, just take his word for it.

Much of the problem seems to be an uncertainty and concern about what drugs, especially those that have to be taken on a regular basis do to you – a concern that was not only manifest amongst those with lower levels of education and knowledge.[35] Mrs Butler had this to say when asked whether she had thought of using any other method of contraception (than the cap):

Well, John says I ought to use the pill, you know, but the pill doesn't appeal to me at all. Its rather silly, I suppose, really, but at the time when I was interested in farming they used to give these type of drugs to cows. Its very difficult in the winter to get a heifer to come on heat you see, to spot her so you can take her to the bull, so they used to give heifers this thing . . . In the 1940s it was quite a new thing and very interesting 'cos you can make the heifer come on heat just when you wanted to, and the idea of me taking drugs of this sort is repugnant. I think one's personality depends tremendously on one's hormones and I don't want mine mucked about with. The thought of feeling pregnant all the time without producing anything at the end of it doesn't appeal to me at all, I must say.

Nor indeed have the medical profession been unconcerned about the health risks of the pill, and in 1967-8 they thought it only slightly risky than the I.U.D. and definitely riskier than the cap.[36] They presumably continued to prescribe it so frequently on the grounds of its efficiency, in the belief that the health risks for pregnancy itself were even greater. It may be that the report *Oral Contraceptives and Health* published in 1974 has allayed some of the fears of both medical personnel and public opinion about the pill, yet this will in itself not necessarily have made it more popular.[37] Whilst medical personnel tend to defend the pill on the ground that the risks are less than those associated with pregnancy, the salient point of comparison for the user is almost certainly that of other methods of contraception, and not those of pregnancy per se. Hence any admission of, and publicity for risks from the pill by doctors and scientists, even if these are said to be less than those of pregnancy, may well deter people from using it.

Nevertheless, medical personnel and experts clearly exert an important influence on the methods of contraception of those to whom they give advice even if they do not convert all those who consult them to their opinions.[38] Many people, however, are reluctant to seek professional advice about birth control and this is a second reason why the pill has not been as widely used as one might have expected, for it requires a medical prescription. Glass, for instance, reports a doubling in the proportions seeking professional advice between those married in 1941–50 and those married in 1961–5, yet the proportion in the latter group was still only 41%.[39] Indeed, there can be little doubt that the custom of selling sheaths in barber shops, and more recently in other non-medical 'outlets', has contributed to its popularity, and that in contrast the need for medical prescription deters people from using the pill.[40]

A number of accounts in the pilot sample brought out the way in which men and women feel hesitant about obtaining contraceptives from professionals (and some from any public source). Mrs Osborn, who did not want any children (for the reasons we have described in the previous chapter) displayed this reluctance very clearly. She thought of using the pill, and did ask her doctor to prescribe it, but her doctor was a Catholic and the reaction she got to her request apparently increased her feeling that she ought to want children, and her reluctance to seek professional advice. Moreover, her husband was unwilling to go out and buy the sheath. The following exchange describes her difficulties.

INTERVIEWER: I've got a list here of methods of birth control, did you use any in fact when you were first married?

MRS O.: Let me see, oh the pill, the oral. Yes that's what I tried and that was making me ill.

I: Ah, I see, you tried this when you first got married?

MRS O.: I did, yes. I, you know, I kept taking them, but I felt I had the flu all the while, and you won't get my husband going in the shop buying anything so . . .

I: So how did you think of starting taking the pill?

MRS O.: Well, I couldn't ask my doctor because she's a Catholic, and I didn't know that, I sort of put my foot in it, and then what I did, my sister was getting them, and she was expecting, and she sent me her prescription and I was using that.

I: So how long in fact did you go on using the pill?

MRS O.: Oh, let me see, I married in April, well as far as – right till I left them off when I – up till when I was expecting.

I: So you were taking them even when you got pregnant?

MRS O.: Oh no, that's what done it you see.

I: You stopped just before?

MRS O.: Well, October I think. I stopped and I immediately fell. Immediately I mean that's what done it you see, you should never leave off.

I: So when you left off, did you think of using any other form at all, or what did you think?

MRS O.: Yes, I thought about – you see, when you're married according to your doctor, you know, they think well, you know, you should love children, you should want them, and I said 'well, its a bit of a hard job, you won't get my husband to go into a shop' so it was up to me every time. And I thought well, I'd try different pills, but after, you know, I didn't know what to do.

I: And the doctor didn't suggest any other method for you then, at the time?

MRS O.: No. I don't want to change 'cos, she's a good doctor, and she won't help in any way. You know, ask her and she says, 'Don't ask me that', so its a bit awkward.

The problem was no easier once she had had the first unplanned pregnancy, because of her feeling that she was asking for something that a professional would think she did not have a right to. Asked about birth control after the first child, she said:

Well, I wasn't going to take the pill again 'cos it made me ill and my husband wouldn't do nothing, and 'course, being a funny doctor I didn't want to – well, she's not funny – being that religion, I didn't want to ask her again, and if you go down the family planning clinic they usually, well, I've never been down there, but I should imagine they'd tell me 'Why are you moaning about one', you know I thought probably you'd have to have about six or seven, and so I thought well, we'll just have to be careful, you know, that's what we thought.

After another unplanned pregnancy, due, she thought, to not using withdrawal 'on very odd occasions, you know. Aggravating, but just that once, most frustrating to think that, you know, just that, and the next month, you know, you're expecting'. She still found the idea of approaching the family planning clinic difficult:

I thought about, you know, going down the family planning clinic, and then getting something done about it properly, you know, but the loop, I don't think is in Ipswich, and what put me off was – I thought about the cap, see, but what put me off, was that you have to fit it in yourself, and all that, and that put me off a bit, and keep going down there, I thought it's horrible enough without having to keep repeat – going down there and that. Ooh, it put me off. And I wouldn't go into the shop and buy anything for me husband and all, I say its' enough, bad enough going in there and buying something for meself without, you know, I can't, I'd die.

Here she adds to the previous reason for not going to the Clinic two more. First, the prospect of having to use the cap which she does not like as a method; and second, the ordeal of having to keep going down to the clinic. She felt she might brave it once, but not regularly.

After her third unplanned pregnancy in three years, this time after completely regular use of withdrawal, her desire to avoid a further pregnancy was very great. The prospect of the family planning clinic had not, however, become any more attractive. She raised yet another problem, 'the trouble is that going down that family clinic I've got to get a doctor's certificate I'm afraid. I don't suppose you know anything about that do you?' Here, finally, a mistaken idea (which the interviewer attempted to remedy) combines with her dislike of the cap, her reluctance to get professional help with contraception (reinforced by her doctor's initial response to her request for the pill), and the practical difficulty of actually getting down to the clinic (which increased as her family size increased), to become an almost insurmountable hurdle. Since Mrs Osborn's third child was only 13 days old when she was interviewed we do not know which turned out to be the greater: her desire not to have any more children or her dislike of the prospect of the family planning clinic. Of course, part of the problem was Mrs Osborn's ambivalence about having children, as well as her lack of knowledge about family planning clinics. Nevertheless, she displayed an underlying anxiety about seeking professional help about birth control that was itself a deterrent to successful contraception.

There are a number of factors that would seem to lie behind reluctance to use professional help in obtaining contraception. The first is the sense that birth control is not really a medical problem. Mrs Osborn suggests this in her belief that the family planning clinic is only for those with six or seven children – i.e. those with 'real' or 'serious' problems. You go to a doctor when things are wrong, not when things are normal and in a sense routine. Doctors themselves seem to have felt somewhat uncertain about their role in the matter when they questioned the system of payment for prescribing contraceptives, which they seemed to feel was not obviously part of their 'essential' business. Second, and related to this, to seek professional help with birth control may seem to involve an implicit admission that you want sex for pleasure not for procreation (which may produce a sense of guilt), a feeling that Mrs Osborn clearly had. She felt she ought to be having children and that she must be selfish to want to avoid childbirth. Third, differences in social status between doctor and patient may make discussing a 'private' topic like birth control seem an especial ordeal.[41] And finally, getting contraceptives through doctors and clinics requires forethought and organisation about sex that may seem antithetical to the ideas of spontaneity and passion that surround the conventional images of it, a point that the manufacturers of sheaths regard as important in maintaining the demand for them.[42]

The planning and forethought that contraception involves is almost certainly one factor that discourages use of a wide range of contraceptives, even the sheath. Only withdrawal does not require some anticipation of intercourse and some planning for it by one or other partner, by obtaining some form of contraception in advance; but withdrawal is objectionable to many couples on other grounds.[43] Hostility to contraception because the planning it requires seems incompatible with sexual spontaneity was specifically mentioned by some of our sample. A husband put the argument forcefully, when asked whether he had used any of the methods of contraception on our checklist when he had first married.

Not really, no. No, we didn't. We agreed—I used 'D' [withdrawal] because, well when you're first married, all these other things, you want about twenty-four hours notice, don't you. When you're first married you don't want to worry about that, do you. If you believe in sex, as sex should be, you don't sort of make an appointment, do you; you either indulge in it at the time you feel like it, or go without. I don't think you want to sort of write to your wife to make an appointment.

After having their first child sooner than they intended, he started using the sheath as well as withdrawal but still felt that contraception made sex 'organised' and 'pre-planned'. Later (after further contraceptive failure) his wife started taking the pill, which, though it required planning, did not, he thought, interfere with sexual spontaneity.

We have already pointed out that the emphasis on planning for the future that is an important feature of the desire for a better life, is likely to produce efficient contraceptive use. Nevertheless, as some of the pilot sample's comments have brought out, ideas about planning are highly complex and there is no necessary reason to believe that most people's willingness to plan is uniform for different areas of activity, or that, for instance, a dislike of planning for sex is necessarily associated with a reluctance to plan other areas of activity. Moreover, as the husband quoted above came to realise, it is possible with certain methods of contraception to make a distinction between planning contraception and planning sex.

One further factor that may have discouraged the use of the pill is the fact that it is a method controlled by the woman. Though it is true that in many circumstances men and women are likely to feel that effectiveness is more important than whether the method is a male or a female one, especially, for instance, when one method of contraception has been proved to be unreliable, if there is a preference either way it is more likely to be that the man should take the responsibility for contraception. The only relevant question in the survey asked who took decisions about birth control. Fifty-one per cent said that at marriage either both of them did, or that sometimes one did and sometimes the other; 20% said that the husband took any decisions and 8% the wife. As many as 21% said that neither of them did. However the matter, like that of settling questions of family size and spacing, is equally subject to a variety of conflicting ideas: ideas which may give the husband the deciding role in the matter, or the wife, or emphasise the importance of coming to a joint decision. Nevertheless, the material from the pilot study suggests that being responsible for birth control is more likely to be regarded as a matter for the husband than that of deciding family size and spacing, since it is often seen as one aspect of the sexual sphere in which the man is expected to take the initiative. We had the impression that for the wife to be held to have the main responsibility for birth control the issue has to be defined more as one of having children, than of sex, a hurdle that was often only overcome, as with the husband quoted above, after contraceptive failure. Certainly from the comments made in the pilot, the belief that the man should be responsible for contraception seemed to be part of a general ideology of male dominance within the family. One couple started using contraception after their third child was born. When the wife was asked why they had chosen that particular method (the sheath) she said: 'Well, its what my husband, he decided to use that one.' When questioned whether they had talked about the matter she said, 'No, not really, I didn't care what happened as long as I had no more.' Not surprisingly, when asked who she had felt at the time should take responsibility for contraception, she remarked 'Well, I left it all to me husband.' Her conception of the roles of husband and wife shows the 'segregation' she expects between them. When asked what she thought were the main things a husband had to do she commented:

Well, the main thing is to work, and do the decorating, occasionally keeping the children in trim, he don't interfere too much, but occasionally they want someone a bit stronger than I am; I'm strict to a degree, but in a way they can wrap me round their finger. I can't be too hard with them, so occasionally he's got to intervene, and lay the law down.

Asked about the main things a wife has to do, she said:

Well, the main thing to my husband is being at home when he come in, because he hate coming in and I'm not here, though I suppose what he love is just me being here, and having his meals ready, just looking after the children.

However, those who accept more segregated relationships do not always use male methods, for as we have said, the desire for an effective method may increase, and lead to the use of a female one. Two accidental pregnancies later, this woman started using the pill with some reservations about the possible health risks. Her ideas about who should take responsibility for birth control had to make a pragmatic adjustment to the change, about which she sounded resigned. Asked about who she felt should take responsibility for birth control she said, 'Well I'm taking it now, because I make sure to have my pills.'

There are other factors, too, that have discouraged people from using the pill, as well as certain advantages that it has over other methods, which together contribute to the particular pattern of contraception that has been observed in the post-war period.[44] However, the points that we have considered so far illustrate the sorts of problems and objections that the use of any method of contraception, even a highly reliable one, may involve, and show how we can account both for the differing preferences for particular methods and for the regularity with which contraception is used over a particular period of time, as well as for the failure of some couples to use any method at all at certain periods in their married lives, even though they do not want a child. Furthermore, this consideration of some of the problems of certain methods of contraception also reinforces the point made by others that it is important to have a wide variety of methods of contraception available, if the regular use of contraception is to be encouraged.

13. Trends in family size and spacing

We have attempted in the last four chapters to examine in detail some of the influences on patterns of childbearing in post-war England. In this final chapter we want to draw together the various ideas we have outlined in these and earlier chapters by considering how we can start to explain the specific trends in childbearing of the post-war period.

The customary explanation of short-term trends in fertility is economic: the level of births is said to respond to the level of economic activity; in times of economic growth they will increase, in times of economic depression they will decline. Our own analysis indicates that at least in post-war England economic conditions must, as other commentators have argued, have contributed to the increase in marital fertility during the period 1956 to 1964 and to the subsequent decline. But this is not because the population has been adjusting itself to the level of available resources by means of changes in the level of fertility, or because economic growth or decline, by changing both the level of household resources and the cost of children, has been changing the number that maximises each couple or household's utility. Neither the Malthusian nor the utilitarian attempt to link economic factors in the fertility is satisfactory. Both pay insufficient attention to the way in which individuals give meaning to the situations in which they find themselves and base their actions on such meanings and interpretations. Hence both too readily assume it is possible to produce some general theory of population or fertility, and ignore the social and historical context in which the actions that affect childbearing occur. The result is a theoretical language into which occurrences can be translated *ex post facto*, rather than an explanatory account that can be subjected to any satisfactory empirical test. It does not follow, however, that economic factors can have played no part in the changes in fertility in post-war England; rather that on the one hand, we need to establish rather than assume their importance, and that on the other hand, in so far as economic factors do influence fertility, they do so because couples *believe* and *accept* that it is important to take such factors into account when making decisions that influence their childbearing. Their impact is not necessary and inevitable but a question of the concerns, interests and beliefs of men and women in the society.

Our own data show that economic factors must have influenced patterns of childbearing in post-war England for two reasons. First, many men and women have felt it was necessary and desirable to take *some* account of their financial and material circumstances when planning their families.

Couples have, for instance, been especially likely to consider such circumstances in deciding when to start having a family and when deciding how many children to have altogether. Second, some couples give especially high priority to their material standards of living and are therefore likely to be especially sensitive to their financial and material circumstances, which are likely to be foremost in their calculations about having children. In consequence, the quantity and tempo of their childbearing is especially responsive to changes in the economic conditions of the country which affect their own financial and material circumstances. In periods of affluence and rapid economic growth, for instance, parents who might otherwise have stopped at two children are likely to feel freer to have a third child, either making a definite decision to have another one, or putting less effort into the task of avoiding an unplanned pregnancy. In contrast, in periods of economic recession which affect them personally, they are likely to feel much more strongly that they cannot go beyond the limit of two. Some may even feel that they cannot afford more than one child, and feel constrained to break the normative boundaries of family size. Similarly, changing economic conditions can also affect *when* a couple start a family, if they do not have one already.

However, economic changes that affect the financial and material circumstances of couples are not the only changing conditions that may affect patterns of childbearing because couples take them into account when making decisions about having children. Those of other ideological persuasions are likely to be influenced by other, related, socio-economic changes. For example, in so far as economic growth within the society during the 1950s and 1960s may have created more opportunity to achieve social mobility, this would have meant that those anxious to improve their social status and that of their families, also felt somewhat less pressure to avoid an additional pregnancy (though as we have argued above there would be more arguments for their not having another child than for those of a more materialist persuasion). Correspondingly, any tightening of avenues of mobility would strengthen the case for only having two children, though it would probably not tip the balance in favour of only one child. Likewise the childbearing of those who give priority to an active life must be affected to some extent by socio-economic changes that alter the available opportunities for jobs outside the home and other activities which provide grounds for the limitation of family size.

Such links between socio-economic conditions and decisions about family size and spacing, together with the impact of such conditions on marriage, must account for much of the correlation that has been frequently observed between birth or fertility rates and various economic indicators over the short-term – indicators that measure more or less imperfectly some of the rather different economic conditions to which couples are responsive in making decisions when having children.[1] They must also account, in part, therefore, for the rise in fertility from 1956 to 1964 and the decline that followed, although no single economic indicator is perfectly related to changes in fertility. Nor, on our argument, should we expect such a thing. The level of unemployment is, for instance, often reasonably seen as an important index of the current economic condition of the country. Its effect on patterns of childbearing is far from simple. To those who experience it, if childbearing is not completed, it may be an especially strong argument for avoiding pregnancy, but not all will find the argument equally strong, and some may even see it as an additional reason for turning to the family as a source of pleasure and satisfaction, and feel more willing to have another child.

It is, moreover, how individuals perceive and assess their present and future circumstances, as well as the importance that they attach to them when making decisions about family size and spacing that counts, and measures of unemployment, levels of productivity, prices, and so forth provide a poor measure of these. This means that if, for instance, unemployment starts to increase and creates a climate of pessimism and uncertainty about the future, its effects on the level of childbearing are likely to extend well beyond those who are actually unemployed. In that respect the significant thing about the period from the mid-1950s to the mid-1960s is the fact that it was a period in which many people seem to have *felt* themselves to be well off materially and financially, thought that their employment was secure, and expected their affluence to continue.[2] Harold Macmillan's phrase, 'You've never had it so good' used in the election campaign of 1959, symbolised and reflected what appears to have been a common feeling: a surge of optimism and confidence and sense of material affluence after the depression of the 1930s and the uncertainty and austerity of the 1940s and early 1950s (rationing did not end finally, for instance, until 1954), born apparently out of economic growth and high levels of employment.

The mid 1950s marked a turning point in post-war England, as in a number of other countries in Western Europe, in this respect, as a number of observers have pointed out. Landes, for example, writing in 1968, commented that it was about the mid 1950s that 'observers became aware that Europe was no longer a convalescent',[3] and elaborated on the changes like this:

It was this sustained and powerful expansion of the 1950s that made the deepest impression on contemporaries and has continued to dominate our image of post-war economic history. Not that rates of growth were higher in this period than before: indeed, the contrary was true. But what had happened before was recovery, with all its precariousness and dependency, and one could argue that Europe was simply making up for lost time; whereas now Europe was moving ahead on its own, and every year brought a new record output. Between 1938 and 1963 the aggregate gross national product of Western Europe, measured at constant prices, increased more than two and a half times.[4]

It is true, of course, that England's economic performance during these years was not as good as that of some European countries, and not as good, in the opinion of some, as it could have been. Moreover there were some signs that indicated, especially with hindsight, that the solution to all the countries' economic problems had not been found.[5] Yet optimism and confidence were the keynote of the period: the affluent society had arrived and seemed to promise a rosy future.[6] It has, indeed, been described as 'the age of illusion'.

By the mid 1960s there were definite signs of trouble and difficulty: a gradual accumulation of events suggested both that the dream of perpetual and sustained economic growth that had begun to seem possible in advanced capitalist societies was not likely to be realised, and that the order and absence of conflict that political leaders had attempted to establish might also be threatened. Certainly in England there were clear signs that all was not perfect economically. Full employment, which had seemed the most substantial achievement of the period was threatened by an increase in unemployment in 1962-3, (though it at no time reached the levels of this decade); moreover England's frequent balance of payments problem recurred producing a major crisis in 1964 which led eventually to devaluation in 1967. By the second half of the 1960s economic growth itself had started to slow down in England and other European countries, and although there was some improvement late in the decade, the optimism and certainty of sustained economic growth was by then somewhat shaken. Furthermore, there was a growing feeling that the fruits of rapid economic growth were not all beneficial: not only were there increasing fears about pollution, the exhaustion of natural resources and so on (that were explicitly linked to rapid economic as well as rapid population growth), but there was also concern about the extent to which economic growth could solve all social and political ills (some argued it had not eradicated inequalities of wealth and unemployment, or given sufficient support to the welfare state, others that it did not encourage the hard work and sacrifice that were necessary to sustain economic growth in the longer term). Such concerns were also reflected in the political sphere where there were signs of change, uncertainty and insecurity. At home Macmillan's resignation in October 1963, following closely on the shock of the Profumo affair, was in turn followed by the electoral defeat of the Conservatives in 1964 (albeit by a narrow margin) after 13 years in power, and then by a more clear-cut victory by the Labour Party in 1966. Such changes, together with the death of Churchill in 1965, combined to create (as well as reflecting) a sense that a political era had ended, and that change and new leadership were needed: the post-war optimism, confidence and sense of certainty seemed to be gone.[8] International events also played a part. The Bay of Pigs crisis in October 1962 not only reawakened old fears of international war, exacerbated by the new fear of nuclear warfare, but highlighted the power of the United States and the U.S.S.R. when compared with that of smaller countries like England. De Gaulle's refusal to admit Britain to membership of the E.E.C. the following year increased the sense of subordination and political uncertainty, the sense 'that Britain had come to the end of one phase without offering any clear indication of the shape of the next'.[9]

Such changes in public feeling over the 1950s and 1960s certainly affected the level of births by affecting individuals' assessments of their social and economic circumstances, and hence their plans for the realisation of particular ideological objectives. Equally, if not more importantly they could also have contributed to certain other ideological changes which would themselves have directly affected patterns of childbearing over the period. A number of salient ideological changes may have occurred during the period. First, there may have been some change in the conventions that govern the way in which people think about, and make decisions about having children. A striking feature of the decision making about having children of those we studied was the way in which the calculations involved were normally encapsulated – encapsulated by an underlying acceptance of the necessity and value of family life, so that most people when they married started off with the assumption that having children was an essential and important part of married life. In consequence, their thinking about children was usually bounded in two respects. On the one hand by the premise that it was essential to have *some* children, and on the other hand by the assumption that calculations about family size and spacing should consider the interests of the family and its members, not solely personal interests. In that sense decisions about having children were typically family-centred, considering what was to the good and benefit of, or feasible for the family members – for the parents and children – and paid little attention to the personal pleasures and satisfactions of the individuals concerned, except in their role as parents.

It is, of course, difficult to establish with any certainty either from our own pilot data or from other available sources whether there has been much change in either of these two related constraints on decisions about having children, which reflect and indicate the value and importance that has been attached to children and family life in our society. We suspect, however, that there has been some change in both during the post-war period. First, it seems likely that the assumption that if you marry you will have some children is somewhat less taken for granted than it once was, although the standard beliefs that back up the assumption have little changed or may even seem to have more force than they did. (In so far, for instance, as more people question the need to marry and see having children as the only justification for marrying, they are likely to see an even closer connection between marriage and having children than before, and hence are even more likely to feel that the idea of marriage without children is anomalous.) Nevertheless, though we do not think that there has been much weakening of the belief that children are an essential part of married life, we suspect that there has been more willingness to question the belief, and hence more need to rehearse the arguments for having some children. The conclusion is usually the same but is less taken for granted than before, and consequently potentially more open to change. This is probably one reason for the increase in the proportions remaining childless during the early years of marriage in recent years, which is likely to be reflected (though we expect to a lesser extent), in the proportions remaining childless when the child-bearing period is completed. But it is not the only one. Some of the childlessness in the early years of mariage must have been due to financial and material constraints, and is unlikely to result in couples remaining childless throughout marriage.

Second, it seems probable that couples are somewhat more likely to consider decisions about having children in terms of their personal interests and satisfactions and less exclusively in terms of the possible advantages and disadvantages to the family unit. This is no doubt one further factor that has encouraged more couples to remain childless over the decade. But including alternative pleasures and satisfactions to those one may gain as a parent in one's calculations does not necessarily mean that an individual is always more likely to want fewer children or none at all, than if the calculation is made on a more restricted basis. The outcome depends on what alternative sources of satisfaction are or can be included in the equation, and how all possibilities, including having children or another child are valued. If, for instance, fewer 'career' openings are available to women because of high unemployment and economic recession, then women who do consider children and careers as to some extent alternatives may be encouraged to have more children rather than less. Hence, one consequence of putting decisions about having children in a broader context is that the level of fertility of those who do would be more sensitive to social and economic changes and, therefore, potentially more volatile.

A number of factors presumably influence the willingness to consider decisions about having children in the context of alternatives. First, the degree of control over fertility that is possible with the available repertoire of methods of contraception. In this sense the pill, though a far from perfect method of contraception and used less widely than might be expected, has brought about a transformation in contraception that makes it qualitatively distinct from other methods. It permits, for the first time, married couples to choose to remain childless or to structure their family as they wish, with a high degree of certainty. It therefore also permits them to treat marriage without children as a practical and serious possibility, as well as allowing them to be more confident that they can have only the number of children they intend and no more. Of course, irrespective of its ideological impact the pill must have reduced the proportion of pregnancies due to contraceptive accidents in the second half of the 1960s, and has therefore facilitated the decline in the birth rate since 1965. Nevertheless, we do not think that this provides a complete or satisfactory explanation of that decline.

Second, there is the question of the extent to which 'individual' versus 'collective' values are dominant within the society. We have argued elsewhere, using the same dichotomy, that in a society widely governed by individualist values and beliefs the family has remained one of the few institutions governed primarily by collective ones.[10] A willingness to consider having children in the light of one's own personal interests and satisfactions can be seen as further encroachment of individualist ideas into family relations: an encroachment that, if it continues, would be comparable to the change in which the selection of a marriage partner became, in principle, a matter of personal rather than familial choice.[11]

Third, we must consider to what extent alternative pleasures to having children are available for both men and women. The availability and nature of alternatives not only affects, in our view, the outcome of any calculation about children that takes them into account, it also affects whether other possibilities are taken into consideration in the first place. Industrialisation and economic development have, over the long term, produced social and economic changes that have undoubtedly created more opportunities for activities, interests and pleasures that can be carried on outside family life. Work, travel, the acquisition of material goods, sport and so on, though they are frequently carried out alongside family activities, provide opportunities that, to an increasing extent, do not demand a familial context and may even conflict with it. Whether they will continue to be available (the monetary costs of some may become prohibitive) and whether they will continue to be considered enjoyable, is impossible to predict. The idea that people will come to think of children and family life (either in its existing form or new ones) as more and more of a haven from the competition and stresses of life in advanced industrial societies may sound cliched and exaggerated, yet it is far from impossible. In our view an increasing commitment to children and family life in some form is no less likely than a decline.

Another possibility is that there has been some change over the post-war period in the precise nature of the ideological perspectives and images of family life that we have outlined, with consequent changes in the ideas about family size and spacing with which they are associated; it could also be that new ideological perspectives which have implications for ideas about family size and spacing have developed. Our own study does not provide us with the right sort of information to establish the latter, and without more detailed information we would not want to speculate about such developments. However, our data, along with that from other sources, suggests that there has been some transformation in certain of the ideological perspectives that we have outlined, which may have contributed to changes in family size and spacing of the post-war period. On the one hand, as we have already argued, the image of family life of those who give high priority to their material standard of living seems to have a less domestic focus than formerly, and the material orientation of those marrying more recently is less home-centred than of those marrying in the late 1940s and 1950s. This change increases, if anything, the arguments for having a small family, and may provide more reason for having no children at all, or starting a family later. It is a change that is to a large extent the result of technological developments both in transport and domestic consumer durables: the latter at first increasing the involvement in and commitment to the home, and later permitting more activity outside it.

On the other hand there is some evidence that the belief in an active life has also been transformed over the post-war period; that it has become less puritanical and more hedonistic than formerly, and that 'experience' has become a more central component of the ideology – changes that themselves have complex origins relating both to the secularisation of society and to economic growth and affluence. An ideological transformation of this type is likely to affect ideas about having children since it is, in itself (though this runs counter to other changes) likely to make an individual more likely to want both to have some children, in order to have the experience of being a parent, and even to have a large family, since, given the individualist nature of the ideology, each child will be held to provide a new and different experience.

Finally, changes in patterns of childbearing in England over the post-war period could have been produced in part by changes in the relative salience of the different ideological perspectives we have described and hence the chances of their dominating an individual's way of thinking about family life. Again any such change is difficult to document. There are, however, a number of possibilities. First, whilst it seems likely, as we have already argued, that the economic depression of the 1930s and the austerity of the 1940s encouraged a material orientation, it seems likely that the affluence and the economic and social oportunities of the later 1950s and the 1960s itself made such an orientation less likely. We would expect that those brought up during the latter period would be less likely to attach as much importance to their material standard of living (at least as long as it remained relatively good and secure), or indeed to be dominated by an overriding concern to make a better life in the future, and be more likely, for instance, to focus on the task of creating an active life for themselves and their families. Equally, in so far as in periods of affluence and economic growth there is less chance that individuals will be frustrated in their attainment of particular goals, there will be fewer seeking the solitude and escape of a quiet life.

Much of what we have said in this chapter about the influences on patterns of childbearing in post-war England can only be suggestive. Nonetheless we hope that it will serve both to illustrate the complexity of the processes that underly observed changes in fertility, and to direct attention to the way in which men and women think about family life and having children, assess their social and economic circumstances, and make decisions that affect their childbearing. Our arguments here reinforce, therefore, the methodological claims of the second part of the book. For if the structure and nature of our account of marriage and childbearing is proper, then we have to accept that ever more sophisticated statistical techniques based on positivist assumptions will not provide the answer to the sociologists' explanatory questions: they will only direct their attention away from the nature of people's ideas and beliefs which must be an integral part of sociological explanation and understanding.

Appendix A.   The samples

I: The pilot sample

The sample of 50 women was drawn from the birth registers for Ipswich, to which the Medical Officer of Health kindly gave us access. From the registers we drew a random sample of the names of ten mothers each of whom had had a child in one of the five years, 1957, 1959, 1961, 1963 and 1965, to ensure that our sample contained women who had had children at different times during the increase in births that had begun in the mid-1950s. For each woman we drew a second name to provide a replacement if we were unable to contact the first.

The response rate for the original sample was 78.1% with a refusal rate of 17.2%, and a no contact rate, due to couples successively not being in of 4.7%. Those couples who had moved away and so could not be interviewed are not included in these calculations. In effect we had to sample 64 people to obtain the required 50.

The sample we obtained by this procedure, though not totally unsuited to our purposes, had some distinct biases. First, it only included women who had had at least one child. Second, though in theory it could have included illegitimate births, it did not, and all the women we interviewed were married. Third, the sample was biased towards couples with large families. This is because women with more children apear more frequently in the birth registers and so have a higher chance of appearing in the sample. However, this bias helped to ensure that the sample contained some women with large families (at any given time the majority of couples have small families since many of them are incomplete). As Table A:1 shows, despite this bias over half our sample had families of only one or two children. Fourth, the association between duration of marriage and family size is exaggerated by our sampling technique. There was less chance for women married a long time who had had small families, than those married the same length of time who had had larger families, to appear in the sample, since those with smaller families would be more likely to have completed their childbearing by then.

TABLE A:1   *Pilot sample: family size and duration of marriage*

Duration of marriage (completed years)	Family size				All family sizes
	1	2	3	4 +	
0–4	3	2	1	0	6
5–9	0	9	4	0	13
10–14	2	12	6	2	22
15 +	0	0	3	6	9
All marriage durations	5	23	14	8	50

Finally, the bias towards large families in the sample also meant that groups in the population that have large families were more likely to be included in the sample. If

259

we assume the situation in 1961 applied to those we sampled this would have been groups such as self-employed professional workers, farmers who were managers and employers, the unskilled manual workers and agricultural workers – groups both high and low on the occupational scale. The distribution of the sample by socio-economic group is shown in Table A:2.

TABLE A:2   *Pilot sample: distribution by socio-economic group*

Socio-economic group	No.	%
1 Employers and managers	5	10
2 Professional workers	3	6
3 Intermediate non-manual and own-account workers	6	12
4 Lower non-manual workers and foremen	8	16
5 Skilled and semi-skilled workers	23	46
6 Unskilled and unemployed workers	5	10

Note: The socio-economic groupings used here have been combined from those used in the Census as follows:

(1) S.E.G.s 1, 2, and 13.

(2) S.E.G.s 3 and 4.

(3) S.E.G.s 5, 6, 12, and 14.

(4) S.E.G.s 7 and 8.

(5) S.E.G.s 9, 10, 15, and 16.

(6) S.E.G.s 11, 17, and 18.

II: The survey sample

The sample for the survey was obtained by the following procedure. First the addresses of 3,600 households were drawn from the electoral register for the County Borough of Ipswich for 1969, since we had calculated that we would need, on average, to approach twelve households in order to obtain one couple satisfying the necessary characteristics. Each listed household was then contacted to establish whether there was an eligible married couple living at that address, whether or not their specific names were on our list. Our calculation of the proportion of eligible couples we would find amongst the 3,600 households proved to be incorrect and the figure was closer to nine households for one eligible couple, with the 3,600 households producing 419 eligible couples. This gave us a large, and as it turned out essential latitude for refusals. As Table A:3 indicates an interview was obtained with one or both partners from only 290 of these couples. This represents a refusal rate of 31%. The same table also shows that both husband and wife were fully interviewed together in 234 out of the 290 cases.

A refusal rate of 31% is a high one; it can be explained by a number of factors. Two obvious possibilities are the subject matter of the interview and its length. Neither we suspect played much of a part in producing the high refusal rate; potential informants were only told the interview would be about family life and having children, and not specifically that contraception would be covered, and the question of the exact length was not discussed unless raised by the informant, which was not very often. Moreover both factors were present for the pilot study when the refusal rate was lower. More important were two other factors. On the one hand, there was our desire to interview both husband and wife together. This not only restricted the times when an interview could be arranged to the informants' convenience, but also meant that reluctance on the part of either partner could prejudice the chance of an interview, and so increase the overall proportion of refusals. On the other hand, there is some evidence to suggest that there has been an

TABLE A:3 *Survey sample: eligibility, refusal rate and who was interviewed*

	No.	%
(a) Eligible couples in 3,600 households		
Total eligible couples	419	11.6
Households with no eligible couples	3,128	86.9
Screening refused at household	12	0.3
No contact made at household	41	1.2
Total	3,600	100.0
(b) Refusal rate in eligible couples		
Refused to be interviewed	129	30.8
One or both spouses interviewed	290	69.2
Total	419	100.0
(c) Who was interviewed		
Couple together	234	80.7
Wife fully interviewed, husband partially	9	3.1
Wife only	43	14.8
Husband only	2	0.7
Other variations	2	0.7
Total	290	100.0

increasing reluctance amongst the population to be interviewed for social surveys.[1] In addition it may well be that the interviewers were not especially anxious to avoid refusals, though we stressed the importance of keeping the proportion low, and also may not have been especially skilful in keeping the rate to a minimum.

Use of the electoral register as a sampling frame allowed one potentially important source of bias. Since they then included only those aged 21 or over, any household in which the husband and wife were still both under 21 was excluded. However, there can have been relatively few such couples, since the proportion of marriages where both partners are under 21 is small, and in many cases one or other of the partners of those eligible for our sample would have been over 21 by the date of the electoral register. We do not think, therefore, that this bias was in practice very serious.

The distribution of our sample couples, and those who refused to be interviewed, by marriage cohort, age, family size and socio-economic group is given in Table A:4. Somewhat more of the couples we interviewed, 164 as opposed to 126, belonged to the more recent cohort, a discrepancy that may be partly accounted for by our eligibility criteria since women from the older marriage cohorts were more likely to be over 45, divorced or separated by the time of the interview. However eligible couples from the 1950s cohort were more likely to refuse than those from the 1960s one: 73 eligible couples from the earlier cohort refused to be interviewed in contrast to 56 from the later one, so that couples from the earlier cohort were almost certainly under-represented.

TABLE A:4   *Characteristics of the survey sample and of eligible couples who refused to be interviewed*

	Sample couples		Refusals	
	No.	%	No.	%
Cohort:				
3–7 years	164	57	56	43
13–17 years	126	43	73	57
Total	290	100	129	100
Wife's age last birthday:				
20–4	54	19	13	10
25–9	90	31	22	17
30–4	47	16	20	16
35–9	73	25	27	21
40–4	26	9	19	15
Not known	0	0	28	22
Total	290	100	290	100
Current family size:				
0	36	12	10	8
1	50	17	25	19
2	117	40	45	35
3	51	18	12	9
4	20	7	10	8
5 +	15	6	8	7
Not known	0	0	19	15
Total	290	100	129	100
Husband's current occupation:				
Non-manual workers	111	38	39	30
Manual workers	178	62	73	57
Not known	1	0	16	13
Total	290	100	129	100

Despite this discrepancy the figures for family size show little significant difference between those who were interviewed and those who refused, although it has to be remembered there was a relatively high proportion of cases amongst the refusals where information about family size is lacking. There is however some divergence in the distribution of the refusals by socio-economic group when compared with the sample. Manual workers and their wives appear to have been more likely to have refused to take part in the survey than non-manual workers. Again, however, a relatively high proportion (13%) of the refusals provided no information about husband's occupation and this could easily account for the discrepancy. Furthermore the nature of occupational information was often different. The respondents' information was generally provided by the husbands themselves whereas the information for those who refused was more often provided by the wives on the doorstep. Hence the reliability of such information is likely to be lower than that obtained in the full interviews.

Appendix B. Interview schedule for the pilot study

I would like to talk about your family and about how you come to have the number of children that you do. Some of the things that I want us to talk about may seem rather personal, but it is important for us to know what you think about these things, and everything that you say will be entirely confidential. We hope to write a report afterwards but we would not use your own name in it.

I: Children

1 First let us talk about the family as it is now. Tell me about your children.
    (Probe for the following if not given)
    2 How many do you have?
    3 How old are they?
    4 Are they boys or girls?
    (Write down ages and sexes.)
5 Do you intend to have any more?

II: Children's education

1 And are they at school?
    (If yes)
    2 Which school are they at?
    3 What sort of school is that?
    4 Do the other children round here go there?
    5 How are they getting on?
    6 Do they like it?
    7 What do you think of it as a school?
    8 And what sort of school do you think they will go to next?
        (If no)
        9 And where do you think they will go to school?
        10 What makes you think they will go there?
        11 What do you think of it as a school?
12 Would you rather your children could go to any other school?
13 Why is that?
14 And how important do you think education is for children?
15 What makes you think that?

III: Children – perceptions

1 And what about your children? What are they like as individuals?
2 Are they like one another?
3 Have you any particular ideas about how you want to bring your children up?
4 What about your husband, does he have the same ideas?
5 What do you think your husband feels about the children and about family life in general?

6   Do you or don't you think that:
   (a)   One of the most important things in life is to have children?
   (b)   Having many children is a lot of trouble and is not worth it?
   (c)   The more children a family has the happier it is?
   (d)   Everything considered it is better to have few children?

IV: Husband's work

1   And what about your husband/you (if husband present), what do you do?
2   Can you tell me more exactly what he does?
3   Who does he work for?
4   And how does he like his work?
5   And what about you, do you think it is a good job for him, or would you rather he were doing something else?
6   Do you and your husband talk about his work?

V: Wife's work

1   And do you go out to work at all or take work in?
   (If yes)
   2   What do you do?
   3   What exactly does that involve?
   4   Who do you work for?
   5   Do you like the work you are doing?
   6   And does doing this work create any problems or difficulties for you?
   7   What does your husband think about your job?
      (If no)
      8   Have you considered going out to work?
      9   What have you thought about it?
10 What does your husband say about the idea of you going out to work?
11 Is it something you have talked about much?

VI: Family life

1   And how do you think you all get on as a family?
2   Do you ever wish that family life was different in any sort of way?
3   How would you like it to be?
4   What sorts of things do you do as a family? Are there things that you do all together?
5   Do just you and your husband ever go out together?
6   Where might you go together?
7   How often do you think you go out together?
8   Do you wish you went out together more often?
9   And what about your husband what do you think he would think about this?
10 Do you find you talk together as a family much?
11 Do you think you compare your family life with that of other people at all?
12 What sort of differences do you think there are?
13 What sort of people do you compare your family life with?
14 Do you think the way you do things in your family is different from the way your
   (a) parents, (b) brothers and sisters, (c) friends, (d) neighbours, do things?
      (for any differences)
      15 In what way are they different?

16 Do you think you mind what other people think of you and your family?

VII: Family of origin – wife's

Can we now look right back to your own childhood,
1   Tell me first about your parents. How did you get on with them as a child?
2   What did your father do?
3   What sort of job was that exactly?
4   How did he like his job, was he satisfied with it?
5   How many brothers and sisters did you have?
6   And where did you come in the family?
7   And how did you get on with your brothers and sisters?
8   And were you particularly close to one of them in particular?
9   Do you think you were happy as a child?
10 And what about the way you were brought up, was that different from the way you are trying to bring up your own children?
11 Tell me how it is different.
12 Did your parents talk to you much and tell you things?
13 Did they, for instance, talk about sex with you ever?

VIII: Family of origin – husband's

1   And what about your husband's parents, how did he get on with them as a child?
2   What job did his father have?
3   What sort of job was that exactly?
4   And do you know how he liked his job, was he satisfied with it?
5   And how many brothers and sisters did your husband have?
6   And where did he come in the family?
7   Do you know if he was particularly close to one member of his family in particular?
8   How did he get on with his brothers and sisters?
9   Do you think he was happy as a child?
10 And what about the way he was brought up, was that different from the way you are trying to bring up your own children?
11 Tell me how it was different?
12 Do you know whether his parents talked to him much and told him things?

IX: Education and training

1   What about your own education, how long were you at school?
2   What sort of school were you at?
3   What did you think of it?
4   And did you have any further education or training?
5   What was that exactly?
6   When was that?
7   What did you think of that?
8   And what about your husband's education, how long was he at school?
9   What sort of school was he at?
10 What did he think of it?
11 And did he have any further education or training?
12 What was that exactly?

13 When was that?
14 And do you know what he thought of it?
15 And do you have any regrets about your own or your husband's education?
16 Do you think your husband has any regrets about his own or your education?
17 And how important an influence do you think your own and your husband's education has been on your way of life?

X: Marriage

And now I want you to think back to the time of your marriage. Try and forget about the present and what things are like now, and remember what it was like then and what you thought and felt.
1 Neither of you have been married before?
    (If married before)
      2 Can you give me the dates of your first marriage?
3 Can you tell me the exact date of your (present) marriage?
4 How old were you and your husband then?
5 How did you first meet your husband?
6 When was this?
7 How long was it before you started talking of marriage?
8 At what stage did you decide to get married?
9 What do you think made you wait that length of time before marrying?
10 Often you can see a reason why someone got married at a particular time in their lives. For instance to escape from their parents, a job they didn't like, or something like that. Can you see a reason why you got married at that time in your life?
11 What about your husband, can you see why he got married at that time, looking back on it?
12 Before you got married, can you remember at all what you thought marriage would be like?
13 Did you talk about what it might be like with your husband before you got married?
14 What did you say?
15 What were the things that you talked about most together between deciding to get married and your wedding? What were the important things for you during that period?
16 And do you know what your husband's main concerns were at this time?
17 What did both your families think about your getting married?
18 Were other people you knew getting married at that time? Who, for instance?
19 Did you talk to other people about getting married, to your family or friends?
20 Any particular things that they said, can you remember?
21 And were there any other important things happening in your lives or those of your families at this time?
22 What about your husband's work, what had he been doing since finishing school/training?
23 And what about your work, where had you been working since you finished school/training?
24 And what about money at that time, how was that before you got married for both of you?
25 Did you worry at all about the cost of being married rather than single?
26 Did either of you save up to get married? What were you saving for?

27 Do you think you yourself made plans about life after marriage, or did you think you would just see what happened?
28 And what about your husband, did he make plans?
29 What sort of plans did you make?

XI: After marriage

Let us now look at the period after you first got married.

Concerns
1 And when you first got married what do you think were the important things for you at the time?
2 And were there any particular worries that you had?
3 And what do you think were the important things for your husband in this period after you first got married?
4 And were there any particular worries that he had?

Residence
1 And where did you live when you first got married?
2 How many rooms did you have?
3 How did you come to live there?
4 Were you satisfied with this as a place to live in?
5 How long did you think you would stay there when you first moved there?
6 Did you think of living anywhere else or have a chance to?
7 What did you think of it as an area to live in? Why was that?
8 Did you move at all before having your first child? (IF YES, elicit information as above).

Networks
Now still thinking back to that time as I want to get as full a picture as I can of your life then.
1 Can you tell me which other people apart from your husband you saw at all regularly?
        (For each person mentioned ask)
    2   And how often would you say that you saw them at this time?
    3   And where did they/he/she live at this time?
    4   How far away was that?
        (For friends)
        5   How did you come to be friends with them?
            (For friends and brothers and sisters)
            6   What jobs did they and their husbands have?
            (Enquire for the following if not mentioned: parents, husband's brothers and sisters, other relatives, friends, neighbours)
7 And did you see your [. . .] at all at this time?
        (If no particular friends at this time)
    8   And why do you think you had no special friends at this time?

Activities
1 And what were you and your husband spending your time on in this period after you were first married?
        (for any activity)

2 And were there any other activities which you or your husband were involved in at this time? (Probe for details as above).
3 And did either of you belong to any clubs at that time?
    (If yes)
       4 What sort of club was this? (Probe for details as above).

Marital relationship
1 And thinking about your husband as he was then, can you tell me what sort of person he was?
2 So what would you say were his good points at this time?
3 And what do you think were his bad points at this time?
4 What were the things he enjoyed?
5 And how about yourself at this time, what sort of person were you then?
6 So what would you say your good points were at this time?
7 And what would you say were your bad points at this time?
8 And what sort of things did you enjoy when you first got married?
9 And how do you think you and your husband got on at this time when you were first married?
10 Did you have any particular problems at this time in your relationship?
11 How much did you talk about things when you got married?
12 How much do you think you understood each other's feelings and reactions at this time?
13 And what about sex when you first got married, how was that?
14 Did it lead to any disagreement between you?
    (If yes)
       15 So what happened?
16 Is sex something that you talked about together at this time?
17 And can you tell me who did the different things between yourselves at this time?
18 Who, for instance, paid the bills?
19 And what happened about the housework? Who did that?
20 And who did the shopping?
    (Where wife responsible)
       21 And did your husband help you at all?
22 And how did you decide things at this time, can you remember?
    (If does not respond)
       23 Can you tell me something you decided at this time and tell me how you decided this? Say something you had to buy.
24 And was that how you usually decided things?

Occupation
1 And what was your husband's job when you were first married, was it the same as before?
    (If different)
    When did he change?
       2 Can you tell me more about the job he was doing at this time then?
       3 And why did he change his job?
4 And do you know whether he was entirely satisfied with this job or did he consider other jobs?
5 How good do you think you felt his job was compared with those of other people at this time?
6 What sort of people do you think had similar jobs to your husband when you got married?

7   And did you work when you got married? (If no) Why not?
8   What was your job then, was it the same one?
9   How satisfied were you with your job then?
10 And how important would you say that working was to you at this time?

Finance

1   Do you mind giving me a rough idea of how much you and your husband were earning in this period after you were first married?
2   Was that before or after paying things like national insurance?
3   And was there any other money coming into the house at all at this time?
4   Did you get regular housekeeping money?
5   And how did you feel you were doing at this time financially, can you remember?
6   Were you worried at all about money at that time, can you remember?
7   Did you feel the money that you had coming in was enough to manage on?
8   Do you think you felt better off, worse off, or about the same financially, as before marriage?
9   How well off, did you feel compared with other people financially at this time?
10 Did you feel there were people doing noticeably better or doing noticeably worse than you financially at this time?
11 Who were these people? What sort of jobs might they have had?
12 And who do you think were the people who were in a similar position to yourselves financially at this time?
13 Where do you think you got the ideas you had at that time about how much money you needed to manage on?
14 And can you remember what you were spending your money on at this time?
15 Were there particular things at that time that you were trying to save up for?
16 And was there anything you particularly wanted and felt you couldn't afford?
17 What were these things? Have you got a TV, washing machine, fridge, car?
18 At what stage did you get that?

Future

1   How do you think you saw the future at this time?
2   Were there any particular things that you wanted to happen or things that you tried to plan for?
3   How did you think at that time, that your husband would do in future at work?
4   And how did you feel you would do financially in the future?
    Did you feel you would be better off, worse off, or about the same?
5   Did you have any ideas about living anywhere else in the future?

Family size intentions

1   And can you remember whether you had any ideas about having children at this time?
2   What were these ideas? (If not mentioned) How many children did you want?
3   And what do you think your husband's ideas were? (If not mentioned) How many children did he want?
4   Did you discuss your ideas at all?
        (If different ideas)
        5   What about the fact that you had different ideas, how did you feel this would work itself out?

6   Had you always thought this way?
      (If yes)
      7   And had you and your husband talked about this before you got
           married?
8   How clear or how vague do you think these ideas were for both of you at this
    time when you were first married?
9   Can you remember a time when these ideas became firm intentions?
      (If have intentions)
      10 And how important do you think having children was for you then? And
           how important was it how many you had?
      11 And for your husband?
12 And what do you think made you have these ideas/intentions?
13 And what do you think made your husband have these ideas/intentions? Why
    didn't you want more children?
14 Why did you think [. . .] would be a good number of children for you? Why
    didn't you want less?
15 And why do you think your husband thought [. . .] would be a good number of
    children?
      (If no ideas at this stage)
      16 And why do you think it was that you/your husband didn't have any
           ideas about having children at this stage?
17 And do you think that if for some reason you could not have ended up with
    this number you would rather have ended up with more or less?
18 And what about your husband?
19 And what do you think influenced you and your husband at this time in your
    ideas about children?
20 Did you discuss with anyone else at this time your ideas about having a family or
    how many they were intending to have?
      (If yes, what did they say?)
21 And did you think at all whether you wanted boys or girls or didn't this matter
    to you?
22 Why did you want this?
23 And what about your husband, did he want boys or girls or didn't this matter
    to him?
24 And why did he want this?
25 And did you have any ideas about when you wanted your first child?
      (If no), Why was that do you think?
26 And is this what your husband thought?
27 And did you actually intend to have it then?
28 What made you think it would be a good idea to have it then?
29 And did you have any ideas about when you wanted your other children?
      (If no), Why was that do you think?
30 What were these ideas?
31 Why did you think this would be good spacing?

Contraception
1   Did you think of using any form of birth control at all at this stage?
2   Did you discuss the question of birth control with your husband?
3   What did you both say about it?
4   So did you start using birth control at this stage?
      (If yes)

I wonder if you would mind telling me which method on my list you started using. You can tell me by the letter if you like.

(If no) Why not?

5   Exactly when did you start?
6   Which method did you start using?
7   What do you think gave you the idea of using that method?
8   Did you and your husband agree on the method to be used?
9   What did you and your husband think of it as a method?
10 Did you expect to be successful using it?
11 Did you get any advice about methods from say a doctor or a clinic?
        (If yes)
        12 What did they say?
13 Did you talk about birth control with anyone else?
14 What did they say?
15 Can you remember what you felt at this time about who should take the responsibility for birth control?
16 Why do you think you felt that?
17 Have you always thought this?
18 How much do you think you knew at the time of the different methods of birth control at this time. Perhaps you could tell me which of the ones on the list you knew of?
19 How do you think you heard of these methods?
20 Can you remember any particular ideas you had about the different methods at this time?
21 Where do you think you had got the ideas that you had at this time about birth control from?

Pregnancy
1   So when was your first child born?
2   Was this your first pregnancy?
3   Why do you think you became pregnant at this particular time?
4   And how did you feel about becoming pregnant then?
5   Were your family or friends having children at this time?
        (If contraception users in the previous interval)
        6   And had you stopped using birth control in order to get pregnant?
        7   When had you stopped exactly?
        8   So how long was it between your stopping and your getting pregnant?
        9   And how regularly had you used the method?
        10 Did you ever take chances?
        11 Had you used any other method at all during the interval?
                (If birth control not stopped in order to conceive)
                12 So what do you think the failure was due to?
        (If blames method)
        13 You don't think there could have been an occasion when you didn't use control and got pregnant?
        (If a birth)
14 And once you had had this baby, how did you feel, were you pleased to have had it then?
15 And how much difference do you think it made to your lives having this baby? What sort of difference did it make?
16 And how much help did you get from other people, from your family and friends?

XII: Subsequent intervals

And now let us look at the interval between your [. . .] and your [. . .] pregnancy/ after your last birth. Can we look and see how this was different from the previous interval. Firstly let us see what was happening at this time.

Concerns
1 And at this time, what do you think were the important things for you?
2 And were there any particular worries that you had?
3 And what do you think were the important things for your husband in this period between your [. . .] and [. . .] children/after your last pregnancy?
4 And were there any particular worries that he had?

Residence
1 And did you move at all in the time up to your next pregnancy/now?
    (If yes)
    When did you move?
    2 Where did you move to?
    3 How many rooms did you have?
    4 How did you come to move?
    5 Were you satisfied with this place to live in?
    6 And how long did you think you would stay in this place once you moved there?
    7 What did you think of it as an area to live in?
8 Did you think of living anywhere else in this period or have a chance to?

Networks
1 You told me who you had been seeing regularly in the time up to your last pregnancy, did you stop seeing any of these people in this period, or did you see any of them less or more than before?
    (For any changes)
    2 Why was this do you think?
3 And were there any other people that you or your husband started seeing at all regularly that you hadn't been seeing before?
    (If yes)
    4 Who were these people?
    5 How often would you say that you saw them at this time?
    6 Did you go and see them or did they come and see you?
    7 And where did they/he/she live?
    8 How far away was that?
    9 What jobs did they have?

Activities
1 And were there any changes in how you or your husband spent your time during this period, did you have less or more time to spend on things you have already mentioned?
2 Did you start any new activities at this time, or drop other ones?
    (For any changes)
    3 And why do you think this happened?
    (For new activities)
    4 And how much time did you/he spend on this?
    5 How much time did you spend on this and how important was it to you/him?

6   Did either of you belong to any clubs at this time?

Marital relationship

1   And what about your husband at this time do you think he had changed at all in what you felt were his good and bad points, did the last pregnancy make any difference?

2   And what about yourself, do you think you changed at all in what were your good and bad points after the last [. . .] pregnancy?

3   Do you think the things that your husband enjoyed and gave him pleasure were at all different at this time?

4   And do you think that the things you enjoyed and gave you pleasure at this time were at all different?

5   And how do you think you and your husband were getting on at this stage in your married life?

6   Did you have any particular problems at this time in your relationship?

7   What sort of things did you talk about together at this time, can you remember?

8   Do you think there had been any changes in the extent to which you understood each other's thoughts and feelings in different situations?

9   And what about sex at this time, after your [. . .] child, did that alter at all?

10   Do you think either you or your husband's feelings about it changed at all?

11   Did it lead to any disagreement at this time between you?
        (If yes)
        12 So what happened?

13   Was sex something that you talked about together at this time?

14   And were there any changes in who did the different things in the family now that you had this [. . .] child?

15   Who looked after the children?

16   Who disciplined the children?

17   And were there any changes in how you decided something after this child was born?

18   How did you decide things about the children for instance?

Occupation

1   And what was your husband's job in this period between your [. . .] and [. . .] births/after your last birth, was it the same as before?
        (If different)
        2   So when did he change his job?
        3   And what exactly was his new job?
        4   Why did he leave his previous job?

5   And do you know whether he was entirely satisfied with his job during this period or did he consider other jobs at all?

6   And how good do you think his job was during this period?
        (If new job in the interval)
        7   And in this job what sort of people do you think had similar jobs to your husband?
        8   And did your husband change jobs again at all in this period!
        (If yes get details as above)

(If wife working before)

9   And did you go on working during this period?
        (If yes)
        10 Did you keep the same job?
                (If no)

11 Why did you stop working at this stage?
(If different job)
12 And what was your new job?
13 How satisfied were you with it?
14 Did it create any problems for you?
15 And how important would you say that working was to you at this time?

Finance

1 Do you mind giving me a rough idea of how much both of you/your husband was earning in this period between your [. . .] and [. . .] children/after your last child?
2 Was that before or after deductions?
3 And was there any other money coming into the house at the time?
4 How did you feel you were doing at this time financially, can you remember?
5 Were you worried at all at this time about money can you remember?
6 You felt that the money that you had coming in was enough to manage on can you remember?
7 Do you think you felt better off, worse off or about the same as before that child was born?
How well off did you feel compared with other people at this time?
8 Did you feel there were people doing better or worse than you financially at this time?
9 Who were these people?
10 What did you feel about this?
11 Why was that?
12 And who did you think were the people who were in a similar position to yourselves financially at this time?
13 What do you think influenced at this time in how much money you needed to manage on?
14 Did you notice more how other people were doing now you had [. . .] children? Who were the people whose finances you noticed?
15 And can you remember what you were spending your money on in this period after your [. . .] child was born?
16 Was there anything in particular that you were trying to save up for at this time?
17 And was there anything you particularly wanted and felt that you couldn't afford?
18 What were these things?

Future

1 How did you see the future at this time?
2 Were there any particular things that you wanted to happen or that you were trying to plan for?
3 How did you think at the time that your husband would do in the future at work?
4 And how did you feel you would do financially in the future, did you feel you would be better off, worse off, or about the same?
5 And did you have any ideas about living anywhere else in the future?

Family size intentions

1 And after you had had this [. . .] child/pregnancy (if not a live birth) what were your ideas about having children were they the same?
2 And what about your husband, were his ideas the same?

(If different for either)

   3   What were you/your husband's ideas then at this time?

   4   What do you think gave you these ideas?

   5   Why did you/your husband think that this would be a good number of children for you?

6 Did you talk at all about your ideas about family size at this stage?

7 And do you think your ideas became more or less clear after having this [. . .] child/pregnancy or were they about the same?

   (If more or less clear)

   8   Why do you think this was?

9 And do you think the ideas that you had at this stage were what you intended to do?

10 And how important do you think these ideas/intentions were for you at this stage?

   What if you couldn't have another?

   (If no ideas at this stage)

   11 And why do you think you/your husband didn't have any ideas about having children at this stage?

12 And did it matter to you at this stage whether you had boys or girls?

13 And did it matter to your husband?

   (For either)

   14 Why do you think that was?

15 And did you have any ideas about when you wanted your next child?

16 And is this what your husband thought?

17 Why did you want it then?

18 And was this when you intended to have it?

19 And did you have any ideas about the spacing of other children at this time?

20 What were these ideas?

21 Why did you think that would be good spacing?

22 (If after last intended child) Is there any chance of your deciding for another?

Contraception

(If contraceptive users in the previous interval)

1 So did you start using birth control again after this child/pregnancy?

   (If yes)

   2   Exactly when did you start?

   3   And did you go on using the same method?

      (If yes)

      4   What so you think made you go on with that method?

      4a Did you consider other methods?

         (If no)

         5   Which method did you start using?

         6 Why do you think you chose this method?

         7 Why do you think you didn't stick to the previous method?

         8 Did you get any advice about using this method? What did you think of it as a method?

9 And did you expect to be successful using this method at this time?

   (If no)

   10 And why do you think you stopped using birth control at this stage?

   11 Did you expect to use it again at a later date?

   12 When was this?

(If control not used before)
13 And did you start using birth control at this stage?
> (If yes)
> 14 Exactly when did you start?
> 15 What do you think made you start at this stage?
> 16 Which method did you start using?
> 17 Why do you think you started using that method?
> 18 Did you and your husband agree on the method to be used?
> 19 What did you think of it as a method?
> 20 Did you expect to be successful using it?
> 21 Did you get any advice about methods to be used?
> > (If no)
> > 22 Why do you think you didn't start using birth control?
> > 23 Did you intend to start using it at any later stage?

(All users)
24 And how regularly did you use the method between your [. . .] and [. . .] children/after your last child?
(If not regular), Why do you think you didn't use it regularly?
25 Did you ever take chances?
26 Had you used any other methods during the interval?
> (If yes)
> 27 What other methods had you used?
> 28 How often had you used them?
29 Did you talk about birth control with anyone else at this stage?
30 What did they say?
31 Can you remember what you felt at this stage about who should take the responsibility for birth control?
32 Why did you feel that?
33 And can you tell me if you knew of any more methods of birth control during this stage, are there any on this list that you first heard of at this time?
34 How did you come to hear of these methods?
35 (For period after last birth) Do you think you will stick to this method in the future?

Pregnancy
1 So when did you next become pregnant?
2 Why do you think you became pregnant at that particular time?
3 Were your friends or family having children at this time?
4 How did you feel about becoming pregnant then?
> (If contraceptive users in the previous interval)
> 5 And had you stopped using control in order to get pregnant?
> 6 When had you stopped exactly?
> 7 So how long was it between your stopping and getting pregnant?
> > (If birth control not stopped in order to conceive)
> > 8 So what do you think the failure was due to?
> > > (If blames method)
> > > 9 You don't think there could have been an occasion when you didn't use control and got pregnant?

(If a birth)
10 And when exactly was this child born?
11 And once you had this baby, how did you feel, were you pleased to have had it then?

13 And how much difference did it make to your lives having this baby? Did it make as much difference as having the first child?
14 And how much help did you get (any help) from other people, from your parents, brothers and sisters, friends and neighbours?

(Repeat Section XII for each pregnancy)

XIII: Pregnancy – general

And can I ask you one or two more questions about being pregnant?
1 And are there any other times when you have been pregnant or thought you have been pregnant, but haven't had a full pregnancy with a live birth?
2 And have you ever had any reason to think you might have difficulty in getting pregnant?
    (If yes)
        3 When was this?
        4 What made you think you might have difficulty?
        5 Did you or your husband seek any advice?
        6 And did this alter your ideas about having children at all?
7 And how do you feel when you are pregnant, do you feel happier, more satisfied, more worried?
8 And what about your usual tasks when you are pregnant, do you feel that you should keep these up?
9 Does being pregnant make you worried about your health?
10 Does the idea of being pregnant seem something natural to you? (If no) why not?
11 And who do you think knows how to handle the situation of pregnancy best, the mother or the doctor?

XIV: Future – general

1 In general would you say that it is better to make plans for most things in life or is it better to leave them and see what happens?
2 Is a family something you should plan for?
3 In practice do you make plans in advance or do you take things as they come?
4 And your husband?
5 Have you any ideas about what jobs you would like your children to do?
6 And what about your husband, do you think he has any particular ideas for them?
7 Do you think a child should follow in his father's footsteps?
8 Do you plan to go to work at all in the future/change your job?
9 When might that be?
10 What sort of job might you get?
11 What do you think you will feel like when the children leave home?
12 And do you think your husband will change his job again?
13 Do you think he would like to?
14 What might he do?
15 What sort of lives do you think your children are going to have?

XV: Family size

1 What do you think is the ideal number of children for the average family?
2 What do you think makes that a good number?
3 What about the ideal for people like yourselves?

4 What makes that a good number?
5 Why in fact do you think people have different numbers of children?
> (If finance given as a reason)
>> 6 But families with much the same amount of money coming in still want different numbers of children, why do you think that is?
7 How many children to you seems a large family?
8 And how many children to you seems a small family?
9 And what sort of people do you think have what you call a large family?
10 And what sort of people do you think have what you call a small family?
11 What if you had [. . .] children (two more than the present intended number) what difference do you think it would have made?
12 And what if you had [. . .] children (two less, if possible, than the intended number, but at least one), what difference do you think it would have made?
13 And what if you had had no children, what difference do you think that would have made?
14 At what stage in their lives do you like children best? Why is that?
15 What are the main pleasures that you get from your children?

XVI: Family life – general

1 And what do you think are the main things a husband has to do in the family?
2 And what do you think are the main things a wife has to do in the family?
3 And what do you think a good daughter would be like?
4 And what do you think a good son would be like?
5 What do you feel are the important things in keeping a family ticking over?
6 And what things make family life more difficult?
7 What do you think have been the main changes in family life over the last twenty-five years?
> (If changes in family size not mentioned)
>> 8 What about the number of children that people have, do you think people have larger or smaller families than twenty-five years ago? [. . .] than ten years ago?
>> 9 Why do you think that is?
10 What sort of things make you anxious or worried?
11 And do you have any anxieties about being a mother?
12 What sort of things make your husband anxious or worried?
13 Do you ever wonder whether you are a selfish person?

XVII: Social class

1 Some people think you can divide the country into different groups of people, how would you divide people in Britain if you had to?
2 (If classes not mentioned) Some people divide Britain into classes, into which classes would you divide people in Britain if you had to?
3 And where would you put yourself?
4 Do you think your position has changed at all during your marriage?
5 Is that the same as your family or friends?
6 Why would you put yourselves/them there?
7 Do you in fact think this is an important difference between people in Britain!
8 What sort of difference do you think it makes to the people in the different groups?

XVIII: Religion and politics

1 And do either of you have any religion? Which is that?
2 And how important would you say it is to you/your husband/both of you?
3 Do you go to church at all?
       (If yes)
       4   How often do you go?
5 And what do you think makes you/your husband/both of you [. . .] (whatever religion)?
6 What sort of difference do you think it makes to your life?
7 Is religion something you and your husband ever talk about? About how often?
8 And do either of you vote at elections?
9 Do you mind saying which party you vote for?
10 What do you think makes you vote for that party?
11 Have your politics changed at all since you have been married?
12 Do either of you actually belong to the party?
13 Do you think your politics are the same as those of your family and friends?
14 How interested would you say you and your husband are in politics?
15 Is politics something you and your husband ever talk about? About how often?

XIX: Children – repeat

And finally, do you mind if we go over those questions again that I asked you earlier about children?
1   (a)   Do you or don't you think that in life there are many things more important than having children?
    (b)   Do you or don't you think that having many children is a burden, but worth the trouble?
    (c)   Do you or don't you think that the fewer the children a family has the happier it is?
    (d)   Do you or don't you think that everything considered it is best to have many children?

List of contraceptive methods shown to respondents.
A   Safe period; rhythm
B   Abstinence; no intercourse
C   Rubber; condom; sheath
D   Withdrawal
E   Diaphragm; cap
F   Douche
G   Jelly; cream
H   Suppositories
I   Foam tablets
J   Sponge; tampon
K   Pill
L   I.U.D.; the coil; the loop

Notes

Chapter 1. Introduction.
1. Mamdani (1972), p.78.
2. Turnbull (1972), p.136.
3. Quoted in Fest (1972), p.398.
4. From the selection of extracts in Pohlman (1973), p.283.
5. Quoted in Branson and Heinemann (1973), p.183.
6. The development of demography is documented in Lorimer (1959) and Glass (1973).
7. Registration and Census data provides, of course, more accurate information about family size, and the timing and spacing of births. Likewise as we point out later, other studies such as those of Glass (1971), Cartwright (1970), and Woolf (1971) offer more reliable data about contraceptive use in England at the end of the 1960s.
8. Eversley (1959) argued that a new alignment of demography with sociology was taking place to replace the former tie with economics. However, the development of a new tradition of economic theories of fertility based on utilitarian ideas has re-established the old alignment with economics, if it was ever greatly disturbed.
9. Eversley (*ibid.*, pp.11-12) implies that population theory and demography, which he takes to be exclusively a discipline concerned with measurement, need to be distinguished. We take population theory to be, at least in principle, part of the subject matter of demography.
10. Cf. our discussion of surveys in Chapter 7, and previous research on fertility in Chapter 5.
11. Hawthorn and Busfield (1968a), pp.169-76.
12. Office of Population Censuses and Surveys, *Population Trends,* I, Table 12, HMSO, 1975.
13. Registrar General (1975), *Statistical Review of England and Wales, 1973,* Part II, Table DI.
14. *Loc. cit.*
15. Population Panel (1973).
16. See for instance Wrigley (1966)
17. Clark (1967), p.64.
18. Habakkuk (1971), p.26.
19. Deane and Cole (1962), p.127.
20. The evidence is discussed by Habakkuk (1971), pp.54-5.
21. *Ibid.,* p. 56.
22. See Matras (1965); Lewis-Faning (1949).
23. Patterns of marriage in Europe and elsewhere are discussed by Hajnal (1965).
24. We calculated (Hawthorn and Busfield (1968a), using period data, that over 50% of total annual fertility was achieved by women married less than five years, and over 80% by women married less than ten, between the years 1951-62.
25. Registrar General (1975), *Statistical Review of England and Wales, 1973,* Part II, Table K.
26. *Ibid.,* Table L.
27. We have discussed these changes at greater length in Hawthorn and Busfield (1968a), and Busfield and Hawthorn (1971).
28. Registrar General (1975), *Quarterly Return for England and Wales,* 30 June 1974, p.46.
29. A point made by Glass (1971), p.191.

30. The most recent example, which provoked a furore was Sir Keith Joseph's 'remoralisation' speech at Birmingham. (See, *The Times,* 19 October 1974).
31. General Register Officer (1959), *Census 1951: Fertility Tables.*
32. See Wynn (1972), especially Chapter 7.
33. Registrar General (1975), *Quarterly Return for England and Wales,* 30 June 1974, p.45.
34. For calculations of mean birth intervals for 1951 to 1962 based on period data see Hawthorn and Busfield (1968a).
35. Some of the evidence is discussed by Glass (1971), p.198.
36. Registrar General (1975), *Statistical Review of England and Wales, 1945-73.*
37. *Ibid.*
38. Registrar General (1975), *Statistical Review of England and Wales, 1973,* Part II, Table D.1.
39. These are described by a number of authors; see, for example Clark (1967).
40. Population change in France is discussed in detail in Aries (1971).
41. See Glass (1968). One interesting exception is Italy where the mean age at marriage for both men and women, though not exceptionally high, has not yet declined significantly (in the period 1964-6 the mean age at first marriage was 28.1 for men and 24.4 for women).
42. Glass (1968).
43. *Ibid.*
44. Hauser (1971).
45. Some of the data are discussed by Hawthorn (1970), pp.10-14.
46. Sullerot (1971), pp.63-4.
47. See Aries (1962). Of course his time span is a long one, but his analysis points to some of the changes in ideas about childhood that need to be considered.
48. The impact of feminism on the decline in fertility in the second half of the nineteenth century has been analysed by Banks and Banks (1964), who argue that its importance was not very great. We cannot however, assume that this is always the case.
49. Adams and Meidam (1968); Altus (1966).
50. Sears, Maccoby and Levin (1957).
51. See, for instance, Feldman (1971).
52. Young and Willmott (1973), p.90.
53. The correlation has been pointed to by Hill, Stycos and Back (1959); Rainwater (1965).

Chapter 2. Malthusian theories of population.

1. See the interesting history of ideas about fertility by Eversley (1959).
2. His work is examined by a number of authors: Flew (1970); Glass (1953); Davis (1955); Spengler (1945), as well as Eversley (1959) himself.
3. Flew (1970), p.87.
4. *Ibid.*, p.73.
5. *Ibid.*, p.243.
6. *Ibid.*, p.244.
7. Davis (1963).
8. *Ibid.*, p.351.
9. Eversley (1959), p.2.
10. Davis (1963), and Banks (1954).
11. Blake (1961; 1968).

12. Habakkuk (1971).
13. See the classical statement of Carr-Saunders (1922). For a more recent discussion see Taylor (1970), and Douglas (1966).
14. Wynne-Edwards (1962).
15. Malthus' influence on Darwin is discussed by Flew (1970), pp.48-51.
16. *Ibid.*, p.26.
17. *Ibid.*, p.29.
18. Davis (1963).
19. Habakkuk (1971).
20. *Ibid.*, p.10.
21. Wrigley (1969).
22. Habakkuk (1971), p.12.
23. *Ibid.*, p.15.
24. It does not agree in some particulars, for instance, with the account in Chambers (1972).
25. As Eversley (1959) shows. See pp.249-54.
26. Habakkuk (1971), p.20.
27. Mortality is, of course, at times directly the result of human agency. Chambers (1972) points out that 'Exposure in the streets, desertion by parents, and a deliberate destruction of infant life by parish authorities were everyday occurrences in London, perhaps especially in the first half of the eighteenth century.' (p.78.)
28. Habakkuk (1971), p.16.
29. Braudel (1973), p.38.
30. *Ibid.*, p.xiv.

Chapter 3. Utilitarian theories of fertility.

1. Some of the main theoretical formulations of this type are to be found in Leibenstein (1957); Okun (1958); Becker (1960); Easterlin (1969); Schultz (1969); Hawthorn (1970); Willis (1973). The approach as a whole is often referred to as 'new home economics'.
2. Becker (1965) and later authors – Lancaster (1966), Willis (1973) – have argued that it is 'commodities' rather than conventional economic goods that are the true objects of family utility. The former differ from the latter, according to these authors, in being produced by combining time supplied by family members with goods and services purchased in the market.
3. Though the use of couples, households or families as the unit of analysis instead of individuals is in some respects appropriate, it raises a number of problems, since invariably additional assumptions about the inter-relationships between units are entailed, and in practice, as Ryder (1973, p.566) points out, the composite unit tends to be treated as if it were a single individual.
4. Leibenstein (1957); Okun (1958); Becker (1960).
5. See especially Mincer (1963), and Becker (1965).
6. Willis' (1973) model is an example of this.
7. See for instance Easterlin (1969) and Michael (1973).
8. Easterlin (1969). For a long list of suggestions see Namboodiri (1972).
9. Brief critiques are to be found in Duesenberry (1960) and Ryder (1973).
10. Blake (1968).
11. Simon (1957), pp.196-7.
12. Easterlin (1969), p.147.

13. Willis (1973), p.519.
14. *Ibid.*, p.517.
15. *Ibid.*, p.519.
16. Becker (1960), p.210.
17. Willis (1973), p.517.
18. See for instance Robbins (1935); Dobb (1937); Friedman (1953); Koopmans (1957); Little (1957); Nagel (1963); Nell (1972); Hollis and Ryan (1973); Hollis and Nell (1975).
19. Nagel (1963), *passim.*
20. *Ibid.*, p.211.
21. This is the formulation as presented and attacked by Nell (1972).
22. Becker (1960; 1965); Mincer (1963); Willis (1973).
23. See the comment made by Schultz (1973), p.57.
24. Many of the correlations are discussed by Simon (1969).
25. Becker (1960); Easterlin (1969).
26. Blake (1968) in her critique of Becker's theory pointed out that there is little evidence of a positive association between *desired* family size and income either. But Becker could well argue that statements about desired family size do not properly control for differences in contraceptive knowledge.
27. Ben-Porath (1973), p.S203.
28. See for instance Willis (1973); Gardner (1973).
29. A number of attempts to do this are discussed by Espenshade (1972).
30. Willis (1973), p.S48.
31. *Ibid.*, p.S48.
32. One exception is to be found in Gronau's (1973) discussion of the price of time to women.
33. We take it as axiomatic that in order to demonstrate that a theory's predictions fit the facts it has to be possible to demonstrate that they do not.
34. A point emphasised by Simon (1957) in his discussion of the traditional model of economic man. See especially pp.196-206.
35. A point that Willis (1973) himself makes: 'Caution', he says 'must be exercised in accepting the explanation of fertility behaviour provided by this model, because the mechanism by which the empirical regularity is generated need not correspond exactly or even chiefly to the one posited in theoretical model' (p.S53).
36. Robbins (1935), pp.126-7.
37. Nell (1972), pp.77-8.
38. Both Easterlin (1969) and Hawthorn (1970), though they have different ideas about the relation between norms and tastes (Easterlin equates the two), suggest that the two types of explanation are not incompatible. Our own analysis suggests that they are.
39. Blake (1968), for instance, points to numerous differences.
40. Willis (1973, p.S16) for one, lists several, though as Ryder (1973, p.567) points out he by no means tackles all or even many of the problems they raise.
41. See, for instance, Douglas (1966); Lorimer (1958).
42. In theory it is possible to extend the models to include 'resources' such as energy, love, patience and so on. In practice to do so would involve making even more problematic assumptions than the inclusion of differences in the price of, and availability of time has done.
43. Some of the problems with the assumption that utilities are comparable are discussed by Little (1957).
44. Becker (1960), p.215.

45. This is quoted in Klein (1965), p.148.
46. Simon (1957), p.198.
47. Eversley (1959), p.2.
48. One outcome of the failure to examine the relations between units is that the possible *interdependence* of utilities is ignored. The problem of the interdependence of the utilities of different family members are briefly discussed by Willis (1973), (pp.518-19), but in effect he ignores it by creating a single utility function of the individual type for the famly as a whole.
49. Simon (1957), Chapter 14.
50. As our comments here indicate we do not agree with Hawthorn (1974) that 'as an ideal type the fiction of economic man (and wife) is a useful one to match against reality'.
51. Ryder (1973), p.566.
52. See, for instance, Nell (1972), and Hunt and Schwartz (1972), for critiques of utilitarian ideas in economics, and Parsons (1949; 1937) for a critique of their use in sociology. Hollis and Nell (1975) critically examine the basis of all utilitarian philosophies.
53. The importance of this criterion is argued by a number of authors. See, for instance, Harré and Secord (1972), Chapter II.

Chapter 4. The foundations for a theory

1. There are a few sociological theories of population and fertility that attempt to move away from the Malthusian and utilitarian approaches; most of them are unsatisfactory and we do not intend to consider them in any detail here.
2. The term is, of course, taken from Gouldner (1971).
3. Eversley (1959), p.277.
4. Most social scientists accept this, though behaviourist psychologists have shown a remarkable reluctance to do so; they do not agree about its implications.
5. The way in which we have to examine meanings in order to identify actions is discussed by Taylor (1964), for example.
6. Some of these differences are discussed in more detail in Chapter 10.
7. We would obviously include utilitarian theorists here, but oversimple notions of rationality are common in sociology.
8. Eversley (1959), Chapter IV.
9. Blau and Duncan (1967), for instance, in their discussion of the possible association between social mobility and fertility mention several hypotheses that might account for an association between the two, including the idea that ambition may lead to the postponement of marriage and childbearing; but they do not consider whether the hypotheses are plausible for contemporary industrial society.
10. An emphasis on the social character of human action is often held to be the hallmark of sociology. Dumont (1965) for instance says 'Sociology begins in earnest with what I would call the 'sociological aperception', i.e. the perception by the student of himself as a social being, as opposed to a self sufficient individual' (p.16).
11. A phrase that gained wider currency with the publication of Berger and Luckman's book, *The Social Construction of Reality* (1966).
12. See, for example, Parsons (1951).
13. Some of the points we make are raised by Lockwood (1956); Wrong (1966); Mann (1970).
14. Dahrendorf (1973).

15. Giddens (1974), p.8. See also Schutz (1967).
16. Berger and Luckmann (1966) amongst others, make this point.
17. See especially Chapter 11.
18. See for instance Rose (1962), p.10.
19. Lane (1974), p.24.
20. The difference emerges from the material in Chapter 10.
21. Clearly we owe this point and the notion of 'taken for granted' beliefs to ethnomethodology. See Garfinkel (1967).
22. An actor's systems of meaning differ in character from the systems of thought developed in science; in particular they are not subject to the same pressures for coherence, clarity, internal consistency, and so on. (Schutz, 1967; Garfinkel, 1960).
23. See, for instance Zajonc (1960).
24. The issue is discussed in numerous places, see: Nagel (1961); Popper (1963); Emmet and MacIntyre (1970); Ryan (1973); Giddens (1974).
25. Winch (1958).
26. MacIntyre (1967); Davidson (1963).
27. The problem is outlined by Walsh (1972) for example.
28. Jarvie (1973).
29. Gellner (1974).

Chapter 5. A natural history of the research

1. Hammond (1964) goes some way to fill the gap, though the accounts of the research activity are not presented in the context of research findings. See also Fletcher (1974). Natural histories of research are recommended by Cicourel (1964, Chapter 2), amongst others.
2. Sloman (1964).
3. Two comments from Lord Annan's recent report (1974) are of interest in this context. The first (p.5) claims that Essex has established a reputation for research; 'Essex' he asserts 'is outstanding among the new Universities for its record in research.' The second records that many members of the academic staff feel that research has not only been given high priority, but too high a one: 'The majority of my correspondents among the academic staff who considered the matter believe that the balance [between teaching and research] is tipped too far towards research and, in particular, that the man who is really prepared to devote his time to students is penalised and has less chance of promotion than the one who amasses a pile of publications. Essex may be unusual among new Universities to demand from young lecturers evidence of completed research within five years of employment.'
4. Hawthorn (1965).
5. *Ibid.*, p.5.
6. The following passages are taken from a personal communication from Geoffrey Hawthorn (April 1975) reconstructing his reasons for doing the research.
7. Hawthorn (1965), p.1.
8. Goldthorpe et al. (1968a; 1968b; 1969).
9. Hawthorn and Busfield (1968a).
10. See Westoff et al. (1961; 1963); Whelpton and Kiser (1950; 1952; 1954; 1958; 1964); Freedman et al. (1959).
11. Hawthorn (1968).
12. Hawthorn and Busfield (1966a).
13. *Ibid.*, p.204.

14. We nowhere, for instance, demonstrated the value of distinguishing between macro- and micro-aggregrate levels, or for that matter between the material cultural and environment.
15. Hawthorn (1968).
16. See Wynne-Edwards (1962) and Banks (1954). As we have argued in Chapter 2 Malthus attempts just such a combination but the exercise is doomed to failure.
17. Hawthorn and Busfield (1968b).
18. See Galtung (1966).
19. Hawthorn and Busfield (1968b), pp.7-8. The works referred to are Banks (1954); Rainwater (1960; 1965); Easterlin (1962).
20. *Ibid.*, p.8.
21. See Calhoun (1962).
22. Rainwater (1960; 1965); Hill et al. (1959).
23. Bott (1957).
24. Whelpton et al. (1966).
25. Hawthorn and Busfield (1968b).
26. See Macintyre (1962; 1967).
27. Rainwater (1965).
28. Patterns of sexual intercourse did not seem likely to be an explanatory factor, in its own right, we thought, since it was the *desire* to control childbearing that counted.
29. See our discussion of religion in our first summary of the literature (Hawthorn and Busfield 1968a).
30. Moser and Scott (1961).
31. Hawthorn and Busfield (1968b).
32. Galtung (1967).
33. Personal Communication, April 1975.
34. Woolf (1971).
35. Hawthorn (1970).
36. *Ibid.*, especially Chapters 4 and 6.
37. Hawthorn and Paddon (1971); Busfield (1974).
38. Davis and Blake (1956).
39. Theoretical models like that of Glasser and Lachenbruch (1968) had shown the potential impact on conception of varying patterns of intercourse.
40. Woolf (1971).

Chapter 6. A chapter of errors.
1. Galtung (1967), p.131.
2. Some studies have shown extremely poor recall of events such as spending time in hospital, even after a very short period of time. Many of the studies are discussed by Cannell and Kahn (1968).
3. Here, as elsewhere, we were constrained by the way in which the statistics were collected to shift the boundaries of our universe. Our demographic statistics referred to England and Wales, the analysis of towns to Britain.
4. Office of Population Censuses and Surveys (1973), *Census 1971, County Reports: East Suffolk;* Ipswich County Borough Council (1972b), pp.5-7.
5. Department of Employment Gazette (1973 and earlier).
6. Ipswich County Borough Council (1972c).
7. Moser and Scott (1961).
8. Office of Population Censuses and Surveys (1973), *Census 1971, County Reports: East Suffolk;* Office of Population Censuses and Surveys (1974) *Age, Marital Condition and General Tables.*

9.   Ipswich County Borough Council (1972c).
10.   Office of Population Censuses and Surveys (1973), *Census 1971, County Reports: East Suffolk;* Office of Population Censuses and Surveys (1974), *Age, Marital Condition and General Tables.*
11.   Ipswich Couny Borough Council (1972a).
12.   Though even this is not entirely correct, since we know that some of the survey sample, for instance, came from the West Indies. It also means that there is a gap between the demographic statistics which relate to England and Wales and the social conditions and culture that we have studied which we think are best termed English.
13.   The first was produced by combining the Registrar General's Socio-Economic groups so that instead of the original 18 there remained only eight (plus one category for the unemployed). The other was a reconstruction by Peter Townsend from what remained of the original classification prepared by David Glass for the social mobility study in 1949 (Glass, 1954), which attempted to make finer distinctions in the middle range of occupations and made use (partly for this reason) of data on income.
14.   There were one or two significant exceptions amongst our coders and it should be emphasised that where coding was poor the blame did not normally lie with the coders.
15.   Of course, there have been changes in the S.S.R.C. since then; we suspect however, that underbudgetting is still a problem. In particular, since applicants may well feel (perhaps wrongly) that a small budget is more likely to be acceptable than a high one, it is especially important that funding agencies should be on the look out for this.

Chapter 7. Survey research.
1.   This is Giddens' (1974, p.3.) description of the term. A useful discussion of positivism is to be found in Kolakowski (1973).
2.   We have based these questions on the sort of justifications for using survey techniques commonly found in methodology textbooks.
3.   Cicourel (1964) passim. What he says applies, of course, to data collection as well as analysis.
4.   Austin (1961).
5.   See, for instance, Hindess (1973).
6.   Cicourel (1967; 1974).
7.   A useful discussion of a similar problem in the study of personality is Allport (1962) who contrasts 'dimensional' and 'morphogenic' approaches.
8.   The problems of scaling and measurement are discussed by Blalock (1960).
9.   The problems of making inferences from tests of significance are discussed by Selvin (1957).
10.   Willer and Willer (1973), p.53.
11.   The foundations of survey procedures are examined in some detail by Willer and Willer (*ibid.*).
12.   Selvin (1957), p.522.
13.   *loc. cit.*
14.   *loc. cit.*
15.   Biological statisticians have developed a number of techniques, such as probit and tobit analysis, to handle variables. They present specific problems of their own and have attracted virtually no attention from social scientists.
16.   Cf. the arguments in Part I of this book.

17. Which is part of Cicourel's argument (1964).
18. See, for instance, Hyman, et al., (1954).
19. More thorough testing of our questionnaire would probably have shown us that the question was not being interpreted as we intended. Even if it had, it would have been difficult to find a question that would be interpreted uniformly throughout the sample.
20. See Chapter 4 above.
21. The techniques used are described in Appendix C of the third and final volume of the study (Goldthorpe, et al., 1969, pp.200-2.).
22. The point is discussed by Platt (1971).

Chapter 8. Marriage.
 1. Here and throughout the final section of the book we have adopted the convention of using the present tense when describing the ideas and beliefs we identified at the time we carried out our study. As we make clear elsewhere some of these ideas and beliefs may have changed by now.
 2. One of us, (Busfield, 1972), has discussed the reasons for the association at greater length elsewhere.
 3. Royal Anthropological Institute (1951).
 4. Hajnal (1965).
 5. The argument is spelled out by Glass (1968). Both he and Hajnal talk of a revolution in patterns of marriage in the post-war period.
 6. There is a more detailed discussion of the stigmatisation of illegitimacy in Busfield (1974a, pp.15-16).
 7. Some of the problems are discussed by Abrams and McCulloch (1974).
 8. It would be interesting to compare differing beliefs as to whether having a wife is an advantage in gaining or maintaining power and status in various contexts (cf. the discussion as to whether being a bachelor was a political advantage or disadvantage for Edward Heath). Hitler apparently felt strongly that 'in view of the decisive importance of women in the elections he could not afford to marry', (Fest, 1972). Naval wisdom apparently has it that 'you mustn't marry as a lieutenant, you may marry as a lieutenant commander, and you must marry as a commander'.
 9. Mair (1971).
10. Clearly any judgement depends on the point of time that you take for comparison, and the standards that you apply. In Victorian England the *appearance* of having a respectable, moral life was all important.
11. Registrar General (1974), *Statistical Review of England and Wales, 1972,* Part II.
12. *Ibid.*
14. The point was suggested by Robert Chester.
15. This can be inferred from the Census figures for family size by duration of marriage and socio-economic group. General Register Office, (1966).
16. The trends are described in Bain, Bacon and Pimlott (1972, pp.99-101).
17. This is one reason why a war brings about important changes in the nature of the employed population.
18. Presumably the decline in domestic service occupations may also have encouraged men to marry, since unless they continued to live in their family of origin, or married, domestic help would be difficult to obtain.
19. For a recent picture see Graham Greene's autobiography, *A Sort of Life.*
20. The trends are outlined by Halsey (1972).
21. Hajnal (1965), p.133.

22. Habakkuk, (1971), p.11.
23. Banks (1954).
24. One obvious change is that families are now smaller on average. Quite what affect this has had on *standards* is more difficult to determine.
25. Housing was mentioned far more frequently in connection with marriage than with having children *per se;* for most people, married life means family life hence it is marriage that raises the question of housing and is presumably most directly affected by the state of the housing market.
26. See Rollet (1972), Table 10:20, p.307.
27. The contrast with some of the passages cited in Banks (1954) is very striking.
28. Though the effectiveness of the cushioning varies over time, and has recently been less good.
29. This point is discussed in more detail in Busfield (1972).

Chapter 9. Thinking about children.

1   The possible influence of changes in contraceptive technology on ideas about family size is considered in Chapter 12.
2. This is because the Census only asks questions about the fertility of women who have been married at some time and it is not possible to make the necessary calculations from the information provided by the Registrar General.
3. Registrar General (1974), *Statistical Review of England and Wales,* 1972, Part II, Table QQc.
4. In using the data from the pilot study we have to rely on comments about children made by those who already have one or more; nevertheless there is every reason to suppose that these ideas are familiar to those who have not yet had children as well as to those who have.
5. Chester (1972).
6. Townsend (1963).
7. Dennis, Henriques and Slaughter (1969), p.238.
8. In the survey when asked 'What sort of disadvantages are there in having children?' as many as 42% of wives and 38% of husbands who gave a specific answer to the question, said there were no disadvantages in having children. Of those who saw some disadvantages what we categorised as the 'social restriction' of children was most commonly mentioned (by well over half of them).
9. See some of the material in Lorimer (1958).
10. This illustrated in a study by MacIntyre (1974) of the 'pregnancy careers' of single women.
11. This was Mrs Osborn whose contraceptive difficulties are described in more detail in Chapter 12.
12. This is illustrated by data from the recent Family Intentions study (Woolf, 1971). Asked the number of children they considered ideal for those with 'no particular worries about money', as many as 41% of women said that four children was ideal, only 22% said two, and less than one per cent (the absolute figure is not given) less than two. In contrast, asked the number of children ideal for families 'like yourselves', 60% said two and only 13% said four or more. The mean difference between the two ideals was in the order of one child. This also indicates that many people felt that finance was a salient issue when selecting the 'ideal' size of family.
13. For Europe see Stoetzel (1955) and Glass (1962; 1965); for the United States see Freedman et al. (1959); Whelpton et al. (1966); Blake (1966) and Ryder and Westoff (1967).

14. The figures, however, fall between those from the two questions from the Family Intentions study (Woolf, 1971), rather than being closer to those for the ideals for families with 'no particular worries about money' as one might expect.

15. The corresponding figures from the Family Intentions study are 12% for the question on ideals if there were 'no particular worries about money', and almost certainly less than that for ideals for families 'like yourselves'. With this question only 2% thought less than two children ideal and only 13% four *or more*. (Unfortunately the tables for this question do not distinguish the proportion regarding four children as ideal from those who chose a larger number.) (*Ibid.*, pp 13-14.)

16. The Family Intentions Study does not give the numbers or percentages for each size of family now wanted, only averages (*Ibid.*, Chapter 2).

17. The initial unpopularity of a family size of three as a specific preference was also noted by Cartwright (1970), p.10.

18. Rainwater (1965) makes a distinction between child-centred and parent-centred reasons for limiting family size which we attempted to incorporate into our coding for reasons offered for ideal and desired family size. We are now, however, unhappy with the assumption that reference to providing adequately for children is child-centred whereas a reference to how much it costs to bring children up is adult-centred. Moreover in many cases it is not very clear to which category a reason should be assigned.

19. *Ibid.,* pp.140-1.

20. *Ibid.*, *passim.*

21. Hawthorn and Busfield (1968b), p.21.

22. Though this type of hypothetical question is not at all satisfactory.

23. Such ideas present an interesting facet of our data which we have not attempted to analyse in detail here (see, however, Busfield, 1974a) since they are salient to childbearing itself only when they lead a couple to have more children than they would otherwise in order to have one of a specific sex, which the evidence suggests is not all that common (Freedman et al., 1960).

24. Cf. the point noted above that it was the 'social restriction' of children that was the more frequently mentioned disadvantage amongst the survey sample.

25. The point is made by a number of authors see, for instance, Hawthorn (1974).

26. This finding is again consistent in overall terms with that from the Family Intentions study, (Woolf, 1971, pp.49-50) however, she found that women married under the age of 20 most commonly said they wanted a child within a year of marriage, a finding that was not matched in our own data; however our question was only asked of those who were *not* pregnant at marriage or within the first three months.

27. The idea here, that you should not be too old when you have children, was mentioned by others. The beliefs on which it is based reflect to a large extent the ideas about the implications of having children that we have already described: that children require companionship, energy, patience and attention, all of which it is assumed become more difficult to provide if parents bear their children rather late in life.

28. Woolf (1971, p.50) comments about her sample's reaction to the interval between the first and second birth (for those who had had a second child without any intervening unsuccessful pregnancies), 'no specific length of interval was thought more "right" than others—except around the two year mark'.

29.   Only 8% of husbands in the survey and 4% of wives who attempted to give some reason for their preferences about the spacing of births gave an answer that we categorised as 'no real reason—nice'.
30.   We should perhaps re-emphasise here that to accept that resources exert some influence over decisions about family size does not require us to adopt the approach of utilitarian theories to the question of explaining that influence.
31.   Rainwater (1965), p.150.
32.   *loc. cit.*

Chapter 10. Images of family life
1.   See for instance, Banks (1954); Lorimer (1958) and Mamdani (1972).
2.   Glass (1971, p.195), for example, having accepted there are differences in values relating to desired family size, proceeds to point out first, that the differences are not unconnected to differences in birth control practice, and second that 'In Britain at present the values relating to family size do not appear to differ very markedly', and suggests that the narrow range of family sizes is evidence of this. The implication is that we need pay little attention to differences in values. But there are a number of problems with this argument. First, the range of family sizes (desired or actual) may be small, but even a difference of one child is significant demographically, and if this is a matter of different values it is worth studying. Second, relatively small differences in family size *may* result from considerable differences in underlying values. Third, the connection between birth-control practice and differences in desires about family size may itself be in part the result of differences in underlying values, as our own study suggests.
3.   An emphasis on these values in social relations is usually held by sociologists to be crucial elements in a 'collective' ideology. The contrast between collective and individualist values are discussed in a number of places. See, for instance, Parsons (1956); Dumont (1965); and Lukes (1973).
4.   Sociologists and others have pointed out that a collective ideology is often associated with hierarchical values, since an emphasis on the need and importance of groups solidarity and support is appropriate to a situation where positions and places in the social order are differentiated and ranked hierarchically, and where everyone 'knows his place'.
5.   It is interesting, but not surprising, that little study has been made of women's perceptions of the social structure, which we cannot assume to be the same as men's.
6.   For each ideological perspective that we outline we have selected one case that in our view best illustrates the ideas and beliefs of that perspective.
7.   The same points are also illustrated by her comments about having sex with her husband: 'I think the actual act is something that you cannot get closer, you can't be more than one at the time, it's something that you can't get any closer to. I think that if you get along with your husband, and he gets along with you, it is something that makes you much closer. You've got the feeling that you're almost one.' Asked what her husband felt she said, 'the same. It is his way of showing his actual, not devotion, I don't want to use sloppy words, but it his actual way of showing he is solely for us as a family. That's how I look at it.'
8.   Hence though the hard work of extra children is not denied, it is treated as part of one's duties as a parent, and is therefore acceptable. Moreover parents of large families, as do others, often point out that in a large family the younger ones help the older ones, thereby reducing the burden extra children create.

9. It is interesting that parents remarking that a child or a baby is 'ours' or that they feel that 'he's yours' seemed to be more common amongst those whose ideas about family life were primarily based on a collective ideology. Such a remark within this perspective indicates, not so much a sense of possession, as a sense that a child is a member of one's own group – he's 'one of us'.

10. Her descriptions of herself and her husband are also instructive in this respect. Of her husband, she said, 'He is big, awkward, kind, rough, very rough, but very kind and very human, very understanding, not very clever, but a very nice person.' Of herself she said, 'I think I try to be on a level the same to everybody. I try to understand other people. I think I'm fairly patient. I'm more patient now than I was ten years ago, but nothing exciting.'

11. One or two parents of this ideological persuasion pointed out that you could be more economical and less wasteful of material goods if you had a larger family, implying both that material standards were not lowered as much with a larger family as other thought, and that squandering material resources was not desirable. One said 'You'll pass the clothes down, you benefit by it that way, and I mean I think it's just as cheap to cook for a lot as it is to cook for a few. I think you waste more, you know, if you've got a smaller family, you tend to cook too much, whereby with a larger family it do get eaten up, and you don't get no waste.'

12. For we would expect to find the hierarchical values that we have already pointed out tend to be associated with a collective ideology, reflected in ideas about relations within the family, as well as in ideas about the broader features of the social order.

13. Lockwood (1966), p.260.

14. Members of the survey sample who claimed that they wanted a higher standard of living than their parents (78% of husbands and wives for whom we have a definite answer) were more likely to want a smaller family than those who said they wanted the same standard of living as their parents (78% of husbands and 71% of wives desiring a higher standard of living than their parents wanted two children or less at marriage, compared with 59% of husbands and 56% of wives desiring only the same standard of living as their parents). However, wanting a higher standard of living than one's parents is a far from perfect indicator of materialism as we have described it, since it tells us nothing about the priority that is attached to one's standard of living, or indeed, whether that was interpreted in material terms.

15. The standard image of the material life has almost certainly become less home-centred over the post-war period, with the change coming in the sixties: a point to which we return in the final chapter.

16. Mr Carter was at pains to point out (perhaps because it was out of character, or in terms of our analysis, incongruent with his ideology) that his most recent job change had not been for money, but to have more time at home.

17. It was Mr Carter who was quoted in the previous chapter (see page 154), as an illustration of the willingness to consider the satisfactions from children in the context of alternatives.

18. A few explicitly linked their own deprivations in childhood, to the economic conditions of the time. One man, for instance, having described vividly and bitterly how his father had died in 1938 when work was still difficult, (he had got a job laying cables and could not afford to take time off when he was ill), also felt bitter about the fact that he had won a scholarship to the grammar school in 1935 'when the Depression was on' but his parents couldn't afford to send him. He himself was determined that his children shouldn't be denied that

opportunity: 'it doesn't matter what sacrifices we make'. His orientation to education, however, as to other things was primarily material. Of money he said, 'it does make every difference from the start to the finish, as how your whole life is run, from the start to the finish'. Our argument that the economic conditions experienced in childhood may influence the individual's ideological perspective needs to be distinguished from Easterlin's (1966) thesis that the standard of living of individuals experienced in childhood, when compared with the one they can achieve as an adult influence their family size.

19. See Lockwood (1966).
20. Lockwood (*ibid.*) sees privatisation as the crucial factor, but though this may be important some of our cases suggested it was not essential.
12. The last two are clearly a secular relic of the protestant ethic. The ideology as a whole has played an important part in English society. It has played, for instance, a central role in the educational system, and was the foundation of Butler's 1944 Education Act.
22. Klein (1965), p.300.
23. The importance she attached to self-control (which made any failure to achieve it a disaster for her) were evidenced in numerous ways. Not only had she and her husband restricted intercourse very rigidly before they had the accidental pregnancy, but after it they virtually abstained altogether, and had intercourse only once or twice a year (this was partly but by no means entirely due to the deterioration in their relationship that followed that pregnancy). Mrs Kowski also described an event relating to their marriage in which 'head had ruled heart', when she had met someone else to whom she felt strongly attracted just before they married, but had allowed herself to be persuaded by her father that she should not change her wedding plans.
24. She was disappointed in her husband in other ways, too, and compared him unfavourably with her father: 'I find I compare my marriage with that of my parents and often unfavourably, you know. I sort of think that my father was a real daddy, everything a daddy should be, although I never realised as a child, but now I'm grown up and I find the little things that my husband does not do, I realise what a wonderful father I had, so helpful domestically in the home.'
25. Quoted in Klein (1965), p.429.
26. *Ibid.*, p.417.
27. Jackson & Marsden (1966).
28. *Ibid.*, p.67-70.
29. This is a common and widely discussed theme in English history; see Thompson (1963) and Halevy's *A History of the English People in 1815.*
30. Hence the ideology makes certain assumptions about human nature, which are essentially positive and optimistic: humans if given freedom will be able to act in autonomous, creative ways. It is interesting that psychologists in stressing an underlying desire for 'self-actualisation' ignore the ideological nature of this idea.
31. And she is optimistic about its effects on her children. As she said, 'I know there is a lot of propoganda that one shouldn't have too many because we are getting over-populated and that sort of thing, but I'm arrogant enough to think that mine would be a help in the world rather than a drag on it.'
32. See Lockwood (1966).
33. These are discussed by Klein (1965), Chapter 6.
34. Merton (1967), Chapters 4 and 5.
35. We discuss disagreement between husband and wife and its impact on contraceptive use in more detail in the following chapter.

36. Her dislike of conflict was brought out in other comments.
37. Unfortunately Mrs Walker was not asked, due to an oversight of the interviewer, whom she thought *should* take responsibility for birth control, and the information on her ideas about birth control is generally sparse, as she was rather unforthcoming on the subject, and was not pressed by the interviewer (perhaps because from time to time she made hostile comments about being interviewed, and said she did not know what her husband would think when she told him about the interview. Did she resent the intrusion of the interviewer into her 'private' life, yet feel unable to refuse an interview to avoid trouble?)
38. Her father was a bricklayer, she was the eldest child, and felt they were 'such a happy family'. She went to a secondary school and left at 15, when she started as a pre-student nurse. Apart from that we know little about her life before marriage, and could only speculate as to what produced her current way of thinking.
39. Merton (1957), p.185.
40. *Ibid.*, p.151.

Chapter 11. Uncertainty, negotiation and change.

1. It is, of course, somewhat easier to make successful aggregate predictions in times of social and economic stability, as the efforts based on fertility expectations have shown. See, for instance, Whelpton, Campbell and Patterson (1966).
2. Mr Jones felt very stongly that life was what you made it, and felt that most people failed to use their opportunities: 'Man creates the headaches. Everyone could have everything. Everyone wishes to do things, but what do they do? Give man an opportunity and he throws it away.'
3. Certainly other studies have shown that it may be considered economically advantageous to have a larger family; see, for example, Mamdani's (1972) discussion of ideas about children in India.
4. Some studies show very clearly the way in which expectations relate to age; Laurence Wylie's *Village in the Vaucluse* (1961) is one example.
5. The point has been made elsewhere. Hill, Stycos and Back (1959) in their report of a study of childbearing in Puerto Rico in the early 1950s examined the 'consistency' of family size preferences, arguing that inconsistency in preferences was primarily due to ambivalence and not to indifference, and showed that for their sample consistency in preferences was positively related to regularity of contraceptive use.
6. Five per cent of husbands and 6% of wives said they had not known how many children they wanted at marriage, and an additional 7% of husbands and 9% of wives said they had been undecided at that time between either two or three children, or three or four. The question was 'At this time, and taking all your circumstances into account, how many children did you actually want?'
7. Only 3% of both husbands and wives did not know how many children they wanted when interviewed, and only 4% of husbands and 6% of wives were undecided between either two or three children, or three and four.
8. Of course the length of time between marriage and the time of the interview varied considerably.
9. Hill, Stycos and Back (1959), for example, argue that 'consensus' in ideas (having the same ones), is not enough to ensure efficient contraceptive use, there must also be 'concordance' (diffusion and joint decision making).
10. The association between our three variables: sharing of activities, discussion, and decision making was low.

11. Quoted in Klein (1965), pp. 440-1.
12. Her ideas about family life are discussed in section I of Chapter 10.
13. This means, of course, that simple questions in surveys about who makes decisions about having children have little value.
14. It does not necessarily reduce a spouse's conflict and uncertainty about having children, if the decision is left to him or her. Those who feel uncertain may well prefer not to have to make the choice.
15. The important thing for those who want a quiet life is to please their partner, and avoid conflict. They will therefore be inclined to accept whichever belief legitimates their partner making the decisions.

Chapter 12. Controlling births.

1. A number of attempts have been made to estimate the extent of different types of infecundity. See, for instance Woolf (1971); Lewis-Faning (1940); Whelpton, Campbell and Patterson (1966).
2. Our own data showed that at marriage some two-thirds of those using birth control claimed to be using it 'every time', whilst about four out of every five users made such a claim in relation to the time when interviewed.
3. Monopolies and Mergers Commission (1975), p.8.
4. One effect of a reduction in the age at marriage is that with methods that have less than perfect efficiency in use, there is more chance of unplanned pregnancies.
5. See Lewis-Faning (1949); Rowntree and Pierce (1961); Glass (1971); Woolf (1971).
6. The change in methods used by different marriage cohorts (including the constancy in the use of the sheath) is clearly illustrated in figure 4.4 of the Family Intentions study, (Woolf, 1971), p.84. We understand that Ann Cartwright's recent study of fertility (which is not yet published) has shown considerably greater use of the pill amongst the most recent marriage cohorts.
7. Woolf (1971), p.84.
8. We cannot be certain that all those who use the pill early in marriage will continue to do so throughout. Recent medical opinion indicates that the risks in using the pill increase with age.
9. Matras (1965); Lewis-Faning (1949).
10. The precise level of use is difficult to estimate; however the figures for the proportions using it in the late 1960s suggest that less than one in ten couples (where the wife was under 45) would have been using the pill around that time.
11. Wrigley (1966).
12. It could be that women feel somewhat more strongly about their family size and spacing preferences than men, since they are more likely to be affected by decisions about having children.
13. We did ask people how 'definite' they felt about their preferences but this is a poor measure of their strength.
14. We have made no attempt in this chapter to discuss abortion. This is because when the research was planned legal abortion was not available. However the points that we make about other methods of contraception in the rest of this chapter can be extended to cover abortion either legal or illegal, though some of the necessary data is lacking.
15. There is little information about the extent of knowledge of how to obtain particular methods of contraception. It is interesting, however, that several of our interviewers reported that they had been asked a variety of questions about contraception, including questions about how to obtain different methods.

16. Hence, one way in which contraceptive technology can have an impact on childbearing is by reducing the knowledge that is necessary for effective use.
17. Our own questions about knowledge of contraception in both the survey and the pilot were similarly restricted in scope and in the use of a checklist.
18. Cartwright (1970), p.28.
19. *Loc. cit.*
20. *Ibid.*, p.29.
21. *Ibid.*, p.143.
22. To parents, the extent of their children's knowledge in comparison with their own at a similar age may make it seem greater than it is.
23. Schofield's (1968) study suggests that teenagers' knowledge of birth control in the early 1960s was far from perfect.
24. The problem of interpreting the answers to these questions provides a good example of the inadequacy of survey data.
25. Doctors seem reluctant to raise the problems of contraception unless they perceive some definite social or health problems; see Cartwright (1970), pp. 51-2.
26. The 'Grapevine' project designed to disseminate contraceptive information through more informal channels is based on this premise.
27. The Monopolies and Mergers Commission (1975) report on the supply of sheaths describes some of the past and present limitations on the advertising of contraceptives.
28. Of those who said they *never* discussed birth control some 27% were using the pill and some 57% the sheath. Of those who said they *often* discussed birth control some 22% were using the pill and some 70% the sheath.
29. Hill, Stycos and Back (1959), for instance, have pointed to the association.
30. Unfortunately we asked few questions that were specifically intended to elicit ideas about different methods of contraception.
31. The influence of religion is discussed by Cartwright (1970), Chapter 13.
32. Some 63% of the mothers in Ann Cartwright's (1970) sample (*Ibid.*, p.30) thought that the pill was the most reliable method of contraception. The method mentioned next most frequently was the sheath, with 14% of mothers saying it was the most reliable method.
33. 77% of the general practitioners interviewed in Ann Cartwright's study said they most often advised the pill (*Ibid.*, p.75).
34. *Ibid.*, p.144.
35. Cartwright (*Ibid.*, p.197) reports 'no difference between middle- and working-class mothers in their views on the health risks of the pill though slightly more middle- than working-class mothers thought it might cause people to put on weight or get too fat'.
36. *Ibid.*, p.75.
37. Royal College of General Practitioners (1974).
38. Responsiveness to doctors' advice is briefly discussed by Cartwright. (1970), p.61.
39. Glass (1971), p.193.
40. This was due in part to the restriction imposed on any form of display or advertising of contraceptives in chemists, and to the fact that the London Rubber Company, the main manufacturers of sheaths in Britain already distributed goods to barber shops. They estimated that 'in 1972 about 26% of retail sales of its sheaths were made through chemists, about 29% through barbers, about 12% through drug and surgical stores, about 10% through vending machines and about 8% through mail-order houses. The rest of the retail sales were accounted for principally by sales through market traders, grocery shops and clinics.' Monopolies and Mergers Commission (1975), p.24.

41. This is presumably one of the most important reasons for the class differentials in use of professional advice on birth control.
42. Monopolies and Mergers Commission (1975), p. 57.
43. Some of its perceived disadvantages are listed by Cartwright (1970) p.31.
44. Some of them are discussed by Cartwright (1970), Chapter 3.

Chapter 13. Trends in family size and spacing.
1. See Simon (1969); Silver (1965a; 1965b); Busfield and Hawthorn (1971).
2. A number of books discuss the period (or parts of it); for example, Bogdanor and Skidelsky (1970); McKie and Cook (1972); Postan (1967); Youngson (1968); Landes (1969); Webb (1969); Thomson (1965).
3. Landes (1969), p.498.
4. *Ibid.*, p.497.
5. Youngson (1968).
6. A phrase that J. K. Galbraith's book, *The Affluent Society,* published in 1958 did much to publicise.
7. Anthony Crosland in the following passage from *The Future of Socialism* (1956) illustrates this note of optimism perfectly. 'The persistence of full employment for more than a decade of peace has now largely cured the depression psychosis which dominated industrial attitudes, with such insidious results, in the inter-war period. The business community accepts the fact that prosperity is here to stay, not only because full employment will be maintained, but also because we have entered a period of rapid growth in personal incomes and consumption . . . Such primary poverty as remains will disappear within a decade, given our present rate of economic growth; and the contemporary mixed economy is characterised by high levels both of employment and productivity and by a reasonable degree of stability.' This passage is quoted in McKie and Cook (1972), p.1.
8. The Labour Party talked of the 'thirteen wasted years' in the 1964 election campaign.
9. Thomson (1965), p.270.
10. Busfield (1974b).
11. We do not mean to imply here that there is any simple linear increase in the acceptance of individualist ideas whether in the family or elsewhere.

Appendix A.
1. Young and Wilmot (1973), p.294.

References

Abrams, P. and McCulloch, A., (1974). 'Men, women and communes', Paper given at the British Sociological Association Conference, 1974.

Adams, B. N. and Meidam, M. T. (1968). 'Economics, Family Structure and College Attendance', *American Journal of Sociology,* 74, pp.239-9.

Allport, G. W. (1962). 'The general and the unique in psychological science', *Journal of Personality,* 30, pp.405-22.

Altus, W. D., (1966). 'Birth order and its sequalae', *Science,* 151, pp. 44-9.

Annan, Lord (1974). *Report of the Disturbances in the University of Essex,* University of Essex.

Aries, P. (1962). *Centuries of Childhood,* New York: Vintage Books.
    (1971). *Histoire des Populations Francaises,* Paris: Editions du Seuil.

Austin, J. L. (1961). *Philosophical Papers,* London: Oxford University Press.
Bain, G. S., Bacon, R. and Pimlott, J. (1972). 'The Labour Force', in A. H. Halsey (ed.), *Trends in British Society since 1900,* London: Macmillan.
Banks, J. A. (1954). *Prosperity and Parenthood,* London: Routledge and Kegan Paul.
Banks, J. A. and Banks, O. (1964). *Feminism and Family Planning in Victorian England,* Liverpool: Liverpool University Press.
Becker, G. S. (1960). 'An economic analysis of fertility', in National Bureau of Economic Research, *Demographic and Economic Change in Developed Countries,* Princeton: Princeton University Press.
  (1965). 'A theory of the allocation of time', *The Economic Journal,* 75, pp.493-517.
Ben-Porath, Y. (1973). 'Economic Analysis of Fertility in Israel: point and counterpoint', *Journal of Political Economy,* 81, pp.S202-S237.
Berger, P. L. and Luckmann, T. (1966). *The Social Construction of Reality,* New York: Doubleday.
Blake, J. (1961). *Family Structure in Jamaica,* Glencoe: Free Press.
  (1966). 'Ideal family size among white Americans: a quarter of century's evidence'. *Demography,* 3, pp.154-73.
  (1968). 'Are babies consumer durables?', *Population Studies,* 22, pp.5-25.
Blalock, H. M. (1960). *Social Statistics,* New York: McGraw-Hill.
Blau, P. M. and Duncan, O. D. (1967). *The American Occupational Structure,* New York: John Wiley.
Bogdanor, V. and Skidelsky, R. (eds.), (1970). *The Age of Affluence, 1951-1964,* London: Macmillan.
Bott, E. (1957). *Family and Social Network,* London: Tavistock.
Branson, N. and Heinemann, M. (1973). *Britain in the Nineteen Thirties,* London: Panther.
Braudel, F. (1973). *Capitalism and Material Life 1400-1800,* London: Weidenfeld and Nicholson.
Busfield, J. (1972). 'Age at Marriage and Family Size: social causation and social selection hypothesis', *Journal of Biosocial Science,* 4, pp.117-34.
  (1974a). 'Ideologies and Reproduction', in Richards, M. P. M. (ed.), *The Integration of a Child into a Social World,* London: Cambridge University Press.
  (1974b). 'Family Ideology and Family Pathology', in N. Armistead, (ed.), *Reconstructing Social Psychology,* Harmondsworth: Penguin Books.
Busfield, J. and Hawthorn, G. (1971). 'Some social determinants of recent trends in British fertility', *Journal of Biosocial Science Supplement,* 3, pp.65-7.
Calhoun, J. B. (1962). *The Ecology and Sociology of the Norway Rat,* Washington: U.S. Department of Health, Education and Welfare.
Cannell, C. F. and Kahn, R. L. (1968). 'Interviewing', in Lindzey, G. and Aronson, E. (eds.), *The Handbook of Social Psychology,* second edition, Vol. II, Reading: Addison-Wesley, pp.526-95.
Carr-Saunders, A. (1922). *The Population Problem,* Oxford: Clarendon Press.
Cartwright, A. (1970). *Parents and Family Planning Services,* London: Routledge and Kegan Paul.
Chambers, J. D. (1972). *Population, Economy and Society in Pre-Industrial England,* Oxford: Oxford University Press.
Chester, R. (1972). 'Is there a relationship between childlessness and mental breakdown?', *Journal of Biosocial Science,* 4, pp.443-54.
Cicourel, A. V. (1964). *Method and Measurement in Sociology,* Glencoe: Free Press.
  (1967). 'Fertility, family planning and the social organisation of family life: some methodological issues', *Journal of Social Issues,* 23, pp.57-81.
  (1974). *Theory and Method in a Study of Argentine Fertility,* New York: John Wiley.

Clark, C. (1967). *Population Growth and Land Use,* London: Macmillan.

Crosland, C. A. R. (1956). *The Future of Socialism,* London: Johnathan Cape.

Dahrendorf, R. (1973). *Homo Sociologicus,* London: Routledge and Kegan Paul.

Davidson, D. (1963). 'Actions, reasons and causes', *Journal of Philosophy,* 60, pp.685-700.

Davis, K. (1955). 'Malthus and the theory of population', in Lazarsfeld, P. F., and Rosenberg, M. (eds.), *The Language of Social Research,* Glencoe: Free Press.

  (1963). 'The theory of change and response in modern demographic history', *Population Index,* 29, pp.345-66.

Davis, K. and Blake J. (1956). 'Social structure and fertility: an analytic framework', *Economic Development and Cultural Change,* 4, pp.211-35.

Deane, P. and Cole, W. A. (1961). *British Economic Growth 1688—1959,* London: Cambridge University Press.

Dennis, N., Henriques, F. and Slaughter, C. (1969), *Coal is our Life,* second edition, London: Tavistock.

Department of Employment Gazette (1973 and earlier). London: H.M.S.O.

Dobb, M. (1937). 'The trend of modern economics', in *Political Economy and Capitalism,* London: Routledge and Kegan Paul.

Douglas, M. (1966). 'Population control in primitive groups', *British Journal of Sociology,* 17, pp. 263-73.

Duesenberry, J. S. (1960). 'Comment', in National Bureau for Economic Research, *Demographic and Economic Change in Developed Countries,* Princeton: Princeton University Press, pp.231-4.

Dumont, L. (1965). 'The modern conception of the individual', *Contributions to Indian Sociology,* 8, pp.13-61.

Easterlin, R. A. (1962). 'The American baby boom in historical perspective', National Bureau of Economic Research, New York. Occasional Paper, No.79.

  (1966). 'On the relation of economic factors to recent and projected fertility changes', *Demography,* 3, pp.131-53.

  (1969). 'Towards a socio-economic theory of fertility: a survey of recent research on economic factors in American fertility', in Behrman, S. J., Corsa, L., Freedman, R. (eds.), *Fertility and Family Planning: A World View,* Ann Arbor: University of Michigan Press.

Emmett, D. and MacIntyre, A. (eds.), (1970). *Sociological Theory and Philosophical Analysis,* London: Macmillan.

Espenshade, T. J. (1972). 'The price of children and socio-economic theories of fertility', *Population Studies,* 26, pp.207-21.

Eversley, D. E. C. (1959). *Social Theories of Fertility and the Malthusian Debate,* Oxford: Clarendon Press.

Feldman, H. (1971). 'The effects of children on the family', in A. Michel (ed.), *Family Issues of Employed Women in Europe and America,* Leiden: E. J. Brill.

Fest, J. C. (1972). *The Face of the Third Reich,* Harmondsworth: Penguin.

Fletcher, C. (1974). *Beneath the Surface,* London: Routledge and Kegan Paul.

Flew, A. (ed.), (1970). *Malthus: An Essay on the Principle of Population,* Harmondsworth: Penguin.

Freedman, D. S., Freedman, R. and Whelpton, P. K. (1960). 'Size of family and preference for children of each sex', *American Journal of Sociology,* 66, pp.141-6.

Freedman, R., Whelpton, P. K. and Campbell, A. A. (1959). *Family Planning Sterility, and Population Growth,* New York: McGraw-Hill.

Friedman, M. (1953). *Essays in Positive Economics,* Chicago: University of Chicago Press.

Galbraith, J. K. (1958). *The Affluent Society,* London, Hamish Hamilton.

Galtung, J. (1966). 'Rank and social integration; a multi-dimensional approach', in Berger, P., Zelditch, M. and Anderson, B., *Sociological Theories in Progress,* Boston: Houghton Mifflin, pp.145-98.

———(1967). *Theory and Methods of Social Research,* London: George Allen and Unwin

Gardner, B. (1973). 'Economics of the size of North Carolina rural families', *Journal of Political Economy,* 81, pp.S99-S122.

Garfinkel, H. (1960). 'Rational properties of scientific and common-sense activities', *Behavioural Science,* 5, pp.72-83.

———(1967). *Studies in Ethnomethodology,* Englewood Cliffs: Prentice Hall.

Gellner, E. (1974). 'The new idealism – cause and meaning in the social sciences', in A. Giddens (ed.), *Positivism and Sociology,* London: Heinemann.

General Register Office (1959). *Census 1951, Fertility Tables,* London: H.M.S.O.

———(1966). *Census 1961, Fertility Tables,* London: H.M.S.O.

Giddens, A. (ed.), (1974). *Positivism and Sociology,* London: Heinemann.

Glass, D. V. (1953). *Introduction to Malthus,* London: Watts.

———(1954). *Social Mobility in Britain,* London: Routledge and Kegan Paul.

———(1962). 'Family limitation in Europe: a survey of recent studies', in Kiser, C.V. (ed.), *Research in Family Planning,* Princeton: Princeton University Press.

———(1968). 'Fertility trends in Europe since the Second World War', *Population Studies,* 22, pp.103-46.

———(1971). 'The components of natural increase in England and Wales', in the first report from the select committee on science and technology, *Population of the United Kingdom,* London: H.M.S.O.

———(1973). *Numbering the People,* Farnborough: Saxon House.

Glasser, J. H. and Làchenbruch, P. A. (1968), 'Observations on the relationship between frequency and timing of intercourse and the probability of conception', *Population Studies,* 22, p.399.

Goldthorpe, J., Lockwood, D., Bechhofer, F. and Platt, J. (1968). *The Affluent Worker: Political Attitudes and Behaviour,* London: Cambridge University Press.

———(1968). *The Affluent Worker: Industrial Attitudes and Behaviour,* London: Cambridge University Press.

———(1969). *The Affluent Worker in the Class Structure,* London: Cambridge University Press.

Gouldner, A. (1971). *The Coming Crisis of Western Sociology,* London: Heinemann.

Gronau, R. (1973). 'The effect of children on the housewife's value of time', *Journal of Political Economy,* 81, pp.S168-S199.

Habakkuk, H. J. (1971). *Population Growth and Economic Development since 1750.* Leicester: Leicester University Press.

Hajnal, J. (1965). 'European Marriage patterns in Perspective', in Glass, D. V. and Eversley, D. E. C. (eds.), *Population in History.* London: Edward Arnold.

Halsey, A. H. (1972). 'Higher Education', in A. H. Halsey (ed.), *Trends in British Society since 1900,* London: Macmillan.

Hammond, P.E. (ed.), (1964). *Sociologists at Work,* New York. Basic Books.

Harré, R. and Secord, P. F. (1972). *The Explanation of Social Behaviour,* Oxford: Basil Blackwell.

Hauser, P. (1971). 'Testimony before special subcommittee, U.S. Senate', in E. Pohlman (ed.), *Population: A Clash of Prophets,* New York: Mentor Books.

Hawthorn, G. (1965). 'Statement of a proposed research project for consideration for departmental support; 1965-6, Mimeo, University of Essex.

(1968). 'Explaining human fertility', *Sociology,* 2, p.65-78.

(1970). *The Sociology of Fertility,* London: Collier-Macmillan.

(1974). 'Family size and spacing in recent English cohorts', in Leggatt, T. (ed.), *Sociological Theory and Survey Research,* London: Sage.

Hawthorn, G. and Busfield, J. (1968a). 'A sociological approach to British fertility', in Gould, J. (ed.), *Penguin Social Sciences Survey 1968,* Harmondsworth: Penguin.

(1968b). 'Some Social determinants of family size: report of a pilot study'. Mimeo, University of Essex.

Hawthorn, G. and Paddon, M. (1971), 'Work, family and fertility', *Human Relations,* 24, pp.611-28.

(forthcoming). *Having.Children,* London: Cambridge University Press.

Hill, R., Stycos, J. M. and Back, K. W. (1959). *The Family and Population Control,* Chapel Hill: University of North Carolina Press.

Hindess, B. (1973). *The Use of Official Statistics,* London: Macmillan.

Hollis, M. and Nell, E. (1975). *Rational Economic Man,* London: Cambridge University Press.

Hollis, M. and Ryan, A. (1973). 'Deductive explanation in the social sciences', *The Aristotelian Society, Supplementary Volume,* 47, pp.147-85.

Hunt, E. K. and Schwartz, J. G. (1972), (eds.). *A Critique of Economic Theory,* Harmondsworth: Penguin Books.

Hyman, H. et. al. (1954). *Interviewing in Social Research,* Chicago: University of Chucago Press.

Ipswich County Borough Council, East Suffolk County Council (1972a). *Structure Plan for the Ipswich Sub-Region: Population.* Ipswich.

(1972b). *Structure Plan for the Ipswich Sub-Region: Employment.* Ipswich.

(1972c). *Structure Plan for the Ipswich Sub-Region: Housing.* Ipswich.

Jackson, B. and Marsden, D. (1966). *Education and the Working Class.* Harmondsworth: Penguin Books.

Jarvie, I. C. (1973). *Concepts and Society,* London: Routledge and Kegan Paul.

Klein, J. (1965). *Samples from English Cultures,* London: Routledge and Kegan Paul.

Kolakowski, L. (1973). *Positivist Philosophy,* Harmondsworth: Penguin Books.

Koopmans, T. (1957). *Three Essays on the State of Economic Science,* New York: McGraw-Hill.

Lancaster, K. J. (1966). 'A new approach to consumer theory', *Journal of Political Economy,* 74, pp. 132-57.

Landes, D. S. (1969). *The Unbound Prometheus,* London: Cambridge University Press.

Lane, M. (ed.), (1970). *Structuralism.* London: Cape.

Leibenstein, H. (1957). *Economic Backwardness and Economic Growth,* New York: John Wiley.

Lewis-Faning, E. (1949). *Report of an Enquiry into Family Limitations and its Influence on Human Fertility during the past fifty years.* London: H.M.S.O.

Little, I. M. D. (1957). *A Critique of Welfare Economics,* Second edition, London: Oxford University Press.

Lockwood, D. (1956). 'Some Remarks on the Social System', *British Journal of Sociology,* 7, pp.134-46.

(1966). 'Sources of variation in working class images of society', *Sociological Review,* 14, pp.249-67.

Lorimer, F. (1958). *Culture and Human Fertility,* Paris: UNESCO.

   (1959). 'The development of demography', in Hauser, P. M., and Duncan, O. D., *The Study of Population,* Chicago: University of Chicago Press.

Lukes, S. (1973). *Individualism,* Oxford: Basil Blackwell.

McKie, D. and Cook, C. (1972). *The Decade of Disillusion,* London: Macmillan.

MacIntyre, A. (1962). 'A mistake about causalty in social science', in P. Laslett and W. G. Runciman (eds.), *Philosophy, Politics and Society,* Oxford: Basil Blackwell.

   (1967). 'The Idea of a Social Science', *Proceedings of the Aristotelian Society,* Supplementary Volume, 61, p.95-114.

MacIntyre, S. (1974). 'Who wants babies? The social construction of instincts'. Paper given at the British Sociological Association Conference, 1974.

Mair, L. (1971). *Marriage,* Harmondsworth: Penguin Books.

Mamdani, M. (1972). *The Myth of Population Control,* New York: Monthly Review Press.

Mann, M. (1970). 'The social cohesion of liberal democracy', *American Sociological Review,* 35, p.423-39.

Matras, J. (1965). 'Social strategies of family formation: data for British female cohorts born 1831-1906', *Population Studies,* 19, pp.167-81.

Michael, R. T. (1973). 'Education and the derived demand for children', *Journal of Political Economy,* 81, pp.S128-S164.

Mincer, J. (1963). 'Market prices, opportunity costs, and income effects', in Christ, C. et. al., *Measurement in Economics,* Stanford: Stanford University Press.

Monopolies and Mergers Commission (1975). *Contraceptive Sheaths: A report on the supply of contraceptive sheaths in the United Kingdom,* London: H.M.S.O.

Moser, C. A. and Scott, W. (1961). *British Towns,* Edinburgh: Oliver and Boyd.

Nagel, E. (1961). *The Structure of Science,* London: Routledge and Kegan Paul.

   (1963). 'Assumptions in Economic Theory', *American Economic Review,* 53, Supplementary Volume, pp.214-8.

Namboodiri, N. K. (1972). 'Some observations on the economic framework for fertility analysis', *Population Studies,* 26, pp.185-206.

Nell, E. (1972). 'Economics: the revival of Political Economy', in Blackburn, R. (ed.), *Ideology in Social Science',* London: Fontana.

Office of Population Censuses and Surveys (1973). *Census 1971, County Reports: East Suffolk,* London: H.M.S.O.

   (1974). *Census 1971: Age, Marital Conditions and General Tables,* London, H.M.S.O.

   (1975). *Population Trends, 1,* London: H.M.S.O.

Okun, B. (1958). *Trends in Birth Rates in the United States since 1870,* Baltimore: The John Hopkins Press.

Parsons, T. (1937). *The Structure of Social Action,* New York: McGraw-Hill.

   (1949). ·'the rise and decline of economic man', *Journal of General Education,* 4, pp.47-53.

   (1951). *The Social System,* London: Routledge and Kegan Paul.

   (1956). *Family, Socialisation and Interaction Process,* London: Routledge and Kegan Paul.

Pearce, D. (1975). 'Births and family formation patterns', in Office of Population Censuses and Surveys: *Population Trends, 1,* Autumn 1975, London: H.M.S.O., pp.6-8.

Platt, J. (1971). 'Variations in answers on different questions on perceptions of class', *Sociological Review,* 19, pp. 409-19.

Pohlman, E. (ed.), (1973), *Population: A Clash of Prophets,* New York: Mentor Books.

Popper, K. (1963). *Conjectures and Refutations,* London: Routledge & Kegan Paul.

Population Panel (1973). *Report,* London: H.M.S.O.

Postan, M. M. (1967). *An Economic History of Western Europe, 1945-1964,* London: Methuen.

Rainwater, L. (1960). *And the Poor get Children,* Chicago: Quadrangle.

(1965). *Family Design: Marital Sexuality, Family Size and Contraception,* Chicago: Aldine.

Registrar General (1974). *Quarterly Return for England and Wales, 30 June, 1974.* London: H.M.S.O.

(1974). *Statistical Review of England and Wales, 1972,* Part II, London: H.M.S.O.

(1975). *Statistical Review of England and Wales, 1973,* Part II. London: H.M.S.O.

Robbins, L. (1935). *An Essay on the Nature and Significance of Economic Science,* Second Edition, London: Macmillan.

Rollett, C. (1972). 'Housing', in A. H. Halsey (ed.), *Trends in British Society since 1900,* London: Macmillan.

Rose, A. M. (1962). 'A systematic summary of symbolic interaction theory', in A. M. Rose (ed.), *Human Behaviour and Social Processes,* London: Routledge and Kegan Paul.

Rowntree, G. and Pierce, R. (1961-2). 'Birth Control in Britain', *Population Studies,* 15, pp.3-31 and 121-60.

Royal Anthropological Institute (1951). *Notes and Queries on Anthropology, Sixth edition.* London: Routledge and Kegan Paul.

Royal College of General Practitioners (1974). *Oral Contraceptives and Health,* London: Pitman.

Ryan, A. (ed.), (1973). *The Philosophy of Social Action,* London: Oxford University Press.

Ryder, N. (1973). 'Comment', *Journal of Political Economy,* 81, pp. S65-9.

Ryder, N. B. and Westoff, C. F. (1967). 'The trend of expected parity in the United States, 1955, 1960, 1965', *Population Index,* 33, pp.153-67.

Schofield, M. (1968). *The Sexual Behaviour of Young People,* Harmondsworth: Penguin Books.

Schultz, T. P. (1969). 'An economic model of family planning and fertility', *Journal of Political Economy,* 77, pp.153-80.

Schultz, T. W. (1973). 'The value of children: an economic perspective', *Journal of Political Economy,* 81, pp.S2-S13.

Schutz, A. (1967a). *Collected Papers,* Vol. 1. *The Problem of Social Reality.* The Hague: Nijhoff.

(1967b). 'Common sense and scientific interpretations of human action', in A. Schutz, *Collected Papers,* Vol. 1. The Hague: Nijhoff, pp. 3-47.

Sears, R. R., Maccoby, E. E. and Levin, H. (1957). *Patterns of Child Rearing,* Evanston, Ill: Row, Peterson.

Selvin, H. C. (1957). 'A critique of tests of significance in survey research', *American Sociological Review,* 22, pp. 519-27.

Silver, M. (1965a). 'Births, marriages and business cycles in the United States', *Journal of Political Economy,* 73, pp.237-55.

(1965b). 'Births, marriages and income fluctuations in the United Kingdom and Japan', *Economic and Cultural Change,* 14, pp.302-15.

Simon, H. A. (1957). *Models of Man,* New York: Wiley.

Simon, J. L. (1969). 'The Effect of income on fertility', *Population Studies,* 23, pp.327-41.

Sloman, A. (1964). *A University in the Making,* London: British Broadcasting Corporation.

Spengler, J. J. (1945)., 'Malthus's total population theory: a restatement and reappraisal', *Canadian Journal of Economics and Political Science*, 11, pp.83-110.

Stoetzel, J. (1955). 'Les attitudes et la conjuncture demographique: La dimension ideale de la famille', *Proceedings of the World Population Conference, 1954*, New York: United Nations.

Sullerot, E. (1971). *Woman, Society and Change*, London: Weidenfeld and Nicolson.

Taylor, C. (1964). *The Explanation of Behaviour*, London: Routledge and Kegan Paul.

Taylor, L. R. (ed.), (1970). *The Optimum Population for Britain*, London: Academic Press.

Thompson, E. P. (1963). *The Making of the English Working Class*, New York: Pantheon.

Thomson, D. (1965). *England in the Twentieth Century*, Harmondsworth: Penguin Books.

Townsend, P., (1963). *The Family Life of Old People*, Harmondsworth: Penguin Books.

Turnbull, C. M. (1972). *The Mountain People*, New York: Simon and Schuster.

Walsh, D. (1972). 'Sociology and the Social World', in P. Filmer, M. Phillipson, D. Silverman and D. Walsh, *New Directions in Sociological Theory*, London: Collier-Macmillan.

Webb, R. K. (1969). *Modern England*, London: Allen and Unwin.

Westoff, C. F., Potter, R. G. and Sagi, P. C. (1963). *The Third Child*, Princeton: Princeton University Press.

Westoff, C. F., Potter, R. G., Sagi, P. C. and Mishler, E. G. (1961). *Family Growth in Metropolitan America*, Princeton: Princeton University Press.

Whelpton, P. K. and Kiser, C. V. (eds.), (1950; 1952; 1954; 1958; 1964). *Social and Psychological Factors Affecting Fertility*, New York: Milbank Memorial Fund.

Whelpton, P. K., Campbell, A. A. and Patterson, J. E. (1966). *Fertility and Family Planning in the United States*, Princeton: Princeton University Press.

Winch, P. (1958). *The Idea of a Social Science*, London: Routledge and Kegan Paul.

Willer, D. and Willer, J. (1973). *Systematic Empiricism: Critique of a Pseudo-Science*, New Jersey: Prentice hall.

Willis, R. J. (1973). 'A new approach to the economic theory of fertility behaviour', *Journal of Political Economy*, 81, pp.S14-S64.

Woolf, M. (1971). *Family Intentions,* London: H.M.S.O.

Wrigley, E. A. (1966). 'Family limitation in pre-industrial England', *Economic History Review*, Second Series, 19, pp. 82-109.

(1969). *Population and History*, London: Weidenfeld and Nicholson.

Wylie, L. (1961). *Village in the Vaucluse*, Second Edition, Cambridge, Mass. Havard University Press.

Wynn, M. (1972). *Family Policy*, Harmondsworth: Penguin Books.

Wrong, D. H. (1963). 'The oversocialised conception of man in modern sociology', *American Sociological Review*, 26, pp.184-93.

Wynne-Edwards, V. C. (1962). *Animal Dispersion in Relation to Social Behaviour*, Edinburgh: Oliver and Boyd.

Young, M. and Willmott, P. (1973). *The Symmetrical Family*, London: Routledge and Kegan Paul.

Youngston, A. J. (1968). *Britain's Economic Growth, 1920-66*, Second Edition, London: Allen and Unwin.

Zajonc, R. B. (1960), 'Balance, Congruity and Dissonance', *Public Opinion Quarterly*, 24, pp.280-96.

Index

Subject Index